Historical Milton

Historical Milton

Manuscript, Print, and Political Culture in Revolutionary England

Thomas Fulton

University of Massachusetts Press
Amherst and Boston

LC 2010037298
ISBN 978-1-55849-845-7 (paper); 844-0 (library cloth)

Designed by Dennis Anderson
Set in Adobe Garamond Pro by Westchester Book
Printed and bound by Thomson-Shore, Inc.

Library of Congress Cataloging-in-Publication Data

Fulton, Thomas (Thomas Chandler)
Historical Milton : manuscript, print, and political culture in revolutionary England /
Thomas Fulton.
    p. cm.—(Studies in print culture and the history of the book)
(Massachusetts studies in early modern culture)
Includes bibliographical references and index.
ISBN 978-1-55849-845-7 (pbk. : alk. paper)—
ISBN 978-1-55849-844-0 (library cloth : alk. paper)
1. Milton, John, 1608–1674—Notebooks, sketchbooks, etc.
2. Milton, John, 1608–1674—Manuscripts.
3. Milton, John, 1608–1674—Political and social views.
4. Milton, John, 1608–1674—Books and reading.
5. Polemics in literature.   6. Commonplace-books—History.
7. Books and reading—England—History—17th century.
8. Political culture—England—History—17th century.   I. Title.
PR3592.P64F86 2010
821'.4—dc22

                      2010037298

British Library Cataloguing in Publication data are available.

for Jessica

Contents

Illustrations

For the complete text of the "Digression," see Thomas Fulton, "John Milton's 'Digression' in *The History of Britain:* An Online Facsimile Edition of Harvard MS Eng 901," which can be viewed at http://scholarworks.umass.edu/umpress/hm.

Acknowledgments

THIS BOOK would never have been possible were it not for the kind support—academic and material—of the Rutgers English Department, chaired at different times by Richard Miller and Kate Flint. They both advised me in crucial ways and, along with Deans Ann Fabian and Barry Qualls, enabled me to obtain support essential to the completion of this project. The Rutgers University Research Council provided additional support toward the publication costs, for which I am very grateful. I am also grateful for grants from the Folger Shakespeare Library that enabled me to attend a conference on British Political Thought and to study rhetoric with John Guillory, and for a fellowship from the National Endowment for the Humanities.

From a list that is too long to provide in detail here, I have enjoyed considerable intellectual support from my colleagues and students at Rutgers. Ann Baynes Coiro has advised me on countless occasions and has read my work with great insight. Michael McKeon commented on several chapters, offering sharp and helpful criticism. I owe thanks to too many graduate students to name here, but I should single out Colleen Rosenfeld for her exceptional insight as a research assistant. Among the many others who have given advice, I'd like to thank Emily Bartels, Stacy Klein, Jonathan Kramnick, Jackie Miller, Ron Levao, and Henry Turner.

While this book has almost no relation to the dissertation I wrote at Yale under the direction of Annabel Patterson and John Rogers, I have benefited enormously from their mentoring. Annabel Patterson has read and criticized countless revisions and reconstructions, and has profoundly shaped the new project's evolution and structure. I will greatly miss the many conversations and arguments over lunch that forged the material for several of these chapters. If she does not agree with the final product, this will, I hope, be cause for many more lunches. I also owe a great deal to Lawrence Manley, Blair Hoxby, Miaja Jannsson (who has since provided parliamentary and paleographic advice), and David Quint, who has since provided valuable observations and saved me from several errors. My early research benefited from support from fellowships from the Beinecke Rare Book and Manuscript Library, the Barbara E. and Richard J. Franke Foundation, and the Mellon Foundation. I have also benefited from the advice of Kathryn James, curator at the Beinecke Library.

Parts of chapter 3 appeared in a different form in *English Literary Renaissance* (2004), and I am grateful for permission to reuse it here.

I thank audiences at various meetings: the members of the Milton Seminar in 2004 for their helpful comments on an early synopsis of this project, especially Nigel Smith; participants in the biannual conferences on John Milton at Middle Tennessee State University; participants of the panels on commonplaces and notebooks at the 2008 meeting of the Renaissance Society of America in Chicago, especially Ann Blair, Peter Stallybrass, and Elizabeth Yale; the Milton Symposium in London, especially Martin Dzelzainis; the Forms of Writing Conference at Columbia, especially Adam Hooks; and the helpful audience at the Oxford Early Modern Seminar, especially William Poole and Sharon Achinstein, who gave essential advice on framing the project. Will Poole's forthcoming edition of Milton's Commonplace Book will be a major asset to Milton studies and to the history of reading. I am grateful for his generosity in sharing his archival and bibliographic knowledge, which enabled a great many improvements to this book. I also owe thanks to the Oxford librarian Mary Clapinson, who shared her vast knowledge of seventeenth-century readers and reading material. The kind hospitality and intellectual vigor of many others at Oxford—particularly Nicholas Perkins, Kirsty Milne, and David Norbrook—made research all the more productive and enjoyable.

I owe a major debt to John Shawcross, who provoked me to rethink some of my assertions, and whose eagle eye caught several mistakes in my analysis of manuscript evidence. Nicholas McDowell offered essential advice on chapter 5 and kindly shared sections of his forthcoming edition of *The Tenure of Kings and Magistrates*. Ray Lurie also caught many bibliographical mistakes. I also thank Arthur Kinney, Carol Betsch, Mary Bellino, and especially Bruce Wilcox at University of Massachusetts Press, and the helpful reports of two readers.

My family has also been very supportive. I owe a special debt to Margaretta Lyon Fulton, mother and humanities editor extraordinaire, who has given me more than I can account for, but who also read this work with great professional attention and made invaluable suggestions and corrections. My parents have not only been supportive, but have provided exceptionally good conversation and companionship over the years. I thank my family generally for many varieties of encouragement: Chandler Fulton, Elaine Fulton, Margot

Robert, William Fulton, Kaysh Shinn, Richard Brantley, Diana Brantley, and two children born in the process, Gabriel and David. I thank Paul Robert for rescuing a forgotten manuscript from a cabin deep in the Maine woods, and my parents for providing said cabin. Jessica Brantley has taught me more about manuscript culture than I probably could have figured out on my own, and has made my thinking and writing vastly better than it would otherwise have been. With these many good people to help, I should like to say that no blunders remain, but all of them, where they do, are my own.

Abbreviations and Texts

BL   British Library

CB   Milton's Commonplace Book, BL MS Additional 36354, reproduced in facsimile in 1876, and printed in original languages in Alfred J. Horwood, *A Common-place Book of John Milton* (London, 1877). To facilitate use with multiple editions and to retain Milton's organizational structure, Milton's original page numbers are supplied with those of *CPW.*

CPW   *Complete Prose Works of John Milton.* Edited by Don M. Wolfe et al. 8 vols. New Haven: Yale University Press, 1953–82.

CSP   *Complete Shorter Poems.* Edited by John Carey. Rev. 2nd ed. London: Longman, 2007.

PW   *Milton: Political Writings.* Edited by Martin Dzelzainis. Cambridge: Cambridge University Press, 1991.

WJM   *The Works of John Milton.* Edited by Frank Allen Patterson et al. 18 vols. New York: Columbia University Press, 1931–38.

Historical Milton

Introduction

Mr. Milton in Aldersgate Street hase written many good books a great traveler and full of projects and inventions.
Samuel Hartlib, 1643

In the past twenty years, research on the history of the book has produced an increasingly detailed sense of how the technologies of reading—such as notebooks, libraries, and practices of annotation—shaped the ways readers confronted texts, collected information from them, and recirculated this information in their own writing. Historians of early modern reading, in particular, have explored the traces of reading left in early modern books, manuscripts, and notebooks, both by attending to individual readers and also by surveying the ways in which certain books or authors were read.[1] Case studies of readers who left extensive records—Ben Jonson, John Dee, Gabriel Harvey, and William Drake, among others—have illustrated the historically different ways in which books were used.[2] Seeking to fill in spaces left in the larger picture by such individual studies, others have explored large archives of used books to see what patterns of anonymous annotation these reveal.[3] This combination of broad archaeologies of reading with detailed individual studies has reinforced collectively a sense that early modern systems of circulation, indexing, reading, and interpretation differ radically from modern ones, in ways that should be taken into account in the historical recovery of a text's meaning.

Studies of Milton have taken less advantage of these advances in the history of the book than have other subdisciplines within early modern studies.[4] Unlike the well-documented libraries of such figures as John Locke, the Countess of Bridgewater, or Henry VIII, which have enabled scholars to draw revealing conclusions about these figures' intellectual endeavors, Milton's physical library is something we have almost no evidence of: there are extant only seven books bearing an authentic "ex libris" of one sort or another.[5] Yet Milton remains a particularly valuable subject for students of the history of reading because he frequently makes precise references to his reading, and also because his private research notes have survived. Preserved in a bound manuscript known as his Commonplace Book, this body of notes is the most comprehensive manuscript record of reading notes we have of a major early modern poet in England. The notebook also provides a rare window on the production process of polemical literature, for, as far as I have been able to find, it is the only political notebook known to have belonged to an anti-Stuart writer during the period of the English Civil War.[6] As such it is not just an invaluable resource for students of early modern literature, but also an aid to understanding early modern political culture more generally, as it offers access to one writer's methods of research and provides opportunities for comparison between private study and public rhetorical performance.

This study focuses on the relationship between the manuscript evidence of Milton's thinking and its public representation in his printed works. We are fortunate to have an unusually rich archive for understanding this relationship: in addition to Milton's Commonplace Book, there is extant a manuscript "Digression," a fantastically trenchant analysis of English politics that accompanied his printed *History of Britain;* the manuscript of *De Doctrina Christiana,* too heretical to be printed while Milton lived and for sometime after; a collection of poetic manuscripts and drafts; and several political poems that existed only in manuscript during his lifetime. I will focus especially on the first two of these manuscripts, the Commonplace Book and the "Digression," both written mostly in the 1640s during the tumultuous period of the civil war. These manuscripts have suffered from an unfortunate but understandable neglect, given the bias toward print that has characterized critical priorities until the 1990s. But if we understand their vital role in this writer's intellectual production, their function and *raison d'être,* we can also see print culture from a revealing perspective, especially the printed texts that are chronologically proximate—*Areopagitica* (1644), *The Tenure of Kings and Magistrates* (1649), the *Observations upon the Articles of Peace* (1649), *Eikonoklastes* (1649), and the great Latin address to Europe, *Pro Populo Anglicano Defensio* (1651). Although the scope of this project will not allow me to trace the whole history of Milton's political writing, nor, indeed, the history of book culture in seventeenth-century England, I hope that the conjunction of these two fields of inquiry will shed new light on each: on the ways in which an early modern writer organized and extracted ideas from his reading, on the fundamental differences between the manuscript records of thought and print material, and on the implications of these habits of reading on the interpretation of early modern texts. Often considered only within the corpus of Milton's writing, Milton's manuscripts deserve special attention not only as physical objects (that is, how and why they assume the form they do), but also as representatives of a larger manuscript and commonplace-book culture.

Although manuscript culture has increasingly interested early modern scholars, the task of "imagining a world where manuscripts were a *normal* mode of literary communication rather than an occasional exception or aberration" as Peter Beal has argued, still "has far to go."[7] My first chapter, therefore, is a brief overview of some of the problems facing the study of Milton's manuscripts within the larger reading culture and how these two most basic forms of material evidence, the scribal and the printed, were treated in cultural and legal terms. Even during the chaotic period of the civil war in the 1640s, attitudes about print regulation as represented by legislative actions, church authorities, and fiery polemicists were at times remarkably severe. Part of the challenge in gauging the differences between manuscript and print evidence lies in understanding how much this repressive language shaped the conditions of writing and, in turn, how much cultural and political impositions on the conditions of writing shaped Milton's own arguments—in *Areopagitica* and elsewhere—about the nature of representation. Manuscripts like Milton's "Digression" in *The History of Britain* or *De Doctrina Christiana* took the material forms they did in part because of specific political shifts and policies regarding the regulation of ideas. These manuscripts seem to have been designed or at least considered for print in their original conceptions, but for political reasons they needed to remain in manuscript form. But texts took different material forms for reasons that were not tied to particular shifts or changes in regulation, and written material was frequently produced not with some printed end in sight but for a context in which its manuscript form served the text's most immediate purposes. A handwritten sonnet to be delivered on the battlefield—such as Milton's "On ye Lord Gen. Fairfax at ye seige of Colchester"—employs a profoundly different rhetorical system from, say, a cheaply printed pamphlet, or a beautifully bound treatise, or a short incendiary text scrawled on the pages of a personal commonplace book.

Investigations in the history of reading have produced many revealing case studies, such as those of John Dee, Gabriel Harvey, and Ben Jonson. My second chapter, on Milton's Commonplace Book, contributes to such studies and to our sense of how Milton gathered information from his reading. I examine the collection of evidence showing not just a record of reading, but also, with the combined evidence of Milton's prose works, the ways in which he organized the knowledge gained from his research and deployed it in public arguments. Milton certainly developed political arguments by finding himself in new circumstances, but his work was not simply occasionalist. His Commonplace Book reveals a focused program of research about the nature of political constitutions, and his positions were often at least partially forged outside of the heat of polemical production. This manuscript notebook also reveals a different kind of political research from that suggested by the two predominant models describing Milton's political thought—classical humanism or political theology—and, perhaps even more importantly, a different kind of research and intended use of that research than that normally practiced. The elements that make up the core of his political argument are not "commonplaces" in the normal sense of the term—truisms drawn from culturally legitimated authorities such as Cicero or Calvin. Nor are they made up of Erasmian *sententiae*, the predominant form of commonplacing in the early modern period. As I argue, Milton is probably influenced by Jean Bodin's criticism of the Erasmian style of note-taking in *Methodus ad Facilem Historiarum Cognitionem* (1566), or *Method for the Easy Comprehension of History*, and favors an analytical assemblage of facts drawn from constitutional history.

For almost twenty years, during the turbulent period of the English Civil War and Interregnum, Milton largely postponed his poetic aspirations to devote himself to polemical, theological, and historical prose. Although this literature has received considerably more attention in recent years, the nature of Milton's political thought *as* political thought—that is, the complex system of ideas that inform his arguments for "civil liberty"—deserves reappraisal. Unlike Thomas Hobbes or James Harrington, Milton did not sit down to write political theory but to address a particular situation with particular adversaries. His public writing during the 1640s took a form that is deeply enmeshed in its discursive and historical context, and he shares a common language with many other pamphleteers at a given moment. These were intellectually competitive conditions, in which a "new persuasiveness of the royalist argument"[8] (for example) had to be countered by a still more persuasive opposing argument, or in which, in the case of the explosion of literature about toleration after 1643, persuasive arguments for suppression and control had to be countered by still more persuasive arguments for liberty. Yet his Commonplace Book indicates a deep interest in political thought that began prior to the outbreak of the civil war, and thus reveals an overlay in his work between a long-term program of reading and note-taking—and the potential writing projects prepared by this process—and the short term, context-driven conditions of polemical writing. Much of Milton's research was conducted under different historical conditions from those in which he put the gathered information to use. Despite the famous headnote to the 1645 edition of *Lycidas,* in which he claims the 1637 poem "foretells the ruine of our corrupted Clergie,"[9] Milton could not have foretold any of these tumultuous upheavals or, indeed, the kinds of texts he would create from his program of research, established sometime around 1637.

Areopagitica demonstrates a complex overlay of long- and short-term reading. Of all of Milton's works, it has attracted the most attention from book historians, since it ranks among the earliest demands for the liberty of printing in England. But *Areopagitica* is about more than books; it is about the way in which information from books is digested. Its core argument therefore is a theory of knowledge, derived from a reinterpretation of the story of the Fall. In chapter 3 I am interested not only in the relationship between his reading notes and the way Milton used his reading in constructing the arguments of the tract, but also in the ways he conceived the political pressures on print culture.[10]

Milton's public polemic is rhetorically complex, often even sustaining contradictory positions in a balance carefully designed to accommodate the views of some readers even while pushing more willing readers to a more challenging position. In *Areopagitica,* he famously argues that books should be treated as malefactors, even as he suggests that such persecution is absurd. *The Tenure of Kings and Magistrates,* rife with contrived contradictions, uses the authority of scriptural arguments and theologians to suggest that it is lawful for magistrates alone to depose a king even while arguing for the absolute sovereignty of the people in deposing without scriptural warrant both magistrate and king. Milton's unpublished work helps reveal how this rhetorical balance functions in the public prose. This is the subject of my fourth chapter, which focuses on the "Digression" in *The History of Britain* and some manuscript poems, which, like the Commonplace Book, serve as interpretive keys to the rhetorical strategies of Milton's printed polemic. The relationship between the "Digression" and *The Tenure of Kings and Magistrates* is particularly revealing, in part (as I argue) because the composition of the "Digression" occurred just prior to that of the printed tract.

The fifth chapter, on *The Tenure of Kings and Magistrates,* continues to examine how Milton's reading habits and methods help us to understand the construction of polemical literature. Here I investigate the ways in which Milton used his political commonplaces and his recent scholarship in British history to forge an argument for popular sovereignty. Crafting a nontheological argument to counter entrenched theological traditions, Milton departs fundamentally from the method of his Presbyterian opponents and from the larger history of Protestant political theology. Like *Areopagitica,* which also has at its core a rational argument that subverts Presbyterian theological traditions, *The Tenure* maintains a complex set of seeming contradictions. Both in and outside of the tract—in his later defenses of the regicide— Milton seems to appeal to the very theological traditions he subverts. The extraordinary range of his reported views has for some readers suggested a writer who was not a "systematic thinker"[11] or entirely in control of his material. I argue instead that these contradictions more often possess a deliberate rhetorical function.

The final chapter continues this exploration of contradiction and rhetorical function through a brief survey of the three surprisingly different tracts written during the first two years of the new republic. Milton is hired essentially as the official counterpropagandist of a teetering administration, a position he seems to grow into even as he slowly loses his sight. The major political work of this period is his masterful satiric rebuttal of a French professor named Salmasius, hired to defend the Stuart monarchy. Written in Latin to address a European audience, *Pro Populo Anglicano Defensio* continues to employ the historical notes from his previous research, adding significant research in the process, but also falling back on classically oriented forms of argument, many of which return him to the kind of Erasmian commonplacing he had avoided through much of his career.

M‍Y STUDY of Milton's reading and writing is greatly indebted to two books involving the revolutionary reader: Kevin Sharpe's *Reading Revolutions* and Sharon Achinstein's *Milton and the Revolutionary Reader*. Sharpe's analysis of William Drake's commonplace books and other manuscript evidence of his reading is at present the only detailed book-length analysis of seventeenth-century political note-taking. This pioneering work has a great deal in common with my own project on a far less extensive manuscript record, and I will endeavor here to draw comparisons between this seventeenth-century reader—among others—and Milton. Drake was born two years before Milton and served as a member of Parliament, although he managed to withdraw himself during much of the strife of the 1640s (he was excluded during Pride's Purge in 1648). Milton's manuscript notes differ in being designed to serve a writer rather than a political operator, and we have the advantage of a printed corpus with which to compare these private notes. Achinstein's attention to the construction of the public reader in pamphlet literature and especially to the rhetorical function of polemical prose has also influenced my exploration of Milton as a reader and writer. Her contextualist approach to the circulation of political ideas seeks to "free English revolutionary thinkers from the bonds imposed by our own search for a consistent revolutionary program."[12] This effort to free our analysis from anachronism is extremely salutary and important to bear in mind at every step in the process: in our search not only for a consistent program, but also for a language that we ourselves recognize as political, according to values and prejudices that have developed since the mid-seventeenth century. Like Achinstein's work and other contextual work on political writing in the seventeenth century, my book has been influenced by Quentin Skinner's emphasis on reading a text "within the framework of its *own* system of communication."[13] Skinner's important criticism of the discipline of intellectual history brought him to suggest that an "attempt to disclose the meaning" of a political tract "must not begin by making an intensive study of the text in itself, but rather by trying to see what relations it bears" to the "existing conventions" of discourse within which it operates.[14] My rethinking of Milton's political writing will also investigate the ways in which Milton's tracts operate within a particular rhetorical framework, but with added attention to what the manuscript evidence of his political thought, and particularly his reading practices—both in the manuscript record and what can be recovered in his writing—reveals about these rhetorical systems. The manuscript notes derived from Milton's reading prior to and during the civil war period, as well as the manuscript of the "Digression," provide a platform from which to survey the rhetorical maneuvering of Milton's public polemics. While not entirely private, these manuscripts were nonetheless constructed for different purposes, and so provide an instructive foil against which to gauge the polemical writing.

Another way Milton's manuscript evidence helps us understand the printed polemic is in the notebook's record of reading itself—not just how the authors read are used, but also how this collected set of authors compares to the body of authors represented in the printed argument. Seventeenth-century writers often wore their reading heavily. Writers used other writers as rhetorical and ideological markers to indicate whence their authority derived or where their alliances stood. Citations in books, which often included chapter and even page numbers, occupied the margins or were inserted in some way into the margins or the body of the text. Some of this marking actually derives from the kinds of commonplace books early modern writers kept: a small pile of crucial passages—biblical, classical, or contemporary—was indexed and kept readily available for a writer to stick in the margins or insert into the text, either as mere citations or in a more discursive engagement. Milton's prose is conspicuously not as "marginal" (a word he once used to describe his opponent William Prynne), nor does he generally seek to compile quotations from the authority of others. But he does engage other writers extensively. His prose, and especially the prose written before his blindness, is riddled with complex citations of a host of writers and texts, most of which fall into five general categories: scripture, literary texts such as Chaucer or Shakespeare, Greek and Roman classics, Reformation-era Protestant theologians, and (to a surprisingly great extent) historians of many nationalities and epochs, although mostly of the late sixteenth century. My aim is to understand how he uses these materials to construct a political argument and to engage in a rhetorical interchange. Political theory and rhetorical maneuverings are often almost inextricable modes of discourse, but they occupy fundamentally different categories of argument that require careful demarcation.

This book is therefore concerned with not only the material forms that thoughts take, but also with the rhetorical textures of these different forms. The manuscript evidence of Milton's political thought shows him to be conducting a form of political analysis that is historically oriented on a level that has not been fully appreciated. Milton's field of reference is also considerably more international than the powerfully nationalistic orientation of his English tracts might suggest. The very fact that there are rather striking differences between the manuscripts and printed texts in his treatment of authors, contemporary views, or theological and political positions should compel us, I believe, to search for patterns that would aid interpretation. In the most extreme cases, these differences suggest patterns of concealment and disingenuity in his polemical work that reveal where and how much Milton sought persuasive function over intrinsic truth.[15]

In addition to the many languages of political thought, there are two basic categories of discourse, increasingly recognized in the early modern period as separate: rhetoric, a form of argument chiefly designed to persuade audiences toward a position in which the speaker holds an interest, and reason, a form of argument bent on unraveling philosophic truth.[16] Unlike Hobbes, Milton does not systematically separate these two categories in his work, although there are discursive elements in his polemical work to which he is philosophically committed, and others to which he is not, and in these the presentation of opinions, values, and authorities are oriented toward the perceived values of his audience, often quite different from his own. The art of speaking indirectly when acting as a political advisor was highly cultivated in the early modern period, and we run some danger of anachronism if we view Milton's polemics through a lens distorted by modern values about rhetoric.

Along with the emerging distinction between rhetorically oriented and rationally oriented forms of argument, the basic languages of political thought underwent major changes during the 1640s, in the context of wars waged between constitutionalist parliamentarians and the English monarchy, between the bishops and the Puritans, and between the Presbyterians and independent factions of Puritanism. The rich variety of discourses mirrors the complexity of this history: English constitutionalists sought to write a history of precedent for parliamentary right, civic humanists reinforced these arguments by appealing to classical republicanism, divine-right monarchists drew from a tradition of Protestant political theology, and opponents fought back using theological and scripturally oriented arguments to support resistance and even deposition. At the same time, in concert with the Hobbesian rejection of rhetoric and embrace of "reason," new political languages appealed to the study of nature rather than custom, theological traditions, scripture, or classical models. Although our conception of Milton's participation in this variety of political discourses has undergone revision, the nature of Milton's politics has been predominantly viewed in two distinct ways: he is considered on the one hand a civic humanist who extols the "ancient liberty" of classical republicanism, and on the other a religious thinker whose politics, like his other convictions, derive from scriptural interpretation. In a study of the topic published in 2006, for example, one scholar asserts that Milton "immersed himself in the literature and writings of the classical republicans" and "also sought answers in scripture."[17] While Milton certainly engaged in exegetical argumentation in his politics, although often for the purposes of refutation, this established notion of his immersion in the classics is not supported by the evidence.

Yet this bifurcated view of the poet's politics stretches back to the Romantics and even before, with the balance of critical interest usually leaning toward Milton's classical politics.[18] One early assessment of Milton's political reading has resonated ever since. The early biographer John Aubrey surmised that Milton's antimonarchist "zeal" derived from his "being so conversant in Livy and the Roman authors and the greatnes he saw donne by the Roman commonwealth & the virtue of their great commanders."[19] This assessment follows Hobbes's famous judgment that the revolutionaries had been spurred on by emulation of the ancient republicans taught in English schools. Aubrey was a close acquaintance of Hobbes and a lifelong admirer, and, as Martin Dzelzainis points out, he had access to the manuscript of *Behemoth* long before it was published.[20] Aubrey's assertion probably derives more from Hobbes than from any Miltonic text, especially given the similarity of its allusions to action rather than theory, and in its single example of Livy, who is not a central part of Milton's political imagination (the historian is mentioned only twice in Milton's English prose, although Livy has an appropriately stronger presence in the Latin polemic *Pro Populo Anglicano Defensio*).[21] Aubrey's observation that Milton admired the "greatnes" done by the "great commanders" echoes Hobbes's ironic appraisal of the "great actions" done in the "glorious name of liberty" by ancient republicans: "There were an exceeding great number of men of the better sort," Hobbes wrote in *Behemoth,* "that had been so educated, as that in their youth having read the books written by famous men of the ancient Grecian and Roman commonwealths concerning their polity and great actions; in which books the popular government was extolled by that glorious name of liberty, and monarchy disgraced by the name of tyranny; they became there by in love with their forms of government."[22] This theory of influence reflects tellingly on Hobbes's perception of his own unusual methodology and its origins. For although he had every advantage the English school system could offer, including the mastery of Greek and Latin at an early age, he was not himself "of the better sort," which may account for his being insulated from the imitation (dangerous in his view) of those "famous" ancient writers and the great actions recounted.

Hobbes's observation of the classical influence on revolutionary ideology is genuinely important on many levels, not least for what it suggests about Hobbes's nonclassical ideological orientation. Milton's particular relationship to classical politics, however, deserves reconsideration. The assumption that he relied heavily on classical precedents has had an enduring legacy, but it is not the most immediate set of vocabularies informing his writing. Although Milton's experience as a student and as a teacher would certainly have inculcated in him the knowledge of classical republicanism that leaves its trace in his work, this trace represents only part of a much larger and more recent program of research, dedicated largely to a reading of history. Curiously enough, as I discuss in chapter 3, it is *Areopagitica* that contains the most forceful language of classical republicanism in Milton's printed work of the 1640s—the manuscripts being still more openly republican—yet even there the classical tradition remains only one of several kinds of argument and rhetoric employed. The major political polemic of the period, *The Tenure of Kings and Magistrates,* shows a diminished investment in classical and especially Roman republicanism—though this is at least partially because Milton seems to be strategically muting the republicanism evident in his manuscripts. Although there are a few suggestive echoes of Cicero in *The Tenure,* for example, the Roman republican is not explicitly mentioned.[23] There is one distinct but uncited echo of the Roman historian Sallust that derives from a passage later used explicitly on the title page of *Eikonoklastes.*[24] And although Aristotle is invoked as among "the best of Political writers" (*CPW* 3:202), Milton mentions him only once in the first edition of the tract. Indeed, the particular passage from the *Nicomachean Ethics* quoted in the first edition happens also to be the only reference to this classical thinker in his Commonplace Book, where the reference glosses a more extensive citation to Thomas Smith, whom Milton also uses more extensively in the regicide tract.[25] It seems clear that he transferred this Aristotelian commonplace from the margin of his notes in the process of moving a number of ideas from more modern authorities. (In the second edition of the tract, Milton refers to Aristotle a second time, significantly calling him "one of the best interpreters of nature"; *CPW* 3:204). Beyond Aristotle, there are only four other cited classical references in *The Tenure*. These are mostly literary, occurring in brief mentions of Livy and Trajan, and in explications of dramatic passages from Euripides and Seneca. There is also an important reference to the neo-Roman *Institutes* of Justinian (*CPW* 3:206).

This short list of classical references should be tallied against two much more dominant reading sources: biblical and historical. There are, as I show in chapter 5, thirty cited or explicit scriptural references, a figure excluding several repetitions, especially of lines from Romans 13, and at least one example drawn from the Apocrypha. Nor does this tally include the scriptural references in the passages from theological authorities added to the second edition. There are thirteen named citations to recent English and European authorities, and another dozen unattributed facts drawn directly from authorities cited in his notes but not in the tract, bringing the total number of historians to at least twenty-five. In spite of Milton's classical training, then, it is fair to say that this formative treatise on civil liberty is not primarily informed by reading the ancients. It also seems fair to conjecture, despite his praise of Aristotle and a few recognizable uses of Cicero, that Milton did not think classical politics were of primary importance in achieving the desired rhetorical effect for his English audience at this moment. So what, really, is foundational to Milton's powerful expression of popular sovereignty in early 1649, and to his political argument more generally?

The nature of our study of Milton's politics itself deserves reassessment. Mere tallying such as this will not produce a fully accurate measure of what went into Milton's mind, or indeed how it functioned once it was there. But it does provide some gauge of what he thought valuable and of what he thought his readers would value. If merely for the purpose of testing presumption, it seems imperative that we begin by studying Milton's ideas not according to what we expect him to have read, but according to what we know him to have read, and to the ways in which he took information and ideas from this reading. Admittedly, what we know Milton to have read is only the tip of the iceberg, and research into the material evidence for the ways in which he constructed texts should never occlude consideration of phenomena for which we have much less concrete evidence: the exchange of ideas through conversation, for example, or the many formative books that may not appear in his writing or in his notes. Yet, to invoke comparison with archeology, it is essential to begin with the fragments of evidence that still exist, with the hope that once the recoverable shards are set into place, the gaps may be sketched in with greater accuracy.

The purpose of grounding an investigation of Milton's rhetoric and politics in a study of his Commonplace Book—apart from its chronological primacy—is to reconstruct our conception of his printed polemics according to his recorded engagement with a large body of reading material. Of course, his published work contains records of reading and uses of authorities that may or may not have appeared in his notes: the interest here is in what the differences between these reveal. Milton began taking notes in the "Political Index" of his Commonplace Book before writing any of the political tracts; indeed, he structures the notebook and begins to take political notes before the civil war, before he has a concrete sense of how the ideas would be employed. He continues to read political history with particular intensity throughout the early 1640s, even when he is not immediately engaged in composing political tracts. But here arises the central challenge facing any study of Milton's politics: just what is political? It could be argued that virtually all of Milton's works are political, especially the prose. The antiprelatical prose, for example, participates in the Puritan critique of the prelacy central to the overthrow of government in the early 1640s. And Milton's arguments for domestic freedom in the divorce tracts participate in a debate about authority that derives much of its strength from its revolutionary context.

I have attempted here to define "politics" as Milton himself does, using the set of categories recognized under the Political Index in his Commonplace Book, and as he also uses the category in subsequent writing. Milton organized his Commonplace Book into three indexes: *Index Ethicus, Index Economicus,* and *Index Politicus.* Milton also recommends this same order—Ethics, Economics, and Politics—for the education of youth, such as those he himself trained from about 1641 to 1646.[26] By a coincidental collusion of political history and private method, the ordering of this Commonplace Book—set in place long before Milton's polemical career—somewhat mirrors the seemingly prescribed structure of this career, which Milton describes later, in 1654, as being structured by the "three varieties of liberty": "ecclesiastical liberty, domestic or personal liberty, and civil liberty" (*CPW* 4:624). Milton also uses these three categories to identify the principal areas of reform in the midst of his tripartite division of labors. In *Areopagitica* he argues that "It is not the unfrocking of a Priest, the unmitring of a Bishop, and the removing him from off the *Presbyterian* shoulders that will make us a happy Nation, no, if other things as great in the Church, and in the rule of life both economical and politicall be not lookt into and reform'd, we have lookt so long upon the blaze that *Zuinglius* and *Calvin* hath beacon'd up to us, that we are stark blind."[27] Reflecting his indexes, the "economical and politicall" constitute a fairly discrete segment of Milton's career in the 1640s; the widest of them, the economic, also includes ideas about the education of youth, which Milton pursued in *Of Education* (1644) and in the projects which occupied him during the hiatus in his polemic career from 1645 to 1649. When Milton writes this in 1644, he had looked into the "rule of life" economical, in the sense that he had written much that derived from his *Index Economicus* in the Commonplace Book, but he would wait several years before becoming a forceful voice in the "rule of life" political. Although the manner in which Milton would execute these projects was hardly predetermined, his retrospective claim in 1654 that he had been long planning to write on domestic and political subjects is fundamentally accurate, especially in the case of politics, since his extensive research on this subject had begun a decade or more before writing *The Tenure of Kings and Magistrates* (1649). It is this tract in which Milton sees himself in 1654 as inaugurating his work on politics and civil liberty, and this tract also uses the information gathered in the Political Index much more intensively than any other—and it is therefore of vital interest to this book.[28]

Something of a categorical anomaly, *Areopagitica* is nonetheless central in Milton's early political writing for several reasons, the most fundamental being that Milton categorizes the subjects of the tract as "political" in his notes, even though his 1654 account of his trajectory vaguely lists it among the works on "domestic or personal liberty." *Areopagitica* mixes the language of politics classically conceived with the more modern discourses of toleration and freedom of expression, thus demonstrating how these two ideological forces were at work at the same time. Milton's own participation in the tolerationist debate is particularly important, since a strong rationalist form of argument emerges in his writing that challenges the method as well as the theology of traditional forms of Protestantism, and in particular that of the majority of his Puritan contemporaries.

"Politics" for this study is therefore limited by Milton's own defined categories: it is that which pertains to the nature of sovereignty, the limitations placed on sovereignty by laws and by the rights of those ruled. Politics is also concerned with the forms government takes, which fall, like other categories in Milton's system, into a binary of monarchic or republican structures. Following the parameters created by the Commonplace Book itself, then, my investigation focuses on the political work created through the recorded process of Milton's reading and reuse. Milton integrated the political notes from his Commonplace Book in *Areopagitica* in relatively small but significant ways, in great numbers in *The Tenure of Kings and Magistrates,* and then to a diminishing extent in a few of the subsequent political tracts before his complete blindness in 1652: in the government publication that included Milton's anonymous *Observations upon the Articles of Peace,* which is not an individual tract but part of a government publication, *Eikonoklastes,* and *Pro Populo Anglicano Defensio.* Milton writes these last few tracts in a different voice, since the new regime hired him as a spokesman for their policies and views. These commissioned tracts serve different purposes even while they each seek to defend the regicide and the legitimacy of a new government: the anonymous *Observations* is a commissioned repudiation of an attempted collaboration of Irish and royalist forces; *Eikonoklastes* is a refutation of the king's supposed self-defense; and *Pro Populo Anglicano Defensio* is a Latin defense of the regicide against a major French monarchist theorist. Milton went blind in 1652, and stopped using his notebook seriously after this point—which is not to say that he stopped getting information from books after his blindness, or that he no longer benefited from the memory of the reading once recorded in his notes. But evidence suggests that the notebook itself, long held to be in continuous use with the help of amanuenses, in fact fell out of use as an active research tool in both senses after 1652—it is not actively collecting new information, and not being used in a measurable or significant manner to recycle old information. It is at the end of Milton's active use of this manuscript, then, that I have chosen to end the book—since this is not a general intellectual history or source study, but an inquiry into a specific relationship between manuscript notes and their use and implications. There is, of course, much more political writing after this major divide in the poet's biography—a few engagements with Cromwell's experimental Protectorate, and a burst of productivity at the eve of the Restoration, which represent for the blind writer yet another transformation in reading technologies as well as methodology, thought, and context, all of which deserve attention in a different book.

Chapter 1

A Material History of Texts
in Milton's England

What Printing-presses yield we think good store,
But what is writ by hand we reverence more.
John Donne, "De Libro cum Mutuaretur Impresso"

[The Parliamentarian defense] is then but making use of some *dull expressions* found
in an old *worm-eaten Record*, . . . delivered in Arguments, or some *dark Sentences* taken
out of a *rotten Manuscript*.
[Charles Dallison,] *The Royalist's Defence* (1648)

THE WRITING of literary history is complicated by the fact that what
remains of the past bears only a partial relation to what actually existed. This
problem is far more severe for the earliest stages of literary history, where—to
take the most famous example—the chance survival of a single flame-scorched
manuscript now known as *Beowulf* must represent an otherwise lost cultural record. Outside of British Library MS Cotton Vitellius A.xv, there are
no traces left of this longest poem in Old English—not a single reference to
the story exists in any other remaining artifact.[1] It is therefore nearly impossible to know its date, whether it was a work known by a large group of
people, whether it was unique in its form or broadly representative. What we
have of early English literary history may be largely a patchwork of anoma-
lies. Similarly, what we know of Ricardian alliterative verse and especially
alliterative romance is heavily dependent on the survival of a single manuscript containing the only known copies of poems now titled *Pearl, Clean-
ness, Patience,* and *Sir Gawain and the Green Knight.*[2] The generic record of the
English medieval morality "tradition" exists largely because of the chance survival of a single volume, the Macro manuscript now at the Folger Library,
which contains three of the remaining four or five vernacular morality plays
written before 1500.[3] While some sense of a much greater spread of this generic form is suggested by the Tudor Interlude, we can hardly be confident

that the plays preserved in this manuscript are representative, even though they happen to be among the only complete representatives.

These fundamental evidentiary problems become far less severe in the seventeenth century, in part because the revolution in print mechanized production and brought with it a system of legal records (from the Stationers' Company) that aided its preservation. Manuscripts, and sometimes literally "rotten" manuscripts, would slowly lose their value as conveyers of texts. Yet in spite of shifts in technology, manuscripts continued as an important alternate method of textual production throughout the early modern period, and the fragility and uncertainties of the manuscript record, while less marked, continue to plague our understanding of surviving manuscripts' relative value and function. The fact that just one reading notebook of Milton's survived, for example, does not mean that it was the only one he had, nor does its survival indicate that its value is greater than other now lost notebooks. A notebook of this sort, of course, is meant only to exist in manuscript. The problem of piecing together literary remains becomes all the more challenging for texts that categorically existed or might have existed in both print and manuscript formats, such as the political sonnets, the "Digression," or *De Doctrina Christiana*. Here we have the additional concern, particularly when the evidence is thin, of addressing some basic problems that would not trouble the interpretation of printed texts: just how were these meant to be read? Were they originally meant to circulate, and how? Are they unfinished, and possibly unvalued drafts, or highly valued representations, perhaps more telling or more truthful than those that found their way into print? If so, why were they not put into print?

This chapter surveys the evidence of several of Milton's remaining manuscripts, how they operated in context, and how they and other controversial manuscripts might have been treated. As the two epigraphs to the chapter suggest, manuscripts held profoundly different values even in the early modern period. In spite of the ironic context of Donne's now famous aphorism—Donne had lent a friend a printed book which was torn apart by children and replaced with a manuscript copy—the lines suggest a reality affirmed in his own practice, in which all but three of his poems were circulated only in manuscript while he lived, and in numbers probably greater than any other early modern English poet: there are now over four thousand manuscript texts, which is but a fraction of what must have existed.[4] (Survival rates vary in puzzling ways: in spite of the value they must have had even then, the survival rate of English poems originating from Donne's own hand is mind-bogglingly low: only one, the "Letter to the Lady Carey, and Mrs Riche," and it was not discovered until 1970.)[5] Scribal circulation was the central mode of publication for poets like Donne, Thomas Traherne, Andrew Marvell, or Katherine Phillips, most of whose poetry was not printed until after their deaths. While seventeenth-century authors might still be reluctant to face the stigma inherent in the wide publicity of print, texts "writ by hand" possessed a special authenticity. Indeed, many genres of early modern writing are inextricably bound to the material form of the manuscript, particularly the common genre of the verse letter, such as Donne's "Letter to Lady Carey," or Milton's epistolary sonnets and poems.[6] These are poems whose primary speech act occurs between the poet and the addressee in a rhetorical relationship that would not function properly if it were initially open to a large readership, since the conditions of privacy provide assurance of the text's authenticity.

In spite of the special quality of authenticity intrinsic to some scribal production, as the epigraph from Charles Dallison's *Royalist Defence* illustrates, manuscripts could by contrast seem far less authentic or authoritative. Writing in the last year of Charles I's life, Dallison takes on the antiquarian work of a parliamentary theorist (perhaps John Selden) who had used information gleaned from manuscript sources. Parliamentary antiquarianism had already a substantial history of challenging royal prerogatives through archival research, and Milton himself would make use of some manuscripts in his republican polemic, such as an "ancient manuscript . . . titled Modus Parlamenti," the ninth-century British historian Nennius, and a manuscript on Llan Daff which Milton had used in *The History of Britain,* possibly obtained through Selden.[7] Dallison's polemical attack on his parliamentarian opponent reveals the potential weakness inherent in the material form of his sources: this political scholarship is "but making use of some *dull expressions* found in an old *worm-eaten Record,* . . . taken out of a *rotten Manuscript.*" Dallison goes on to impugn this unnamed parliamentarian's use of print sources as well, suggesting a tiered conception of textual authenticity, in which manuscripts are at the bottom, and anonymous printed books with obscure origins are almost as bad: "If any *printed Book* be daigned the mentioning, it must not be the *known authentique Authours,* reporting the resolutions of the Court of Justice, nor such as shew the common and constant practice of the Kingdome, which is the Law it self, but some *antiquated* thing whose *Authour* is unknowne, and his meaning as *obscure.*"[8] Manuscripts remained the most unreliable for being potentially inauthentic, authorless, of unknown origin, and empty of the assurance provided by the assumed regulatory system of the Stationers' Company. Their use, Dallison implies, represents a kind of scofflaw scholarship. Using a manuscript required ascertaining its credibility; a printed text came already credentialed. When in a context removed from heightened polemical rhetoric, the Restoration Secretary of State, Sir Joseph Williamson, took notes from his reading of history, citing from a printed text was simple: "out of Stowe's cronicle"; but citing from a manuscript required some credentialing: "out of an unknowne MS but of good credit."[9]

The Janus-faced quality of a manuscript's textual authenticity emerges in the fascinating publication history of Donne's treatise on suicide, *Biathanatos*. Donne circulated this scribal book among a few friends. As he wrote in 1619 to one of them, Sir Robert Ker: "because it is upon a misinterpretable subject, I have always gone so near suppressing it, as that it is onely not burnt. . . . Keep it, I pray, with some jealousie; let any that your discretion admits to the sight of it, know the date of it; and that it is a Book written by *Jack Donne,* and not by *Dr. Donne.*"[10] Donne operates in a category of textual distribution that cannot properly be called "publication" even though the manuscript is reproduced and has circulation. The text is maintained in a special category of scribal circulation in part because its content is highly valued by the author: it is, as Donne wrote to Sir Edward Herbert ten years prior, the only defense of this doctrine ever written. Herbert's library, Donne hoped, would provide a home for it, since "Authors of all complexions" are there preserved.[11] This manuscript possessed a special kind of authenticity; it is presented as a private meditation, in which the author's contemplation of a personal subject remains largely unimpeded by the consideration of its public reception.

Yet when *Biathanatos* was put into print against Donne's wishes some years after his death in the mid-1640s, it was done so precisely in order to preserve its authenticity. Its status as a manuscript made it vulnerable to misuse, largely because it was on a "misinterpretable subject." The very quality that originally kept it in manuscript seems to have forced it into print. As John Donne the younger writes in the preface, "it was writ long since, by my Father, and by him, forbid both the Presse, and the Fire; neither had I subjected it now, to the publique view, but that, I could finde no certaine way to defend it from the one, but by committing it to the other." In order to prevent this treatise from being burned, Donne the younger put it into print in his father's name. Donne's son had been under suspicion by the parliamentary party in the early 1640s, and, as he recounted, "my Study having been often searched, all my Books (and al-most my braines, by their continuall allarums) sequestred, for the use of the Committee; two dangers appeared more eminently to hover over this, being then a Manuscript; a danger of being utterly lost, and a danger of being utterly found; and fathered, by some of those wild Atheists, who, as if they came into the World by conquest, owne all other mens Wits."[12] The manuscript might thus be stolen or "lost," and stolen or "found" by a "wild

Atheist" whose illegitimate fathering would corrupt it enough to make it worthy of the fire, either literally or metaphorically.

This split vision of a manuscript's special authenticity and its high potential for inauthenticity is similar to that which modern readers bring, sometimes by necessity, to handwritten texts. The text titled *De Doctrina Christiana* and attributed to Milton (London, National Archives, SP 9/61), for example, has been historically received on a spectrum of extremes between fundamentally inauthentic and profoundly revelatory. While the contents of this manuscript are not central to this study, its textual history offers an instructive comparison for the others. The "Digression" in *The History of Britain,* now at the Houghton Library at Harvard University (MS Eng 901 [Lobby XI.2.69]), has also been approached with a set of doubts about its date and authenticity, and doubts about whether it should be read as a kind of temporary expression, a discarded draft, or a valued and revealing text. The notes in Milton's extant Commonplace Book, now housed in the British Library (MS Additional 36354), while different generically, are nonetheless subject to uncertainties related to their physical form. Even Milton's commonwealth sonnets, omitted from the volume of poems printed a year before his death, have been treated in diametrically opposing ways according to what that gesture of omission implies about their value. Preserved in the Trinity College Manuscript at Cambridge (MS R.3.4) and published posthumously in a different form, these sonnets raise the most basic question of determining textual authority. For even from a purely editorial standpoint, manuscripts might assume wildly different values, where some editors prefer the printed text when a manuscript copy exists, sometimes out of respect for what the early modern reader would have experienced. With Milton's sonnets, the manuscript has been generally preferred to print, to the degree that the heavily deleted but still legible titles of the sonnets in manuscript—not just those omitted in 1673, but the others as well—have been mostly restored in modern editions, producing a strange hybrid of manuscript and print versions of these poems that never existed collectively. This is an editorial tradition that presumes that authorial intention can be recovered from the manuscript history, or in some cases that the author's intentions should be overruled. Even when a manuscript is clearly authoritative, there can be startling differences between manuscript and print. The fair copy of book 1 of *Paradise Lost* now at the Pierpont Morgan Library differs in small respects from the printed text with alarming frequency: the 798 lines of manuscript differ from the printed text at over a thousand places.[13] Authorial agency remains nearly impossible to reconstruct: the differences in the print version may indicate authorized changes, or changes introduced by stationers in the printer's shop.

In course of this study, I will generally favor a Donnean respect for the manuscript record over a Dallisonian prejudice toward the authenticity of print. But I am aware of the danger of placing too much weight on what are at times rather thin material remains. The purpose of this brief survey of the evidence, therefore, is to consider the various ways in which Milton and his contemporaries valued manuscripts, and what political and social pressures may have dictated the choices between scribal and print production. Milton operated in a world where both printed books and manuscripts were used to embody texts of various forms. Often, as Harold Love has observed, "texts of great political and intellectual importance were deliberately reserved for the scribal medium."[14] This is certainly true of *Biathanatos,* and of texts that were essentially created for controlled scribal circulation. But how much might scribal circulation have been on Milton's mind in composing what remained in manuscript at his death? How much did the changing political climate dictate what he felt he could or could not put into print? And how much did he seek to push against such constraints?

Although manuscript texts would generally have far less circulation, they could be churned out in multiple editions. In the famous case of Machiavelli, the printing of *Il Principe* and *I Discorsi* was illegal during the reigns of Elizabeth and James, and the extensive English knowledge of Machiavelli may at least be partially explained by the circulation of manuscript translations of *The Prince,* seven copies of which surfaced to scholarly notice in the twentieth century.[15] Manuscripts were the mode of circulation for controversial English writers as well. The vast majority of the contentious prose of Sir Walter Raleigh, an author Milton claimed to put into print, circulated in manuscript.[16] The first political tract of Thomas Hobbes, *The Elements of Law,* in some instances over four hundred manuscript pages long, was allegedly distributed to members of Parliament on the eve of the civil war. As Noel Malcolm writes, the evidence "suggests a form of clandestine publication by a production-line of copyists."[17] Hobbes's treatise had (according to its author) been in the hands of "many gentlemen," and "occasioned much Talk of the Author,"[18] who, in fear of his life because of this text, soon fled to France. Although Hobbes may have overestimated the danger to himself, Manwaring had recently been sent to the Tower for arguing for absolutism—and, according to Aubrey, for preaching Hobbes's "doctrine."[19] A remarkable number of manuscript copies of *The Elements of Law* still exist (at least nine from the early 1640s), suggesting that considerable scribal industry accompanied this polemical effort.[20] Of course, manuscripts served purposes other than avoiding the authorities. In an intricate twist of political and publication history, Hobbes produced a beautiful scribal copy of the *Leviathan* on vellum to give to Charles II soon after the book went into print in 1651, per-haps because he feared justifiably that the text would be perceived as sup-porting Cromwell and the new government in England.[21] Again because of his views, despite some strategic changes in the manuscript version, in late 1651 Hobbes was "compell'd secretly to fly out of Paris" under threat, and returned to England.[22]

Research into early modern manuscript culture is complicated by the fact that while the archive is vast, its terrain is made impossible by crevasses of lost evidence. Once manuscripts were superannuated by print, there was little sense in preserving the rudimentary form—not at least until it was old enough to be valued by museums and antiquarians. We have no idea how many copies of *The Prince* were created in manuscript, or of Hobbes's *Elements of Law,* or indeed of Milton's "Digression" in *The History of Britain.* Part of the difficulty lies not merely in the severe paucity of evidence, but in the nature of the technology used to produce it. We need only one copy of a printed text—or even a record that it was printed—to know generally that it was designed to be produced, and for a fairly wide audience. One copy of a manuscript, however, can be much less instructive. In Milton's case, we have examples of each within his own corpus: there is only one remaining copy of *Epitaphium Damonis* (1639?), which is enough to tell us that the work was multiply reproduced, and presumably with authorial oversight, yet the one copy of the "Digression" in *The History of Britain* contains very little intrin-sic information about its reproduction or its authenticity.[23]

Yet print history has its pitfalls as well. In some cases, printed texts have left a surprisingly scant record: there are some printed books for which only one copy remains, or for which there is notice in the Stationers' Register, but no extant printed copy, suggesting that many books remain as yet unfound or uncatalogued. There were many books for which there was no notice in the Stationers' Register, as was the case for 50 percent of the extant books printed in the first decade of the seventeenth century.[24] By 1644, the Register recorded approximately only 20 percent of the total number of books and pamphlets published.[25] Many seventeenth-century printed pamphlets are known only from the single copy preserved in George Thomason's collection now in the British Library. In some cases, advertisements tell of books for which no other record remains. This is true for Milton: an 1656 advertise-ment for books for sale by Edward Farnham lists a lost work titled *The Works of Milton concearning Divorce, digested into one volume.*[26]

An undetermined number of print runs have vanished from the record en-tirely. McKenzie suggests that the number of books listed in the Wing short-title catalog from 1641 to 1700 may represent a mere "sixty to seventy percent of the titles and editions actually published."[27] Print runs ranged from some-where around four hundred or lower, as was probably the case with Milton's *Epitaphium Damonis,* to an upward limit of around fifteen hundred copies (as was contractually the case for *Paradise Lost*), which means that in many in-stances less than 1 percent of the evidence survives.[28] But while we can be fairly sure with most printed texts that hundreds of copies were produced, we can only say, to invoke the example of Machiavelli, that some number greater than seven manuscript copies of *The Prince* were *probably* made. The number is surely substantially greater than seven, yet "substantially" provides little empirical satisfaction. Although medievalists are quite familiar with this problem, the evidentiary strength (and sometimes false assurance) provided by print machinery makes manuscripts of the post-Gutenberg era seem by comparison all the more frustratingly incapable of measurement. Unlike the products of print, books made by hand were not overseen by authorities, so information about them is consequently much harder to trace—manuscripts are not registered, and they rarely include indications of provenance or dates, or names of scriptoriums or scribes. Texts that circulated in manuscript also come in a wide variety of forms: sometimes they take the form of an integral whole, as in the case of Hobbes's *Elements of Law,* but often prose tracts were copied into a miscellaneous collection of other notes and texts, and some-times only in a fragmentary manner.[29]

The production and reception of Milton's manuscripts, although more confined than the *Elements of Law,* remain nonetheless hard to categorize, even with the assistance of Harold Love's useful categories. In Love's view, the physical manuscript took three basic forms: an authorial holograph, a scribal copy, or a copy made by an individual wishing to possess the text. Most of Milton's writing before his blindness—including the vast majority of the en-tries in his Commonplace Book—is in autograph, and most of the writing that is not in his hand is made by a scribe or by an amanuensis taking dicta-tion. Milton's manuscripts were produced in a complex process, and the roles of the amanuenses who took dictation and the scribes who produced fair copies need to be more sharply distinguished—indeed, because of these com-plications, it may make sense to add "amanuensis" to Love's list as a fourth category, since even writers who were not blind used amanuenses. These dis-tinctions are particularly important with regard to the manuscript of the "Digression," which seems to be the work of a scribe rather than a personal col-lector (since it is overseen and corrected in the hand of another scribe), and it also seems—though this remains undetermined—that it is a scribal hand copying the idiosyncratic spelling of Milton's autograph, which (if true) would alone date the original to a period prior to the onset of Milton's blindness in

1652.[30] In the Commonplace Book, entries that are not in Milton's hand could be those of an amanuensis taking dictation, as is usually thought. Yet differences in the function, style, and level of expertise of some of these entries suggest other possibilities: that they are the additions of friends, researchers, or students invited to contribute. In addition to the physical aspects of a manuscript, Love also formulated three related categories for describing a manuscript's purpose: "author publication, entrepreneurial publication, and user publication."[31] These divisions provide an excellent platform for thinking categorically, yet it is often hard with limited evidence to comprehend what the intended form of publication of a given manuscript might have been. Milton's manuscripts are probably mostly authorial—meant for limited circulation if any—though some manuscripts may move toward the entrepreneurial. Although there are only two witnesses of the "Digression"—one manuscript copy and one printed copy that derives from another manuscript source—it seems designed for limited circulation.[32]

The current term "scribal publication" may have the unintended problem of blurring the boundaries between scribal and print circulation. As Margaret Ezell points out, the term "implies that the mode and motive of writing were the same as for print, to achieve a public audience, with a different type of ink."[33] Certainly, many texts achieved a similarly public audience; as Sir Roger L'Estrange complained of Libels in 1675, "not one of forty ever comes to the Presse, and yet by the help of Transcripts, they are well nigh as Publique."[34] Yet in Milton's case, "publication" is not a useful term for most of his scribal output, although he should not be viewed as one who saw print as the only form his writing would ultimately assume.[35] We know that some of his work circulated in manuscript, such as *A Maske Presented at Ludlow Castle* (now known as *Comus*), which seems to have first gone anonymously into print (or so Henry Lawes tells us) only because Lawes's hands grew so tired with copying it that he was forced to give it to the press.[36] Milton's "On Time" was first circulated with the instructions "Upon a Clocke Case, or Dyall," as it appears in a manuscript now housed in the Bodleian (similar instructions are later crossed out in the Trinity MS).[37] A copy of "On the Marchionesse of Whinchester" was copied into a poetic commonplace book, attributed to "Jo. Milton of Chr: Coll Cambr."[38] Sonnet 7 was sent in a letter to a friend that exists in draft in the Trinity Manuscript.[39] Milton's Hobson poems "circulated for many years in manuscript, and were sometimes transcribed by people who did not know or who did not care to know the author's identity."[40] Milton's early poetry was shared with his friends in scribal form in both England and Italy, where he also received poetry in manuscript. In Florence, as James Turner has written, "the Academician Antonio

Malatesti presented him with a manuscript of his own lewd sonnets, evidently responding to the English visitor's interests."[41]

We lack manuscript copies outside of the Trinity Manuscript for the occasional poetry written during the civil war and commonwealth periods with the unsurprising exception of the poem written to the Bodleian librarian John Rouse, which exists in a presentation copy at the Bodleian, possibly in the hand of Milton's nephew John Phillips and corrected by the poet.[42] But the other poems written during this period would very likely have enjoyed some scribal circulation. The sonnet titled "On his dore when ye Citty expected an assault," written in a scribal hand in the Trinity Manuscript, with the title then changed in Milton's hand, was likely reproduced by the same scribe; it appears to be a finished copy rather than one created from dictation, and possibly created in the process of additional scribal copying.[43] Copies were surely sent to the eponymous recipients of epistolary verse, such as Sonnet 13 to Henry Lawes in "Feb.9.1645 [i.e., 1646]," which exists in three versions in the Trinity collection, and one, attributed to J. Milton, was published in 1648 with Lawes's *Choice Psalmes*—a publication which poignantly shows the complexity of relations during this period, and Milton's lack of control over his scribal texts, as the volume is conspicuously dedicated to Charles I, imprisoned and soon to be executed.[44] This version of the poem bears the same title, "To my Friend Mr. Henry Lawes," as the first draft in the Trinity Manuscript, suggesting that the copy sent to Lawes derived from Milton's original. The sonnet to Lawes is the only epistolary sonnet that retained its title in print; the rest have the titles struck through in the manuscript. The occasional title "*To Mr. Lawes, on his Aires*"[45] may have been retained to counteract the radicalism of the untitled sonnets. Sonnet 14, with the title "On ye religious memorie of Mrs Catharine Thomason my christian freind deceas'd 16 Decem. 1646,"[46] canceled in the manuscript and omitted as well from print, was likely sent to Milton's friend the bookseller and collector, George Thomason, although we lack scribal copies outside of the Trinity drafts. We similarly lack manuscript copies outside of the Trinity version of the sonnet addressed to Henry Vane in 1652, although it appeared anonymously in a biography of Vane in 1662, suggesting that the biographer used the copy sent to Vane: "The Character of this deceased Statesman," he wrote, "I shall exhibit to you in a paper of Verses, composed by a learned Gentleman, and sent him, *Iul* 3. 1652."[47]

Perhaps the most suggestive story of Milton's manuscripts is that told by the Quaker Thomas Ellwood, on whom Milton bestowed a manuscript copy of his epic in 1665. "After some common discourses had passed between us," Ellwood recounts, "he called for a manuscript of his; which being delivered to me, bidding me take it home with me, and read it at my leisure; and when I had so done, return it to him with my judgment thereupon. When I came home, and had set myself to read it, I found it was that excellent poem which he entitled 'Paradise Lost.'"[48] It is extremely unlikely that Milton would have relinquished indefinitely the only copy of a poem he may still have been revising. It seems more likely that this was a scribal copy designed to be circulated among friends. As well as being highly versed in the mechanical arts of print publication, the blind writer had employed a large number of scribes for over a decade, and could easily have produced scribal copies for private circulation.

The number of manuscripts in proportion to printed texts that would have crossed Milton's own desk, either in single sheets, like the "paper of Verses" sent to Vane, or in bound codices, remains unclear. But there are significant examples. Milton put into print a manuscript to which he seems to have supplied both author and title in 1658, an act that reveals much about his conception of contemporary manuscript culture. Sir Walter Raleigh's supposed *Cabinet-Council,* a collection of extracts and commonplaces from Machiavelli, Lipsius, Bodin, and others, is actually not by Raleigh, but by a compiler with the initials "T.B." Not one of the nine extant manuscripts of this text attribute it to Raleigh save one, and this attribution is added well after Milton put it into print.[49] This manuscript was in its original Elizabethan and Jacobean contexts an especially fitting text to circulate in manuscript, not only because of its extensive borrowings from *The Prince,* but also because the scribal form could more easily promote its value as a collection of semi-secret counsels. Some extant copies advertise elegantly the special quality of their contents: the copy at the Huntington, for example, owned by the Earl of Bridgewater, is an example of exceptional scribal craftsmanship, on large 8-by-12-inch paper, and bound in vellum with gold inlay, with red marginal lines and large margins for notes—making Milton's quarto print production appear quite scrappy by comparison.[50] Milton may well have known Raleigh was not the author—indeed, the evidence suggests this—but given the fungibility of authorship in manuscript culture, he could have created this attribution for urgent political purposes and for the simple aim of selling the book, since publishers would have been far less interested in a large Elizabethan advice book by an anonymous author. Indeed, it would not be inconsistent with Milton's transformative use of authors, as I will argue, for him to have forcibly linked these views to Raleigh, hero of the anti-Stuart cause and much admired by Cromwell.[51] This spurious attribution may have been facilitated by the fact that it is not an "authored" work in the modern sense of the word; it deserves the distinction used in medieval manuscript culture of a *compilator* or "compiler," a writer whose authorial status lies somewhere between the copyist (*scriptor*) and the author (*auctor*).[52] This was true of Lipsius's own *Politica,* which, as he wrote, "were but a well-arranged register of accounts or COMMONPLACES."[53] As the Elizabethan compiler T.B. himself wrote, in an introductory passage significantly omitted from Milton's version, "I have here (without method or precise order and not unlike to him that gathereth stones, tymber, yron, and other stuffe for a builder) collected together certen authorities, Maximes, and examples, to be applied disposed, and squared unto suche accidentes as th[e] affairs of tyme and proceeding of men shall give occasion."[54] These are not original ideas, but "gathered" commonplaces and passages distilled from the work of others.

Milton's account of the manuscript from which he created the *Cabinet-Council* seems therefore all the more interesting. Among other things, he rewrites the story so as to present himself as a seeing rather than a blind man: "I had the *Manuscript* of this *Treatise,* Written by Sir *Walter Raleigh,* many years in my hands, and finding it lately by chance among other Books and Papers, upon reading thereof, I thought it a kinde of injury to withhold longer the work of so eminent an Author from the Publick; it being both answerable in Stile to other Works of his already Extant, as far as the subject would permit, and given me for a true Copy by a Learned Man at his Death, who had Collected several such peices."[55] There is little evidence provided even here that the attribution is certain: that the "style" is answerable is hardly proof, especially with the disclaimer "as far as the subject would permit" and the dubious assurance that the knowledge of its provenance died with the unnamed man who gave it to him. His use of "publick" here is particularly important in discerning the categories of publication he himself imagined to be in play. For Milton, although such a manuscript clearly had circulation, it is essentially in a non-"public," controlled form.

Milton had other "such pieces" that stood on the verge of becoming public, should the conditions of publication change—including, of course, his own writing. We know, for example, of his acquisition of an inflammatory manuscript by Jean Bodin, *Colloquium Heptaplomeres* (ca. 1588), which was not set into print for over two hundred years, in spite of at least one suppressed attempt in the early eighteenth century.[56] The *Colloquium* is a massive work of philosophical prose—one copy now at the British Library runs to 594 pages[57]—showing the extraordinary industry that could be put into the semi-secret circulation of an important although scandalous work.[58] Bodin's manuscript is significant not only for the tolerationist position it espouses, but also for its sympathetic treatment of many so-called heresies that would be of interest to Milton: mortalism, anti-Trinitarianism, and free-will anti-Calvinism.

The dialogic work included representatives of different religions and belief systems: Catholicism, Calvinism, Lutheranism, Islam, Judaism, natural philosophy, and skepticism. Its many possessors in the seventeenth century include Hugo Grotius, who obtained a copy in 1634,[59] and it has been speculated that Milton obtained the manuscript in Europe in 1638 (also when he met Grotius).[60] This is certainly possible, although our first knowledge of his possession derives from a letter of Hartlib's in 1658, and from another correspondence we know that Milton then sent it sometime before 1662 to a friend in Germany, probably John Dury.[61] Henry Oldenburg, mutual friend of Hartlib and Milton, wrote Hartlib of how he had finally come across a copy of the manuscript, which he nonetheless deemed "not a book fit to be printed."[62] As Oldenburg reports of the manuscript, "If I can get a Copist, I intend, God willing, to have it wholly transcribed, though it will cost much time and trouble . . . The piece . . . containeth almost six quires of paper; wch will not be written out nor in a day nor in a week."[63] Oldenburg's devoted interest in material whose suppression from print he nonetheless endorses is related to a phenomenon James Turner describes as "libertine reading," when a reader and writer admits "the proscribed into the sphere of discourse"[64]—in this case, it is a protected sphere inhabited by himself, his friends, and a connected network of private readers. Such networking structures and production methods were well established, and deserve to be taken into account when considering the mechanisms of censorship, since print is only one form in which texts circulated. While some of these texts may have crossed into the world of print—or attempted that crossing—others were assumed "not fit to be printed" by the readers and entrepreneurial publishers, even without input from the authorities, and circulated scribally as highly valued—if scandalous and scandalizing—texts.

Although most of Milton's reading would have been in print, manuscripts played an important if not rather charged role in carrying information that was either "lewd," as in the case of the Italian sonnets, or politically and religiously risky. Bodin's manuscript was most risky because of its sympathetic treatment of anti-Trinitarianism, a heresy associated with Socinianism. Milton's first brushes with this theologically dangerous position may have been in the late 1630s, perhaps from John Hales, generally thought to be the "learned friend" "Mr. H." mentioned in a 1638 letter to Milton from Henry Wotton, who had formerly served as English ambassador in Venice and advised Milton on his Italian travels.[65] Milton visited Wotton and probably Hales at Eton College, some five miles from his home in Horton. The recent discovery of the manuscript shelf-list of Hales's library, which Milton may well have had access to, reveals an extensive collection of Socinian books among other printed and manuscript texts of interest.[66] Hales kept on his study wall a portrait of the Arminian political philosopher Hugo Grotius—whom Milton would soon visit—and was a member of the "Great Tew Circle," a group of intellectuals that met throughout the 1630s to form "an esoteric graduate reading party in the country" at the house of Viscount Falkland, described by Aubrey as the "first Socinian in England."[67] These readers included such luminaries as Robert Boyle, William Chillingworth, Edward Hyde (the Earl of Clarendon), Ben Jonson, Thomas Hobbes, John Suckling, Edmund Waller, and others, with celebrity visits from Grotius.[68] In 1636 Hales wrote a short manuscript tract concerning "Schisme and Schismaticks" in the form of a letter to William Chillingworth that circulated widely to readers such as Joseph Mede, Samuel Hartlib, members of Parliament, and even (presumably against Hales's wishes) Archbishop Laud.[69] Like many other members of the Great Tew Circle, Hales gained the reputation of a Socinian, although perhaps merely for writing sympathetically about anti-Trinitarianism. Hartlib had sent the tract to Mede, and Mede's 1638 letter in response reveals the incendiary nature of the manuscript's contents: "I have looked it but once over. But any more free or particular censure thereof than what I have already given look not for, lest I be censured my self. 'Tis an argument wherein a wise man will not be too free in discovering himself *pro* or *con,* but reserved."[70] Hales's tract was later printed in 1642, when a breakdown of censorship had made such publication possible.

Toleration tracts often circulated in manuscript largely because they entertained the possibility that a "heresy" like anti-Trinitarianism might not in fact be heretical. For similar reasons "heretical" tracts and treatises, such as Milton's *De Doctrina Christiana,* were often tolerationist. The relationship between heresy and toleration had a substantial history. One of the earliest works of tolerationist thinking after the Reformation, Sebastian Castellio's *Historia de Morte Serveti,* appeared in manuscript in Basel in 1553, shortly after the anti-Trinitarian Michael Servetus was burned at the stake through the mutual efforts of the Inquisition and John Calvin.[71] Castellio's tract finally went into print posthumously in 1612 with another book that circulated widely in manuscript, *Contra Libellum Calvini* or Against Calvin's Book, in Which He Tries to Show Heretics Should Be Coerced by the Right of the Sword.[72] Castellio's response to Beza's *De Haereticis,* titled Concerning the Non-punishment of Heretics by the Civil Magistrate, also circulated in both Latin and French manuscripts and was not printed until 1971.[73] The persecution of Servetus caused other writers to take up the cause of toleration, such as Guillaume Postel, whose work *Apologia pro Serveto* circulated widely in manuscript (ca. 1553; printed in 1748). Bodin may have also been specifically motivated by the persecution of Servetus, as he seems to have left Geneva in 1553, and later composed the *Colloquium Heptaplomeres,* which treats Castellio with sympathy.[74] Indeed, Bodin's *Colloquium* is allegedly based on a series of conversations held in Venice and recorded by Postel.[75] Anti-Trinitarianism has a fairly pronounced place in this treatise, since Bodin's most sympathetic character Salomon refutes the Trinity, as it has (according to him) no scriptural support.[76] Even Grotius circulated a (now lost) manuscript on toleration, *Meletius,* which apparently "gravely shocked the orthodox."[77]

There is thus a considerable history of radical prose tracts that circulated in manuscript, as well as a history of manuscripts written to defend anti-Trinitarianism and toleration under a governmental position of intolerance supported by Calvinism. This history of intolerance is one of the contexts in which Milton's own writing—both manuscript and print—deserves further scrutiny. The most famous of his manuscripts, what Milton himself termed his "best and richest possession," is *De Doctrina Christiana.* And yet the problems of authenticity inherent to manuscripts have plagued no Miltonic manuscript more than this theological treatise. Some critics have argued that this is a profoundly revealing and authentic representation of the author's ideas, and thus an interpretive key to the more ambiguous theological representations of *Paradise Lost* and other more public texts, while others have argued that the manuscript contains much less authentic and even possibly inauthentic views. It has been argued that perhaps the main scribe of the manuscript was simply Milton's student, in a work "begun under Milton's tutelage and amplified abroad under religiously eccentric authorities, or that he copied the work of someone now unknown to us, producing a manuscript that the blind man felt obliged to improve modestly."[78] Although this position represents what is now an extreme position, the fact that the manuscript is scribally produced has been a source of broader concern. As John Shawcross has flatly asserted, "anyone familiar with the manuscript of *De Doctrina Christiana* cannot be happy with the assumption that the text in Daniel Skinner's hand is a reliable copy of the manuscript that Milton produced through Picard and the other amanuenses, any more than one can rely on their work; or that the manuscript represents what Milton would have approved publishing."[79]

Sometimes treated as a kind of private work for the author's own edification, *De Doctrina Christiana* shows conceptual and physical signs of being created with an audience in mind, and it may have had some circulation beyond the many amanuenses, copyists, and friends that Milton worked with.[80] The manuscript records a complex overlay of composition and correction, in which one partially extant base manuscript, elegantly created by the professional scribe Jeremie Picard, is entirely replaced in a first section by Daniel Skinner, who may have been preparing it posthumously for press, and at any rate disposed of or passed on the long section originally copied by Picard in the late 1650s. Picard's own scribal copy, although heavily revised, has an ornate formal layout that shows it to be a fair copy rather than one produced from dictation, and thus itself the product of revision and recopying. Picard used three scribal fonts, employing a large font for emphasis and a small italic script for proof texts, the labor of which could not have been enjoyed by a blind writer who commissioned this work, except to know that it would be clearly read by others.[81] The physical evidence suggests a collaborative process of production, and one that involved both readers and editorial assistants. In addition to these two main hands, there is writing in the hands of several others that may number as high as eleven contributors, each of which make an addition or correction.[82]

Moreover, the prefatory pages indicate some sense of Milton's aim to publish the treatise, although expressed in remarkably conditional terms: "*If* I communicate the result of my inquiries to the world at large . . . *if* . . . I readily give as wide a circulation as possible to what I esteem my best and richest possession, I hope to meet with a candid reception from all parties, and that none at least will take unjust offence, even though many things should be brought to light which will at once be seen to differ from certain received opinions" (*WJM* 14:9, emphasis added).[83] That Milton considers giving it "as wide a circulation as possible" suggests a distinct consciousness of narrower kind of circulation, which it may have been intended to have, depending on the conditions of publication. This conditional phrasing seems out of place in a printed version of the text, and may indeed have been meant for revision should the text have gone into print. Milton's unusual frankness about circulation continues in his words about concealment: "Concealment is not my object; it is to the learned that I address myself, or if it be thought that the learned are not the best umpires and judges of such things, I should at least wish to submit my opinions to men of a mature and manly understanding" (11).[84] The words about concealment seem conceptually as well as historically paradoxical: given that this is an act of open disclosure to a reader, the unnecessary words about concealment seem all the more conscious of the fact that concealment may, in spite of Milton's hopes, *have* to be an object, as it had been for a substantial tradition of other texts espousing anti-Trinitarianism. And yet Milton makes it abundantly clear that he writes with an audience in mind: he recounts, for example, that he "thought fit to scrutinize and ascertain for myself the several points of my religious belief," and then turns to suggest the same to the reader: "it is in the hope that others, who have a similar wish of improving themselves, may be thereby invited to pursue the same method" (5). Clearly, this is a work designed for "others."

Yet for significant periods of Milton's career, the circulation of certain ideas would have to be highly circumscribed, and concealment of one sort or another would be a high priority. This was true even in the putatively free days of the civil war and interregnum, as after the 1648 "Ordinance for the Punishing of Blasphemies and Heresies," which deemed that those "Printing" and even "Writing" anti-Trinitarian ideas "shall suffer pains of death." The distinction in this legal document between the printing and writing— between print or manuscript evidence—suggests that beyond even the cultural and formal differences these physical forms of representation had different legal statuses: the idea here being that even private evidence of belief was, in this case, equally culpable. Anti-Trinitarianism remained only part of a host of positions forbidden under threat of death, and the ordinance went on to spell out other, less damning offenses. For Arminianism, the ordinance seemed less interested in private manifestations of belief than public disclosure: those who sought to "publish or maintain . . . that man by Nature hath free will to turn to God"—a position that could have been pinned on Milton's *Areopagitica* (1644)—would be "committed to prison."[85] This brief history of extremist rule in England was less effective in the persecution of bodies than it was in psychological fearmongering. The Socinians Paul Best and John Biddle were imprisoned, but never executed or burned at the stake, although they were threatened.[86] But a constant strain of extremist rhetoric advocating the persecution of heretics resonated through the print warfare of this period as well as in legislation.[87] Milton was frequently included in fanatical lists of heresies and their practitioners for his views on divorce, and might well have been included for views that he had not disclosed to the public.[88] In December 1648 the same Parliament that enacted the persecutory laws was overthrown (or "purged"), which dramatically altered the course of policy, and may have prevented the severe ordinance of the summer from being put more fully into practice.

These moments of extreme governmental control deserve attention in our reconstruction of Milton's positions and his method of representing them— both physical and rhetorical—in this period. It is indeed the period in which, as I argue in chapter 5, Milton wrote the dark "Digression," and subsequently, after Pride's Purge of the same persecutory Parliament, the more optimistic *Tenure of Kings and Magistrates*. Milton evidently watched the governmental prohibitions keenly, and seemed ready in a changeable climate to respond to the lifting of them. As Martin Dzelzainis has shown, on August 10, 1650, the day after the earlier Ordinance was replaced with the relatively lenient

Blasphemy Act—a day he precisely remembered nine years later—Milton, now working for the government, licensed the Racovian Catechism, a Socinian document espousing anti-Trinitarianism.[89] In spite of his caution, Milton still managed to get in some trouble. The publisher was first investigated, and then Milton was interrogated, and he defended himself (according to a contemporary report) by citing his credentials as a published defendant, in *Areopagitica,* of the position "that men should refrain from forbidding books."[90] Just as he seems to have waited for a favorable moment to publish the Racovian Catechism, Milton must have imagined a safer time for publication when he began composing the unfinished manuscript of *De Doctrina Christiana,* and wrote casually that "concealment" was not his object. Indeed, as a recent study of the manuscript has argued, Milton probably sought ardently to conceal the manuscript at the Restoration.[91]

If the manuscript of *De Doctrina Christiana* had not been found in 1823, or had not been shown with a strong degree of certainty to be authentic (a scholarly process that has taken nearly two centuries), our understanding of Milton's theological beliefs would stand on far more speculative grounds, and in many cases take an entirely different form.[92] This is especially true of anti-Trinitarianism, the most persecuted belief in the period, a view carefully hidden in Milton's printed work.[93] In some cases, such as that of mortalism, Milton in *De Doctrina Christiana* "adopts minority positions that seem at odds with his other writings."[94] As Balachandra Rajan has pointed out, the idea of Creation *ex deo* is "scarcely discernable in *Paradise Lost.*"[95] It was once surmised that the seemingly different and more ambiguous representations of theology in *Paradise Lost* represented a change in the author's opinions or affirmed the inauthenticity of the manuscript.[96] It is now more often thought that this change represents the conditions of writing, as Milton suggests in a self-reflexive moment in *Paradise Lost,* describing himself as "fallen on evil days . . . and with dangers compassed round."[97]

These same "evil days" are responsible, I would argue, for keeping a good deal of Milton's important writing, as well as his unwritten views, from seeing the light of print. At the Restoration, the Act of Indemnity and Oblivion mandated that "all names and terms of distinction" of the civil war period will be "put to utter oblivion."[98] The Printing Act of 1662 reinstituted many of the regulatory measures of the Stuart government before the civil wars (particularly the Star Chamber decree of 1637).[99] In addition to general legal measures, Milton's own *Eikonoklastes* and *Pro Populo Anglicano Defensio* were singled out in a royal proclamation with John Goodwin's *Obstructours of Justice,* to be called in and burned. The proclamation states that the books "contained sundry Treasonable Passages against Us and Our Government, and most Impious endeavors to justifie the horrid and unmatchable Murther of Our late Dear Father, of Glorious Memory." According to the Proclamation, "the said *John Milton,* and *John Goodwin,* are both fled, or so obscure themselves, that no endeavors used for their apprehension can take effect, whereby they might be brought to Legal Tryal, and deservedly receive condigne punishment for their Treasons and Offences."[100] While Milton endured only a short stay in prison, Goodwin suffered far worse: excepted from the Bill of Indemnity on June 18, 1660, he went into hiding and died in 1665.

The Act of Oblivion, the Printing Act, and the singular treatment of Milton are major factors in understanding why Milton's manuscript work was either self-censored or censored, and it suggests that the work published may have taken a very different form had it not been for these prohibitions. These events supply the easiest explanation for why several of Milton's sonnets, to turn to the example of his poems, were not published in his name during his lifetime. Yet in part because we have no record of censorship (as we do for other Miltonic texts), these manuscript poems have been subject to a vexed set of questions. The best texts of the sonnets to Fairfax, Cromwell, and Cyriack Skinner (a sonnet that mentions the condemned *Pro Populo*), exist in the Trinity Manuscript. They appear posthumously in a quite different form, tucked into a collection of Miltonic papers published by Edward Phillips at the end of the seventeenth century, *The Letters of State, written by Mr. John Milton* (1694), and again in John Toland's *Life of Milton* (1699).[101] The sonnet to Vane, also omitted from Milton's collected poems in 1673, appeared anonymously in [George Sikes], *The Life and Death of Sir Henry Vane* (1662); Vane was excepted from the Bill of Indemnity and executed. The four poems in the Trinity Manuscript may have been excised against Milton's wishes, or perhaps, as Annabel Patterson has argued, Milton "chose not to publish," in order to keep his "poetry from being contaminated by [the ideas of] his polemical prose."[102]

The four unacknowledged sonnets pose something of an editorial problem as well as an interpretive one. Yet a number of small particulars suggest that they had a life outside of Milton's poetic notebook, that Milton did not willingly abandon them there, but instead had hoped late in life to print them with the rest of his poems. Since there is significant evidence that Milton sent several other poems to their addressees—to Rouse, Lawes, and Vane, for example—it seems safe to conclude that the excised poems circulated in the most primary sense. Indeed, the differences between the Trinity manuscript and the 1694 printing of these poems are quite extensive, not just in accidentals or missing words and phrases, but also in frequent phrasing differences, suggesting they derive from different manuscript originals, or from copying and recopying.[103] In one instance in the poem to Vane, a word crossed out in the Trinity Manuscript shows up in print in these late posthumous editions, showing that this poem must have circulated in different forms. The word "right" is crossed out and replaced with "firm" in Milton's manuscript, and yet it seems to have first circulated in some manner with "right," since this excised word shows up in both of the print editions of the 1690s.[104]

If Milton had wished to dissociate his poetic corpus from his polemical writing, he would probably have cut the two sonnets that are explicitly on his pamphleteering: Sonnet 11, which boldly begins, "I did but prompt the age to quit thire clogs / By the knowne rules of ancient liberty," and Sonnet 12, which begins, "A booke was writ of late call'd Tetrachordon," which had the earlier, canceled wording "I writt a book"—a correction made by a scribal hand, suggesting that these slight changes of wording were part of the process of making the texts safer to print.[105] Instead, all that is cut is the challenging title to Sonnet 11, "On the detraction w[ch] follow'd upon my writing certain treatises," not canceled (as the epistolary titles are) in the manuscript, but instead written again in what appears to be a fair copy of the poems in a non-Miltonic hand, with the instructions: "these sonnets follow y[e] 10. in y[e] printed booke," which refers to the 1645 edition of the poems. That these are instructions to a stationer rather than simply an owner of the printed poems (to insert the manuscript at Sonnet 10) is suggested by further instructions for the ordering: "to come in as is directed in the leafe before" and "to come in heer turn over the leafe," which include the excluded poems originally titled "On y[e] Lord Gen. Fairfax at y[e] seige of Colchester," "To the Lord Generall Cromwell May 1652 / On the proposalls of certaine ministers at y[e] Committee for Propagation of the Gospell" and "To S[r] Henry Vane the younger."[106] All of these titles are canceled, like the canceled titles of the earlier poems that made it into the 1645 edition, and instead given sequential numbers that follow the earlier printed sequence. Yet they never made it into print, and the numbering is accordingly altered at some late stage of the publication process.

Milton thus seems to have endeavored to publish the four commonwealth poems, but was prevented or changed his mind because it was dangerous to do so, not for aesthetic reasons. Vane, Fairfax, and Cromwell, whose corpse had been disinterred and hoisted to public view in 1661, were erstwhile heroes of the Good Old Cause. Their names alone—and especially Cromwell's or Vane's, coming from Milton—would have been enough to give pause to the publisher. (When the publisher of the poems of Marvell, hardly as vilified a figure, made the mistake of including Marvell's Cromwell poems in the posthumous *Miscellaneous Poems* (1681), the publisher was arrested and the sheets were removed; the poems survive today in only two known copies.)[107]

In the sonnet to Skinner, Milton refers to a work that had been recalled and burned, when he recalls that he lost his eyes "In liberty's defence, my noble task, / Of which all Europe talks from side to side." Republican sentiments resonate in the highly suggestive line in the sonnet to Fairfax, "O yet a nobler task awaits thy hand" (line 9).[108] The sonnet to Vane, like that to Fairfax, contains markedly republican language, a distinctive feature of Milton's manuscript texts. A "better senator ne'er held / The helm of Rome" (l. 3) than Vane, who is described as moving by the "two main nerves" of war, "iron and gold" (ll. 7–8). These lines seem to derive from a Machiavellian entry in his Commonplace Book, an extremely rare application of Milton's Machiavellian notes, especially those in a scribal hand. In the Economic Index, a scribe wrote "Against riches Machiavelli argues rightly that 'riches are not the nerves of war as is generally believed'" [CB 148, *CPW* 1:414–45]). The political language and names that could associate these poems and their recipients with the overthrow of the Stuart government is surely what barred them from print. As the language of the Act of Oblivion specified, "all names and terms of distinction" from the civil war were to be erased.

The "Digression" in *The History of Britain* shares some of the language of the political sonnets (particularly the sonnet to Fairfax, as I argue in chapter 4), and it too seems likely to have been omitted from print publication for political reasons. Once appropriately called "the frankest reflections of the greatest poet of his age on the greatest upheaval of seventeenth-century England,"[109] the manuscript demonstrates the peculiarly paradoxical nature of texts that often assume a manuscript form: the frankest reflections, yet preserved in an extremely unstable form—a form that lends itself to profound uncertainties as to how these reflections are to be read. Like *De Doctrina Christiana,* it shows signs of having been designed and copied for an audience, although in this case just the fit and very few indeed.[110] Milton may have written this trenchant piece of historical analysis thinking that he might publish it, but in fact he did not, and its ideas sharply differ from any he did publish. Moreover, the "Digression" seems to comprise only a portion of the unpublished remains of the *History;* there is record of a lost stash of material excised by the censor held by Milton's friend the Earl of Anglesey. Edward Phillips records in his biography that in 1670 Milton "finisht and publisht his History of our Nation till the Conquest, all compleat so far as he went, some Passages only excepted, which, being thought too sharp against the Clergy, could not pass the Hand of the Licencer, were in the Hands of the late Earl of *Anglesey* while he liv'd; where at present is uncertain."[111]

Shortly after these apparently unsuccessful attempts to sneak political or religious criticism by the licenser in his publication of *The History of Britain*

(1670), Milton seems, as Stephen Dobranski has argued, to have developed an elaborate method of slipping criticism into print. While the precise origins of the *Omissa*—some ten lines inserted late in the printing process of *Samson Agonistes* (1671)—cannot be known for certain, the print history suggests an author versed in the art of circumventing licensers, eager to circulate dissenting material. As Dobranski suggests, two basic hypotheses may be drawn from the evidence of the *Omissa:* either that "Milton slipped in these ten lines after having the book licensed on July 2, 1670, in an attempt to avoid the licenser's censure and emphasize the poem as a political allegory," or that "a licenser initially suppressed this and/or other passages" and thus "Milton may have been using the *Omissa* to defy the government's stricture."[112] The second of these choices seems less likely, since Milton could then have been charged with committing an act of open defiance rather than an innocent act (or so he could claim) of last minute revision. But the fact that he had just preserved "some excepted passages" of the *History* from the censoring hands of the licenser strongly encourages the first of Dobranski's reconstructions.[113] The "Digression" in *The History of Britain* seems to perform the same function in manuscript—and perhaps was designed to perform the same function—as the added *Omissa* does to *Samson Agonistes.*

Milton was continuously at battle with the mechanisms of prohibition which sought (often quite inconsistently) to define the limits of what was printable: in spite of a Licensing Order of 1643, for example, Milton refused to obtain a license to publish divorce tracts, and wrote a major polemic against licensing. Shortly thereafter, perhaps in part because the extremists included his views among the heresies that deserved persecution, Milton retreated from print culture to write several texts including some that would remain in manuscript until after his death. Even when he was put in a position of licenser, he put into print a text that immediately invited governmental action. At the Restoration, he was frequently at odds with print regulation. That even his first venture into print, *Paradise Lost* (1667), was printed at all is a testament to his skill in working with publishers; he returned in fact to a family business that had published several political tracts.[114] As John Toland wrote, "We had like to be eternally depriv'd of this Treasure by the Ignorance or Malace of the Licenser; who, among other frivolous Exceptions, would needs suppress the whole Poem for imaginary Treason in the following lines" (*Paradise Lost,* 1, 594–99):

> As when the Sun new ris'n
> Looks through the Horizontal misty Air

Shorn of his Beams, or from behind the Moon
In dim Eclips disastrous twilight sheds
On half the Nations, and with fear of change
Perplexes Monarchs.[115]

We unfortunately do not know what other "frivolous Exceptions" were either excised or included, but Milton's manuscripts continued to be challenged by licenser. When Milton sought to publish a *History of Britain,* it contained passages that "could not pass the Hand of the Licencer." It seems possible that some effort to circumvent the licenser may account for both the manuscript "Digression" and the *Omissa;* certainly the single extant copy of the manuscript "Digression" would perform this function.

The material evidence concerning Milton's two largest prose projects, *De Doctrina Christiana* and *The History of Britain,* indicate a pattern of composition in which Milton wrote with the idea that the conditions of publication would become more lenient. In the case of the theological treatise, he may have also written with the idea, suggested in the conditional clauses of the introduction to *De Doctrina Christiana,* that his work could have a circulation that was *not* "as wide as possible"—such as the circulation enjoyed by Donne's *Biathanatos* or Bodin's *Colloquium Heptaplomeres.* Like these texts, Milton's manuscripts may not have been entirely private, nor were they designed to be, although they have a character much unlike those texts Milton chose to put into print. The distinction here must therefore not be strictly between public and private, but between public and various forms of nonpublic—often a form of nonpublic that bordered on becoming public should the conditions of publication change.

Even Milton's Commonplace Book, to which I now turn, more clearly designed for private scholarly use, may have had some in-house circulation among friends and students. Like the many hands in *De Doctrina Christiana,* it too has many scribal visitations, where individual contributors make as few as one or two entries—possibly at times directed by Milton, but often not. This manuscript also had a posthumous life and readership. A later seventeenth-century owner of the manuscript continued to make entries: not as presumptuous acts of defacement or unauthorized intrusions in another's notebook as we now might view them, but as such books customarily found use. Yet in spite of these limited acts of circulation, the notebook allows us to venture as close as is possible to the private, unpublished Milton.

Chapter 2

Combing the Annals of Barbarians

The Commonplace Book and Milton's Political Scholarship

When a man would looke he should vent something of his owne, as ever in a set speech the manner is with him that knows anything, he, lest we should take notice of his stupidity, declares it by Alphabet, and referres us to odde remnants of his topicks.
Milton, *Apology against a Pamphlet*

THERE ARE limits to what source study can reveal about the derivation of a writer's ideas, even when we are fortunate enough to have a substantial collection of notes from that writer. Yet even in the most straightforward ways, Milton's collection of notes, titled the Commonplace Book shortly after its discovery in 1874, remains an unusually rich resource, in part because the evidence of his private research suggests a different intellectual enterprise from that which he conducted publicly. Many entries reveal a Milton absent from his public self-presentation, such as the strongly voiced opinion that it would be "absurd beyond measure"[1] to prohibit the dramatic arts, suggesting that Milton stood at a more substantial distance from Puritan contemporaries than might be judged by his public discourse. Had the manuscript not been discovered, posterity would also have been left with a very different picture of what Milton read and what he took to be important from this reading. While Milton speaks only disparagingly of the bogeyman "Machiavell" in his public work, for example, there are several excerpts from the Italian writer in his Commonplace Book that suggest he regarded Machiavelli as a valued resource. The contrast reveals that Milton's public treatment of this authority—among many others—must be treated with caution.

The Commonplace Book also shows that Milton was invested in the problems of civil liberty long before the composition of *The Tenure of Kings and Magistrates* (1649), which Milton considered his first tract on the subject. He had begun a serious program of research on topics that take a prominent place in this tract before he wrote the antiprelatical tracts and in some cases before the outbreak of the first Bishops' War in 1639. The close connection between this research and his political work complicates the view that Milton invented himself as a political writer as a response to the pressures of immediate circumstance. Much of the potential in this unusual record remains unrealized in part because the 1876 facsimile is quite rare, and modern print editions cannot easily recapture Milton's system of note-taking, his chronologically layered entries and marginal comments, or the manner of the additions made in the hands of several others. Although important work was done in the early- and mid-twentieth century, few comprehensive investigations of the manuscript have since appeared.[2] The notebook has instead been usefully mined to illustrate the sources for particular ideas, although often without considering how these passages functioned in the manuscript, or the divergent ways in which Milton represented ideas in the different media of printed polemic and manuscript notes.

Following Lisa Jardine and Anthony Grafton's seminal article on Gabriel Harvey's methods of reading and the pioneering work on commonplacing by Ann Moss and Ann Blair in the mid-1990s, scholars have investigated the ways in which information, phrases, sententiae, and other expressive material were gathered from texts and recycled.[3] This research allows us to understand how much the conventions of note-taking in early modern England might have compelled Milton to record what he does, and it also provides a clearer sense of how he moves against these conventions. The increasingly well-drawn history of the use of commonplace books also suggests that the status of the entries made by other hands in Milton's Commonplace Book, some twenty-seven entries by seven scribes (or more, if posthumous use is included) ought to be reconsidered. Once these essential parameters are roughly established—in addition, of course, to the most basic facts of the work's chronology—it becomes possible to reexamine the relationship between Milton's system of notes and the printed texts it was used to create.

The Political Index constitutes by far the largest portion of Milton's Commonplace Book, although it was not originally planned as such. In structuring the book, Milton left himself a series of blank pages for each index: *Ethicus* starts on page 1, *Economicus* on page 101, and *Politicus* on page 177, ending on page 247, with an index or table of topics at the end (figure 2.1). *Ethicus* thus has exactly a hundred pages, and *Economicus* and *Politicus* are each left about seventy-five pages, thus leaving domestic and political subjects 75 percent of the space devoted to ethics.[4] Yet over time this apportioning of space was not representative of actual use, and the accumulated notes develop very different proportions from the space initially allotted them, with a major shift occurring in the early 1640s, when the political entries become far more numerous— ultimately taking over three times the space of the others. Many pages in each

Figure 2.1. The Index of Milton's Commonplace Book, showing the structure of the notebook as Milton set it up initially, the chronological layers of topics as they were added, and the substantial gaps he left for the addition of new topics. From Milton's handwriting, ordering, and ink, it is clear that the first two topics in the Political Index were "Respublica" and "Rex." Unlike the Ethical and Economic Indexes, where substantial gaps for new topics are provided in the very beginning of the indexing system (perhaps suggesting that primary importance had yet to be determined), "Respublica" begins on the first page of the Political Index. The Index has several topics added that are not in Milton's hand, such as those from pages 197 to 205, which are by Lord Preston, except the topic on 198, "Varius Reipub. Status," or "Various Forms of Government," which is in the hand of a "Machiavelli Scribe," possibly John Phillips. BL MS Additional 36354, p. 251. © The British Library Board.

Leges

Savanarola escendogli mandato una scommunica da Roma non l'ubbe
di dicendo in sua difesa una bella parabola, la quale si proua cho side
piu tosto ubbedire alla intentione delle leggi che alla parole. l.1. p.48-49
rinouation della chiesa.

Lambard saith that laws were first deris'd to bound and limit the power of
governours, that they might not make lust thire judge, and might thire minister
avarice. c.3.

Some say they ought to have reasons added to them. il legislatore dee rende ragione del suo
decreto diminuisce l'autorità sua, però il suddito s'attacca alla ragione ad
doltta, e quando grade haver'l miso l'opra l'havor aplo l'ebata la virtual
P.960. Alfred turnd the old laws into english. I would he live now to redus of thy norman
sta. p.80 gibbrish. the laws of Molmutius, as Holmsh. p.15. and of Quene Martia. see Holinshed. in the raigne of Sisilius the son of Guintoline. p. 19. was also of the wes-
Saxons & made many laws Holinshed. l.6.c.1. and he it was that made that
shamefull, and unworthy law of peter pence. renew'd also by the murderer
Offa the Mercian so thinking to expiate his horrid sins. Holinshed. l.6.c.4.

De iure naturali, gentiu et ciuili quid statuam iurisperiti. vide Iustinian institut. l.1. tit.2.

Edward the Confessor reduct the laws to fewer, might them, and set out under that
name of the common law. Holinsh. l.8.c.4.

Lawyers opinions turn with the times for private ends. Speed. 614. 615. Rich 2. but
there md it to be civilly & p.616.

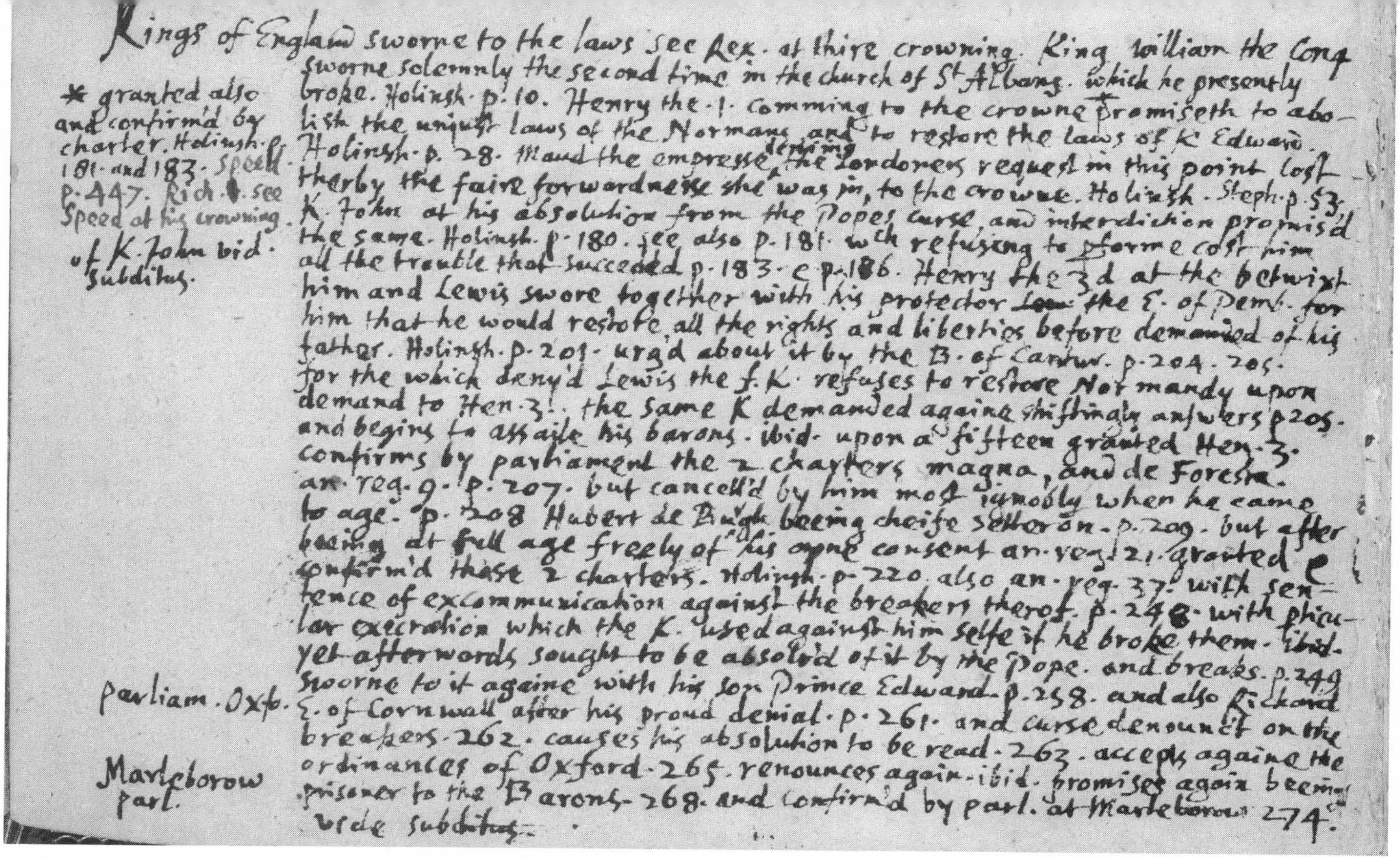

Figure 2.2. "Laws" from Milton's Commonplace Book, showing one of many clustered entries to Holinshed's *Chronicles*, in which Milton seeks to cite multiple instances of English kings being sworn to the laws at their coronation. The page contains a few cross-references, "vide Subditus" and "see Rex," which provide access to related passages. The third entry on this page, crowded by the second and fourth, was clearly written after, showing that the sequence is not determined by chronology. BL MS Additional 3634, p. 179. © The British Library Board.

of the book's three sections remain blank. The *Index Ethicus* contains roughly 64 entries, the *Index Economicus* contains 67 entries, and the *Index Politicus* contains 236 entries.[5] Out of the 95 authors quoted, 66 appear in the Political Index.[6] Although the topics are all designated in Latin, most of the entries are in English, with about a third in Latin, and some in Italian.

Precisely when Milton acquired this codex of 254 blank pages and organized it into a note-filing system remains something of a mystery.[7] While it is possible that the careful diminutive hand of the first entries belongs to the early 1630s, it seems far more likely that they were begun during his independent studies after he left Cambridge, around 1637, when he was still using the distinctive Greek ε common to datable manuscripts of this period.[8] The style of handwriting and other evidence suggest that the vast majority of the entries occur after 1638; the ultimate terminus for this majority is easy to determine, since Milton could no longer see to write after the early months of 1652.[9] The bulk of the entries seem to fall into the period from about 1639 to perhaps as late as 1648, with many falling in the years 1639 to 1641. This dating, much of which remains speculative, has been established by such evidence as the extensive use of Holinshed in *Of Reformation* (1641), the relative position of entries on the page (see figure 2.2), and the placement of citations from recently published books.

It has long been thought that for the period after his blindness Milton simply continued using his Commonplace Book with the help of amanuenses, with the dates of these entries traditionally set from 1650 to 1665. The presumed function of these additions as strictly the work of amanuenses taking dictation for a blind writer has contributed to a misconception that the Commonplace Book was in unvarying use throughout Milton's career.[10] There are many reasons to reassess this view, one being that it seems unlikely that Milton would have used the book so sporadically during this period. The small handful of entries that have been attributed to the late 1650s or after have little recognizable relation to Milton's work at this time, thus giving no explanation for why the blind writer would have instructed a copyist—and a different one almost every other time—to take out his notebook for a brief entry after years of nonuse. Unlike the entries in Milton's own hand, few of these fit Milton's structured reading agenda or style of entry. John Shawcross has suggested that most if not all of the amanuenses were his former or current students, and that their notes may have been made during the period when Milton took up several students, between 1642 and 1647.[11] There are a couple of entries that almost certainly came after this, made by Jeremie Picard in 1657 or 1658, one of which corresponds to additions made to *Pro Populo Anglicano Defensio,* which appeared in an extended edition in 1658. This entry, shown in figure 2.3, supplies an extremely rare correlation between the notebook and Milton's blind period, yet it suggests more about his working relationship with scribes than it does about the Commonplace Book, since it seems not to have been made *prior* to the editorial changes in the text in 1657 or 1658: the changes are an expansion of an earlier citation to Augustine in the *Defensio,* not generated from the Commonplace Book but from other Augustinian passages in the 1651 text. In this unusual case, the notebook seems not to have supplied the reference to a piece of finished writing, the norm for Milton's own entries, but rather the other way around. The kind of un-Miltonic entry made here by Picard—casual, complementary, not agenda-driven—seems the pattern of many of the scattered entries made by various members of Milton's scribal team.

Although commonplace books were by and large private, they were sometimes shared, a fact that bears weight in determining just how to consider entries in Milton's book that are not in his hand. Most of these are recognizable as the work of the same people Milton used as scribes and amanuenses, but the hand of Lord Preston is demonstrably posthumous. All of these posthumous notes are omitted from the Columbia and Yale editions, suggesting a canonicity in the remaining scribal entries. But it may be asked whether the other contributions to the book were made under conditions of far less supervision, either by invitation, or—as in the case of Preston—in a casual continuance that was not unusual. It is dangerous to suggest, as is often done, that these entries attest to Milton's "writing" and "reading,"[12] as if there is no doubt that Milton would only have let someone write in his Commonplace Book under the strictest supervision; indeed, it is evident that many contributions cannot derive from direct dictation. Some of theses entries are jejune and out of place, full of cancellations and mistakes, suggesting that they are not the work of amanuenses properly speaking, but of students, friends, or assistants operating with considerable freedom. Since the entries by hands contemporary with Milton account for less than 10 percent of the Political Index, this is not of major consequence here, although over half of these (14 out of 22) are from Machiavelli's *Discorsi.*

The entries from the *Discorsi,* since they are more extensive, professional, and pertinent, were likely made under different circumstances from the others. These students or scribes behave more like researchers, although still not recognizably as amanuenses. The entries from the *Discorsi* are more commonly

Rex

De regibus Britannis inquit Gildas, ungebant reges, non
Scum. p. 119. contra quàm nunc vulgo æstimat, quosmmqꝫ
scilicet reges dei unctos esse.

Si in principatu positio aliqua est servitus, magis proprio servus est qui præ-
est, quam qui subest: Augusti. de Civit. Dei lib. 19. cap. 14.
sieriuos fortasse princey tuan Profes. et Mirowne et loc offendiy Siua aulor
ball rith Ranges gg olynque their houvure et empohery iuxto threseldey
Go th Communicat et profitable example of ys. Bodin. de F. Aug. Roub. L. 2. c7. p. 229.

Successio.

Come Dipoi = si commincio a fare il principe per successioni, e non per electione subito cominicarono gli henri.
a degenerare dai loro antichi, e lasciando l'opere virtuose pensarono chi i principi
non havessino a fare altro che superare gli altri Di sontuosità edi lascivia e d'ogni
altra qualità Dilicina M......

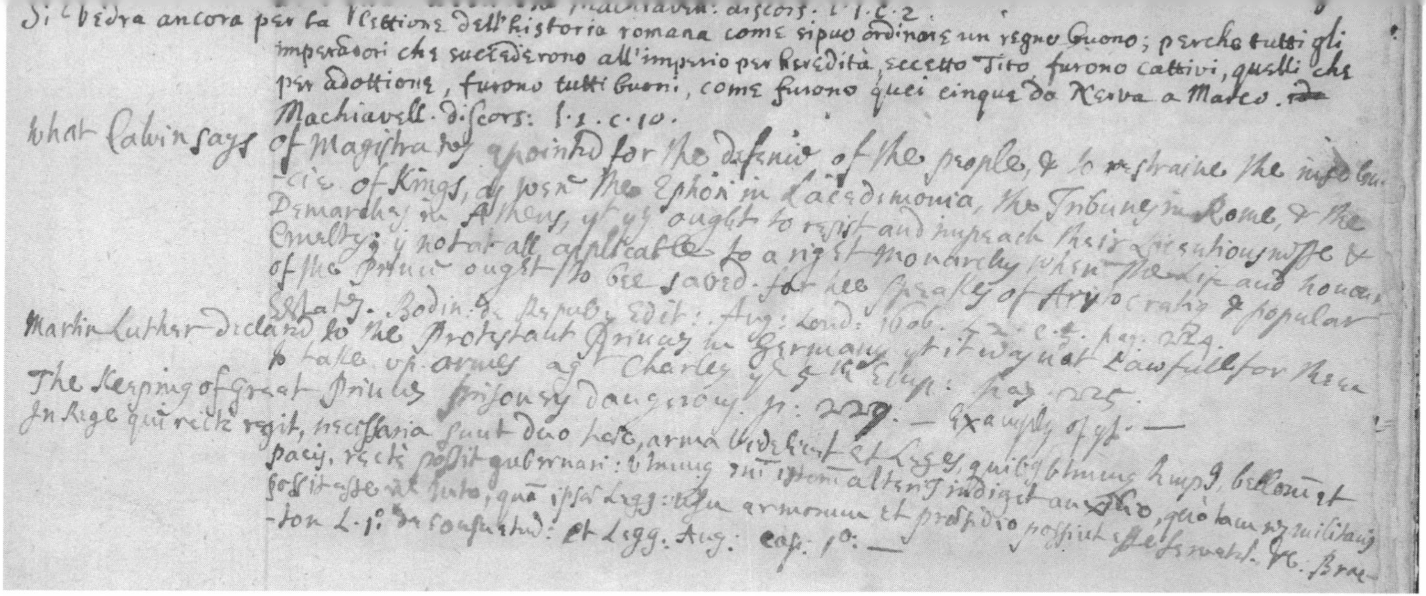

Figure 2.3. Scribal entries by Picard, a "Machiavelli Scribe," and Lord Preston. All of the entries on this page, except for the first entry and the topic of "Rex"—the fourth and last page devoted to this subject—are in hands other than Milton's. Picard's entry from Augustine is in the elegant scribal hand second from the top. Preston's entries—"What Calvin says"—are particularly significant for what they reveal about Milton's categorically different record of reading. BL MS Additional 36354, p. 195 (detail). © The British Library Board.

intermixed with Milton's own, and more frequently under Milton's written topics rather than under topics created by a scribe. One of these scribes has the recognizable hand of Milton's nephew Edward Phillips, who, with his brother John, studied formally with Milton for six years, and may have continued less formally after 1646. The second "Machiavelli Scribe" is arguably John Phillips. Instead of deriving from Milton's blindness after 1652, these Machiavellian entries seem more likely to date some time in the late 1640s, prior not just to Milton's blindness, but also to the execution of the king in 1649. One such example considers a question that seems far more appropriately asked before the execution than after: "Whether it is permissible to kill him. Against a bad ruler there is no other remedy than the sword. 'To cure the ills of the people, words suffice, and against those of the prince the sword is necessary.' Macchiavel. Discors. c[hapter] 58. Book 1" (CB 185, *CPW* 1:456). In spite of its pertinence, this potent entry follows a convention in commonplacing that Milton's own entries seldom do: it extracts from Machiavelli a sententia: a pithy, quotable aphorism that might be committed to memory and inserted into one's own speech or writing.

Milton's Commonplace Book and the Conventions of Note-Taking

Commonplace books offered a system of recall such that excerpted arguments could be easily accessed under topical headings. The use and style of these headings derived from a notion of "topics" that had evolved from Greek and Roman models. Aristotelian topics concerned the rhetorical methods to be used in argument, rather than the arguments themselves, and while some of the methodological directions of Aristotle still shaped the constructions of rhetorical commonplaces, Renaissance humanists followed the sense of topics as it was used by Roman rhetoricians such as Cicero, for whom the topic was not a method of argument so much as the content of the argument itself.[13] Accordingly, Gabriel Harvey wrote that he favored Cicero's *Topics* over Aristotle's "for civil use . . . and for public application (*praxis*) of arguments."[14]

Particularly informative to the structure of Milton's note-taking was Aristotle's idea of opposites in rhetorical persuasion, articulated first in the long list of common topics (*topoi*) in *On Rhetoric:* "One line of positive proof is based upon consideration of the opposite of the thing in question. Observe whether that opposite has the opposite quality. If it has not, you refute the original proposition; if it has, you establish it."[15] Milton promotes this technique in his textbook *Art of Logic,*[16] one of the pedagogical projects undertaken during his retreat from public debate in the years from 1645 to 1648.

In the chapter "On the Adverse," Milton explains how Cicero, Ramus, and Aristotle treated contraries:

> Aristotle defines contraries (for so he called the adverse in Categories 6 [6.6a17–18]) 'as those things which are at the greatest distance within the same genus'; and again in Categories 8 [11.14a14–15] he says that 'contraries are either in the same species or in the same genus.' Cicero follows him in the *Topics* and Galen in *De optima secta*. But in truth the adverse, as Aristotle teaches in his chapter on contraries, not only differ most widely in the same genus, as do white and black, but also in contrary genera, as do justice and injustice; or the genera themselves, as good and evil, virtue and vice. (*CPW* 8:262–63)

Each of these opposites has a correlative in Milton's Commonplace Book, which begins with the opposing topics "Moral Evil" and "of the Good Man"; "Virtue," and then a set of vices: "Avarice," "Gluttony," and "Lust" (CB 4, 5, 6, 12, 13, 14). In the *Art of Logic*, Milton further cites Tibullus' use of the opposites "Liberty" and "Servitude" (*CPW* 8:263), topics that Milton uses in his own Commonplace Book, among many other contraries: "Lenity," "Severity"; "Lust," "Chastity"; "Riches," "Poverty." Milton's interest in representing opposing arguments also transcends the topic headings, for even within a given topic he might examine both sides of an issue without apparent bias.

The entries in the Commonplace Book allow us to see Milton reading and thinking, largely through surveying his process of selecting and assembling arguments. The individual entries consist of passages recorded from Milton's research, sometimes accompanied by a short commentary that represents either his own opinion or a paraphrase of the cited author, usually with a precise enough citation to the author, work, and page that the edition can be traced. The entries often contain sufficient information to be reused in subsequent argument with rewriting, although some entries require a return to the indicated source should the material need to be quoted. While it is hard to tell what factors formed each set of entries, their relative completeness may be dictated in part by the accessibility of the books. All of the reading notes taken from the parliamentary theorist Thomas Smith, for example, although *De Republica Anglorum* was quite popular, suggest that Milton may have been using a source outside of his own collection, as they are recorded in such a way as to make returning to the books unnecessary, and citations to Smith in Milton's printed work seem to come directly from the notebook. Whereas the minimal notes from Holinshed, De Thou, Justinian, Stow, or Chaucer suggest a kind of index providing quick access to his own library.

In the case of Chaucer, it is possible to chart the course of Milton's reading through the *Canterbury Tales* at some point in the early 1640s. Since a few of these entries come from a fairly small portion of Chaucer's narrative, the process of reading can be followed with some accuracy. For some authors, such as Holinshed, for whom Milton often records large clusters of entries in one sitting, it seems clear that Milton marked passages for citation in the books as he read, and then turned to his notes to record these marked passages. Thus, as William Poole observes, "we can only reconstruct the order of Milton's review of his reading, and not the order of his reading itself."[17] Yet in the case of the *Canterbury Tales,* the order of Chaucer's narrative itself allows for some safe presumptions about sequence. And while we cannot know in every case whether he marked passages or excerpted while he read, the essential evidence of reading remains. The earliest recorded passage from the *Canterbury Tales* was made under an established Latin topic heading with a thoroughly Miltonic presentation of opposites: "Marriage see of Divorce." Here, after some two dozen previously entered sources, Milton wrote "the discommodities of mariage. See Chaucer marchants tale, and wife of Baths prologue."[18] Reading forward in the *Wife of Bath's Tale,* Milton then marked or perhaps flipped directly to another established topic heading "Nobility," which then had only two other entries, to write simply "See Chaucer wife of Baths tale fol. 36," and then, reading forward only a few more lines on that page in Chaucer, Milton marked a passage to be recorded under a topic with only one previous entry, "Poverty," where he wrote "See Chaucer. no poverty but sin. wife of Baths tale. p. 36."[19] Since little of this manuscript notation is itself quotable—in the case of "Nobility," there is nothing here to indicate what Chaucer or the Wife of Bath says about nobility—Milton probably meant the terse entries to serve as bookmarks for a text to which he had easy access. The views of the Wife of Bath coexist on a seemingly equal plane with those around her—with a book of Greek and Roman law compiled and edited by Johann Löwenklau and Paolo Sarpi's history of the Council of Trent, a juxtaposition that demonstrates the notebook's virtually indiscriminate commingling of genres and tones.

Whether discursive or perfunctory, the notes in the Commonplace Book are by nature casual and unfinished, and thus provide a rare window into a writer's private intellectual history. Yet despite the informal and unformed status of the notes, they conform on some level to traditions of self-organization in the early modern period, which gives them a constructedness and generic quality of their own. At the same time, Milton's Commonplace Book deviates considerably from the structure and purpose of some well-established conventions of early modern commonplacing. The notes taken here are mostly not "commonplaces" as the term was often understood, but ideas, facts, and the interpretation of history. The notebook is therefore much less an arsenal designed for rhetorical reuse so much as it is a research tool designed to help solve questions about history and, by extension, the present. To be sure, passages and citations would find reuse, and their manner of reuse is vital to understanding Milton's composition process and his rhetorical negotiation with other writers. But the reuse of notes based on facts drawn from history serves a very different function from the reuse of sayings and authorities.

The vogue for commonplacing in both Latin and the vernacular grew to such an extent that in the sixteenth and early seventeenth century books were increasingly printed with passages already marked for extraction and reuse. Junius Lipsius's monarchist *Politica* (1589) came equipped with its quotations "clearly marked typographically" in italics, to show (in the words of Ann Moss) that they were "eminently extractable, as indeed they have already been."[20] Lipsius shows his own process of composition as an example to be imitated: "The spider's web [*textus*] is no whit the better," he wrote, "because it spins it from its own entrails; and my text no whit the worse because, as does the bee, I gather its components from other authors' flowers." Addressing the reader directly, Lipsius instructed imperiously: "These are COMMONPLACES, under which you should duly register extracts from what you have read or will read on the same subject. Look and imitate."[21] Unlike Milton, Lipsius employs classical commonplaces from a host of sources, with passages from writers like Tacitus and Sallust carefully chosen so as to omit republican sentiment or the ambiguous treatment of imperial power.[22] When Lipsius was translated into English in 1594, small pentagonal stars are used so that "sentences" can be "distinguished."[23]

The recent work of Peter Stallybrass and Zachary Lesser has detailed the ways in which the commonplacing of English poets flourished around the turn of the seventeenth century, which saw a series of published commonplace books with excerpts under topic headings from English poets such as Shakespeare, Drayton, and Chapman.[24] These include two major productions, each with alphabetically ordered topics, *Englands Parnassus; or, The Choycest Flowers of our Moderne Poets* and *Bel-vedére; or, The Garden of the Muses,* both published in 1600. Publishers involved in the production of these collections were also involved in marking the sententious passages in such texts as Shakespeare's *Lucrece* (1594) or the first quarto edition of *Hamlet.*[25] These are appropriately the two Shakespearean texts singled out by Gabriel Harvey in his famous marginal notes in Speght's Chaucer as able to "please the wiser sort."[26] Even passages in Holinshed—Milton's most cited source in his Commonplace Book—came with italicized sententiae that, as András Kiséry has shown, Shakespeare preserved in at least one occasion in the first folio edition of *Henry V.*[27] Like the 1603 *Hamlet,* the elaborate 1605 edition of Jonson's *Sejanus* also came with inverted commas to indicate sententious passages to be copied and commonplaced, and in this case we know of one reader contemporary to Milton—William Drake—who dutifully copied into his notebook the passages marked for extraction.[28] Fittingly for Drake, the sentences in Sejanus are often, like Lipsius's, political advice, aphorisms pertaining to politics—advice to the king from an advisor like Polonius or a Machiavel like Sejanus. In the same marginal passage that Harvey praises *Hamlet,* he compliments "Daniels peece of the Chronicle" as "a fine, sententious, & politique peece of poetrie."[29] For Harvey, as for many of these writers, "sententious" and "politique" often went hand in hand.

Unlike Lipsius, who borrowed from others, the English poets are themselves usually the authors of these marked commonplaces—and clearly strove to be. The cultural role of commonplace books and even the market itself reinforced a style of literary production that privileged sententiousness and language packed with deportable phrases and axioms. Jonson claimed that he had discharged the offices of a tragic writer in *Sejanus* through the "fullness and frequency of Sentence."[30] The "Sentence," often synonymous with the maxim, aphorism, or apothegm, refers in this case to an essential element in ancient tragedy, which came to Renaissance tragedians largely by way of Seneca. Neoclassical tragedy used sententiae in imitation, and in printed editions of such playwrights as Giraldi Cinzio and Robert Garnier they were similarly set off by inverted commas.[31] When Thomas Kyd translated Garnier's *Cornelia* (1594), he maintained Garnier's markers, but also offset the sentences in rhyme. Like Kyd, and perhaps following him, Jonson emphasized the sententiae with both material and literary markings. Unlike the blank verse of most of *Sejanus,* these marked passages feature aphoristic abstractions set in strongly endstopped couplets. Thus, in words that may derive from Machiavelli's *Prince,* Jonson's Sabinus pronounces that tyrants' arts "Are to give flatterers grace, accusers power, / That those may seem to kill whom they devour," or later: "When power, that may command, so much descends, / Their bondage, whom it stoops to, it intends."[32] What is striking about these commonplaces is the sheer portability of these separable units of language. Polonius becomes the source for utterly credible advice; Sejanus or the Wife of Bath might be mined for their wisdom on politics or on the "discommodities of marriage." In part because Renaissance authors are "conditioned to argue *in utramque partem*—on both sides of the question,"[33] as Joel Altman wrote of the compositional structures of English drama, the original

The faults and many mo committed through the negligence of Adam Scriuener, notwithstanding Chaucers great charge to the contrary, might haue ben amended in the text it selfe, if time had serued : Whereas now no more, then the Prologues only, are in that sort corrected : which fell out so, because they were last printed, Sentences also, which are many and excellent in this Poet, might haue ben noted in the margent with some marke, which now must be left to the search of the Reader : of whom we craue in Chaucers behalfe that, which Chaucer in the end of one of his books requesteth for himselfe,

Qui legis, emendes autorem, non reprehendas.

Lo
O

FINIS.

gabrielis haruij, et amicorum ⸳ 1598 ⸳
Un raro assai piu, che Cento mediocri ⸳

Figure 2.4. "Sentences . . . now must be left to the search of the Reader": Harvey's annotated copy of Thomas Speght's Chaucer (1598), with Harvey's commonplacing marks in the margin. BL Additional MS 42518, fol. 435v. © The British Library Board.

context, speaker, and generic tone matter less than the rhetorical force of the sentence.

Yet Milton's own reading places far less value on rhetorical formulation, even where the ideas themselves may still have the same separable portability. Some evidence of the portability of ideas can be found in Milton's use of Chaucer, and he in fact cites from an edition produced around the height of the vogue for marked sententiae. Perhaps because Chaucer used the same rhymed pentameter that marked English sentences in tragedy, he was similarly promoted as a master of the sentence, a compositional strategy that had the added benefit of ready extractability. In the first edition of Speght's Chaucer (1598), Speght laments on a corrections page that "Sentences," "which are many and excellent in this Poet, might have ben noted in the margent with some marke, which now must be left to the search of the Reader" (see figure 2.4). Speght's comment wonderfully suggests that premarked commonplaces—imitating in print the annotations readers habitually made in pen—would provide readers with the option of simply skimming a text for excisable words of wisdom.

We know that Milton used the second edition of 1602, because his citations match the later edition's changed foliation. Here Speght rectified the

☞ That he is gentle that doth gentle deedis.
And therfore deare husbond,J thus conclude,
All were it that mine auncetors were rude,
Yet may that high God,and so hope J,
Graunt me grace to liue vertuously :
☞ Then am J gentle,when J begin
To liue vertuously,and leauen sin.
    And there as ye of pouertie me repreue,
The high God,on whom that we beleue,
In wilfull pouerte chese to lead his life:
And certes,euery man,maid,and wife
May vnderstond,Jesu heauen king
Ne would not chese a vicious liuing.
☞   Glad pouert is an honest thing certaine,
This woll Seneck and other clerkes saine.
☞ Who so would hold him paid of his pouert,
J hold him rich,all had he not a shert.
☞ He that coueteth is a full poore wight,
For he would han that is not in his might.
☞ But who ꝑ nought hath,ne coueteth to haue,
Is rich,although ye hold him but a knaue.
Uery pouert is sinne properly.

Figure 2.5. Manicules in Milton's Chaucer. This is the same edition of Chaucer that Milton used, with "sentences and proverbs noted," as it advertises on the title page. The manicules indicating extractible sentences are peppered across the pages that Milton cites in his notebook and in his prose, but Milton never seems tempted by marked sententiae. *The Workes of our Ancient and Lerned English Poet* (1602), fol. 36v. Beinecke Rare Book and Manuscript Library, Yale University.

lack of notation, and accordingly promoted the "Sentences and proverbs,"[34] which were marked in this new edition by the marginal pointing hand William Sherman calls a "manicule."[35] It is unlikely that Milton valued these markers, as he does not follow them. When Milton cites the treatment of poverty in the *Wife of Bath's Tale,* there is a manicule pointing, as shown in figure 2.5, to the couplet, and not the final line that takes Milton's interest:

> But who yᵗ nought hath, ne coveteth to have,
> Is rich, although ye hold him but a knave.
> Very povert is sinne properly. (fol. 36v)

Milton's "no poverty but sin" is a close paraphrase of the last unmarked line—it may perhaps qualify as an aphorism, and it is about as close as one gets in Milton's notes to a traditional "commonplace." In Milton's final citation from Chaucer, a passage from the *Physician's Tale*, Milton accurately quotes three lines pertaining to the topic of the education of youth, and in this case the passage is not valued as sententious by Chaucer's seventeenth-century editor, nor does it seem to be valued for the language, so much as for the ideas, by Milton.[36] Milton cites concretely from the *Canterbury Tales* a few times in his printed work, all in pamphlets written at the probable time of his manuscript entries: several references appear in *Of Reformation*, and a glancing reference occurs in *Animadversions*, both written in 1641. In *Of Reformation*, where Milton actually quotes Chaucer, he does so from the "merry Frier" as described in the General Prologue, and then twice at length from the spurious *Plowman's Tale*,[37] which Milton treats as Chaucerian, all to argue that England has been "forewarn'd at home by our renowned Chaucer, and from abroad by the great and learned Padre Paolo" (*CPW* 1:595)—reflecting the same juxtaposition of authors in his notes.

In none of the cases in his Commonplace Book or in his printed prose does Milton seem remotely drawn by passages marked by manicules suggesting reusable sententious material. Thus, while these early citations in Milton's prose come somewhat close to conventional English commonplacing habits, Milton is much less interested—indeed he is at significant times quite averse—to aphorisms and sententiousness. In fact, the words "sententiously" and "sententious" appear only once each in Milton's entire corpus of printed poetry and prose, the first used to describe the king's rhetoric in *Eikonoklastes* and the second in Satan's mouth in *Paradise Regained*, tempting the Son with the rhetorical power of "brief sententious precepts"[38]—in conspicuous opposition to Milton's far from "brief" enjambed style. These examples suggest a deep connection between the inventions in political argument represented in Milton's concerted deviation from the Erasmian and Lipsian norm and the inventions in prosody that especially characterize the late poems. Even in the material he collects from his reading, Milton seems averse to the qualities of "sententious" representation that Jonson embraces, reinforced through the predominant, prescribed, and even market-driven methods of commonplacing.

The defining difference in style between the Cavalier Sons of Ben and Milton thus seems to emerge not just as a practice of writing, but as a practice of reading.

STUDENTS IN English schools were trained to keep commonplace books as a way of building a structured system of information that would help in the construction of an argument of any sort. Most education manuals included some injunction that "schollars may be sure ever to have store of matter, or to find of a sudden where to turne to fit matter for every Theame," and "every schollar should have his Common-place booke written."[39] John Brinsley's *Ludus Literarius* (1612) cites as prime examples Erasmus's *Adages* and "Tulies sentences," and then suggests "the rules in Erasmus *de Copia*" as a key to commonplace-book construction.[40] The pedagogical tradition of commonplace books had deep roots in the curriculum of Milton's own grammar school, St. Paul's, devised by John Colet with the help of Erasmus and others, and Erasmus dedicates *De Copia,* a system for training rhetorical virtuosity, to Colet for use in his new school.[41] Under the rubric "Commonplaces," Erasmus explains the value of the *exempla* gathered in a commonplace book: "Thus, as one should obtain the greatest and most varied number of these possible and have them always at hand. . . . *Exempla* are also drawn from the differences in authors, for example: From historians, from poets, and among the latter, from the comedians, tragic poets, epigrammatic, heroic, and bucolic poets; from the writers of philosophy, of whom there are several groups; from the theologians; from sacred volumes."[42]

Milton does indeed cull from a variety of sources, although there are important omissions from Erasmus's list, as well as a large disproportion in the numbers drawn from history. As would be expected, Erasmus stresses the classics as a highly valued source, but he is willing to concede "even" the value of more contemporary writers: "Thus a great number and variety of these should be gathered for each one of the places, gathered not only from every type of Greek and Latin author, but even from the annals of the barbarians, and in fact from the common talk of the crowd."[43] In an unusual deviation from this tradition, Milton's own notes are almost entirely from barbarians—from the ancient barbarians that Erasmus's whimsical words may intend, such as Gildas or Bede, but also from more current *Annales,* such as those of Stow and Camden. In addition to his heavy use of historical reading, Milton has also a different purpose from Erasmus's: rather than assembling aphorisms or apothegms from other writers, Milton is focused on facts or ideas.

Another school, the Rivington, advocated the pedagogical use of commonplace books in its charter: "The elder sort must be taught how to refer

every thing they read to some common place, as to virtue, vice, learning, patience, adversity, prosperity, war, peace &c. for which purpose they must
have paper books ready to write them in. But the eldest sort that are ready to
be ministers, must be diligently practiced and perfect in Calvin's Catechism
and Institutions, and the New Testament, which the Master shall declare
unto them; and especially the Epistles to Timothy." [44] As Mohl writes, "Milton's *Commonplace Book* . . . is so typical of this plan as to make one wonder
whether he did not begin his note-taking at St. Paul's." [45] This is true in so far
as the topic headings are concerned, many of which—such as "Virtue" and
"Avarice"—appear in Milton's Ethical Index as well, but Milton's notebook
has not a single passage from the New Testament or the Old, nor indeed one
from Calvin or any other major Reformation theologian besides Peter
Martyr. Luther appears, but from an account provided in Johann Sleidan's
history, suggesting Milton may not have accessed Luther directly. Milton
would obviously have put some of relevant theological entries in his now lost
Theological Index, but along with the lack of classical citations, these omissions point again to a different purpose of note-taking than that recom-
mended by Erasmus and the English pedagogical tradition.

The Renaissance meaning of "commonplace" originates in the Greek concept of *topos* or *topoi,* often translated as "topics," although the words "place"
or "locus," and hence the Latin *communes loci,* capture Aristotle's sense of an
idea occupying a mental space that can be accessed for the advantage of argument. [46] The system of note-taking thus worked in concert with early modern
conceptions of the art of memory, since the literal position or place of an idea
was essential to its capacity for recall. Excerpts from reading material were
essential to the process of memorization. As the prolific humanist pedagogue
Jeremias Drexel wrote, "Great labor places so many images of things in this
treasury of memory; but no amount of labor has managed to preserve them
there for long without excerpts." [47] Lord Preston, the man who posthumously
added entries in Milton's Commonplace Book, accordingly called his own
reading notebook a collection of "excerpta." [48]

Milton's collection of facts or concepts rather than aphoristic phrases
distinguishes his research activities from many other commonplacers of the
period, even more than does the remarkably historical predominance of his
sources. One of the features distinguishing the entries of the non-Miltonic
hands in the Commonplace Book, including those of Lord Preston, is that
they are rhetorically focused excerpts rather than facts and interpretive
notes from history. William Drake reads many of the same writers as Milton
does, although not with the same object. As Sharpe writes, "Drake drew
on the known classical and humanist sources that distilled knowledge and

experience into aphorisms." [49] Drake seeks to distill bits of quotable or *usable* knowledge that can be accessed and reused in a packaged form. Like Harvey's, Drake's reading is "studied for actions," for how it might be used to function, advance, and advise in the political worlds of Parliament and the court.[50] Drake follows a tradition in creating political aphorisms and maxims shown in such texts as Roger Dallington's *Aphorismes Civill and Militarie,* dedicated to Charles I, or Raleigh's *Maxims of State,* initially dedicated to Prince Henry, or the manuscript that Milton obtained and printed as Raleigh's *Cabinet-Council,* originally dedicated to a member of the Elizabethan Privy Council, all of which are essentially polished commonplace books put into print.[51]

Milton worked against this tradition, which he clearly found trivializing. He criticized one writer for cutting Tacitus, as Lipsius had done, "into slivers and steaks," and he wrote scornfully of the "super-politick Aphorisme," and "all the Tribe of *Aphorismers,* and *Politicasters.*"[52] In his short tract on educational reform, Milton complained of poorly educated youth, too well prepared to find themselves at court reading "tyrannous aphorismes" that "appear to them the highest points of wisdom" (*CPW* 2:375–76). In *Eikonoklastes,* Milton writes that "matters of this moment" should not be decided by "curtal Aphorisms" (*CPW* 3:496). These passages further suggest a self-conscious differentiation in his own commonplacing from those "narrow intellectuals of quotationists and common placers" (*CPW* 2:230).

We cannot know for certain what the precise sources are behind Milton's structured reading agenda, but one iconic figure whose opposition to Erasmus's style of research is extremely likely, either through immediate influence or through curricular agendas that he helped to initiate. This is the French political writer Jean Bodin. Bodin's *Methodus ad Facilem Historiarum Cognitionem,* or *Method for the Easy Comprehension of History,* lays out a plan for a directed and voluminous study of history, which includes instructions for taking notes from an orderly, chronological system of historical reading. The *Methodus* went through thirteen editions in Latin between 1566 and 1650, and was partially translated by Thomas Heywood in 1609; it appears with some frequency in private libraries and in the listed books in Cambridge Inventories.[53] It exerted a formidable influence on English writers of history, such as John Speed, Samuel Daniel, William Camden, and John Selden.[54] And while a Bodinian style of reading is far less common in extant commonplace books, there are some known exceptions. The remaining commonplace books of Sir Robert Sidney, the younger brother of Sir Philip and grandfather of Algernon Sidney, adhere to Bodin's program of historical reading.[55] This was true also of Sir Robert's son, the second Earl of Leicester, whose commonplace books also show a deep interest in modern history that was not rhetorically oriented.[56] Milton's notebook seems to follow a Bodinian program in three basic ways: in being predominantly historical, in undertaking historical study in a systematic and chronological manner, and in being more interested in deeds and events than in sayings, and especially aphoristic sayings. In addition, Milton's Commonplace Book follows a set of common philosophical divisions that are also found in Bodin: the moral, the domestic, and the political (though these would have been available elsewhere as well).[57] In a chapter titled "the proper arrangement of historical material,"[58] Bodin writes that the "multiplicity and disorder of human activities" and the "abundant supply of histories" mean that history cannot be understood or retained "unless the actions and affairs of men are confined to certain definite types." As Bodin writes, "What scholars . . . are accustomed to do to assist memory in other arts should, I think, be done for history also. That is, common places [*loci communes*] of memorable matters should be placed in certain definite order, so that from these, as from a thesaurus, we may bring forth a variety of examples to direct our acts." The kind of political analysis undertaken by others, according to Bodin, pays too little attention to the facts of history, which he sees as the more important matter of analysis: "Of course we do not lack the studies of erudite men, who from the reading of historical treatises have extracted sagacious *sententiae* known as apothegms [*sententias, que, Apothegmata vocant*] . . . yet only the words have been collected by writers; they have omitted what is implied in plans and in deeds. Some have recorded the sayings and deeds of illustrious men, but rather ineffectively and without orderly arrangement."[59] Bodin is responding to the trend made popular by Erasmus, not only through his pedagogical instructions, through his *Adagia*, but also the *Apophthegmata*, which contain anecdotes and the sayings of famous men from antiquity, translated into French as *Les apophthegmes* in 1539, and into English in 1542 as *Apophthegmes, That Is to Saie, Prompte, Quicke, Wittie and Sentencious Saiynges, of Certain Emperours, Kynges, Capitaines, Philosophiers and Oratours, aswell Grekes, as Romaines.*

Bodin's method demands an alternative to apothegmatic commonplacing. Like many of the writers Milton studied—including de Thou and Hotman—Bodin wrote during and after the French civil wars of religion, a period which had much in common with that of the English civil war. Ann Blair's pioneering book on the subject, *The Theater of Nature: Jean Bodin and Renaissance Science*, reconstructs Bodin's *Universae Naturae Theatrum* (1596) according to his prescription for note-taking and what his now missing commonplace books would have looked like. Blair describes the ways in which "'facts' drawn largely from books . . . increasingly in the Renaissance also incorporated 'experience' of various kinds." [60] Yet in many ways Bodin's theories about gathering facts rather than sententious sayings seem to have had less of an effect on English commonplacing in the seventeenth century than would be expected, given its obvious popularity. Commonplace books that gather facts and experiences were used by natural philosophers such as John Evelyn and John Aubrey, but most political commonplacing of the period was of a different sort. [61] Bodin's massive *De Republica Libri Sex* (1576), translated into English as *The Six Bookes of a Commonweale* (London, 1606), draws on research into nature and history, using examples from history in the way he prescribes it in the *Methodus,* and in a way similar to what Milton would do in his shorter and more context-driven political tracts. As is true of Milton, Bodin's political arguments relied heavily on an elaborate system of notes drawn from historical research.

Bodin advocated a systematic approach to the study of history, organized according to the fundamental divisions of human existence: the self (moral), the family (domestic), and society (civil, political). "The chief activities of men are directed toward defending their common society," and these "interests are divided among civil, domestic, and moral training (civili, domesticica, & morali disciplina): the one teaches him to control himself; the second, his family; the third, the state." [62] These three divisions, the moral, the domestic, and the civil, reflect the structure of Milton's manuscript, divided into moral, domestic, and political indexes.

Bodin suggests that the topics might either be "arranged in each book under headings in this order, or as seems more suitable to each reader." Milton does not follow any prescribed order since he generally added topics as they emerged from his reading, although at times he constructed binaries that impose some direction to this reading. Still, many of Bodin's suggested topics are used: under the moral subjects, Bodin suggests, "The first topic will be the obscurity and the renown of the race; the second, life and death; the third, the conveniences of life; then, riches and poverty . . . later, moral training and, in general, discussion about virtues and vices." Milton's Ethical Index is largely a set of conventional virtues and vices, and "Riches" and "Poverty" appear in his Domestic Index, carrying the general tenor of Bodin: "There will follow a consideration of domestic training, of the mutual love of husband and wife, or the mutual feeling between parents and children." Bodin's divisions of the final section of the proposed notebook, dealing "with civil knowledge," invoke many of the same topics used in Milton's Commonplace Book: "dominion, royal prerogatives and despotic rule . . . proposing or annulling laws; magistrates and private citizens; war and peace." [63]

Whether by direct influence of Bodin, or through the general movements in reading he had helped initiate, Milton had clearly a historically oriented program of reading from the start, a curious direction for an aspiring poet.[64] Indeed, Milton's organization and the historical notes that dominate the notebook suggest a very different kind of career, although certainly not one exclusive of poetry. The notes suggest that Milton had been planning on writing political books (among others) for quite some time, although the final shape these works took would have obviously been unknown to him.

It is possible that Bodin influenced Milton's decision to keep a theological commonplace book, although these were common. The now lost Theological Index is unfortunately the only notebook mentioned by the author himself, and it is not unlikely to have been a different index than that which helped create *De Doctrina Christiana*.[65] In the preface of *De Doctrina Christiana*, Milton explains that he used a commonplace book in the process of composing the theological treatise: "I also started . . . to list under general headings [*locos communes*] all passages from the scriptures which suggested themselves for quotation, so that I might have them ready at hand when necessary."[66] This description supplies a rare view of the composition process of a major work of prose. We also know of this—or another—theological commonplace book from a cross-reference in the extant Commonplace Book. Next to an entry from Machiavelli's *Discorsi*, Milton's nephew Edward Phillips supplies a detailed marginal reference to a missing notebook, referring as well to a topic within it: "Vide Indicem Theologicum de Religione non cogenda," or "See the Theological Index, of not forcing Religion" (CB 197). This is the only reference that actually names this missing index; the others—there are twelve such references in all—merely point to topics and to "the other index," although it seems unlikely, given the orderliness generally represented here and the coherence of these references, that this would indicate a plurality of indices.[67] Some of the subject matter concerning *Areopagitica* would therefore have presumably been found under the topic "Of Not Forcing Religion" in this lost theological notebook, as well as under such entries as "Lenitas" (Leniency) or "Rex" in the secular Commonplace Book.

The Political Index: Omissions and Questions

In spite of the seeming correspondence between Milton's public and private methods of organizing thought, there are significant differences between the authorities he records in his Commonplace Book and those to whom he refers in public discourse. Almost no contemporary writers or books appear in his notes. John Selden is mentioned twice, but only in the domestic section on divorce. There is one contemporary reference to Sir Francis Bacon's *A Wise and Moderate Discourse* (1641), a wartime republication of Bacon in pamphlet form—and a pamphlet that originates on the opposite side from Milton (CB 184, *CPW* 1:450–51). There are no references to influential contemporaries, such as Hugo Grotius, although Milton elsewhere cites him several times, and it seems extremely unlikely that he would not have known his work before seeking him out in Paris in 1638. None of the many contemporaries, Puritan and otherwise, that Milton engages in the political work, such as Herbert Palmer or William Prynne, appears in the Commonplace Book. None of the books cited except Selden and Bacon appears in the Thomason Tracts, and, except for the republication of Bacon, there is no wartime pamphlet literature whatsoever.

The Italian poets enjoy a better representation than the English, with notes on Tasso, Dante, Boccalini, Boccaccio, Berni, Boiardo, Tassoni, and Ariosto. Some of these may well have been recorded during Milton's Italian journey. Milton quotes from Traiano Boccalini's *Ragguagli di Parnaso* (Venice, 1612), notable for its republicanism.[68] Of the English poets of the previous generation there are only a smattering of notes. The only English poetry cited comes from Gower, Chaucer, and the medieval verse chronicler John Hardying. Spenser appears in two passages on the Irish from *A View of the Present State of Ireland,* one on "the wicked policies of divers deputies & governours in Ireland," and one that comments on the need to provide for soldiers after the wars, one of the most pressing issues for the army in the late 1640s (CB 188, 242). Sidney appears in a reference to the debate about the rights of the magistracy in the *Arcadia*—"See also an excellent description of such an Oligarchy of nobles abusing the countnance to the ruin of royal sovranty"[69]—which pertains closely to Milton's argument in *The Tenure,* although it seems to support the position opposite to the one he was finally to take.

The omissions produce even greater surprises. These challenge the conception of Milton as either a classical civic humanist or a political theologian. Milton cites virtually no classical texts, and not a single biblical reference or example from biblical history. There are also few references to the theologians from the previous generation that we would expect to inform a radical Protestant's political thinking. Except for one rather brief reference to Peter Martyr, and a mention of Luther from Sleidan's historical *Commentaries,* not one of the many "foremost theologians" (*CPW* 4:626) Milton boasts to have used in *The Tenure* appears in the Commonplace Book, except in the hand of Lord Preston under Milton's own headings. Milton would promote major Reformation authorities on the title page of the second edition of *The*

Tenure as "the best & learnedest among Protestant Divines asserting the position of this book" (*CPW* 3:189); yet there is no Calvin, Luther, Zwingli, Bucer, or Gilby in the Commonplace Book. The kind of research evidenced by the Commonplace Book is thus not designed to produce anything like the classic texts of Protestant resistance theory, such as the *Vindiciae contra Tyrannos,* Goodman's *How Superior Powers Ought to Be Obeyd,* the works of Gilby, Knox, Ponet, or of many of Milton's contemporaries, such as William Prynne or Sir Robert Filmer, whose works depend on Reformation theology and the extensive use of scripture to justify their claims.

The significant absences in Milton's Commonplace Book are underscored by Lord Preston, who, in his posthumous additions to the Political Index, cites precisely the passage from Calvin's *Institutes* that proved so influential to the history of debate in revolutionary England, and that Milton refutes in *The Tenure of Kings and Magistrates* (see figure 2.3). "What Calvin says of Magistrates apointed for the defence of the people," Preston observes, "and to restrain the insolencie of kings, as the Ephor in Lacedemonia, the Tribunes in Rome, and the Demarches in Athens, that they ought to resist and impeach their Licentiousnesse and cruelty; is not at all applicable in a right monarchy where the life and honour of the Prince ought to be sacred."[70]

The absence of the classics, theologians, scriptural text, and biblical history is remarkable for one who had been trained in a humanist tradition and for one who uses biblical and theological arguments in his political work. One explanation for the missing biblical citations is that they would have gone in the lost *Index Theologicus,* but it seems highly unlikely that Milton would have confined all his biblical references to this category. The inclusion of a handful of theologians argues against the idea that Milton deliberately excluded theologians, even when their writing pertained—as it often did—to politics. And there is no missing index to help explain the paucity of classical references, a mainstay in English political writing and in commonplace-book construction.

There are two possible explanations for these absences. The first is that Milton knew the Bible, Calvin, and the classics so well that he needed no commonplace book to help recall the key arguments from these sources. This explanation has merit, although it was not the habit of other writers to omit classical or biblical exempla because they are well remembered. And the three rather meager classical references in Milton's Commonplace Book tend to negate this possibility: a citation from Aristotle's *Ethics,* one of Milton's most frequently used resources, a citation from Frontinus, common enough in Milton's reading and teaching,[71] and a mention of Caesar through a citation of another writer.[72] Of these only Aristotle falls in the Political Index, in a marginal note supporting a passage from Thomas Smith: "See Arist. Eth. The tyrant seeks what benefits himself, the king what benefits his subjects" (CB 182), a line Milton cites in *The Tenure of Kings and Magistrates,* and one of only a handful of classical references in that tract. The marginal Greek line is also one of the only true aphorisms in Milton's manuscript.

The second, more compelling explanation for the omission of classics and theology is that during the crucial period from the late 1630s to the mid-1640s, Milton is engaged in a different kind of political scholarship, so that to describe him either as a classical civic humanist or a political theologian somewhat misses the mark. Milton engages here in the kind of political work by historical example undertaken by Machiavelli, Guicciardini, Jean Bodin, and Francis Hotman, writers who rely less on religious belief or on the authority of classical writers but rather seek to use historical example and historical precedent to understand the constitutional potential of European societies.

Milton's reading record certainly suggests a more modern and more historically oriented form of argumentation than is usually considered. Yet one might argue that this reading record is not an accurate gauge of the writer's authentic interests because it represents a distorted history of his reading. It may be that Milton was more compelled to record from books that were less familiar to him, in some cases borrowed or consulted in collections when away from home or abroad. Certainly it is a mistake to conclude that references in the Commonplace Book indicate Milton's possession of the books in his personal library.[73] Contrary to the conventional assumption, Milton does seem to have taken the notebook with him on his trip through the continent. A letter from Henry Lawes of 1638 was discovered in the Commonplace Book, in which Lawes supplies Milton with an accompanying document that would give him "sufficient warrant to justify [Milton's] going out of the King's Dominions."[74] Lawes's letter is worn through and torn in many places, and covered with dozens of small ink stains indicating its use as blotting paper, further suggesting that the book and the letter accompanied him on his continental journey.[75] Indeed, given that he had a servant attending him, and that he spent a great deal of time in libraries and bookshops, it seems unlikely that he would not have brought along this valued research tool. There are also many pages missing from the book—though not those with entries, since they are all indexed—suggesting that the blank pages may have been used for other purposes when spare paper was less easily obtained.

A few notes in the Commonplace Book are suggestive of an itinerant scholar, or of one who has not yet set his hands on the book cited. In a note written in the late 1630s, Milton accounts for books that he does not seem to have in front of him, in language indicating that the information comes to him secondhand. The Latin note is recorded under the topic "Rex": "That the authority of a king does not depend upon the Pope, Dante the Florentine wrote in the book whose title is Monarchia; a book which Cardinal Poggietto had burned as an heretical work, as Boccaccio asserts in his life of Dante, in the earlier editions, for in the later ones all mention of that fact was taken out by the inquisitor" (CB 182, *CPW* 1:438). Especially since there is (unusually) no citation, Milton seems to be gathering this information secondhand—perhaps through conversation. But the secondhand nature of this is also suggested in the manner of his recording: "all mention of that fact was taken out by the inquisitor," for example, is not information that comes immediately from the books themselves.

Comments made in a letter to Lukas Holste at the Vatican suggest that Milton was eager to visit libraries and take notes when he could. He thanks Holste in March 1639 for helping him gain admittance to the Vatican Library, where he could "browse through the invaluable collection of Books, and also the numerous Greek Authors in manuscript" (*CPW* 1:333). Later in the same letter Milton reports that he cannot transcribe the passage that Holste had requested from Laurentian Library in Florence: "In illa Bibliotheca, nisi impetrata prius venia, nihil posse exscribi, ne stylum quidem scriptorium admovisse tabulis permissum" ("In that library, unless permission is obtained in advance, nothing can be copied. It is not even permitted to use a stylus [*stylum*] on writing tables [*tabulis*]")—a passage that seems to refer to the erasable writing "tables" referred to in *Hamlet*.[76]

Other entries refer to a book that Milton does not possess, as when he writes, around 1642–44, of "a book entitled *Franco-Gallia*," which he discovers from reading de Thou's *Historiarum Sui Temporis* (Geneva, 1620). Milton again mentions *Francogallia* to support the claim that France had elected monarchs until the time of Hugh Capet—"see the book entitled *Franco-Gallia*," which is quoted "in Thuan. hist book 57, p. 969" (CB 186). Milton has yet to have seen the book, and these notes function in part as a program for future reading. With the same page open in de Thou, Milton seems then to have flipped forward to a new topic, "Of Civil War" (CB 244), writing, "At the time of the siege of Magdeburg a book was written, and was again brought out in France in the year 1574, enlarged with many theories and examples, in which it is shown that subjects are at liberty to ward off by force a force advanced against them contrary to the law, even by magistrates. Thuan. hist Book 57 p. 969." The book, again, is Hotman's short work of secular republicanism, *Francogallia*, which Milton had yet to lay his hands on.[77] It is, however, an important representation of the kind of new political writing that Milton was himself engaged in—based on "examples" and "theories" drawn from history. The subject too would be of great importance to Milton, as Hotman wrote on whether the subjects may revolt even against the magistrates, and whether the subjects may choose their king. Milton did manage to obtain Hotman's work by 1651, probably in the late 1640s, as he works it into both Defences of the English People (*CPW* 4:420–21, *CPW* 4:659). Like de Thou's discussion of Hotman, Sleidan's discussion of Luther's treatment of sedition in *Liber contra Rusticos* (1625) catches Milton's interest, and he notes Luther's opinion, although only from this secondhand source (CB 246). Instead of being a precise representation of Milton's library, then, the Commonplace Book sometimes documents ideas from books that Milton has not yet obtained or seen.

While Milton did not own all of the books referred to in his notebook, this fact contributes only very partially to our understanding of why there is a surprisingly limited correspondence between the proportions of the textual categories cited in the Political Index and those quoted in *The Tenure of Kings and Magistrates*. There is plenty of history in both, but they share only one of the theologians that he garners for his defense in the public tract, and not a single passage from the Bible or scriptural doctrine, except one from Sulpicius Severus, but it uses biblical history as history, rather than doctrine: "Severus says that the name of kings has always been hateful to free peoples, and he condemns the actions of the Hebrews in choosing to exchange their freedom for servitude" (CB 182, *CPW* 1:440). The only theologian quoted in the Political Index is Peter Martyr, and Milton cites precisely the same passage in *The Tenure,* indicating that he did not return to the source when citing Martyr in the regicide tract, possibly also suggesting that he possessed only a record of the source in his notes (CB 185, *CPW* 3:221). Like many of the books cited in the Commonplace Book, this is an old book with a foreign imprint: *In Librum Iudicum D. Petri Martyris Vermilii* (Zurich, 1571), although hardly impossible to obtain.[78] The same is true for Claude de Seissel's *La Grand Monarchie de France* (1519), translated by Sleidan in 1545, which is cited three times in the Commonplace Book and only once again—from the same place in the source—in *The Tenure* (CB 186, *CPW* 1:458, and *CPW* 3:200). Milton also mentions Luther in both the manuscript and *The Tenure*, using a reference to Luther within Sleiden's *Commentaries* (Strassburg, 1555) for his citation in *The Tenure:* "Luther . . . apud Sleidan" (*CPW* 3:243). In this case, however, Milton does go back to the source to provide a fuller passage, suggesting an easy access to Sleidan's *Commentaries* (which Milton cites nine times in his notes), although not to Luther. (In *Tetrachordon,* Milton alludes to Luther as "quoted by Gerard out of the Dutch"; there is in fact no known work of Luther's, as important as he is, in Milton's reading history.)[79] Quoting from notes was a common phenomenon, and commonplace books were designed in part to convey textual excerpts to their eventual place in a formal piece of writing.[80] In some cases, this was for logistical reasons: the source was simply not handy.

The proportion of foreign imprints quoted in the Political Index is 73 percent, which might, in comparison with Locke's library, to give a well-documented example, seem high: here the proportion of non-British imprints is 55 percent.[81] Yet, in comparison with many other gentlemanly libraries for which we have shelf-lists, the low percentage of British imprints in Milton's notes is quite normal, and it may well represent the proportions in Milton's own library.[82] Milton acquired books on his trip through Europe, so he may have made notes from books and also sent them home to take notes from them later. Some of these cited foreign imprints, such as the *Historia Miscella* (1603), published in Ingolstadt, Bavaria—which Milton may have consulted on his continental journey—must have been very rare indeed, as the title does not appear in either the Cambridge Inventories or in the inventories of English Private Libraries, where books are seldom found from Ingolstadt, although books in known English libraries did come predominantly from Europe.[83] Indeed, a lively trade in foreign books occurred in London, and Milton could have obtained many non-British imprints at home as well.[84]

We must conclude, therefore, that while Milton may have occasionally used his notebook for books outside of his library, it was not specifically designated for this purpose. Even if Milton occasionally used the Commonplace Book to store passages that were not available on his shelves, this would not explain the extraordinarily high proportion of historians, since the basic generic proportions of Milton's reading material remain the same whether the rarest books are borrowed or his own. The surprising range of historical reading in Milton's notes remains in a high percentage both for books that may have been borrowed or consulted away from home, and for a substantial core quantity that show every appearance of easy access. Over half of the books in the Commonplace Book are quoted two or fewer times—mostly once—and many of these, such as the *Historia Miscella,* fall into the category of rare editions. The vast majority of passages cited come from books that Milton would likely have owned: Holinshed's *Chronicles* (1587) being by far the most quoted, at approximately sixty-four entries, many of which themselves contain clusters of citations to different pages. These entries are clearly made at many different sittings, if not different years, and they are often useless without easy access to the source. The next most common is the French monarchomach Jacques-Auguste de Thou (1553–1617), whose *History of His Own Times* (*Historiarum Sui Temporis*) first began to appear in 1604.[85] De Thou's five folio volumes and approximately six thousand pages on sixty-four years of French history is a purchase fit for libraries, as even carrying home one of these six books would require some muscle, the whole set a sturdy wheelbarrow. Folio editions and especially multivolume sets came also at a considerable cost.[86] Yet Milton must have had easy access to this history, and very probably owned it, since it is clear that he returns to it on several different occasions in his notes.

While de Thou is the second most cited author in Milton's notes, he is overtly cited only a handful of times in Milton's published prose—this authority is more frequently simply used than cited in the using. William of Malmesbury, cited seven times, is never cited explicitly in the published work. Similarly, except for the unusual case of the short "Postcript," Holinshed is cited by name only once in outside the Commonplace Book, in a marginal note in *The History of Britain*.[87] Yet while Milton does not call upon Holinshed himself as an authority, the facts derived from Holinshed pervade Milton's work,[88] and it is the facts themselves, rather than the authority of the source, that Milton deploys in public debate. The next several major presences in Milton's notes are popular domestic historians, whose works Milton surely had handy, not only because of the number of entries, but because of the richly layered style of these references, with Speed and Stow often inserted, like Aristotle, as marginal glosses. Speed is cited 31–33 times, Stow 22–24 times, and Camden, the fifth most cited, at 19.[89] This core of historical authorities therefore represents a highly directed research agenda, such that the peripheral entries that may have come from other libraries should be seen to indicate the intensity of such a pursuit, rather than as fragments to fill an underdeveloped area of Milton's private library.

The Historical Purpose of the Political Index

Milton's political research is devoted for about a decade to quite an extensive reading in history: Greek and Roman, early Christian, Italian, Russian, French, and English, and especially the latter two. At least 72 percent of the entries in the Political Index are to histories, a figure that increases to 80 percent when the other hands are excluded—not counting individually the many clustered entries to Holinshed, which would increase that statistic to well over 90 percent. As is shown in figure 2.2, Milton has a particular way of using Holinshed with multiple citations within one entry, creating disproportionately long passages on English history. The information gathered from Holinshed is then frequently corroborated with reference to the annals of Speed and Stow. Most of the histories cited represent not one volume but quite substantial collections: gathering information from six thousand folio pages of de Thou, for example, might take several months.

Beyond the evidence of structured research given by the notebook itself, Milton leaves a couple of revealing hints about the method of his reading in his early prose and letters. One such hint can be found in a 1637 letter to Diodati. "By continuing reading," he writes, "I have brought the affairs of the Greeks to the time when they ceased to be Greeks. I have been occupied for a long time by the obscure history of the Italians under the Longobards, Franks, and Germans, to the time when liberty was granted them by Rudolph, King of Germany. From there it will be better to read separately about what each State did by its own Effort."[90] The endeavor of researching such efforts of self-autonomy is evident in many of the entries here, which anatomize states as they are formed by their own self-constitution (or "effort"), often in a struggle between the people and those in power to negotiate a constitution. The Political Index is thus largely a record of how states are constituted by the effort of their representational bodies, in cooperation with—if there was one—a monarch. This idea of the autonomous efforts of states is, it should be emphasized, a nonprovidential view of the way in which political bodies operate, and, in its method of legitimating arguments of right, quite distinct from a Calvinist political outlook.

As is evident from the handwriting, ink, and method of construction, the first two topics that Milton put in the Political Index were "Respublica" and "Rex" (see figure 2.1). These two opposing topics—with "Respublica" in a primary position—were later separated by other topical entries as the book was slowly filled in. The Yale edition translates "Respublica" simply as "The State," but this does not capture the sense of the topical oppositions Milton sought to establish, and "republic" and "monarchy" are standard oppositions. One entry in Latin, written by Milton in the early 1640s, asks whether "Respub. Regno potior"—whether a republic is better than a monarchy— and then cites Machiavelli's *Art of War* in Italian, using the same abbreviated word: "perche delle repub. escano piu huomini eccellenti, che de regni. perche in quelle il piu delle volte si honora la virtu, ne regni si teme. &c" ("because more excellent men come from a commonwealth than from a monarchy; because in the former virtue is honored most of the time and is not feared as in a monarchy, &c"; CB 177, *CPW* 1:421). The question is also posed in English, in an entry rare in the Political Index for its length and for having no stated source. This early exposition on the forms of government is possibly simply Milton's own, jotted down in a rough, truncated syntax in a moment of self-reflection—unusual for the Commonplace Book—though the notes may also derive from a series of phrases taken from Thomas Smith and then transformed a bit by Milton (see figure 2.6).[91] The ideas are central to the structure of Milton's political philosophy, appearing even as late as in Michael's

Index Politicus

Respublica

immutata re efficere civilium esurias edicto sancxit constantinus. Euseb: vita: l. 10. c. 7.

The form of state to be fitted to the peoples disposition some live best under monarchy others otherwise. so that the conversion of commonwealths happen not always through ambition or malice. as among the Romans who after thire infancy were ripe for a more free goverment then monarchy, becom in a manner all fit to be As afterward growne lorruly, and impotent with over much prosperity were either for thire profit, or thire punishment fit to be curbd with a lordly and dreadfull monarchy, wch was the error of the noble Brutus and Cassius who fell themselves of spirit to free a nation but considerd not that the nation was not fit to be free, whilst forget ting thire old justice and fortitude which was made to rule they became slaves to thire owne ambition and luxurie.

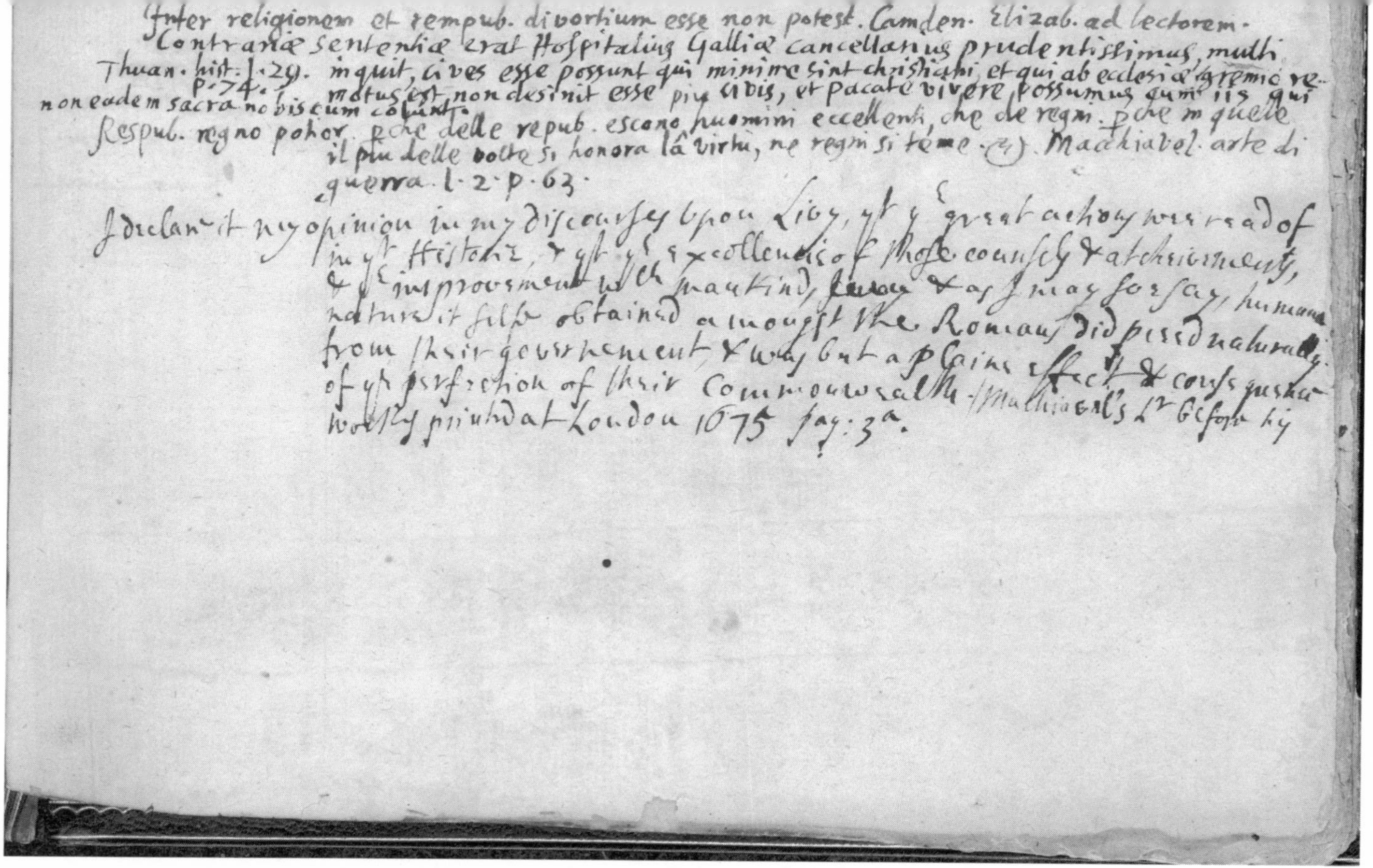

Figure 2.6. The first page of the Political Index of Milton's Commonplace Book, showing an unusually long reflection without citation that may not derive directly from reading material. The first topic in this Index is Respublica, or "Republic." The page illustrates the differences in handwriting, from one of Milton's earliest entries, drawn from Eusebius, in a small neat hand, to Lord Preston's entry at the bottom, drawn from a book of Machiavelli's, "printed at London, 1675." BL MS Additional 36354, p. 177. © The British Library Board.

observations to Adam in *Paradise Lost* on the fitness of societies to embrace political freedom:

> the form of state to be fitted to the peoples disposition some live best under monarchy others otherwise. so that the conversions of commonwealths happen not always through ambition or malice. as among Romans who after thire infancy were ripe for a more free government then monarchy, being in a manner all fit to be Ks. afterward growne unruly, and impotent with overmuch prosperity were either for thire profit, or thire punishment fit to be curb'd with a lordly and dreadfull monarchy; which was the error of the noble Brutus and Cassius who felt themselves of spirit to free an nation but consider'd not that the nation was not fit to be free, whilst forgetting thire old justice and fortitude which was made to rule, they became slaves to thire own ambition and luxurie. (CB 177, *CPW* 1:420)

It is notable that Milton uses the word "conversion" here, as he surely had in mind the Latin noun *conversio, conversionis,* a "turning" or "revolution"—he uses the same word in Latin in the first *Defense* to describe the "revolution": "concerning the execution of the king and the revolution (*conversione*) amongst us" (*PW* 61).

The most vital aspect of this passage in relation to Milton's printed politics lies in the phrase-sentence "so that the conversions of commonwealths happen not always through ambition or malice," which suggests that a conversion of government from a monarchy to a republic—or whatever the nature of the conversion might be—can happen according to the choice of the people about what best suits their needs, rather than through a power struggle based on lesser impulses or hereditary claims. There needs then to be no proof of tyranny or any other kind of proof of illegitimacy to change government: just the determination that the people would benefit more from a different form. In *The Tenure of Kings and Magistrates* Milton would claim that "the people as oft as they shall judge it for the best, [may] either choose him or reject him, retaine him or depose him though no Tyrant, meerly by the liberty and right of free born Men" (*CPW* 3:206). As well as indicating an early contention that the state of government corresponds to the natural conditions of the people, this important reflection also shows an early republican sympathy, although not without some hesitation. A nation such as England may not yet be "fit to be free." This would be Milton's despondent assessment of the English people in the dark "Digression" in *The History of Britain.*

The representation of republicanism, although minor in scope compared to the critical treatment of monarchy, occurs in a series of entries that suggest a bias in Milton's early political thought. And while it is sometimes thought that Milton's consideration of republicanism would have only come after the beheading of Charles—and hence the late dating of the entries from the *Discorsi*—this is clearly not the case. Whether or not the entries to the *Discorsi* were after 1649, Milton knew Machiavelli in a republican fashion before this, as is confirmed by the passage quoted from the *Art of War*—a text in fact bound with the *Discorsi,* as Milton's page numbering reveals. Republican entries from scribes outbalance Milton's own, but this is not a reliable gauge of the date or level of investment. One scribal entry reads, for example: "Republican form. Machiavelli much prefers a republican form to monarchy, citing reasons by no means stupid throughout the 58th chapter of Book 1 of his discors. and in Book 3. chapter 34, where he argues that a republic makes fewer mistakes than a prince does in choosing its magistrates or councilors." This passage is followed by another: "to return a republic to the very source of government, either by enacting good laws or by reducing magistrates to the ranks of ordinary citizens or by restoring the control of things to the decision of the people, is often beneficial. see Machiavel. discours: Book 3 c[hapter] 1, where he says that this is very healthy for a republic just as it is for a mixed government &c" (CB 198, *CPW* 1:477).

There are also such endorsements in Milton's own hand. One particularly important topic is "Libertas," the word used by Cicero to designate the rightful condition of the Roman people.[92] Milton provides a citation to Cuspinian, a Roman "led by love of liberty" to revolt, and then, in the manner of Machiavelli, gives an example of Niccolo Rienzio, not recounted in Cuspinian, whose attempt to regain power and restore Rome to its ancient republican form failed in 1354 (CB 190, *CPW* 1:470).[93] It is not clear from where Milton derives his account of Rienzio (known as Niccolo di Lorenzo or Cola di Renzo). He could have had access to the story from Petrarch or Machiavelli, although from Machiavelli's *Florentine History* rather than from the *Discorsi,* since it does not appear there. Indeed, all of the cited Machiavelli comes from the *Art of War* or the *Discourses,* which happen to be bound in the second of the two volumes of the *Tutte le Opere* that Milton and his scribes used; the first volume contains the *Prince* and the *Florentine History,* neither of which appear in the Commonplace Book.[94] After the republican entry entered under "Libertas," Milton makes a series of important citations to Justinian, and one to Guicciardini.[95]

These are all authors that appear with much greater frequency in Milton's private notes than in his public discourse. Cuspinianus's *Historia Caesarum et Imperatorum Romanorum* (Frankfurt, 1601), the first text cited under "Libertas," appears six times in his notes and is never cited in the printed work, although some history presumably from this source is recounted in the *Defensio Secunda*

(*CPW* 4:683–84). Guicciardini is never cited in his printed work, although he appears twice here. Justinian is cited in his notes eight times (two of these are clustered), and it seems likely from a copy of the *Institutes* that Milton owned, since the citations are very brief, and where the ideas reappear in Milton's printed works, Milton seems to return to the source and works with another part of the *Institutes,* indicating that he knew it well.[96] "For what lawyers declare concerning liberty and slavery see Justinian, Book 1. institut. Tit[le] 3," he writes, for example. At the passage Milton cites, which seems to be "title 5," Justinian writes: "This thing [manumission] affirmed by law the origin of peoples; as, for example, under natural law all men are born free, nor would manumission be known if slavery were unknown. But after slavery invaded free birth by man-made law, there followed the boon of manumission."[97] Milton's statement in *The Tenure of Kings and Magistrates* that "men were naturally born free" (*CPW* 3:198), or that power cannot be taken away "without a violation of thir natural birthright" (202) echo the same rights articulated in the passages cited in the *Institutes.* "Civil law favors liberty" (*CPW* 1:471) Milton writes in the next entry, and then cites Justinian.

But given that England's and most of Europe's political history had been monarchical, the majority of entries concern the nature of kings and tyrants, and the relationships and obligations between these and the people. Again in contrast to a Calvinist outlook, many entries interrogate the problem of divine right from a secular angle, as well as the problems of mixing religion and politics. Milton gives a series of examples in a late 1630s entry under "Rex," on kings as "lords," one of which was later used in *The Tenure:* "Augustus, the founder of the Empire, was unwilling even to be called 'Lord,' for this also is a name of God. I will certainly call the Emperor 'Lord,' but at a time when I am not compelled to say 'Lord' instead of 'God'; otherwise I am free to this extent: my Lord is God alone," &c. Tertull: apologet" (CB 181, *CPW* 1:433). "The Titles of Sov'ran Lord, natural Lord, and the like," Milton later wrote in *The Tenure,* "are either arrogancies, or flatteries, not admitted by Emperours and Kings of best note . . . as appears by Tertullian and others" (*CPW* 3:202). "Kings scarcely recognize themselves as mortals," he observed sometime later under the same topic ("Rex"), "scarcely understand that which pertains to man, except on the day they are made king or on the day they die." This reflection interprets history, rather than simply records what is read. He goes on: "On the former day they feign humanity and gentleness, in the hope of capturing the voice of the people. On the latter, having death before their eyes and in the knowledge of their evil deeds, they confess what is a fact, namely, that they are wretched mortals" (CB 181, *CPW* 1:431–32). On the same question of a king's pretense of divinity, Milton writes under a second heading "Rex" on the following page, also begun in the late 1630s, "Diocletian was the first of the Romans to permit himself to be worshipped," although "others make" the same assertion "about Constantine" (CB 182, *CPW* 1:437). Early Christians, he continues, were offended by this: "What the early Christians decided about this, Justin Martyr, writing to the Emperor Antonius Pius, makes clear in his belief, founded upon the teachings of Christ, that we should give to Caesar the things which are Caesar's and to God the things which are God's; 'therefore,' he says, 'we worship God alone, and in other matters we gladly serve you,' in which he plainly assigns 'worship' to God alone, and 'willing service' to kings. Apology: 2. p 64" (CB 182, *CPW* 1:437).

Legal obligations established at coronation indicate that limitations to a monarch's rule are established at the outset. Under a topic heading "Laws," Milton pursues the vein of the legal foundations of kingship—with a cross-reference "see Rex" (see figure 2.2): "Kings of England sworne to the laws see Rex at thire crowning," after which follows accounts from Holinshed and Speed of twelve kings. Always interested in establishing the original status of a human institution, Milton notes that "Laws were first devis'd to bound and limit the power of governours," citing Lambard (CB 179, *CPW* 1:423).

WHAT KIND of political work was Milton's Political Index preparing him to write? What were his models for this kind of research? And what might he have written, had it not been for the unexpected events that occasioned each political tract, or the incendiary pamphlet wars in which he found himself involved? The preparation in the Commonplace Book suggests that much of the political theology in tracts such as *The Tenure* is reactive, existing largely because he is arguing against contemporaries using these biblical arguments, and not because he seeks fundamentally to ground his own claims in readings of Romans or Samuel. In *The Tenure,* Milton rarely if ever uses the examples from history that he has gathered in the Commonplace Book to rebut any specific point about history in contemporary pamphlets. Rather than refuting his opponents, these historical arguments constitute part of the tract's core arguments about political right.

Milton's models for this kind of historical argument are by no means obvious. To some extent, Milton's work mirrors that of Selden, Coke, and even Filmer, in which a historical and historicist interpretation of English legal history is used to help formulate the grounds for constitutional legitimacy.[98] Yet Milton's own use of history, while it occasionally concerns itself with some of the same historical details,[99] is not legally or nationally constrained in the same way. Nor is his use of historical example meant to provide a precedent for legitimacy, although he certainly endeavors to use historical examples of political right to challenge present conditions or ideologies (such as the idea that the king is unaccountable or above the law, or that the laws are meant to limit subjects).

Milton's historical politics would have been modeled after the work of Italian and French writers as well as English. Given his references to these writers, he had at an early stage acquainted himself with the historical politics of Machiavelli and Guicciardini. Machiavelli's work in the *Discorsi,* in which he used historical evidence to refute many of the claims of Livy—and thus refuses to emulate the classics with which he is nonetheless in dialogue— must have had some claim on Milton's imagination. Two French writers, Jean Bodin and Francis Hotman, may have been still more important, since their work involves northern monarchies and northern religious civil wars. Milton had been reading Bodin's *De Republica Libri Sex* by 1641, as it is cited in the Commonplace Book sometime in the early 1640s and it is also referred to in the *Reason of Church Government* (1642).[100]

Francis Hotman's work, whose full title was translated in the early eighteenth century as *Franco-Gallia; or, An Account of the Ancient Free State of France, and Most Other Parts of Europe before the Loss of their Liberties,*[101] although acquired too late to have been of formative influence, is nonetheless a strong northern model of the kind of work being conducted here. Milton must have acquired *Francogallia* sometime before composing the *Defence,*[102] although it may well have already influenced his thinking in *The History of Britain* and *The Tenure.* Hotman is compelled to write his short treatise because, as he says in the preface, "my unfortunate miserable country has been for almost twelve years burning in flames of civil war." He records that he has "perused all the old French and German Historians that treat of our Francogallia, and collected out of their works a true State of our Commonwealth; in the condition (wherein they agree) it flourished for above a thousand years."[103] This comparison allows Hotman to make a strong case against the recent rise of absolutist forms in France. Hotman begins by setting "forth the estate of Gaul, before it was reduced into the form of a Province by the Romans,"[104] an endeavor very like Milton's own in the "Digression," and in *The Tenure,* in which he uses the state of Britain just after the Romans had left as the earliest reliable account (from Gildas) of British governance. The early rulers of France, were, Hotman finds, "not hereditary, but conferred by the people upon such as had the reputation of being just Men"—a point touched on by Milton a few times in the Commonplace Book.[105]

Beyond simply taking notes and organizing his ideas, Milton seems, then, to be preparing to write a form of historical politics that combine elements of

The History of Britain and *The Tenure of Kings and Magistrates. The History of Britain,* I suspect, was originally more politically oriented in its conception and even in its prepublished form. Milton had intended to carry the *History* beyond the conquest to as far as "the present day" (*CPW* 4:627), and would have therefore used the extensive research in later medieval English history recorded in his notes.

How the Notes Resurface in Print

Milton's printed writing of the 1640s is in direct dialogue with other pamphleteers and at the same time interspersed with material drawn from the idiosyncratic reading recorded in his notes. In composing the polemics, Milton draws from the notes in revealing ways. When he reformulates the notes for public consumption, they often seem to possess the information and meaning that they had in the Commonplace Book, yielding the appearance of having been intended for the argument they end up supporting in print, and thus the transfer seems relatively simple. Yet the notes are also drawn on quite selectively: there are (understandably) no arguments in his public treatises about how Machiavelli prefers a republic, and certainly none that suggests with Machiavelli's backing that the sword is the only way to do away with a bad king. (Though appearing in the Commonplace Book in Milton's hand and that of two others associated with him, Machiavelli is only vilified in his public work, lest Milton suffer the fate of one of his own opponents, whom Milton pilloried for citing Machiavelli: "though Machiavell whom he cites, or any Machiavillian Priest think the contrary.")[106] In his printed work, Milton never repeats his curt dismissal of the idea of closing the theaters alluded to briefly at the beginning of this chapter. This strongly articulated opinion simply does not exist in the public Milton at this time, which in fact does seem—in both its silences and its stated position—to endorse the puritanical policy. Milton's stated public distain for the theater in 1642—the year the theaters were closed—occurs in a passage that responds to the accusation (probably true) that he frequented "playhouses" (*Apology, CPW* 1:886–88). His counter-sneer paints a picture of the theatre as a generally contemptible and even unlawful affair; avoiding the subject of the London theatres, he admits that he had gone with other students at college, but "thought them fools" and "hist" (887). He goes on to treat the theater's closing as acceptable, in a comparative formulation: "For if it be unlawfull to sit and behold a mercenary Comedian personating that which is least unseemely for a hireling to doe, how much more blamefull is it to endure the sight of as vile things acted by persons . . . [in] the ministery" (888). A suggestive contrast occurs in the

Commonplace Book, where, instead of recognizably "Puritan" sentiments, Milton writes in a statement that must either respond to the closing of the theaters, or the talk of such closing: "although the corruptions in the theatre deservedly should be removed, it is by no means necessary for that reason that all practice of the dramatic arts should be completely done away with; on the contrary it would be absurd beyond measure" (*CPW* 1:491, CB 241). The contrast suggests an almost Janus-faced Milton, or one forced by polemical need to play a disingenuous role.

Milton's reconstructions of the historical evidence fall into three patterns. First, the manuscript notes suggest a more pronounced republicanism than appears in print in the 1640s, and Milton softens the republican language when he reuses his notes in print. Second, Milton's emphasis on the idea of individual choice—both rational and political—frequently reshapes the original entries in the Commonplace Book to support the notion of individual free will and an idea of popular sovereignty that is based on the freedom to choose. Unlike the muting of republicanism, which seems a rhetorically strategic alteration to suit the audience, this pattern of revision may reflect a philosophical development in the author. Finally, following a commonplacing convention, Milton transforms the fragmentary borrowings of other writers with opportunistic resourcefulness, often seemingly with the purpose of co-opting another author's politics into his own.[107] An author who acquired a certain cultural value, such as Francis Bacon, Thomas Cartwright, or Calvin, may be deployed to perform a function that opposes that value, thus undermining the ideological system of his opponents.

The political notes in the Commonplace Book resurface in his finished writing in disproportionate ways. In *Areopagitica,* Milton explicitly reuses only four entries in his notes, although several others show him to be preoccupied with the broad range of arguments in the tract. Two entries that are reused in *Areopagitica* are recorded under a topic from the late 1630s or very early 1640s, "Lenitas" (that is, "leniency"),[108] with an unusual subtopic, added in the index as well, on "the prohibition of books." The first of these begins "prohibition of books not the wisest cours," and then quotes Bacon from a posthumous work, *A Wise and Moderate Discourse Concerning Church Affairs* (1641). It is the only contemporary pamphlet quoted in the Commonplace Book, and Milton seems to have drawn from it shortly after its publication, since he cites it, essentially paraphrasing the same idea recorded here, in *Animadversions* (1641; *CPW* 1:668). The passage Milton quotes captures Bacon commonplacing Tacitus, although he cites the Roman historian only as "that wise writer," quoting him in Latin: "*Punitis ingeniis glisscit authoritas* [when ideas are punished, power blazes forth]." The quotation is followed in

Bacon by an explanation much like those found in Erasmus's *Adages*. In a relatively rare act of commonplacing others, Milton copies the Tacitean adage and its following explanation almost precisely, save for a few inconsequential phrases silently trimmed from the original: "and indeed we ever see [it falleth out] that the forbidden writing is thought to be a certaine sparke of truth that flyeth up in the faces of them that seeke to choke and tread it out, whereas a book authorized, is thought to bee but [*temporis voces,*] the language of the time."[109] Milton does not quote Bacon's next sentence, which in 1644 would have undermined his argument: "But in plaine truth," Bacon wrote, "I doe finde to my understanding, these pamphlets as meet to be suppressed as the others." Nor does he include Bacon's subsequent contention that such Puritan pamphleteering seeks "to deface the government of the Church in the persons of the Bishops and Prelates," and has such "dangerous amplifications" "as if the civill government itselfe of this estate, had neere lost the force of its sinewes, and were ready to enter into some confusion, all things being full of faction and disorder."[110] These sharp oppositions to Milton's position are also conveniently omitted when he quotes Bacon in *Areopagitica* as saying "*such authoriz'd books are but the language of the times*" (*CPW* 2:534). Milton's creative misuse of Bacon performs an act of appropriative misquotation that seeks to destabilize its source. Bacon is now an authority supporting Milton's argument against licensing. But this misquotation also seems to enact one of the theories of reading postulated by the tract itself, that reading is an act of culling, and one brings to one's reading a set of convictions that deeply inform what one takes away.

Just after the 1641 Bacon entry is a citation to Paolo Sarpi's *Istoria del Concilio Tridentino* (London, 1619), translated as *The Historie of the Councell of Trent* (1620).[111] It was probably entered between the first and second editions of *The Doctrine and Discipline of Divorce* (in late 1643), since Sarpi appears in the second edition where he had not in the first. Tracking Sarpi yields evidence about the notebook's use—and also reminds us that we cannot depend on its record as an index of when Milton encountered ideas. As Nigel Smith points out, Milton "made more references to Sarpi's *Istoria* in the *Commonplace Book* than to any other text of recent [non-British] European history, with the exception of Bernard de Girard, Seigneur du Haillan's *L'Histoire de France* (first ed., 1576) and Jacques de Thou's *Historia Sui Temporis* (1620,1626)."[112]

Sarpi is an interesting choice of reading for an English Puritan, as he was a Catholic who had hoped to make peace with the Protestants, and was embraced by members of the English Church. Sarpi's *Istoria* is referred to some thirteen times in the Commonplace Book from late 1643. He also seems to influence Milton's earliest polemical work—for example, his painting of the English bishops as being full of "Monkish prohibitions, and expurgatorious indexes, . . . proud Imprimaturs," suggests that Milton was reading Sarpi's shorter work, *The History of the Inquisition,* soon after its appearance in England in 1639.[113] Several years before writing *Areopagitica,* Milton had been introduced to the history of the use of *Imprimatur* ("Let this be printed"), which gave him the opportunity in 1643 to use this bit of book history to show the origins of the word *imprimatur* still used on English title pages, even though it was created by the Inquisition. Sarpi supplies the source for several pages of historical writing in the first part of *Areopagitica,* and, like Bacon, he is introduced with a rare subtopic: "Prohibition of books when first us'd. The storie therof is in yᵉ Councel of Trent Book 6. strait from yᵉ beginning" (CB 184).

In addition to these recent entries in the Political Index that Milton reuses in the tract, there are related entries that show him to have been concerned about censorship and toleration—or the church-state relationship—earlier in his career. In an investigation of publication history mentioned earlier, for example, Milton observes how later editions of Boccaccio's life of Dante had passages removed by the "inquisitor" which revealed that Dante's *De Monarchia* had been burned "as an heretical work" (CB 182, *CPW* 1:438). This sentiment against the act of book burning helps, as I will argue further in the next chapter, in understanding the rhetorical disingenuousness of Milton's statements in *Areopagitica* that seem to favor treating books as malefactors.

A mysterious gap in Milton's polemical output separates *Areopagitica* from the next printed political tract, *The Tenure of Kings and Magistrates,* by four years. When Milton turns to publish *The Tenure,* Colonel Pride had purged Parliament to almost a fifth of its members, and the new "rump" Parliament set about to put the king on trial. In this urgent opportunity for polemical intervention, Milton deploys the storehouse of information in his notes to an astonishing extent. The relationship between the two is so extensive as to almost suggest that the Political Index had been designed for the purposes of this tract. The short first edition of *The Tenure* draws specifically on at least twenty-five entries in the Political Index, with many more related entries. Nearly all of the nonbiblical authorities and the historical events cited in the first edition derive directly from Milton's Commonplace Book. In most cases, although not all, the transfer of information does not require Milton to return to the original source. The composition process is also predetermined by the organization of the notebook: at times Milton employs as many as three entries from a single page in the Commonplace Book on the same page in *The Tenure.*[114]

Milton's use of the Commonplace Book for the political treatises he wrote while he still had his sight continues, after *The Tenure,* although in diminishing numbers. The anonymous government publication, *The Observations upon the Articles of Peace* (1649), utilizes about six entries, *Eikonoklastes* (1649) about five, and *Pro Populo Anglicano Defensio* (1651), twenty-three. Milton uses entries for many of the other works written in the 1640s as well, including the *History of Britain,* the "Digression," and the outlines for "British Tragedies." There are a couple of possible uses after the 1640s and early 1650s, also detailed in the appendixes, but they suggest very rare scribal visitations to the manuscript. The diminishment is not surprising: in a sense, Milton also uses up a great deal of his arsenal of information in the urgency of its first deployment. After his blindness, his consultation of the manuscript is no longer distinctly evident, which suggests that the book fell into disuse—except possibly for an occasional scribal visitation—after 1652.

Chapter 3

Areopagitica
Books, Reading, and Context

You have found and will find that the Greeks and Romans were much less favourable
to tyrants. So too the Jews, if that book of Samuel in which he, 1 Sam. 10, had
described the rights of kingship were extant. This book, so the doctors of the Hebrews
have reported, was torn apart or burnt by kings so that they might exercise tyranny
over their subjects with greater impunity.
Milton, *Pro Populo Anglicano Defensio*

How can we more safely, and with lesse danger scout into the regions of sin and falsity
then by reading all manner of tractats, and hearing all manner of reason?
Milton, *Areopagitica*

CRITICISM OF *Areopagitica* has often sought either to extol the work
as a cornerstone in the foundation of the liberal tradition, or to diminish and
even renounce such claims as misreadings of Milton's more conservative intentions. Following the Whig and Romantic lionization of Milton during
the nineteenth century, traditional readings have seen the tract as "one of the
founding and canonical texts of modern liberalism,"[1] and have even gone so
far as to call it "unique in its period, and perhaps unequalled in the range
of freedom it demands until the *Liberty* of John Stuart Mill."[2] This liberal
humanist account of *Areopagitica*'s position in intellectual history has been
challenged from a postmodern perspective by readers who cast suspicion on
all kinds of discourse—ideological or philosophical—as unconscious instruments of power.[3] Such cynicism may seem almost justified by the fact that
five years after writing *Areopagitica,* with his party now in power, Milton
took a role as licenser ostensibly similar to the one he had railed against.
Some have accordingly suggested that "as Petrograd in 1919 and Havana in
1965, so was Milton's protestant London in 1644,"[4] while others have seen a
complicity in the tract "with the most repellent aspects of fascism."[5] A similarly unsentimental revision of the liberal view of Milton is taken by Stanley

Fish, although from a different perspective. Fish's deconstruction of *Areopagitica*'s many internal contradictions, and his emphasis on such passages as "I deny not, but that it is of greatest concernment . . . to have a vigilant eye how Bookes demeane themselves . . . and thereafter to confine, imprison, and do sharpest justice on them as malefactors" (*CPW* 2:492) brings him to argue that the tract is "not against licensing," and "has almost no interest at all in the 'freedom of the press' . . . [and] does not unambiguously value freedom at all,"[6] and therefore cannot fit into the history in which it has been enlisted.

Part of the difficulty in assessing the quality of freedom in *Areopagitica* is that the tract's arguments fit into at least three categories of liberty: of the press, of conscience, and of the political subject. The recent reassessment of Whig historiography has often focused on one of these forms of liberty to the exclusion of others. Quentin Skinner's *Liberty before Liberalism* (1998), for example, describes Milton's contemporaries as embracing a neo-Roman conception of civil liberty that is not rightly termed "liberal." This important reconsideration mostly omits liberty of conscience, a major part of civil war discourse, but recent work on religious freedom has also tempered the Whiggish habit, as Blair Worden phrases it, of congratulating "the past on becoming more like the present."[7] Revisionist approaches to the history of toleration have argued that the idea of "liberty" itself has been taken out of context, and that Puritan proponents of toleration did not seek liberty in a modern sense.[8] "The claim of liberty of conscience," argues J. C. Davis, "had virtually nothing to do with a claim to direct or manage ourselves"; rather it is a claim to "be free to submit to the governance of God [over] any other authority."[9] Recognizing some overcorrection in this conception of toleration, John Coffey's "post-revisionist"[10] work offers a more balanced account, showing that both religious and philosophical pressures were at play in determining the nature of the debate, and that the policy of persecution, although far more persistent than earlier accounts allowed, was nonetheless dramatically eroded by tolerationist ideology through the course of the seventeenth century.

These recent conversations about the character of toleration and its place in political historiography have provided a more nuanced context within which to understand Milton, although as always he remains hard to place. Readers of *Areopagitica* might immediately detect considerable overadjustment in the idea that toleration had "virtually nothing to do with a claim to direct or manage ourselves," since here liberty of conscience is explicitly packaged with other liberties—with "free writing," "free speaking," and "the liberty to know"—and set with them "above all other liberties." He writes in the beginning that the freedom to express one's grievances freely in the "Commonwealth" is the "utmost bound of civil liberty attain'd, that wise men looke for" (487), presenting his argument as an integral part of a package of political liberties toward which he assumes his audience aspires—indeed, it is the "utmost bound" of such liberties. The now common phrase "civil liberty" was at that point just gaining currency—this is the first attested use in the *OED*, and among the first occurrences in Milton.[11] The buzzword "liberty" itself, used sixteen times in the tract but only twice as modified by "Christian liberty," takes on a form that exceeds the preconditions for free worship: it is, Milton writes, using a civic humanist formulation, "the nurse of all great wits" (559), and the enabler of "the very sound of this which I shall utter" (487). In Milton's encomiastic terms, England is "formost in the atchievements of liberty" (505).

The general language of liberty Milton employs cannot have been separated in his mind from the "liberty" invoked with frequency in the Commonplace Book, where it is more overtly tied to republicanism. Indeed, the two texts together suggest that Milton already favors republicanism, and they suggest that he had hoped that the tract's subtle republicanism would speak to a similar bias in his audience. In entries under the topic "Libertas" written around 1642–44, Milton drew on a few passages from Justinian to show that "Civil law favors liberty" (CB 190). In another entry, he speculates that "it is not likely that a city, led by love of liberty, should do *very noble deeds* [quamvis praeclara facinora] and then regain its freedom when it has been lost. Just as Crescentius of Nomentum was unsuccessful when he tried to restore the old form of the Roman republic" (CB 190, *CPW* 1:470, emphasis added). *Areopagitica*'s description of the "vast city" of London, a "mansion house of liberty," would have figured in Milton's imagination as engaged in a similar revolutionary effort.[12] The phrase early in *Areopagitica* claiming that the parliamentary forces had moved "beyond the manhood of a *Roman* recovery" (487) appeals subtly to the same sense of republican *virtù* endorsed in the manuscript. Milton's notes concerning "a city led by love of liberty" are not in the source material supporting this idea, and thus all the more the material of his own intellectual preoccupations.

Milton associates the liberties of knowing, speaking, writing, and believing in a conspicuously political manner with the parliamentary success against the king, which again suggests a presumptive republican overthrow of the monarchy. Parliament has "purchast us" liberty, provided a "mild, and free, and human government" instead of the "oppressive, arbitrary, and tyrannous" (559) government experienced under the rule of Charles. The language here seems to affirm Milton's later argument in *The Tenure of Kings and Magistrates* that the deposition of the king was in the early 1640s the understood logical outcome of the war. Janel Mueller accordingly sees in *Areopagitica* a "nascent republicanism," a political vocabulary "in its fullest and most precise articulation in the interval between *Of Reformation* and the *Tenure of Kings and Magistrates.*"[13] One could argue that this language is not nascent so much as functionally subdued—it is a presumed system of values that Milton had long been familiar with. In his close analysis of the tract's pervasive republican resonances, David Norbrook has suggested more strongly that the tract constitutes an "early manifesto of English republicanism."[14] While this seems to be the case, rhetorically speaking, of course, there is a difference between early modern political writing and the manifestoes of modernity, which truly bear the sense of "open demonstration." *Areopagitica*'s republicanism exists as a kind of ideological substratum, an established system of ideas to which Milton need not risk explicit application.

Connecting republicanism with arguments for Christian liberty, Victoria Kahn draws attention to another important topic in the Commonplace Book, "Of Religion. To what extent it concerns the state."[15] The entries that follow this topic, two from the *Discorsi* (entered by Edward Phillips) and one from Dante (entered by another scribe), provide an unusual window on the back-stage of Milton's public rhetorical performance:

> Among the most excellent of all mortals are those who instruct the minds of men in true religion, more excellent even than those who have founded, however well, kingdoms and republics by man-made laws. Machiavel. discors Book 1. c[hapter] 10.

> That the combining of ecclesiastical and political government (when, that is to say, the magistrate acts as minister of the Church and the minister of the Church acts as magistrate) is equally destructive to both religion and the State, Dante, the Tuscan pet, shows in his Purgatorio. Cant. 16.

> [Two passages from Dante follow]

> The opinions of men concerning religion should be free in a republic, or indeed under good princes. While Machiavelli praises such princes, he says, among other things, that under them you will see golden times, "where each man can hold and defend the opinion that he wishes." Discors. Book 1. c[hapter] 10. See the Theological Index, Of Not Forcing Religion. (CB 197, *CPW* 1:475–76)

As Kahn points out, these entries suggest that Milton "does not read Machiavelli simply as a secular theorist," but rather sees "the *Discourses* as compatible with his own argument against 'forcing religion.'"[16] Machiavellian republicanism and English freedom of religion thus operate in the same conceptual framework. This piece of evidence should be approached with some caution, since the entries are not as certainly Miltonic as those written in his own hand under "Libertas." But Phillips's cross-reference to Milton's now lost Theological Index suggests (among Phillips's other work for Milton) a special intellectual intimacy, and therefore that this Machiavellian entry, like Milton's own entries from the same volume, is integral to his system of ideas.

There is, then, evidence supporting an affinity between classical republicanism and Milton's arguments for freedom of speech, and between civic humanism and liberty of conscience. This connection complicates the recent position taken by Simone Zurbuchen that early modern republicans gravitated toward a more Erastian position—that is, of a national church.[17] Yet Milton invokes classical republicanism more for rhetorical purposes than philosophical; more to affirm a set of values than to adopt a philosophical system or engage a particular argument about freedom. The Athenian scene from Euripides is translated on the title page, for example, to reinforce Milton's eponymous association with the Athens of Euripides' time. But there is no specific Athenian argument produced to support the claims of toleration or liberty of the press—rather, the argument gains persuasive strength by association. Milton uses the history of ancient Rome in a similar fashion, frequently reinforcing the strength of republican Rome against its corrupt imperial history. The period of history in which Cicero flourished, "so great a father of the commonwealth" (498), was also one in which people were open-minded about the publication of controversial books—but no argument from Cicero is used to support the positions of the tract. Milton holds the Roman republican conditions of liberty in opposition to the persecutory treatment of writers like Ovid, who struggled under the "tyranny in the Roman Empire" (500). Later, Milton points out that Claudius intended to institute the form of licensing eventually established in the Inquisition, but "went not through with" it (504), which provides the compelling impression that the practice belongs to imperial states even more corrupt than Claudius's. As a rare marginal note in Suetonius's Latin confirms, Claudius was "even said to have considered an edict that would allow farting at a banquet" – presumably because suppression is unhealthy.

In spite of the paucity of examples of formal legislation, Milton manages to portray licensing as an imperial rather than a republican motive. The rhetorical appeal to republicanism seems rather surprising, since, as Norbrook points out, Henry Marten had been expelled from Parliament and imprisoned for his republicanism for stating in the House of Commons in August 1643 that "it were better one family be destroyed than many."[18] Marten spoke these words while defending a pamphlet by John Saltmarsh—*Examinations; or, A Discovery of Some Dangerous Positions* (1643)—which had come under examination for its antimonarchist views. Fittingly, perhaps because Milton came to recognize the rhetorical dangers of republicanism, there is far less of an appeal to it in *The Tenure of Kings and Magistrates,* where we would most expect it, and for which there existed a prepared set of republican notes that would remain muted or unused.

In part due to the lack of a concrete body of knowledge in ancient republicanism supporting freedom of the press or freedom of belief, classical republicanism supplies rhetorical texture rather than the philosophical foundation for the liberties Milton advocates. Where there is a firm articulation of these ideas in ancient thought, it is in their negation in Plato's political theory, in which the control of belief and the exclusion of bad texts enabled a greater knowledge of the good and hence greater happiness. Although Milton had earlier applied Plato's ideas in the *Republic* and the *Laws* to his arguments for church government, he now views them as wrongheaded, a system "no City ever yet received" (522). Plato is indeed the most frequently mentioned authority.[19] But while Milton sees his own political argument in line with the Platonic tradition, he invokes the ancient philosopher only to show the diametric opposition between his own theory and that represented in the *Republic.* Like Plato's politics, the center of Milton's argument is about the acquisition of knowledge, but for him a prescribed set of beliefs does not yield knowledge of the good, but no knowledge at all. As he describes in an outline of his argument at the outset of the tract, control of belief will be a "discouragement of all learning, and the stop of Truth, not only by disexercising and blunting our abilities in what we know already, but by hindering and cropping the discovery that might bee yet further made both in religious and civill Wisdome" (491–92).

While clearly colored by republicanism, the tract's central argument about the acquisition of knowledge through written material represents an experiment in self-authenticated reasoning informed by new philosophical trends. As Richard Tuck and others have shown, the language of natural reason and natural law emerged with some intensity in the constitutional debates of 1643.[20] A similar experimentation with method informs the arguments for "Philosophic freedom" (537) in the toleration debates of the following year. In order to counter the well-buttressed commitment to a prescribed religious and social order, Milton and others developed arguments that do not easily conform to the categories that have characterized debate about seventeenth-century political history.[21] The basic rational methods required to make these new arguments are neither classical nor biblical, although Milton engages both in distinctive and unusual ways. Milton's argument for liberty ultimately rests on a philosophical explanation of the acquisition of knowledge. This explanation negates Reformation theology of the servitude of the will that was strongly espoused by his Presbyterian contemporaries—a position on free will that is represented among the earliest entries in his Commonplace Book.[22]

Milton's theory of reason deserves to be more fully contextualized. The work of Ernest Sirluck in the Yale edition of *Areopagitica* has helped provide a sense of the immediate discursive context from which the tract arises, as one among many contemporary pamphlets on liberty of conscience and (to a far lesser extent) on freedom of the press.[23] This scholarship has shown Milton to have a complex engagement with contemporary pamphleteers. In 1644 Milton seems allied with a coalition of Independents and separatists who sought to defend freedom of belief against the parliamentary control established by Presbyterians, who believed in church control of the state, and the Erastians, who believed in state control of the church. In contrast to recent suggestions that Milton's politics are Erastian, I argue that Milton maintains a subtle but strong opposition—as he would later write explicitly—"against *Erastus* and state-tyranie over the church."[24] Part of the task in evaluating Milton's complex and seemingly self-contradicting positions lies in understanding how they coexist with more context-bound rhetorical maneuvers that seek to appeal to the Erastians (such as John Selden) in order to counter the Presbyterian hegemony in Parliament.[25] Milton's approach allows him to raise the toleration question without immediately alienating his Erastian audience, since among other things it avoids the conventional—or what would become conventional—argument separating church and state. Such an argument would have been fully available to Milton, as he had posed the problem among the entries on the first page of his Political Index in the late 1630s or early 1640s with a passage from Camden: "Inter religionem et rempub. divortium esse non potest" ("separation of religion and state is not possible"), to which he later added a remarkable rejoinder in around 1642–44 from Hospital, "the very wise [prudentissimus] chancellor of France"—which is very rare praise in the Commonplace Book: " 'Many,' he says, 'can be citizens who are by no means Christians, and he who is far from the bosom of the Church does not cease to be a loyal citizen, and we can live peacefully with those who do not reverence the same religious rites as we do.' "[26] This is an extraordinarily secular formulation, and worth holding in contrast to the much less allowing tenets of *Areopagitica,* in which Milton remains famously intolerant to Catholics, even when some of his peers and friends (Roger Williams, William Walwyn, and Richard Overton, for example), were more widely

tolerant.[27] Yet Milton's reading places him in a much more continental—
and more widely tolerant—framework. Michel de L'Hospital was a Catholic,
as was de Thou, and thus the "bosom of the Church" in this case is a conspicuously Catholic Church, although he advocated a tolerant French state.[28]
While it is hard to gauge just how much of the disparities between this view
and *Areopagitica* are due to polemical exigencies, it seems clear enough that
what dictates the disparity is not a shift in conviction, but a shift in posture.
Milton could not himself have argued for the rights of all, including non-
Christians, and be taken as seriously by the English readership he hoped to
reach. Nor indeed would he have quoted Hospital in this Protestant tract.
Yet he is clearly far more sympathetic to the ideas of the French statesman—as
the endorsement of Hospital's superlative sagacity suggests—than he lets on
in his printed work.

But while toleration is a central issue of this tract, as has been recently claimed in the work of Stephen Dobranski, Blair Hoxby, and Joseph
Loewenstein, it is a serious mistake to undervalue as either tactical or secondary the argument for the liberty of printing.[29] This is, as its title loudly
proclaims, A SPEECH OF MR. JOHN MILTON *For the Liberty of* UNLICENC'D
PRINTING, *To the* PARLAMENT OF ENGLAND—it is not even immediately
about toleration, although it becomes entrenched in that concern.[30] Sirluck's
important contextualist work in the Yale edition has perhaps had the distort-
ing effect of shifting the tract out of itself: *Areopagitica* is not as much a part
of this whole as this criticism—including my own—would imply.[31] Books
and reading are themselves Milton's subject, in addition to the "heretical" subjects which those books sometimes convey. As Annabel Patterson has pointed
out, the tract uses the word "book" some eighty-five times, and "tract" or "trac-
tate," which appear more toward the end, some thirty-two times.[32] It need
hardly be said that these figures complicate Fish's claim that "books are no
more the subject of the *Areopagitica* than is free speech."[33]

Milton himself elides the two issues, and makes the "Ordinance for the
Regulating of Printing" look as if it is actually about the suppression of heresy. But unlike the 1648 "Ordinance for the Punishing of Blasphemies and
Heresies" that approached the issue of controlling heresy *through* print—where
it became illegal to print certain heresies—the 1643 Ordinance, while related, originated from economic problems faced by the Stationers' Company,
which had petitioned Parliament about trade issues unrelated to the content
of books printed. The issue of controlling heresy is shortly mentioned in
Henry Parker's speech to Parliament on behalf of the Stationers as a side benefit, and religion is also glanced at in the ordinance itself,[34] but the immediate
issue—an issue that Independents might come to believe that a Presbyterian

hegemony could control to their advantage—was not the regulation of opinion, but the regulation of property and trade.[35] Parker does mention, in his speech published in April 1643, that lands like Poland and parts of the Netherlands that do not have regulation see "the poison of *Socinus* and *Arminius* spread[ing] unregarded," and he makes the ill-considered point that "we must in this give Papists their due" for having such an effective machine in the "Inquisition,"[36] which would have horrified Milton—and probably did, given his attack on the Inquisition in the tract, although it is likely he would have made this attack regardless, since he had already recorded this relationship in notes taken from Paolo Sarpi in his Commonplace Book.[37] Yet, in spite of the occasional religious comments in the official documents, it is clear that the monopolizing protection of the Stationers' Company and the maintenance of stable trade, rather than the suppression of heresy, motivates the licensing act of 1643.[38] Milton's recasting of the purposes of this act is suggested in the very belatedness of his response.

Beyond the rhetorical challenges produced by *Areopagitica*'s conflicted parliamentary audience, the tract's complexity mirrors that of the crisis to which it responds. Even while various forces within the Puritan movement vie for ascendancy or sufferance through Parliament, their political battle is itself under siege by royalist armies. Although this is not the tremulous moment of composition Milton experienced two years before in penning a sonnet to be fixed "on his door when the City expected an assault," the outcome of the war in late 1644 remained quite uncertain, with an alternating series of victories and defeats on both sides. Milton's description of London as a city "besieg'd and blockt about, her navigable river infested, inrodes and incursions round, defiance and battell oft rumor'd to be marching up ev'n to her walls" (556–57) reflect this moment of military uncertainty. The proximity of the royalist army was seen by Parliament as well as "possibly culminating in an attack on London."[39] In mid-November (when the tract was published), the parliamentary armies sounded retreat after two battles.[40] In short, at the time of composition, Milton could have little confidence about England's political future. The immediate question of authority over freedom of the press was ensconced within a larger undetermined issue concerning the outcome of the war: who would rule England, and what the nature of that rule might be.

As pragmatically shifty and contingent as it may seem, *Areopagitica* does, however, participate in a distinct polemical effort from a coalition of dissidents writing against the reigning Presbyterian majority. In the years 1643–44, the arguments for toleration suddenly and indelibly entered English political discourse.[41] There were, of course, related forms of toleration that had been brewing on the continent, as in the work of Grotius, Bodin, Postel, and Castellio, which often appeared in manuscript, and the work of Paolo Sarpi, whose manuscripts were smuggled from Venice to be printed in England through the sponsorship of Milton's friend Henry Wotton.[42] Yet the intolerance of Calvinist extremists that had risen to power occasioned a sudden burst of toleration tracts in 1643 and 1644 that would define debate for many years. Perhaps in part as a result of the surprising intolerance of his Puritan contemporaries, Milton's own interest in toleration appears rather suddenly, although both the Commonplace Book and early references in the antiprelatical tracts suggest that he had a steady interest in European and papal instruments of censorship.

The sudden increase in the intensity of the toleration debate in England stems not only from the squabbles of various Puritan sects, but from more impartial considerations that followed in the wake of the first episode of the civil war, begun in the summer of 1642. These writers, whom Sirluck has termed "secularist," look more at the religious causes of the war, and slightly predate the Independent tracts, as in such anonymous pamphlets as *A Short Discourse, Touching the Cause of the Present Unhappy Distractions,* acquired by Thomason in February 1643.[43] The secularists employ the same sequence of argument as Hobbes's *Leviathan:* they begin with the problem of civil war, and then, taking the opposite view to Hobbes, present toleration as the solution. Henry Robinson also uses a secular line of reasoning in *Liberty of Conscience: or the Sole Means to Obtaine Peace and Truth* (March 1644), and then in a major work that probably appeared in September, titled *John the Baptist, Forerunner of Christ Jesus; or, A Necessity for Liberty of Conscience.* Robinson sees intolerance to religious difference as the principal cause of war, and also sees liberty of the press as crucial to the maintenance of liberties and to the discovery of truth.[44] The toleration texts that followed within the next several months came from a largely Independent standpoint. They include Roger Williams's tracts, shaped by his experience of persecution in Massachusetts, although he feared with some foresight that the Independents would come to practice the same intolerance if they were to come to power. In February 1644 Williams anonymously published a short pamphlet titled *Queries of Highest Consideration,* and then in July emerged with a 247-page book on the subject, *The Bloudy Tenet of Persecution,* which ignited intense opposition. As if to illustrate Milton's phrase "as good almost kill a Man as kill a good Book" (*CPW* 2:492), Parliament ordered it burned by the hangman.[45] Those tracts that follow, up to the publication of *Areopagitica* on November 23, are of a more sectarian bent, all with vastly different titles from Milton's: *M.S. to A.S. With A Plea for Libertie of Conscience* (May 1644), attributed to John

Goodwin; Goodwin's sermons in *Theomachia; or, The Grand Imprudence of Men Running the Hazard of Fighting against God* (October 1644); William Walwyn's *The Compassionate Samaritane* (June–July 1644) also attacks the Licensing Order and clearly influences Milton[46]; *A Paraenetick or Humble Addresse to the Parliament and Assembly for (Not Loose, But) Christian Libertie*, by an Assembly Congregationalist; Henry Robinson's work, which may also have influenced Milton, *John the Baptist* (September 1644) and *An Answer to Mr. William Prynn's Twelve Questions* (November 1, 1644). Copious production along these lines continued for some time, especially as negotiations for an Accommodation Order, which would have allowed nonseparating "Assembly" Congregationalists to practice equally with Presbyterians, began to fail.

It is hard to gauge how avidly Milton read his pamphleteering peers, since the concrete references we have in this period are almost always to opponents. But he had his ear to the ground, and this unrecorded reading shapes and advances his writing. One influence in particular, mostly charted by Sirluck, is William Walwyn.[47] In a tract written just prior to *Areopagitica,* Walwyn argues against press regulation. Milton borrows Walwyn's argument that "Truth was not used to feare colours, or to seeke shifts or stratagems for its advancement,"[48] in writing "Truth is strong next to the Almighty; she needs no policies, nor stratagems, nor licencings to make her victorious, those are the shifts and the defenses that error uses" (*CPW* 2:563). The second edition of *The Compassionate Samaritane* (1645) seems in turn to respond to *Areopagitica* (*CPW* 2:551n228).

Though there are strong hints of his thinking on free will and reason in the Commonplace Book, Milton's formative theory of reason emerges also from an intense engagement with tracts published within a period of only weeks or months prior to it. These were collaborative conditions of debate, in which a body of sectarians argued against a group of more conservative Puritans that held a position of legislative power over them. But they are also competitive conditions, in which polemicists battled against increasingly robust Presbyterian polemics that were backed by a long tradition of intolerance in Protestant England and Europe. As a moving part of this fast-paced system of debate and collaboration—the "knowledge in the making" celebrated in various ways throughout the tract—Milton brings an argument implicit in these earlier tracts to its next logical step. Milton's unusual part in this dynamic history illustrates more than just the author's context-dependent process of innovation; it also gives some impression of how sophisticated the exchange of ideas could be through this cheap and high-paced print culture.

Reading and Rereading Plato

Scholars have often noted the turn in *Areopagitica* away from Presbyterianism.[49] A major biography by Gordon Campbell and Thomas Corns has forced us to rethink this history, as it suggests that Milton was not, in fact, deeply rooted in the Presbyterian Puritan heritage as formerly thought, but adopted it quite late, in 1637, before leaving for the continent. Campbell and Corns suggest that Milton writes the antiprelatical tracts as "though he would rather be writing a tolerationist tract" and "has been pushed out of position [that is, out of his non-Calvinist position] by polemical exigencies."[50] While their sense of Milton's being "pushed out of position"—and at times profoundly—is crucial to my own argument, Milton at times engages aspects of the Presbyterian position in ways that are so invested, and the repudiation of these positions in *Areopagitica* so strong, as to suggest a more complex adjustment of position than simply the shifting of rhetoric according to context. The sharp turns in position suggest that some fine-tuning of this important theory may be necessary.

Several elements in *Areopagitica*'s argument represent a full-scale deconstruction of the theopolitical elements of Calvinism. Calvin had a profound influence on the development of theological politics in the north, shaping English concepts of politics both in the English Church and in the Puritan movement. His view of the nature of political obligation derived from a literal reading of scripture and from the theology of predestination. Calvin conceived of an idealized relationship between church and secular authority that gave rise to his term "Christian polity"—or *politia Christiana*—in which there exists "a double 'ministry' of magistrates and pastors, both deriving their authority from God, and both charged with governing the same body of persons, the only possible relationship between them is one of cooperation and mutual restraint."[51]

Calvin was not, of course, the only continental reformer whose ideas were imported to England. Before the Marian exile, Martin Bucer came to England to continue the process of reformation, where he wrote his last political work, *De Regno Christi—On the Kingdom of Christ*—which he dedicated to the Edward VI.[52] The first English translation of this appears in part in Milton's *Judgment of Martin Bucer to Edward the Sixth in his second book of the Kingdom of Christ now englished,* which attempts to capitalize on Bucer's authority as one of the original Protestant reformers. This tract appeared a few months before *Areopagitica,* in early August 1644, and it is addressed only to the "Supreme Court of Parliament"—Milton here gives up on the Westminster Assembly.[53] This newly exclusive address has the further significance of countering the increasingly theocratic state. Bucer espoused a form of theological politics that encapsulates the mixture of utopianism and theology that infused extremist Reformation thought. He used Mosaic law and other social codes derived from scripture as the basis upon which to build his disciplinarian "Christocratic" utopia, or what he referred to as a "respublica Christiana."[54] "No man," he wrote, "can live well and happily except in a Christocratic society," in which living happily, as in Plato's *Republic,* meant living a rule-bound, censored, and disciplined existence.[55] Bucer advocates a Platonic legal control of belief: when malfeasants remain stubbornly irredeemable, "it is proper to remove them from the commonwealth as Plato indicates in his *Politics* [a reference to both the *Republic* and the *Laws*]." As Bucer shows in a formulation repeated throughout *De Regno Christi,* this Platonic code works in concert with Old Testament law: "For the lord has commanded his people quite strictly that they are to drive criminal and incorrigible men from their midst, and to burn them with fire, and thus to wipe out their offensiveness as completely as possible (Deut. 13:5 ff.; 17:2–5; 19:11–21; 21:18–21; 22:13–28; and 24:7)."[56] The lines from Deuteronomy invoked here were the scriptural basis by which heretics were burned, and they figure centrally in the Presbyterian arguments against toleration in the 1640s. Bucer prescribes an intensely disciplinary polity for England, creating one of the sources for the central concept of "discipline" in the Puritan language of reform.[57] Another, more major source for the concept of political, social, and church "discipline" in England—though oddly, Milton does not cite it—is the late part of Calvin's *Institutes of the Christian Religion,* book IV, chapter 12: "The Discipline of the Church: Its Chief Use in Censures and Excommunication."[58]

These conceptions of theological politics deeply informed Milton's early polemics. Milton forges in *The Reason of Church Government* (1642) a merger between Platonic and biblical legalism in imagining a discipline-bound Christian polity. He begins with an analogy comparing his own motivations in formulating the "reason" behind church government with the rhetorical motivations of Plato and Moses. Plato's "advice was, seeing that persuasion certainly is a more winning, and more manlike way to keepe men in obedience than feare, that to such lawes as were of principall moment, there should be us'd as an induction, some well-temper'd discourse, shewing how good, how gainful, how happy it must needs be to live according to honesty and justice," which to do one must "incite, and in a manner, charme the multitude into the love of that which is really good" (*CPW* 1:746). Milton moves to the more ancient (and more sacred) source of Moses, "the only lawgiver we can believe to have been visibly taught of God," who "began with the book of Genesis as a prologue to his laws"—suggesting a generic connection with Plato's *Laws*—"that the nation of the Jews, reading therein the universal goodness of God to all creatures in the creation, and his peculiar favor to them in his election of Abraham, their ancestor, from whom they could derive so many blessings upon themselves, might be moved to obey sincerely by knowing so good a reason of their obedience" (747). Milton combines Platonic utopian politics with Presbyterian "discipline" in his remark that "Discipline" is "so hard to be of mans making, that we may see even in the guidance of a civill state to worldly happinesse, it is not for every learned, or every wise man, though many of them consult in common, to invent or frame a discipline, but if it be at all the worke of man, it must be of such a one as is a true knower of himself" (753). This passage appeals to the concept of a self-knowing philosopher king, able to frame a discipline and lead the state to happiness.

One concept that still aligns Milton with the theocratic Presbyterians in 1642 is "discipline," which he uses as a kind of identity-marker. The need for all forms of discipline is a constant refrain in the early tracts, and often, as above, with a conception of governmental control that extends far wider than the parameters of the church. "There is not that thing in the world of more grave and urgent importance throughout the whole life of man, than is discipline," he writes. "What need I instance? He that hath read with judgement of nations and commonwealths of cities and camps, of peace and war, sea and land, will readily agree that the flourishing and decaying of all civil societies, all the moments and turnings of human occasions, are moved to and fro as upon the axle of discipline." Once again, Milton goes on in a Platonic vein: "And certainly discipline is not only the removal of disorder; but if any visible shape can be given to divine things, the very visible shape and image of virtue. . . . The state also of blessed paradise, though never so perfect, is not therefore left without discipline, whose golden surveying reed marks out and measures every quarter and circuit of New Jerusalem" (752).

In such a conception of civil harmony, disciplined citizens live according to a "prescribed" set of laws, and emulate the disciplinary utopia of "blessed paradise." Not only is Church discipline itself "prescrib'd in the Gospell" (750), but we must live according to "that which is prescrib'd" (752), and to God's "own prescribed discipline" (757). Paradise here is upheld as a sort of ideal, a condition of bliss under discipline. This utopic vision will not be the case for *Areopagitica,* in which the lost paradise becomes a kind of inevitable and even celebrated precondition for modern existence: "God uses not to captivate under a perpetual childhood of prescription," he asserts suggestively, before turning to the Fall, "but trusts [a man] with the gift of reason to be his own chooser" (*CPW* 2:513–14). In the place of a prescriptive system,

Milton adds a startling new claim that revolved around the way human reason worked. The "childhood of prescription" alludes to the Platonic utopianism and legalism that Milton allies with the Presbyterian position, and that he had once evoked more positively in the antiprelatical tracts.

In the space of a couple of years, Milton thus turned sharply from key concepts identifying a long tradition of Puritan and Calvinist political thought, and in systematically repudiating his contemporaries, he seems to be renouncing his former self—particularly around the notions of prescription, discipline, and the utopianism that had long structured godly Protestant theology. Yet, as mentioned, the seeds for this defining turn in *Areopagitica* were already planted in the Commonplace Book. A primary example can be found in a note on the early Christian writer Lactantius (ca. 240–ca. 320), sequentially the second entry in the entire book, under the topic "Moral Evil" in the Ethical Index. Here Milton writes: "Why does God permit evil? So that the reasoning and virtue may be correlated [*ut ratio virtuti constare possit*]. For the good is made known, is made clear, and is exercised by evil. As Lactantius says, Book 5 c[hapter] 7, that reason and intelligence may have the opportunity to exercise themselves by choosing the things that are good, by fleeing from the things that are evil. Lactan de ira dei. c[hapter] 13."[59]

Milton's subversion of the Presbyterian paradigms of theological limitation and political control are shown in his antagonistic representations of "Discipline" and Platonism. The Platonic politics in *Areopagitica* work not only to achieve his present argument, but to deconstruct and refute the theological politics of those he now sees as his opponents. Plato is openly cited seven times in the antiprelatical tracts, all in support of his claims—in contrast to the six references in *Areopagitica,* all in opposition.[60] In *An Apology against a Pamphlet* (1642), Milton invokes a Platonic utopianism that is shot down in 1644: "That grave and noble invention," he writes in the early tract, "which the greatest and sublimest wits in sundry ages, *Plato in Critias,* and our two famous countreymen, the one in his *Utopia,* the other in his *new Atlantis* chose, I may not say as a field, but as a mighty Continent wherein to display the largenesse of their spirits by teaching this our world better and exacter things, then were yet known, or us'd" (*CPW* 1:881). When he returns to these arguments in *Areopagitica* it is to renounce them powerfully: "To sequester out of the world into *Atlantick* and *Eutopian* polities, which never can be drawn into use, will not mend our condition" (*CPW* 2:526). Milton's ideas in *Areopagitica* are often called utopian, but this misreads his explicit rejection of the Platonic political tradition.

In addition to this sharp repudiation of Protestant Platonism, the use of the related term "discipline" diminishes significantly, turning from positive to a negative representation. Milton uses the key term "discipline" pervasively until *The Doctrine and Discipline of Divorce,* which seeks even in its titular alliteration to associate divorce with two key concepts of the strict reformers. "Discipline" occurs twenty-four times in *Of Reformation, Touching Church-Discipline in England,* thirty-six times in *The Reason of Church Government,* and in dwindling numbers in five divorce tracts, in spite of Milton's efforts to show that divorce is a "discipline," five times in *Areopagitica* (yet in a negative sense), and three times in *The Tenure of Kings and Magistrates.* In its many instances in Milton's first antiprelatical tract it almost always appears with a capital D, as in "the forwarding of true Discipline, which are among ourselves" (*CPW* 1:528), or "the Discipline sought." Finally, he speaks famously of the "one right discipline" (*CPW* 1:605), a phrase that suggests that there is only *one* true sect or "discipline" (Presbyterianism). The Milton represented here is not the schismatic tolerationist who would come to promote freedom for all forms of Protestant worship. In *Areopagitica,* there is no "one right discipline," but many. Here, Milton turns against the very concept, constructing the argument with specific allusion to this Presbyterian ideal: "Shut up all youth into the severest discipline that can be exercis'd in any hermitage, ye cannot make them chaste" (*CPW* 2:527). This keyword shows up repeatedly in this manner, as in the statement that "freedom of writing" has been "restrained by a discipline imitated from the Prelates" (541), or in the argument that "he who hears what praying there is for light and clearer knowledge to be sent down among us, would think of other matters to be constituted beyond the discipline of Geneva" (561–62), where the now problematic "discipline of Geneva" stands for the ideal held by reformers—and in particular the Presbyterians—stuck in their tracks. This is one of the moments in the tract where Milton indicates explicitly that there are serious limitations to Calvinism. In the polemic literature that would appear after 1648, after the "Ordinance for the Punishing of Blasphemies and Heresies"— which prescribed the death penalty for anti-Trinitarianism and imprisonment for Arminianism—Milton represented himself ostensibly in a more orthodox manner.

In *Areopagitica,* Milton's politics no longer seek to recapture a happy state of humanity or to build a discipline-bound utopia. Instead, his politics recognize the necessary benefits of leaving the perpetual childhood of *prescription*—a word which itself helped define the role of "discipline" in the Calvinist polity of *Reason of Church Government:* "It is not to be conceiv'd that those eternall effluences of sanctity and love in the glorified Saints should by this meanes be confin'd and cloy'd with repetition of that which is *prescrib'd,* but that our happiness may orbe it selfe into a thousand vagancies of glory and delight."[61] Milton's politics in *Areopagitica* seem in contrast to idealize the state of humanity that has left behind the prescripted happiness of Paradise. For Milton, rational choice is essential to the acquisition of knowledge, and therefore a social structure in which an authority—church or otherwise—determines and prescribes "the good" is impossible. Knowledge of the good cannot be prescribed by an external authority, since knowledge itself is not possible without the active volition of the knower. The legal utopia of the Presbyterians becomes in this view a dystopic world of artificial Adams and predestined puppets.

On the surface, Milton's argument for rational freedom in *Areopagitica* may appear to be no more significant than any other of the multifarious positions that grew from this unusual tract, whose generative forces seem to instantiate what is possible with such freedom. But when placed in the light of its larger discursive context, both religious and philosophical, the singularity of the idea becomes more apparent. For in forging a free-will theory of reason, Milton revokes a central tenet of Reformation Protestantism, which asserted Augustinian depravity over the freedom of Roman Catholic theology. For Puritans, one of the most troubling indicators of the "softening of relations with Rome,"[62] particularly prior to the impeachment of Archbishop Laud, was the Anglican embrace of the Arminian doctrine of free will.[63] Of course this theology came with other practices abhorrent to many Puritans, but it is significant that it was often specifically the theology of free will that raised the most ire. The Puritan Stephen Marshall preached in 1640 of the rotten *Dagon* of mans *free will*."[64] William Prynne argued too that the Arminian doctrine of "free will . . . [was a] total and final apostacie from the state of grace."[65] In his own antiprelatical tracts, Milton himself had suggested, although never with the sneering finality of Prynne, that the Arminian position was untenable.[66] But here, I would argue, he is merely wearing the mask of anti-Arminianism for rhetorical purposes, to situate himself respectably among Puritans even while he refutes the theology of Calvin. He used "Matchiavel" (*CPW* 2:321) the bogeyman in a similar fashion.

As Campbell and Corns have suggested, Milton perhaps never accepted Calvin's view of free will. This is also indicated in the early entry from Lactantius in his notes. If this is the case, as it seems, the arguments for free will in *Areopagitica* would be constructed as they are to keep them free of the prejudices attendant on the weighty theological history—to draw others to this conclusion without immediately indicating theological implications that might block their judgment. For when Milton returns to the question of rational liberty in the Restoration, at a safe distance from the earlier tensions between Laudians and Puritans, he uses this very language to counter the

Calvinist predestination and the Augustinian depravity that had informed Puritan theology. "Reason also is choice," argues God in *Paradise Lost,* and "when Will and Reason" are "made passive," as in Reformation theology, humanity serves "necessity / not mee" (3.108–10). As if in dialogue with misled theologians, God continues, fulfilling part of the theodicy of the narrative: "So [they] were created" free, "nor can justly accuse / Thir maker." God's words become almost comically dismissive, furthering their ironic dislocation from the theological debate they address: "As if Predestination over-rul'd / Thir will, dispos'd by absolute Degree / Or high foreknowledge" (3.111–15). Reformation theology is untenable because it prevents rational liberty. The Reformation theology of predestination, agonizingly constructed on the bedrock of scripture, is refuted on rational rather than scriptural grounds.

Milton begins in 1643 to introduce the concepts of reason and natural law. In the antiprelatical tracts, he sought to understand the correct discipline according to what God prescribed. "Let them chaunt while they will of prerogatives," he wrote in *The Reason of Church Government,* "we shall tell them of Scripture [until] the mighty weaknes of the Gospel throw down the weak mightiness of mans reasoning" (*CPW* 1:827). Here Milton follows the extreme forms of *sola scriptura* practiced by English Presbyterians since Thomas Cartwright. Indeed, the strict biblicism in the Puritan tradition develops in opposition with natural law even in the Elizabethan context. Cartwright is Richard Hooker's chief antagonist in the *Laws of Ecclesiastical Polity.* From Hooker's point of view, the obsession with scripture as a source for all rules upon which humans must base their actions had serious limitations: "Because ye suppose the lawes for which ye strive are found in scripture; but those not, agains which ye strive; and upon this surmise are drawn to hold it as the very maine piller of your whole cause, that *scripture ought to be the only rule of all our actions.*"[67] Against his opponents, Hooker argued that in many cases God's "preceptes comprehended in the lawe of nature, may be otherwise knowne then onely by scripture."[68] In short, the hermeneutics of the strict adherence may limit the scope of human understanding and moral action.[69] In offering a different hermeneutic method, Peter Lake observes, "Hooker was attempting to lead his opponents step by step to a position rather different from the austere biblicism with which they had entered the debate," and in doing so "he was attacking more than the epistemological underpinning of presbyterianism."[70] This extra-biblical method of understanding God's precepts, according to most Puritans, was wrongheaded, and natural law accordingly never appears in the antiprelatical tracts.

The use of natural law enters Milton's discourse when he begins to break openly with the Presbyterians. It also enters his political vocabulary—from its first appearance in the divorce tracts in 1643–44—at the same moment when it had begun to appear frequently in political debate. Richard Tuck views Hobbes in this context as a follower of Selden, who "provided a whole generation of politically active and intelligent Englishmen with a new ideology, which they were able to apply to the most important issue of the day"[71]—the English Civil War. In addition to the pioneering work of Hobbes, a group of English intellectuals—including Selden, William Chillingworth, Dudley Digges, and Henry Parker on the parliamentary side—began to change the nature of political debate. Significantly, an explosion of interest in natural politics occurs during precisely the same debate in which Pocock discerned the origins of English republicanism: that surrounding the *Answer to the Nineteen Propositions* of 1642.[72] Natural law arguments are used in many of the political pamphlets Milton may have seen, which seem to bear the influence of Hobbes, such as John Bramhall's *Serpent Salve* in 1643. In defending Charles I's published response to Parliament's Remonstrance against the parliamentary "Observator" Henry Parker,[73] Bramhall asserts that Charles's "strong judgement seem[s] to be written with a beam of the Sun, and like the principles of Geometry doe rather compel then persuade."[74] Bramhall would later disavow this connection between geometry and politics in ways that suggest an ongoing dialogue with Hobbes. In the famous "catching of Leviathan" chapter of *Castigations of Mr. Hobbes* (London 1657), Bramhall revokes his earlier view, and argues that "State-policy, is not at all like *Arithmetick and Geometry,* which are altogether abstracted from the matter, but much more like *Tennis-play.*"[75] That Milton self-consciously develops his own theory of natural law in line with this emerging political discourse is suggested in a telling rebuke in *Tetrachordon* of Herbert Palmer, a Presbyterian preacher who had denounced Milton's *Doctrine and Discipline of Divorce.* Palmer had written *Scripture and Reason Pleaded for Defensive Armes* in 1643, a parliamentarian tract that responds to the royalists with the vocabulary of natural law. He had since preached to Parliament and the Assembly against Milton's work on divorce, in a sermon published in November 1644, which speaks with horror of those who "plead Conscience" for divorce, such as is written "in a *wicked booke . . . deserving to be burnt,* whose *Author* hath been so *impudent* as to *set his Name* to it, and *dedicate it to your selves . . .* will you grant a *Toleration* for all *this?*"[76] Milton quotes from this passage in the preface to *Tetrachordon* (March 4, 1645), reminding Parliament that "it was preached before ye" in "August last upon a special day of humiliation" (*CPW* 2:580). In Milton's defense of his reasoning, as Barbara Lewalski points out, he avers that "Palmer himself elsewhere used against the king the same natural law argument about revoking covenants that Milton used to legitimize divorce."[77] Milton's rebuke in the preface to *Tetrachordon* suggests that he had been influenced by the new method of argument, although used for a political rather than a domestic subject, even at the time of composition of the divorce tract: "I offer my hand also if need be, to make good the same opinion which I there maintain, by inevitable consequences drawn parallel from his own principal arguments in that of Scripture and Reason; which I shall pardon him, if he can deny, without shaking his own composition to peeces" (582).

In the revised edition of *The Doctrine and Discipline of Divorce* (1644), and in subsequent tracts, Milton employs a new hermeneutic approach.[78] Following Selden and other natural law theorists such as Grotius, Milton uses natural law theory and natural reason to complicate the scriptural prohibitions against divorce.[79] In the revised edition, he writes that scriptural law must be correspondent to the "law of nature": "in the delivery and execution of [God's] Law, especially in the managing of a duty so daily and so familiar as this is wherof we reason, hath plain anough reveal'd himself, and requires the observance therof not otherwise then to the law of nature and of equity imprinted in us seems correspondent" (*CPW* 2:297).[80] In one instance in *Tetrachordon,* Milton writes of Genesis 2:18 that God "presents himself like to a man deliberating" to show that he "intended to found it according to naturall reason, not impulsive command, but that the duty should arise from the reason of it, not the reason be swallow'd up in a reasonlesse duty" (*CPW* 2:595). God's posture of speculation should bring us to conclude that he meant to instill in us the freedom to use our own "natural reason." It was with this conception of God's charge that Milton entered the toleration debate and defended the freedom of the press.

The Immediate Reading Context

Milton clearly read many of the printed "tractats" that shared topics with *Areopagitica.* These approached toleration from several angles and with different methodologies, the most central being scriptural and exegetical. Modeling themselves more after printed sermons than speeches to Parliament, these pamphlets often focus on the scriptural arguments used for persecution (particularly Deuteronomy 13:5 and 17:12).[81] Scriptural exegesis was one of the most popular modes of Puritan polemic, but it was significantly not Milton's central method in *Areopagitica*—besides the suggestive rereading of the Fall. Unlike the densely exegetical language of the divorce tracts composed at this time, or of even *The Tenure of Kings and Magistrates,* which has some eighteen chapter and verse citations among other less explicit allusions, there are no chapter and verse citations in *Areopagitica,* and a less substantial collection of italicized scriptural phrases, which—also in contrast to *The Tenure*—are clustered mostly toward the end. Rather surprisingly, Milton does not attempt to counter the major scriptural precedent for persecution in Deuteronomy, used in the Calvinist theological tradition, although he does write dismissively of the case of burning books in Acts 19, a moment which supplies perhaps the strongest refutation of Fish's claim that Milton supports post-publication censorship: "As for the burning of those Ephesian books by St. *Pauls* converts," he maintains, "It was a privat act, a voluntary act, and leaves us to a voluntary imitation: the men in remorse burnt those books which were their own; the Magistrat by this example is not appointed: these men practiz'd the books, another might perhaps have read them in some sort usefully" (*CPW* 2:514). Acts 19 had been invoked as an instance of worthy governmental action in works like Prynne's *Histrio-Mastix* (1633).[82] The modified position in *Areopagitica* provides a keen example of the tract's rhetorical maneuvering. Readers are now to understand that when Milton averred initially that he did "not deny" that books should be treated "as malefactors," he actually meant this treatment to be private and voluntary, and not a public legal act.

Some pamphlets were philosophical as well as exegetical. Some argued that it was "inforced uniformity"[83] that caused civil war, and some, like Hobbes, that the fragmentation of uniformity that caused it. Henry Robinson, for example, just before being caught up in the cause of the Independents against the Presbyterians, attempted to offer liberty of conscience as a means to bring peace to the two sides—the royalist prelates and the parliamentarian presbyters—of the civil war.[84] Robinson echoes a slightly earlier pamphlet, which views the present state of England as the product of sectarian discord that would not exist if people were allowed to embrace what beliefs they choose. The anonymous *Short Discourse Touching the Cause of the Present Unhappy Distractions . . . and Ready Means to Compose, and Quiet Them* (1643) argues that the present state of war stems from "spirituall" rather "than from temporall interests." To support this position, the author argued primarily that toleration would bring peace and that persecution is wrong. He also provides an additional argument that later writers, particularly Milton, would struggle to elaborate. It concerned the problems incurred by human reason itself, for it recognized that "mans reason cannot be forced by outward violence."[85]

In a simple sense, this problem of explaining why persecution was wrong lay at the very center: of course persecution is ugly, its defenders would argue, but heresy is even uglier, as scripture made clear. Tolerationists first approached this argument, not through a description of "mans reason" itself, but by characterizing the relationship between reason and those beliefs legislated by the state: in short, by painting a picture of just how ugly persecution was. These oppositions to persecution began in earlier—though, as Robinson points out, "seldom thought on"[86]—discussions of toleration. Leonard Busher's book *Religions Peace; or, A Plea for Liberty of Conscience* is among the earliest English treatises on the subject. Printed in Amsterdam in 1614, and again republished in London in 1646 with a preface "To the Presbyterian Reader,"[87] it was coopted into the cause of the Independents, who, like Milton, sought to erode the Presbyterians' compulsory policy of religious conformity. Busher mounts a twofold case against enforced religion: persecution is unjust and tyrannical, and persuasion is a more viable means of bringing people to see the truth than fear. Ministers should be allowed to persuade people of the word of God, "and not, as tyrants, to force and constrain them by persecution."[88]

The strongest piece of persuasion prior to Milton characterized enforced belief through analogy, and as an assault on the believer. Enforced belief, wrote Busher, was a kind of rape: "And herein the bishops commit a greater sin, than if they force the bodies of women and maids against their wills."[89] This way of casting enforced uniformity resurfaces in Roger Williams's *Queries of Highest Consideration:* "since the Common-weale cannot without a spirituall rape force the consciences of all to one Worship, oh that it may never commit that rape, in forcing the consciences of all men to one Worship, which a stronger arme and Sword may soon (as formerly) arise to alter."[90] Wolseley later described forced conscience as "a spiritual rape."[91] The argument yoking intolerance with violent tyranny became a mainstay in tolerationist rhetoric; in *De Doctrina Christiana* Milton would argue that a society without the "liberty" of "winnowing and sifting every doctrine" is a "barbarous tyranny" (*WJM* 14:13).

Against the contention that enforced religion was tyranny, opponents of toleration might justifiably argue that force was (after all) used to control other moral codes of society, that Deuteronomy 13 and 17 demanded the execution of false prophets, and that, without an enforced state religion, society would become schismatic. Schism bred discord, a far more odious social condition than orderly, harmonious conformity. The Presbyterians accordingly argued that the people who would be rightfully "forced to cover their heresies," might instead be encouraged to "rent" the "Mythicall Body of Christ" to pieces, unless set under the "Presbeterian discipline."[92] Milton engages this aspect of the debate, even adopting the same language of dismemberment—suggesting, for example, that the supposedly "fantastic terrors of sect and schism" (*CPW* 2:554) were merely a healthy sign that English society would eventually restore the "torn body of our martyred saint." Presbyterians took the stand that their united church offered "a medium way between Hierarchy, and a Democraticall Government"—extremes represented respectively by the royalist Prelacy and the anarchist Independents—and, as a united Aristocracy, was thus able "to suppresse all Schismes and Divisions."[93] In addition to fragmentation, toleration might allow any number of heretical, dangerous, and self-harming beliefs to circulate. Tolerationists therefore needed a still more "plausible reason,"[94] as one opponent wrote, than mere outrage at the cruelty of punishment. A more plausible and more philosophical solution was advanced by a couple of writers prior to Milton, Walwyn and Robinson.

In a debate with Prynne, Robinson sought to differentiate between the moral codes necessary to the integrity of the state, and those from which it was necessary to allow individuals to choose. Prynne, famous for having lost his ears to the Prelates, now wrote in favor of enforced uniformity under the Presbyterians. In his *Twelve Considerable Serious Questions,* published in September 1644, he argued that it was the right of the state to enforce a given system of church government for the sake of order and conformity. Robinson responded that although there is no divinely established church government, the state has no right to impose one, and that the choice should devolve on the people: "Every particular Christian *ought to have under the Gospel a liberty and latitude, to choose such a forme of Church government,* as he himselfe, for his particular use, in his owne reason and understanding apprehendeth to be according to Gods Word."[95]

Here the connection between choice and reason, which Milton would exploit more fully and consciously, is introduced into the debate. Robinson suggests that a person's understanding is better disposed when given the freedom to choose. He employs the discourse of natural law, which he uses to differentiate between externally dictated moral codes and those beliefs that require voluntary apprehension:

> The selfe same Law of Nature, God, and rectified reason which instructed and warranted all Nations to subject themselves unto some publique forme of Civill government, obliging all persons and societies of men alike, which they conceived most advantagious, doth not warrant us to doe the like in Church affaires; because whatsoever civill action the Civill Magistrate requires, may be performed by the outward man, or else be expiated by penalty without taint of conscience: But the Church government as it aimes at, and regards the Spirituall service and performance, . . . cannot be undergone, or worke upon a mans spirit unlesse he will himself, neither may he be willing thereunto, unlesse he apprehend them to be according to Christs Government and Institution.[96]

Robinson's insight is that the kind of moral understanding at stake in this debate, which "regards the Spirituall service and performance," cannot "worke upon a mans spirit" unless "he will himself." Truth cannot be forced on a person unless that person wills, and that volition is essential to the process of apprehension. In his earlier *Liberty of Conscience,* Robinson similarly connects cognitive volition and human understanding: "Though a man would use all the means which can be prescribed him, and should even himselfe be contented, and desire that such a Religion were the true one, yet it is not in his power to thinke so, and consequently to be of the same in heart, untill his reason and understanding be convinced thereof."[97] While following a prescribed set of beliefs may even be conducive to contentment, a person cannot have the "power to thinke" or understand these beliefs unless his or her reason has properly apprehended them. In *Areopagitica,* Milton pushes these arguments further, to show precisely why a prescribed set of beliefs cannot produce knowledge.

Like Robinson, Walwyn, whose work Milton followed carefully, also sketchingly adumbrates a theory of "mans reason." Walwyn developed an argument for freedom of conscience that derives from the nature of reason itself: "Whatsoever a mans reason doth conclude to be true or false, to be agreeable or disagreeable to Gods Word, that same to that man is his opinion or judgement, and so man is by *his owne reason necessitated to be of that mind he is.*"[98] For Walwyn, it is the way a person comes to a particular belief that determines the accuracy of judgment. A belief that enters the mind by some means other than free reason (coercion or conformity) is epistemologically inferior.

A Rationalist Approach to Civil Liberty

Areopagitica addresses the topic using not just more artful, but also more philosophical prose. Milton's appreciation for the new discourses of political philosophy appears in his commendation of the methodology of Selden, whose use of natural law as well as his Erastianism followed the work of Hobbes.[99] Milton writes that Selden's volume "proves by exquisite reasons and theorems almost mathematically demonstrative, that all opinions, yea errors, known, read, and collated, are of main service and assistance toward the speedy attainment of what is truest" (*CPW* 2:513). It is not entirely clear precisely where this new, Hobbesian or Grotian (and Cartesian) idea of a "mathematically demonstrative" political argument originates for Milton, although it is of interest, I believe, that Galileo's book on the new science of motion and mechanics, published in the same year Milton visited Galileo, is

Discorsi e Dimonstrazioni Matematiche (Leiden, 1638).[100] Beyond the connection to Selden, it is curiously hard to determine a source for this strain in Milton's writing—it is not represented in the Commonplace Book. Yet since this is a method of argument made without appeal to human authorities, it is reasonable that few authorities are cited. And it is not information, the central ingredient in the Commonplace Book, but method, which of course the notebook represents as an instrument of knowledge, but less so in the material of the citations themselves. Milton is drawn to a standard of argumentation in which a social or political problem, such as the one he grapples with now—and claims that Selden, too, undertakes—can be grounded in "exquisite reasons" and provable laws. Selden endorses Milton's idea that unprejudicial reading aids the attainment of knowledge, but Milton loosely connects this small point from Selden's preface with the broader methodology of his work. His use of Selden integrates two issues central to seventeenth-century philosophy: the question of how moral laws might be mathematically demonstrable, and the question of how humans come to the "attainment of what is truest." This latter question occupies the bulk of *Areopagitica,* which becomes as much a treatise on how "to discover onward things more remote from our knowledge" (550) as on toleration and licensing.

Milton's interest in the emerging discourse on method is evinced not only in his initial praise of Selden's laws of nature and in his use of "reason" which began in the divorce tracts, but also when he explicitly suggests a "method" to his own discourse.[101] The tract's sinuous thread of argument at one point illustrates the "ingenuity of Truth" when Milton turns from an unfinished thought and self-consciously comments on his writing. This sudden shift reveals how Truth, "when she gets a free and willing hand, opens herself faster then the pace of method and discours" (521). The idea that truth outstretches "the pace of method and discours," with its seeming allusion to Descartes' *Discours de la Methode* (1637), suggests a conscious relation to such recent attempts to establish a method for determining the truth.[102] The sudden revelation of the "ingenuity of Truth" beyond method, and beyond the pace of rational discourse, indicates a mild defiance of philosophic discourse. The defiance occurs again in more formal terms when Milton privileges Spenser over Aquinas as a "better teacher" (516). Milton's promotion of his tract's own powers of discovery illustrate its general tenets concerning the imposition of external controls on the truth. By his conception, discovery itself depends on liberation from preconceived directives. In this exception to "method and discours" and in the treatment of Spenser's narrative of choice as superior to philosophy, Milton is eager to show that philosophical advances may be achieved within the representational arts. The defense of poetry ensconced within this tract is generically associated with the more formal responses to Plato's banishment of poets, such as that of Sidney.[103] Poetry and even literary polemic is not epistemologically inferior, as Plato had suggested, but an artform in which truth is allowed to shift for itself, and thus outstretch the pace of method and discourse. The process of coming to the truth is thus fundamental to the politics Milton promotes.

Accordingly, Milton starts out in *Areopagitica,* aptly mirroring what he praises in Selden, with "great authorities brought together"—historical examples linking, among other things, licensing with the Inquisition. Here Milton exploits his historical research drawn especially from Paolo Sarpi's *Istoria* (1619) on the history of licensing, prompted by the Commonplace Book. But after he has exhausted the historical examples a discernible shift then occurs in the tract itself—turning like Selden from historical "authorities" to "exquisite reasons," and to a discussion of reason itself. Following the progress of argument in the *Nicomachean Ethics,* Milton proceeds from the idea of maintaining "temperance" to the idea that true knowledge derives only from rational choice: God gave humanity "the gift of reason to be his own chooser" (513–14).[104] Milton's refutation of Plato's epistemology and politics thus comes in appropriately Aristotelian terms. Milton's idea that "reason is but choosing" alludes to Aristotle's cerebral sense of metaphysical (rather than behavioral) choice, which builds on the Platonic distinction between opinion and knowledge, the lower and higher forms of human understanding. "Choice is not common to irrational creatures," wrote Aristotle, "but appetite and anger are. . . . Appetite relates to the pleasant and the painful, choice neither to the painful nor to the pleasant. . . . For this reason too, [choice] cannot be opinion. . . . We choose what we best *know* to be good, but we opine what we do not quite know."[105] Distinguished from the faculties that govern opinion, cognitive choice is the process by which people obtain knowledge. The argument, as suggested, is represented in an early entry in the Commonplace Book to Lactantius: "Reason and intelligence may have the opportunity to exercise themselves by choosing the things that are good, by fleeing from the things that are evil" (CB 4, *CPW* 1:363).

In basing the argument for choice on the nature of reason, asserting that humanity was left with the "gift of reason to be his own chooser," Milton demonstrates that intolerance is not just a violation of a set of nebulous values, but a violation of conditions that are essential to the possession of knowledge. Because reason is so constructed by nature that it must be left free in order to obtain knowledge, it would compromise the nature of human understanding to control or prohibit systems of belief.

Following his explanation of the metaphysics of reason, Milton turns to a theory of knowledge. The natural condition of humanity, he had argued, is one of rational choice, and under such conditions humanity cannot develop "under a perpetuall childhood of prescription" (514). To be in a state of prescription in the civilized world, then, is unnatural. The childhood of prescription suggests Eden, to which he turns directly: "It was from out the rinde of one apple tasted, that the knowledge of good and evil as two twins cleaving together leapt forth into the World. And perhaps this is that doom which Adam fell into of knowing good and evil, that is to say of knowing good by evil" (514).[106] Milton turns from this thought abruptly, to the question of what good and evil are in a state of prescription. "Prescription" had operated as a kind of keyword for the antiprelaticals. For example, *God hath delivered the sword to judge the earth,* Prynne wrote of princes, gesturing toward Romans 13, "and made them servants onely to himselfe, since all other soules must be subject to them by the tenor of his owne Prescription and their first erection as the Scripture witnesseth."[107] Milton's argument against "prescription" had serious implications on several levels, both political and hermeneutic. The argument concerns the correct posture of the individual regarding the prescriptions of both God and the state. On the state level, the Presbyterian control of publication is a prescriptive control of what people should think, limiting (in Milton's view) their ability to act virtuously. But the model originates from a conception of the individual's relationship with God. For Milton, God himself operates less by prescription than his contemporaries were wont to think. "God uses not to captivat under a perpetuall childhood of prescription" suggests that the "prescription" espoused by the Presbyterians in their view of the proper posture of the believer is the same they seek to impose through licensing.

Milton merges the two forms of prescription in a passage that shifts from "Plato's licensing"—which he associates with Presbyterian policy—to God's prescription:

> To sequester out of the world into *Atlantick* and *Eutopian* polities, which never can be drawn into use, will not mend our condition; but to ordain wisely as in this world of evill, in the midd'st whereof God hath plac't us unavoidably. Nor is it *Plato's* licencing of books will doe this, which necessarily pulls along with it so many other kinds of licencing, as will make us all both ridiculous and weary, and yet frustrat.... If every action which is good, or evil in man at ripe years, were under pittance, and prescription, and compulsion, what were vertue but a name, what praise could be then due to welldoing, what grammercy to be sober, just or continent?

The picture of humanity in Paradise, first suggested by a "childhood of pre-scription," develops in language that more forcefully suggests the Fall as a *felix culpa*: "many there be that complain of divin Providence for suffering *Adam* to transgresse, foolish tongues! when God gave him reason, he gave him freedom to choose, for reason is but choosing; he had bin else a meer artificiall *Adam*. . . . God therefore left him free" (526–27). With the faculty of reason, Adam was given the freedom of choice, since the two are interdependent.

The description of Adam's metaphysical freedom, his "freedom to choose, for reason is but choosing," again evokes the Aristotelian notion of rational choice. The use of the gerund—"reason is but *choosing*"—stresses the process itself rather than the knowledge acquired. This rational process Milton later describes as "knowledge in the making" (554). The phrase exemplifies the frequent use of present participles in the text—such as "building," "cutting," "squaring," "hewing"—which predominate over past participles, which would have, as Norbrook writes, "overtones of premature completion,"[108] and thus embody the rhetorical features of the sublime for Longinus. Milton's idea is of reason itself, that it is but *choosing,* where the act, or process of making knowledge is far more important than its static or closed representation. The nature of conception of the truth remains more important than its external representation, just as the posture of the believer in conceiving the truth is more important than the belief professed. This is a theory of representation that maps itself onto Milton's reading habits in distinct ways. Milton's reading practices are less concerned with rhetorical formulation than with facts or ideas, and thus his reading itself fundamentally does not privilege external, fixed representations. More specifically, the commonplacing habits of many of his English contemporaries fostered a particular aesthetic appreciation for the closed sentence, and thus Milton's theory of representation also suits a history of aversion for the "tyrannous aphorismes" (*CPW* 2:375–76) that were transformed into the Jonsonian couplet and into closed, end-stopped verse.

In Milton's ideal picture of the life of the mind, the search for truth is something necessarily fragmented, since epistemological fragmentation causes constant trial and assists in the process of discovery. Milton characterizes his contemporaries' view of original humanity as a mere "artificiall Adam," controlled by the unseen hand of God. Milton's depiction of Adam describes human nature even as it exists now: this is the "doom which *Adam* fell into of knowing good and evil, that is to say of knowing good by evil," he writes, "as therefore the state of man *now* is" (514, emphasis added). This is an "estate of man" or "state of nature" argument such as that which Hobbes used. Milton's contemporaries generally used the prelapsarian condition as described by Reformation theology to analogize the state. Sir Robert Filmer, for example, wrote that "the desire for liberty was the cause of the fall of Adam."[109] William Davenant similarly wrote that political "obedience like the Marriage Yoke, is a restraint more needful and advantagious then liberty; and hath the same reward of pleasant quietnesse, which it anciently had, when *Adam*, till his disobedience, injoy'd Paradise."[110] In claiming that moral knowledge as well as judicature is the province of the sovereign, Hobbes too reverted to a biblical argument: "Cognisance or Judicature of Good and Evill" is "forbidden by the name of the fruit of the tree of Knowledge."[111] For Milton, individuals must be left free to come to moral knowledge themselves. The metaphysical description of human reason—that choice brings us to true knowledge—thus became the cornerstone for his argument.

The idea that externally prescribed "truth" can never instill knowledge is perhaps the most powerful argument for toleration. People conforming to a prescribed body of knowledge may even speak the truth, but, not having arrived there by their own volition, are no closer to knowledge than they are in speaking falsely: "A man may be a heretick in the truth; and if he beleeve things only because his Pastor sayes so, or the Assembly so determins, without knowing other reason, though his belief be true, yet the very truth he holds, becomes his heresie" (*CPW* 2:545). Of the tolerationists prior to Milton, only Walwyn makes a similar argument: "For though the thing may be in it selfe good, yet if it doe not appeare to be so to my conscience, the practice therefore in me is sinfull, which therefore I ought not to be compelled unto."[112] Yet, as David Loewenstein has pointed out, no English contemporary had gone as far as Milton does here, in denying heresy its cultural and institutional value.[113] But the passage also, as Loewenstein points out, strips heresy of its religious and scriptural value, where it is condemned in such central Pauline verses as 2 Peter 2:1, Galations 5:20, or Titus 3:10–11.[114] In keeping with the tract's resolute fluidity, although perhaps also with some awareness of his startling inversion of scripture, Milton suddenly turns to another line of reasoning, that knowledge is actually in a progressive state of flux, which suggests that representation of the truth (if not also the truth itself) must always be changing: "Well knows he who uses to consider, that our faith and knowledge is compar'd in Scripture to a streaming fountain; if her waters flow not in a perpetuall progression, they sick'n into a muddy pool of conformity and tradition" (*CPW* 2:543).[115] Milton's arguments not only suggest the uncertainty and transmutability of external representations, but also enforce the necessity of an ever-changing way of describing these truths—if not an ever-changing truth itself.

Milton's ideas about heresy seem quite radical even in their revolutionary context, and it is clear that he goes well beyond the thinking of other Independents. In spite of its tolerationist purposes, the Independents' *Apologeticall Narration, Humbly Submitted to the Honourable Houses of Parliament* in late 1643 rejected, as Coffey writes, the "ruinous toleration of error and heresy."[116] More extreme efforts to persecute heresy through the 1640s culminated in the Long Parliament's 1648 "Ordinance for the Punishing of Blasphemies and Heresies,"[117] and helped occasion Milton's dark "Digression."

A Republican Rhetoric of Praise

Toward the end of the tract, Milton broadly connects printed knowledge with politics in asserting his own work as an instance of what is possible in a land of true "Philosophic freedom" (537). In the beginning he had promised that "this whole Discourse propos'd will be a certaine testimony" "to all who wish and promote their Countries liberty." "The utmost bound of civill liberty attain'd," he continued, would be "now manifest by the very sound of this which I shall utter, that wee are already in good part arriv'd, and yet from such a steepe disadvantage of tyranny and superstition grounded into our principles" (487). His closing address to the "Lords and Commons" draws a correlation between the free pursuit of knowledge and the "mild, and free, and human government" that the Parliament's "valorous and happy counsels have purchast." Because of this political freedom, English society is able to be "enfranchis'd, enlarg'd and lifted up our apprehensions degrees above themselves." "Ye cannot make us now lesse capable," he continues, "lesse knowing, lesse eagarly pursuing of the truth, unless ye first make your selves, that made us so, less the lovers, lesse the founders of true liberty" (559). Milton draws a concrete connection between the rational models he has depicted and the politics that would enable them.

In this closure, the reader encounters some of Milton's most rhetorically invested and at times disingenuous prose: on a fundamental level, Parliament has not actually purchased "liberty." Nor would it revoke the ordinance against unlicensed publication Milton so strongly denounces. In the last sentence Milton appeals to Parliament to reverse this decision, which he claims was made under false impressions created by the Stationers: "This I know, that errors in a good government and in a bad are equally almost incident; for what Magistrate may not be mis-inform'd, and much the sooner, if liberty of Printing be reduc'd into the power of a few; but to redresse willingly and speedily what hath bin err'd, and in highest autority to esteem a plain advertisement more then others have done a sumptuous bribe, is a vertue (honor'd Lords and Commons) answerable to Your highest actions, and whereof none can participat but greatest and wisest men" (570). Milton uses "advertisement" here in the now obsolete sense of a "written notification" (*OED* 4); thus he suggests the Parliament is to receive his instruction as others, less honorable, might have taken a bribe. To receive his advertisement and revoke the Order, Milton explains, is a "vertue" answerable to Parliament's "highest actions" that are open only to the "greatest" and "wisest"—hyperbole that might have been cloying were it not an expected mode of address.

It is hard to recover the historical nature of rhetorical practice without encountering prejudices that have since emerged. Although a word like "disingenuous" may usefully describe the manner of language use from a postmodern perspective, the values associated with this assessment would not have fully inhered at the time. A relatively esoteric critique of rhetoric does emerge in the 1640s, but it is not until the Restoration—in the watershed moment represented in Thomas Sprat's famous dictum "Eloquence ought to be banish'd out of all *civil Societies*"—that this criticism begins to take root.[118] Yet the critique that emerged in the seventeenth century also existed in the form it did because rhetoric had a vastly more extensive role than it does today. English pedagogy inculcated rhetorical expertise at an early age, and rhetorical techniques of all forms were marshaled in the aid of political writing, especially in advice books to those in power, such as Machiavelli's *Prince,* Erasmus's *Education of a Christian Prince,* or Raleigh's *Maxims of State.* As Lewalski has observed, in *Areopagitica* Milton transforms "the renaissance genre of 'Advice to Princes' into a republican advice to a council."[119] Sharon Achinstein has written that the "ideal rhetor in Renaissance humanistic terms was a great statesman, an advisor to princes" and that there was a "transformation of the Renaissance humanist practice" in Milton's polemics and speeches to the "public," a term Milton uses in his translation of the epigraph from Euripides.[120] Free speech is paramount, and even true speech, but often this speech is more rhetorical than true. "Disingenuous calculation,"[121] as Thomas Corns puts it, is a common feature of English polemical culture—though again, the ethical value that inheres in this judgment is more ours than theirs. One of the principal ways of giving advice to those in power is through what Thomas More called the *obliquus ductus,* the indirect way of meaning something other than what is said, often through the rhetoric of false praise.[122] Earlier examples of the rhetoric of praise are of value in understanding Milton's inheritance. In a revealing letter, Erasmus wrote of his *Panegyricus* to Philip the Handsome (one of the princes he tried to reform through such "pious adulation") that he hoped such rhetorical indirection will reform the "boorish," "erring," "indolent," and even the "hopelessly vicious."[123] While we do not have quite the same kind of evidence for Milton, it is clear, for the purposes of effecting change, that he too would have possessed the rhetorical skills and the cultural backing to praise someone he thought hopelessly vicious.

Political rhetoric can operate in a great number of ways. Often, a passage is not to be taken at its face value, but as it interacts contextually: that is, it has a rhetorical force that acts against other discursive forms and rhetorical conventions. In describing this form of rhetoric, Quentin Skinner uses the example of Machiavelli's seeming authorization of gross immorality in his loaded statement: "Princes must learn when not to be virtuous." Machiavelli means this, Skinner argues, only in a certain rhetorical sense: to "challenge and repudiate an accepted moral commonplace"[124] that was part of the discursive conventions—in this case, the advice book to princes—within which Machiavelli operated. In a similar manner, as I argue in the ensuing chapters, Milton formulates arguments in a way designed to destabilize the conventional constructions of his opponents. This is sometimes undertaken in direct confrontation, but often in a much more indirect manner—a rhetorical Trojan horse, designed to enter the walls of defense and deconstruct ideology from the inside. When Milton writes near the exordium of *Areopagitica,* "I deny not but that it is the greatest concernment in the Church and Commonwealth, to have a vigilant eye how Bookes demean themselves, as well as men; and thereafter to confine, imprison [books], and do sharpest justice on them as malefactors" (492), he is asking his opponents to let down their drawbridge. Milton wrote in the First Prolusion that "the most eminent masters of rhetoric" hold that an orator "must begin by winning the goodwill of his audience; without it he cannot make any impression upon them, nor succeed as he would wish in his cause" (*CPW* 1:218).[125] This exordium is not about truth, nor even about what the truth *ought* to be, but about what Milton thinks his audiences believes as the truth, and wants to hear. To invoke the useful terms of Austin and Habermas, Milton is not interested in locutionary meaning, here, but in illocutionary force.[126] The passage should not be read literally, as it is meant to *function* rhetorically.

When Milton writes in *Areopagitica* that Parliament is full of "the free and ingenuous sort of such as evidently were born to study, and love learning for itself, not for lucre, or any other end, but the service of God and of truth" (541), he is employing a rhetoric of praise that played a fundamental role in addressing those in power. A sense of the epideictic quality of this passage is conveyed not only in its hyperbole, as in the description of parliamentary members as "the ingenuous sort . . . born to study," but also in the carefully inlayed instruction within this praise: they "love learning" (read *politics*) not "for lucre, or any other end." It is significant that the account of this same Parliament in the "Digression" intimates that the members needed exactly the instruction Milton seems to give, as he accuses them of being corrupted by money and power: "the sweetness of briberie and other gaine with the love of rule" (*CPW* 5:445). Their "love" of "learning" is, in truth, a "love of rule." He also accuses them here of taking bribes, when in *Areopagitica* he suggests that honorable men would take counsel as "others" would a "sumptuous bribe" (570).[127] This encomium to the Long Parliament would thus be followed, some years later, by a critique of its failures that could hardly have been sharper: the "Digression" in *The History of Britain*.

Chapter 4

"The Digression" and Milton's
Return to Polemics

Spite and favour determin'd all: hence faction, then treacherie both at home & in the field, ev'ry where wrong & oppression, foule and dishonest things committed daylie.
Milton, "The Digression" in *The History of Britain*

IN EARLY 1649 Milton revisited the polemical battlefield after a long and mysterious absence from public debate. Rushed into print within two weeks after the king's execution, *The Tenure of Kings and Magistrates* marks a return after a hiatus of almost four years—the last two divorce tracts having appeared in March 1645. Milton's only other print publication during this period was an elegant volume of poetry published early in 1646 by Humphrey Moseley, a publisher determined not to get involved in ideological warfare, and bent on emphasizing the courtly connections of Milton's art.[1] Moseley writes in his preface to the volume that "the slightest Pamphlet is now adayes more vendible then the Works of learnedest men," suggesting that the proliferation of pamphlets had debased learning, and even the English language: "It is the love I have to our own Language that hath made me diligent to collect, and set forth such Peeces," as would "renew the wonted honour and esteem of our English tongue."[2] While these are not Milton's words, the poet's own retreat may have been partially motivated by a similar set of values. As Milton laments in a sonnet written during this hiatus, his age hates "Learning worse than Toad or Asp" (*CSP* 309). In the sequel sonnet, he writes of the "barbarous noise" that surrounded him after he had prompted the "age to quit their clogs." This imagined transformation had become instead a prolonged "brawl for freedom" in "a senseless mood," a "waste of wealth and loss of blood" (*CSP* 297).

When viewed in the context of his assertions of unwavering devotion to public affairs and his relatively constant output of polemical prose before 1645 (eleven tracts in the previous four years), Milton's silence in these four years seems a withdrawal from public debate, if not even a retirement. He later insists, in *Pro Populo Anglicano Defensio Secunda* (1654), that he devoted "to this conflict all my talents and all my active powers" (*CPW* 4:622), but this amends a far more conflicted history. In the *Defensio Secunda* he also suggests a teleological design to his political work in the 1640s, culminating in the treatises on civil liberty. In a basic sense, this seems quite plausible: there remained a major arsenal of unused political arguments in the Commonplace Book, waiting for some kind of application. His poetry suggests that he already harbors a sense that the Presbyterians and others had not carried the revolution far enough; as John Leonard shows, in Sonnet 12 Milton accuses the "revolting" Presbyterians of backsliding, a theme he takes up in full force in *The Tenure*.[3] Yet he chose no other venue than this semiprivate mode of expression to work toward reform—if these poems were circulated in manuscript, and it seems likely that some of them were, they probably would have enjoyed only a limited readership. In *Areopagitica* Milton had glorified London as "a shop of war" that "hath not there more anvils and hammers waking, to fashion out the plates and instruments of armed justice in defense of beleaguered Truth, than there be pens and heads there, . . . musing, searching, revolving new notions and ideas wherewith to present," while others "as fast reading, trying all things, assenting to the force of reason and convincement" (*CPW* 2:554). But five months later, Milton himself had ceased to "present" new notions on England's reformation, and his work during this interim suggests a profound disillusionment, if not also the desire to engage different audiences in very different circumstances.

As Annabel Patterson has shown, a Latin verse letter to the Oxford librarian John Rouse that accompanied a gift of his *Poems* in 1647 is particularly suggestive, not only in the expressed desire to "follow" again, as he had in the poems, "his own devious [*devius*] ways aloof from the people,"[4] but also in its lament over the present state of affairs.[5] This scribal verse letter is the only evidence we have of Milton's friendship with Rouse, and presumably his familiarity with the Bodleian itself. Rouse's commitments remain unknown, although there is something suggestive in his purchase of revolutionary pamphlets in 1645, when Oxford was occupied by the king, and in his famous refusal to lend the king a book.[6] Milton's verse epistle to Rouse expresses many of the same attitudes as Moseley's preface to the reader. The "accursed tumults among the citizens" have banished the Muses and "our fostering studies," Milton wrote, "with hardly a retreat" left "anywhere in all the confines of England."[7] In a 1647 letter to his old Florentine acquaintance Carlo Dati, Milton despairs: "Do you think there can be any safe retreat for literary leisure among so many civil battles, so much slaughter, flight, and pillaging of goods?" (*CPW* 2:764). During this four-year hiatus in his polemical career he wrote a few political poems, including an important sonnet to Fairfax, discussed below, written toward the end of the hiatus. But besides such occasional interventions, Milton returned mostly to his interest in education, writing a grammar, a logic, and the beginning, at least, of two histories, *A Brief History of Moscovia,* and *The History of Britain.*[8] All of these works, the poetry and the prose, were published after the Restoration, and of the prose only *The History of Britain*—the longest prose work to be published in his lifetime—has more than a tangential relation to wartime politics.[9] A fragmentary "Digression" to this history, published only in a pirated posthumous edition, has considerably more relevance.

During the late 1640s Milton was at work on the manuscript of the first four books of *The History of Britain,* part of which became excerpted at some point prior to the publication of the *History* in 1670, and given the title "The Digression"—as it appears in its one extant manuscript now at the Houghton Library at Harvard. Milton's original, which would have been in his own hand, was either discarded or lost, and what we have now is a scribal copy, created after the publication of the *History,* when Milton had long been blind. We know that the Harvard manuscript was created after 1670, since it is specifically designed to accompany the printed text. The "Digression" is a comparison between the present state of England and the void that followed the disintegration of Roman rule in ancient Britain; in short, it is a digression on the present, and as such it enacts the kind of comparative study between past and present that motivates entries in the Commonplace Book and their reuse in subsequent tracts. Milton himself does not assign a date to the events and people he describes in this present—indeed both the moment described and the moment of composition remain a matter of conjecture. Yet careful examination of the context can, I believe, locate Milton's excursus in a short period between the political stalemate following the end of the Second Civil War and Pride's Purge of Parliament on December 6, 1648. Ironically, the short "Digression" is the least digressive of Milton's enterprises in the four-year interim prior to the composition of *The Tenure of Kings and Magistrates;* indeed, in terms of forthrightness, besides the notes in the Commonplace Book, it is his least digressive political prose.

Milton had left the pamphleteering world in search of different audiences, and he brings himself back into the fray, I would argue, by writing in an unusual genre—a digressive commentary on the present. Written from the standpoint of a historical analyst rather than an advisor to the commonwealth, the manuscript is so openly critical of England's political and religious failures as to suggest a readership very differently conceived from the audience for his political tracts. The manuscript deserves more attention, particularly in relation to *The Tenure of Kings and Magistrates,* not only because of its temporal proximity to the regicide tract, but also because it serves as an example of the extraordinary variety of Milton's supposed views, suggesting that the nature of these views depends largely on his audience. The tracts published between 1643 and 1645 were in several cases addressed specifically to the Parliament and the Westminster Assembly or, finally in *Tetrachordon* in 1645, Milton having broken with the assembly, simply to the Parliament. This is the Parliament, or the "Magistratum," which he said in the *Defensio Secunda* was "sedulously employed [*sedulo agere*]" (*WJM* 8:130) in looking after civil liberty, and therefore, until turning to *The Tenure of Kings and Magistrates,* he had no need to write on the subject. In the "Digression," it is clear that the body of men he was addressing in these tracts he generally deemed despicable, and even criminal—a contradiction so stark that it caused David Masson and Don Wolfe to question the work's authenticity, particularly given the strength of Milton's endorsements of Parliament in *Areopagitica*.[10] Like the Commonplace Book, this manuscript helps provide a sharper sense of the relative weight of the various political arguments in Milton's prose. The two manuscripts function as a sort of internal gauge or norm against which to measure the rhetorical strategies of his printed polemics.

The Artifact and Its Context

One of the reasons why the content of the "Digression" has suffered so much neglect, given its vital interest, is that its moment of composition has been the subject of considerable debate, leaving the text's meaning dependent on an unstable conception of its context.[11] This legacy of chronological instability began with a pirated posthumous publication in 1681, *Mr John Miltons Character of the Long Parliament and Assembly of Divines in MDCXLI,* which, although it appeared only a few decades after the war, inaccurately fixes the context to be 1641. As Nicholas von Maltzahn has shown, this pirated publication is in fact a work of Tory propaganda—Milton's criticism of the parliamentarians being eminently recyclable in the Tory reaction following the Exclusion Crisis—and its false date of 1641 was probably chosen to give the strongest association with the outbreak of the civil war.[12] This posthumous pirated edition was the only version of the work available until the manuscript reappeared late in the nineteenth century, to be acquired by Harvard in 1926 and published in 1932.[13] It has been traditionally thought by such readers as Christopher Hill and French Fogle that the preserved excerpt belongs to some point in the late 1640s prior to Milton's reentry into the public sphere, and prior to the momentous political shift occurring with Pride's Purge in December 1648.[14]

Since the mid-1980s, however, the manuscript has mostly been seen as post-revolutionary, either as looking back from a distance on the exasperating conditions before the revolution of 1648–49, or as looking back on a botched opportunity for revolutionary change. The first of these major reconstructions was undertaken by the historian Austin Woolrych, who argued that the piece echoes the fatalistic sentiments of Milton's last cry for freedom, *The Readie & Easie Way to Establish a Free Commonwealth* (1660), and thus belongs to a very different period from *The History of Britain*.[15] Although Milton does not directly invoke the various Cromwellian regimes and parliaments in the 1650s, in Woolrych's view the manuscript nonetheless comments sweepingly on the failures of the whole interregnum period. In an important study of *The History of Britain,* von Maltzahn consequently argued that most of the first four books of the *History,* including the "Digression," belong to the period in 1649 just after the king's execution, and viewed the text as pronouncing "a final verdict of failure" on "the backsliding government that the Purge brought to an end."[16] More recently, however, Blair Worden has suggested that "the later the date for the composition of the 'Digression' that we propose, the likelier it may be to be correct"—in other words, sometime after the first printing of *Paradise Lost* (1667), up to and perhaps including 1670.[17] In Worden's view the manuscript is not a commentary on the present, but a distant reflection on the late 1640s by a more sagacious political thinker. Not all readers have accepted this post-revolutionary trend in locating the manuscript's context: in a less sustained treatment of the subject, Barbara Lewalski, echoing the speculative assessments of Fogle, Hill, and David Norbrook, argues that the "Digression" belongs to the late months of 1648.[18]

This debate, essentially split between literary scholars and historians—with little agreement among them—is made all the more interesting by the fact that, for each of these eminent scholars, the "Digression" helps significantly to explain a very different moment in British political culture. The fact that so much is at stake in identifying the date of these twelve manuscript pages reinforces, I believe, the significance of their physical form. Since this manuscript supplies such an important key to the political work that follows, my aim is to establish with still greater certainty the date and the immediate context. The knotty problem of the text's context is bound inextricably to problems of interpretation, and therefore fruitfully approached holistically. I investigate the problem of dating still further in my introduction to the online facsimile edition of the "Digression,"[19] where technical issues concerning the date alone may be worked out with still greater precision.

Lɪᴛᴛʟᴇ ɪs known about the origins of the short manuscript, nor is it clear how Milton originally designed it to fit in *The History of Britain*. Its title, "The Digression," might have existed in the manuscript of the *History*—certainly it is treated as a digression even by the chapter that contained it. Yet it does have a distinct quality, both tonally and generically, that distinguishes it as separable from the *History* itself. Milton's model for this rare genre may have been the "Digression" in Guicciardini's *History,* if in part because the Italian writer's "Digression" is reported on its English title page to have been "forbidden the Impression, and effaced out of the Originall by the Inquisition."[20] If this publication history was in Milton's mind, he would more likely have drawn the connection in knowing apprehension that it would be censorable than after its actual censorship from the 1670 edition—if it indeed was one of the passages prevented from appearing. The manuscript has a couple of revealing corrections that seem to be the work of Edward Phillips, who would have been consulting a more authoritative copy, because he adds a line mistakenly omitted by the scribe as a result of eye-skip, a phenomenon that occurs when a copyist is mechanically following the words rather than the sense in copying (see figure 4.1).[21] This scribal evidence, with the fact that the text omits Miltonic passages found in the pirated posthumous text, suggest that more than one copy was in circulation.[22] The twelve pages of handwritten text are designed to fall in the midst of a discussion of the chaos that ensued after the disintegration of Roman domination in fifth-century Britain; it is, the copyist instructs, "To com in Lib. 3. page 110," after a passage which auspiciously ended with the words "from one misery to another" (*CPW* 5:406)—which also suggests that this is a copy of something that would have been cut from the manuscript, rather than an original document, since it postdates the printed book (see figure 4.2). There is also a single blank protective back sheet, suggesting the manuscript was produced with a front and back sheet (like a small pamphlet), and possibly by the bookseller. The offset words "in Miltons History of England," a later addition to the title's symmetrical layout, seem to have been added by a different hand. The pagination supplied here ("page 110") corresponds to the printed text of the first and second printings of *The History of Britain* (1670 and 1671), and suggests, particularly in the expression "to com," that the preserver of the Miltonic excerpt had hoped that it might be restored to its rightful position, either for a select private readership or for posterity.

against themselves) thir intents were cleere to no
other then to have set up a spirituall tyrannie by a
secular power to ye advancing of thir owne authoritie
above ye magistrate; And well did thir disciples ma-
-ifest themselves to be no better principl'd then thir teach-
-ers, trusted with committiships and other gainfull
upon thir commendations for zealous &c as they
offices, stuck not to term them godlie men, but executing
-ing thir places more like childern of the divil, unfaithfully, unjustly, unmercifully, and where not
corruptly, stupidly. So y^t between them ye teachers

Figure 4.1. Detail of page 8 of the "Digression," showing the addition of a missing line, inserted by another hand, which appears to be that of Edward Phillips. Harvard MS Eng 901 (Lobby XI.2.69). By permission of the Houghton Library, Harvard University.

The implications of these brief instructions warrant consideration, as they suggest more than a merely preservationist interest such as would be expressed in "omitted from"; the phrase "to come . . . after these words" is instead the sort a writer would use to instruct readers or printers on where to insert a passage for the purpose of restoration. (The ten-line *Omissa* appended to the 1671 edition of *Samson Agonistes,* for example, uses a similar set of instructions, and instructions to the publisher about the placement of poems in the Trinity manuscript also use "to come.")[23] Some critics have felt that Milton intentionally omitted the "Digression" for reasons of structure and relevancy, and perhaps to some extent as a preemptive act of self-censorship or revision, although he apparently did not omit other passages that were subsequently cut by the censor.[24] Edward Phillips records in his biography that in 1670 Milton "finisht and publisht his History of our Nation till the Conquest, all compleat so far as he went, some Passages only excepted, which, being thought too sharp against the Clergy, could not pass the Hand of the Licencer, were in the Hands of the late Earl of *Anglesey* while he liv'd; where at present is uncertain."[25] Any text in the hands of the Earl of Anglesey was almost certainly part of the extraordinary library he made available to readers.[26] Yet just what "passages" Anglesey's library held remained unclear, since the "Digression" is really a passage rather than "passages," and it is not centrally about

The Digression. / in Miltons History of
England.

O com̃ in lib: 3. page 110. after these words. /
[from one misery to another.]

But because ye gaining or loosing of libertie is ye greatest
change to better or to worse that may befall a nation under
civil goverment, and so discovers, as nothing more, what
degree of understanding, or capacitie, what disposition to
justice and civilitie there is amongst them, I suppose it
will bee many wayes profitable to resume a while the
whole discourse of what happn'd in this Iland soone after
ye Romans gooing out: and to consider wt might bee ye
reason, why, seeing other nations both antient and
modern with extreame hazard & danger have strove
for libertie as a thing invaluable, & by ye purchase thereof have soe onobled thir spirits, as from obscure and
small to grow eminent and glorious commonwealths,
why ye Britans having such a smooth occasion givn ym
to free themselves as ages have not afforded, such a
manumission as never subjects had a fairer, should let
it pass through them as a cordial medcin through a
dying man without ye least effect of sense or natural vigor. And no less to purpose if not more usefully to us it may withal bee enquir'd, since god aft
12 ages and more had drawne so neard a parall-
ell betweene thir state and ours in the late
com -

Figure 4.2. The opening to the "Digression," created from an excerpted section of Milton's *History of Britain*. Given that the title with the instructions for insertion were originally centered, the words "in Miltons History of England" appear to have been added later by another hand. By permission of the Houghton Library, Harvard University.

the "clergy"—and where it is, it is about the Presbyterians associated with the Long Parliament, and not members of the English Church. It seems likely that these excerpts include something more than, or something different from, the discrete text of the "Digression."

What remains clear is that passages of the censored *History*—perhaps all the pages of the censored manuscript—found their way into Anglesey's hands. Anglesey's collection was a well-used private library, arguably "the largest private library of the period—some 30,000 volumes."[27] It reputedly had a major collection of controversial materials—it notoriously held the secret document that revealed the true author of *Eikon Basilike* (the identity was revealed in spite of the government's efforts to destroy the evidence).[28] As is reflected in the sale catalog, the "*whole Library*" was used by "*many Persons of Honour . . . (tho possessed of very great Libraries of their own) [who] had frequent recourse to this for the perusal of many out of the ordinary Road of learning, not elsewhere to be found.*"[29] Andrew Marvell used Anglesey's library in writing his own polemics, and Anglesey used his power to protect Marvell and his bookseller after they found themselves in trouble with Sir Roger L'Estrange for printing the *Rehearsal Transpros'd* without license.[30] After Anglesey's death in 1686, the vast collection was sold off, but a large portion was prohibited from being sold by L'Estrange: "S.ʳ Roger did prohibit the Sale of many Manuscripts, and severall Bookes (but seized upon or tooke more away) as . . . Miltons Iconoclastes in ffrench."[31] Milton's manuscript or manuscripts may have been "seized upon" at this moment—a moment later than L'Estrange's publication of the *Character,* so this would not have been the occasion of that confiscation. Anglesey certainly had a close interest in Milton's subject, writing toward the end of his life that if God would "give life," he "would write a compleat History of England" showing how "the people" were "tenacious . . . allwayes of their liberties" and of how "the clergy have been the worst" in endeavoring to corrupt government.[32] Milton's *History* was also intended, at least as Milton relates in 1654 convincingly (since there is no ulterior gain in his doing so), to trace "in unbroken sequence . . . the history of my country, from the earliest origins even to the present day" (*CPW* 4:627–28). This implies a massive undertaking, but it also implies that the present would have always have been a frame of reference for his history, that an explicit or implicit comparison with the present would have been an integral part of the narrative, and that—as is suggested in the account—the other excised passages were comments that drew a critical comparison with the present.

One of the tantalizing questions about the extant manuscript of the "Digression" is whether it represents something reproduced in scribal form for limited circulation. If so, it may have been available from one of the booksellers' shops in London that sold Milton's *History,* such as those of Spencer Hickman or James Allestry, printer to the Royal Society. Manuscripts were sometimes kept by the booksellers, and lent or reproduced at the buyer's request—for example, Hobbes's posthumously printed *Historical Narration Concerning Heresie and the Punishment Thereof,* which Hobbes apparently wrote in an effort "to deflect a proposed prosecution of *Leviathan*"[33] on the grounds of its supposed atheism in 1666.[34] A letter from Charles Blount shows he had obtained a manuscript copy from Hobbes's bookseller, William Crooke.[35] Sometimes booksellers provided scribal additions to printed books, or finished books that remained incomplete. John Selden's *Historie of Tithes,* halted in the middle of the printing by the Bishop of London in a "whirlwind of anger combined with authority" (as Selden described it in a letter), was then circulated in copies that were "halfe printed and halfe writen."[36] None of these copies is extant. In one remarkable case of scribal completion of a printed book, though, twelve scribally completed copies of Bacon's *Certain Considerations Touching . . . the Church of England* (1604), suppressed in the middle of printing, have survived. Given that these twelve represent the vast majority of extant copies, it seems evident in this case that a large portion of the print-run would have been completed by scribes employed by the printer or bookseller, even after the printer, Thomas Purfoot, was fined and imprisoned.[37] While further research on this phenomenon needs still to be done, it seems quite possible that Milton's "Digression" belongs to a category of "hybrid" productions, in which part of a book is supplied in manuscript form.[38] In the case of the "Digression," it might have been made available as a manuscript inset, available by special arrangement. The manuscript measures 6 by 7½ inches, and the printed *History of Britain* has the same dimensions, with three-sixteenths of an inch to spare (that is, at 6 by 7 11/16).[39] This coincidence of size strongly suggests that the manuscript was produced to fit in the book. The manuscript was not bound, although the extant copy is folded, and since the folding has left tears and wear marks along the crease of each page, it appears to have been folded for a very long time. The folding may have occurred when the extant copy of the manuscript was removed from the printed *History,* which might explain why a later pen added the line "in Miltons History of England" to the title.

Either for the sake of a small private readership, or as a result of an incomplete revision, Milton did not omit indications at the beginning of the third book of the *History* that he would be drawing connections between current and ancient Britain, leading acute readers to expect such a digression. He writes in the introduction to book 3 of the *History,* also originally written in the late 1640s: "The late civil broils had cast us into a condition not much unlike to what the Britans then were in, when the imperial jurisdiction departing hence left them to the sway of thir own Councils; which times by comparing seriously with these later, and that confused Anarchy with this intereign, we may be able from two such remarkable turns of State, producing like events among us, to raise a knowledg of our selves great and weighty" (*CPW* 5:130). After only twelve pages of description of fifth-century Britain in the printed history, the excerpted digression would have begun as a comparison of the early political troubles "with these later." The continuity of narrative toward a digressive discussion shows that Milton did not write the text "as an afterthought" as is sometimes argued.[40] Despite raising such expectations, the omission is not keenly felt, although the Restoration audience is given here the prologue to a comparison between the "late civil broils" and the condition of post-Roman Britain, and some promise of further analysis that would bring "knowledg of ourselves great and weighty." The Restoration context may, of course, be an age too late for such consideration. The use of the word "late" to describe the civil wars was by 1670 becoming relatively unusual; the last civil war having ended twenty-two years before—it is used, however, with particular intensity in 1648.[41] Even here some suggestion of the republicanism of the excised text asserts itself: when "the imperial jurisdiction" departed, they left the British to their "own Councils," offering an opportunity for conciliar, rather than imperial, government. The Restoration reader would have been slightly thrown off, moreover, by the phrases "these later" and especially "this intereign," which might have seemed to indicate the anarchy of *the* Interregnum.[42] In the "Digression" itself, it becomes clear that "*this* intereign" refers not to *the* Interregnum, but to a specific unresolved vacuum of power between the Parliament, the army, and the king prior to Pride's Purge.[43] The phrases "*these* later" and "*this* intereign" further suggest—as I believe was the case—that Milton wrote during a vacuum of power. This chronology is somewhat destabilized by the pluperfect expression "the late civil broils *had* cast us into a condition," probably changed for the 1670 printing from "civil broils *have* cast us into a condition," so as to give some distance from the event. This incomplete revision of verb tenses occurs also in book 2, where—as Blair Worden points out—Milton writes that the "'presbyters of our age . . . *like* well to sit in Assembly on the public stipend, but *liked* not the poverty that caused' their counterparts in early Britain 'to do so'" (*CPW* 5:116, emphasis added).[44] When, in the excised "Digression," Milton began to write on the "late commotions" (*CPW* 5:441) it is with a more distinct sense of their having just happened. In the excised "Digression," "these later" of book 3 becomes "these *lately*," which suggests the temporal proximity of these wars still more keenly: "Of these who swayd most in the late troubles few words as to this point may suffice, they had armies, leaders, and successes to thir wish; but to make use of so great advantages was not their skill. To other causes therefore and not to want of force, or warlike manhood in the Brittans both those and these lately, wee must impu[te] the ill husbanding of those faire opportunities, which might seeme to have put libertie, so long desir'd, like a brid[le] into their hands" (443). Such phrases as "these lately" confirm a sense that the civil wars must have been quite recent.[45] The Parliament and the army had, in 1648, troops, leaders and successes—but, in spite of the victory over the king, they could not grasp "libertie, so long desir'd."

The traditional argument that the "Digression" is a pre-Purge piece of writing was based largely on a conception of *The History of Britain* itself as belonging to the 1647–48 period. This dating of the history was challenged by both Woolrych and von Maltzahn, whose evidence for a 1649 composition of *The History of Britain* lies in Milton's retrospective account in the *Second Defence of the English People* (1654), where the author seems to suggest that he turned to the history after composing his defense of the regicide. As Woolrych argued, "the apparent sense of the relevant passage in the *Defensio secunda* is that he turned to it only after he had written *The Tenure of Kings and Magistrates*."[46] "Apparent," though, is the operative term. Latin often allows for more ambiguity, and here the syntax and tenses are particularly convoluted, producing two contradictory translations in the Yale and Columbia editions. A good deal hinges, too, on the Latin word translated as "turned" in "I turned to the task of tracing the history," which is *converti,* a word that might sensibly be translated as "I returned."[47] Milton explains in the original (the Yale translation follows):

His rebus confectis, cum jam abunde otii existimarem mihi futurum, ad historiam gentis, ab ultima origine repetitam, ad haec usque tempora, si possem, perpetuo filo deducendam me converti: quatuor jam libros absolveram, cum ecce nihil tale cogitantem me, Caroli regno in rempublicam redacto, Concilium Status, quod dicitur, tum primum authoritate Parlamenti constitutum, ad se vocat, meaque opera ad res praesertim externas uti voluit. (*WJM* 8:136–38)

When these works had been completed and I thought that I could look forward to an abundance of leisure, I turned [*converti*] to the task of tracing in unbroken sequence, if I could, the history of my country, from the earliest origins even to the present day. I had already finished four books when the kingdom of Charles was transformed into a republic, and the so-called Council of State, which was then for the first time established by the authority of

Parliament, summoned me, though I was expecting no such event, and desired to employ my services, especially in connection with foreign affairs. (*CPW* 4:627–28)

Even without consideration of just when Milton turned or returned to the history, this chronology is already a bit murky, especially surrounding the issues of when he was employed (March 13) and when the kingdom was officially transformed into a republic (May 19).[48] Although this latter event could be understood in its less official sense of transformation (the beheading of the king), Milton is at pains here to use legal language—in part because the real object of this treatise is to assert at every moment the legitimacy of England's government, and he aims to obviate any potential charges of impropriety. Yet even when it is approached literally as a brief passage of disinterested autobiography, this passage has serious impediments to clarity. His use of the pluperfect in "I had already finished [*absolveram*] four books" seems to indicate that four books of *The History of Britain* were done when Charles was executed. A translation might follow more closely the order of the Latin: "I returned to the task of tracing the history of our race. . . . I had already finished four books, when, having no such thought in my mind, the kingdom of Charles having been transformed into a republic, the Council of State, so it was called, then for the first time constituted by the authority of Parliament, summoned me, and desired my work especially in foreign affairs." This still leaves the chronology vague, and elides the periods of the transformation of government and Milton's new career. The precise chronology sought by posterity is clearly not of interest to the author here—unless, of course, he is deliberately occluding it.

Edward Phillips is sometimes a bit murky on chronology (he misdates Milton's death, for example), so his own account of this composition should be treated with some suspicion. In an account that reflects valuably on the contrast between Milton's "private" work and his public persona, Phillips echoes some of the same ambiguities in Milton's 1654 recollection. He too suggests that Milton *returned* to this project after *The Tenure:* "After [writing *The Tenure*] his thoughts were bent upon retiring again to his own private Studies, and falling upon such subjects as his proper Genius prompted him to Write of, among which was the History of our own Nation, from the Beginning till the Norman Conquest, wherein he had made some progress."[49] Edward's pluperfect "had" looks back to a time of composition prior to the execution.

Regardless of how the passage in the 1654 Defense is translated, it may be that Milton did not remember the precise sequence of composition five years later, nor have reason to be precise about it: in this context, he means to emphasize that he was not seeking promotion in writing *The Tenure of Kings and Magistrates*—"no man ever saw me canvassing for preferment," he writes, or "fixed, with supplicatory look to the doors of the parliament" (*WJM* 8:137). Milton's retelling shows him to be pulled from his private studies when the Council of State asked him to write on their behalf, thus suggesting no connection between the defense of the English republic and the advantages it would bring him. In this way, looking back from 1654, Milton is showing himself to be innocent of the charges he had made against Salmasius in the first *Defence,* that Salmasius was literally paid for his views, which would have been different—and had, in fact, been different, as Milton shows—before the mercenary assignment.[50] In the first of these defenses, *Pro Populo Anglicano Defensio,* Milton lambastes Salmasius with charges of mercenary motives: "But you have, old fox that you are, wished not to be a laughing-stock also, in saying 'a king's defence'; for, as you have sold it, it is no longer yours but is now rightfully 'a king's defence'—indisputably bought for one hundred jacobuses, a huge price, from an absolutely destitute king" (*PW* 55). In the *Defensio Secunda,* Milton insists that he was not looking for a reward from Parliament in order to protect himself from the same compromising charges.

Milton significantly omits that he was also asked to write the so-called *Observations upon the Articles of Peace,* thus suggesting much more leisure than there actually was. Milton was offered the position of Secretary for the Foreign Tongues on March 13, and the anonymous *Observations* was just one of his many assignments.[51] The tract appeared on or before May 16, 1649, just over three months after the publication of *The Tenure of Kings and Magistrates* in mid-February. If the passage in the *Defensio Secunda* were to indicate a fresh start to this historical project, he would have had little over a month to write about 185 pages of British history, a project that he would have had to race to, according to this account, just after the king whose execution he advocated was put on the block. While we might expect some compulsive behavior at this juncture, a new project on this scale seems too incredible. At any rate, other material evidence contradicts this interpretation of the 1654 account. Samuel Hartlib records in his diary in July 1648, through information provided by Theodore Haak, that "Milton is not only writing a Univ. History of Engl. but also an Epitome of all Purchas Volumes."[52] Milton's account in the *Defensio Secunda* should therefore be seen more as an example of his evasiveness—common in this tract, and especially understandable in this context—than as a strict account of composition history.

But the evidence for a 1648 composition of the "Digression" can be determined with still more confidence by the relation between the manuscript's content and its context. Milton's description of the political frustration—and his evident frustration with it—points not to 1649 but to the much less optimistic period prior to Pride's Purge. In one instance he pessimistically compares England's political vigor to that of a dying man: The "purchase" of liberty, now within England's grasp, "having such a smooth occasion to free themselves as ages have not afforded," has nonetheless been let to pass, like "cordial medcin through a dying man without the least effect of sence or natural vigor" (*CPW* 5:441). The "purchase" of liberty within England's grasp refers to the recent "victory" of parliamentary forces against the king, but, to the enormous frustration of Milton and others, nothing was done to realize the potential of this moment. Thus, the "ill husbanding of" such "faire opportunities" (441)—the potential for a true republican settlement—is precisely the topic of the "Digression." Instead, after seven years of conflict, they seemed to Milton no closer to a constitutional change that would insure an essential set of liberties than when they started. The Parliament was once again in a process of making overtures of reconciliation with the king.

Woolrych does allow that, were it not for Milton's puzzling account in the *Defensio Secunda*, 1648 would be the plausible moment of composition, given the condition of political stalemate. His description of the historical moment is of value:

> Commissioners of the two Houses did renew negotiations with him [the King] in the so-called Treaty of Newport, which proceeded on the Isle of Wight from just after mid-September until the Army interrupted it on 6 December. With Fairfax plainly unhappy about violating either the King's or Parliament's authority, with Cromwell lingering over the siege of Pontefract in November and still wrestling with his own conscience as to whether providence required the Army's assistance, and with public feeling running powerfully in favour of an agreement with the King, so that his would-be prosecutors walked in danger of their lives, it is likely enough that Milton went through a period of despondency while the Treaty was in progress.
>
> If one were forced to consider a date in 1648 for the Digression, it would have to fall within that eleven-week period.[53]

These eleven weeks between mid-September and December 6 should be seen as the period of the text's composition. The postulated dates of 1660 or later are too late for Milton to be writing about the "late civil broils" (129) or "these lately" (441); further, he nowhere in the "Digression" mentions any of the parliamentary bodies that had governed since 1648. There are, in addition, several echoes in the "Digression" to Milton's own work of the late 1640s—both in sonnets written just prior, and in the subsequent *Tenure of Kings and Magistrates*—as well as similarities to the work of others in this period. The "Digression" is also, as mentioned, integral to the *History* itself in ways that do not allow it to be seen as an afterthought. Milton began the third book of the *History* with the express intention of digressing.

The same extreme exasperation with the revolutionary efforts and with the Parliament is seen in such texts as the *Petition of 11 September 1648,* written by John Lilburne and others, with the supposed backing of forty thousand signatures.[54] The petition, prompted by an impending parliamentary treaty with the king, complains that Parliament deserted the very cause for which it had taken arms against the king: "Give us leave before you conclude (as by the treaty in hand) to acquaint you: first with the ground and reason which induced us to aid you against the king and his adherents; secondly what our apprehensions are of this treaty; thirdly, what we expected from you and still do most earnestly desire."[55] The petition contains the same language as Milton's "Digression," referring on a few occasions as Milton does to the "late" wars, and the expectations consequent to their success. Like Milton, these revolutionaries express deep misgivings about the Parliament's not realizing its implicit and not-so-implicit intention in undertaking the wars in the first place, that of replacing Charles's version of monarchy with a representative government. This charge of reneging would become central to *The Tenure of Kings and Magistrates,* which needed to justify the act of deposition of this Parliament. The purging of Parliament and the deposition of the king would be justified, according to Milton's argument, because the intention of the war itself—and the near ruin of the country by both king and Parliament—mandated these acts.

Unlike Milton's writing, Lilburne's Leveller tract represents the voices of those who actually served in the military effort, but on many fronts it advocates essentially the same position. While Milton speaks from one step removed, writing distantly of the "armies, leaders, and successes to thir wish" (441), he concurs with Lilburne that these "opportunities" are in the process of being lost. Lilburne and the petitioners protest:

> We know no great cause wherefor we assisted you in *the late wars* but in hope to be delivered by you from so intolerable, so destructive a bondage, so soon as you should through God's blessing upon the armies raised by you be enabled. But to our exceeding grief we have observed that no sooner God vouchsafed you victory and blessed you with success, and thereby enabled you to put us and the whole nation into an absolute condition of freedom and safety, but, according as ye have been accustomed—passing by *the ruin of the*

nation and all that blood that has been spilt by the king and his party—ye be-
take yourselves to a treaty with him, thereby putting him that is but one
single person and a public officer of the commonwealth in competition with
the whole body of the people whom ye represent, not considering that it is
impossible for you to erect any authority equal to yourselves.[56]

Like many of the Leveller apologists, Lilburne uses the philosophical position of *salus populi* (the safety of the people) as a central feature of the argument for popular sovereignty. The maxim *salus populi suprema lex esto*—the
safety of the people is the supreme law—is cited by Cicero from the Law of
the Twelve Tables, and it was invoked in parliamentary discourse just prior
to the onset of the civil war.[57] This argument sometimes appears in Milton's
political formulations, as when he writes in *The Tenure* about how "the
people would be disingag'd" if "the King or Magistrate prov'd unfaithfull to
his trust," or "when any danger threatn'd to have care of the public safety"
(*CPW* 3:200). Although Milton's method of argument depends on historical sources and other authorities not cited in the Leveller tracts, much of
the core elements—public trust, *salus populi*, representative government, and
toleration—remain the same. Lilburne's argument in the *Petition* is that
since "God vouchsafed you victory," the next stage should be the overthrow
of the same government against which they had fought, as Milton would
also argue in *The Tenure:* "If God and a good cause gave them Victory, the
prosecution wherof for the most part, inevitably draws after it the alteration
of Lawes, change of Government, downfal of Princes with their families"
(*CPW* 3:192). The *Petition*, like the "Digression," laments with "exceeding
grief" the seeming inability of Parliament to make this change, given the
extraordinary sacrifice of the country. The monarchy has held the people in
a condition of "intolerable" and "destructive bondage," and despite the war
of liberation from this, Parliament endeavors to set "one single person" in
"competition with the whole body of the people whom ye represent." Milton
takes this republican position in *The Tenure*, arguing that setting "one body
[of the people] inferior to him single . . . were a kinde of treason against the
dignity of mankind to affirm" (*CPW* 3:204). Lilburne writes of "the ruin of
the nation and all that blood that has been spilt"; Milton similarly writes in
the "Digression" of "the ruin of a whole nation" (*CPW* 5:446–47), although
he goes so far as to make the Parliament, even more than the king and his
party, responsible for that condition (yet the point in both texts is that the
Parliament has become part of the king's party). Indeed, in Milton's text
the king is not even mentioned; as he has been vanquished, the responsibility
for the country's welfare resides in the Parliament.

Milton's language and argument is also very close to that of a *Remonstrance* of the army that appeared in November 1648, which articulated a position that would support the formation of a purged Parliament and the trial and execution of the king. The *Remonstrance* expresses deep concern with the progress of the Parliament, and hopes "to hold off impending ruin from an honest people and a good cause."[58] As Milton would in *The Tenure,* the *Remonstrance* argues for popular sovereignty, defining what is potentially an alternative parliamentary body that is truly representative of the people:

> therefore the same [Supreme] Council or Representative Body therein, having the supreme trust, in all such cases where the offence or default is in public officers, abusing or failing their trust, or in any person whatsoever, if the office extend to the prejudice of the public, may call such offenders to account, and distribute punishments to them, either according to the law, where it has provided, or their own judgment where it has not, and they find the offence, though not particularly provided against by particular laws, yet against the general Law of Reason or Nations, and the vindication of the public interest to require justice; and that in such case no person whatsoever may be exempt from such account or punishment.[59]

This passage is also of interest for its extra-legal argument for popular sovereignty, where the people's rational construction, rather than the sovereign, may be above the law. With some ambiguity, Milton will make this same argument in *The Tenure*. Like many pamphlets against both Parliament and king at this point, the *Remonstrance* is full of language calling Parliament as well as the king to account in a more general sense. According to the *Remonstrance,* the king "has been the author and continuer of a most unjust war, and is consequently guilty of all the treason it contains, and of all the innocent blood, spoil and mischief to the kingdom acted or occasioned thereby."[60]

Milton's criticism in the "Digression," however, is leveled at the Parliament itself and their mishandling of the revolt against the king. He writes in a passage that echoes his complaint in the sonnet "I did but prompt the age" of "this waste of wealth and loss of blood," there is now, *after* much "bloodshed" and "vast expense," thanks to these parliamentary failures, the condition of ruin: "as they brought those antient natives to miserie and ruin by libertie which rightly us'd might have made them happie, so brought they these of late after many labours, much blood-shed, & vast expence, to ridiculous frustration" (*CPW* 5:443). Woolrych comments that this complaint "would have seemed utterly extravagant and unjust if written in 1648,"[61] yet it echoes Milton's own contentions in his poetry and the strident voices of his contemporaries at this time. Notably, this is the only moment in the poet's career when he makes precisely this argument. This is also the very level of exasperation required for the forcible overthrow of Parliament that would follow. It took a dangerous and illegal act to put an end to the "ridiculous" impasse between Parliament and king. Milton expresses this frustration in republican terms. He goes on to pose the question why, given that "other nations both antient and modern with extreame hazard & danger have strove for libertie as a thing invaluable, & by the purchase thereof have soe enobl'd their spirits, as from obscure and small to grow eminent and glorious commonwealths," the Britons having "such a smooth occasion giv'n them to free themselves as ages have not afforded, such a manumission as never subjects had a fairer" (441), fail nonetheless to adopt such a state. The word "enobl'd," like the "nobler task" that awaits Fairfax, suggests the virtue (or *virtù*, strength) of a republican.

The "Digression" and *The Tenure of Kings and Magistrates*

As we saw in chapter 2, the historical arguments collected in the Commonplace Book play a major role in the construction of Milton's regicide work. In addition, the composition of *The History of Britain,* and particularly the third book with its digressive analysis, has an especially important role in forging the historical argument of *The Tenure of Kings and Magistrates,* not merely by virtue of its proximity and its depth of historical scrutiny, but also because Milton undertakes in this work the kind of specific comparison with the present that was mostly implicit in records of his research. Moreover, he articulates here a moral indictment against the corrupt members of the Long Parliament and the Westminster Assembly in ways that would justify an overthrow of this Parliament, and further enable him to make a clear argument justifying popular sovereignty—the right to overthrow not just kings but also magistrates—when he reenters public debate.

The "Digression" portrays the character of the Long Parliament and the Westminster Assembly as almost hopelessly corrupt from the outset. The theocratic intentions of the Presbyterian Assembly "were cleere to be no other then to have set up a spir[i]tual tyrannie by a secular power to the advancing of their owne authorit[ie] above the magistate" (447). His criticism of the Presbyterians is damning in the extreme. As Milton writes, "they taught compulsion without convincement (which not long before they so much complaind of as executed unchristianlie against themselves)"—the "New Presbyter" had become "Old Priest writ Large," as in the poem "On the New Forcers of Conscience." Worse, they executed "thir places more like children of the devil, unfaithfully, unjustly, unmercifully, and where not corruptly, stupidly"

(447–49). While there is no explicit description of the 1648 "Ordinance for the Punishing of Blasphemies and Heresies," this act of extreme government intolerance and "spir[i]tual tyrannie" may well be registered here, as we would expect it to be, given the recent work on Milton's anti-Trinitarianism, and his evident response to this severe Presbyterian effort to control belief with the threat of execution.[62]

Indeed, Milton goes on to suggest that this culture of "compulsion without convincement" has actually given "mor cause of blaspheming . . . to the enemies of god and of truth since the first preaching of reformation; which needed most to have begun in the forwardest reformers themselves" (449). This use of "blaspheming" may well gesture toward the "Ordinance for the Punishing of Blastphemies," with the sense that such an order actually gives more cause for "blaspheming." This passage suggests revealingly that the Presbyterians' efforts to suppress blasphemy are counterproductive, but it also—unlike Milton's printed texts—endorses the "forwardest reformers" oppressed by such actions. The rather oblique casting back to the "first preaching of reformation" may allude to such forwardest reformers as Michael Servetus, whose opposition to Calvinist theology in 1553 caused him to suffer the very form of persecution ("the pains of death")[63] now instituted by these English Calvinists, and the rhetoric of persecution from this period, such as Beza's defense of Calvinist intolerance, was used to support the present English extremists.[64] Milton may also be gesturing toward the recent persecution of "forward reformers" under the 1648 ordinance, such as Paul Best or John Biddle.[65] For Milton the Reformation had not gone far enough, and there were other reforming voices that "needed most" to have been in the fore.

Looking back at the actions of Parliament from 1641 to 1648, Milton writes that "the greatest part" of this body of magistrates were motivated by "wealth and ample possessions or bold and active ambition rather then merit had commended to the same place, onc[e] the superficial zeale and popular fumes that acted their new magistracie were cool'd and spent in them" (443). One pronounced difference between this manuscript representation of Milton's political observations and his printed views is in its tone: shorn of all praise for England's potential success, a frequent feature of his printed tracts of this period, the "Digression" is nothing but deeply critical of its failures. In a nutshell account of the speedy moral decay of the Parliament, looking something like Michael's summation of human history to its first protagonist, the screed continues: "Then was justice delai'd & soon after deny'd, spite and favour determin'd all: hence faction, then treacherie both at home & in the field, ev'ry where wrong & oppression, foule and dishonest things committed daylie" (443). He states that the magistrates had irrevocably violated the public trust: "for that faith which ought to bee kept as sacred and inviolable as any thing holy, the public faith, after infinite summs receiv'd & all the wealth of the church, not better imploy'd, but swallow'd up into a private gulfe, was not ere long asham'd to confess bankrupt" (445). Milton made the same complaint in a sonnet written to Fairfax on his siege of Colchester on August 27, 1648, stating that "Public Faith" must be "clear'd from shameful brand / Of Public Fraud" (*CSP* 325, ll. 11–13). This is a remarkably republican sonnet, suggesting that Fairfax move beyond military victory, and use his strength to effect real political change: "O yet a nobler task awaits thy hand" (l. 9).[66] As Honigmann pointed out, "Public Faith" was a term officially used in this period "to refer to a form of National Debt incurred by the Parliament."[67] For Milton, these magistrates have become parasites on the nation, willfully holding it in a condition of political stalemate for the sake of self-enrichment. His use of "now" here again suggests the freshness of this account: "And now besides the sweetness of briberie and other gaine with the love of rule, thir own guiltiness and the dreaded na[me] of just account"—echoing the demands of Levellers and others in the late 1640s—"which the people had long call'd for discover'd plainelie that there were of thir owne nu[m]ber who secretly contrive'd and fomented those troubles and combustions in the land which openly they sate to remedy, & would continually finde such worke, as should keepe them from ever being brought to the terrible stand of laying down thir authoriti[e] for lack of new business, or not drawing it out to any length of time though upon the nesessarie ruin of a whole nation" (445–47). The indictment is so serious as to easily justify Pride's Purge; indeed, it is more specific and arguably more damning than the indictment of either king or Parliament in *The Tenure of Kings and Magistrates*. It is of interest here that "the people" are pitted so definitively against the magistrates.

The people had, in fact, literally called for an "account." Fogle points to Leveller discourse against parliamentary corruption, which focuses particularly on the problem of the army's neglected arrears.[68] Similar charges of corruption and of the need for a "just account" appear in such documents as the anonymous pamphlet *London's Account,* which appeared in February 1647.[69] Although written from the perspective of a royalist, the pamphlet maintains some of the same positions found in populist criticisms of the Parliament, such as those of the Levellers, which is an indicator of how allegiances shifted with astonishing speed in this period. This royalist tract has much in common with Leveller pamphlets and with the more literary and scholarly republicanism in Milton's "Digression." The writer of *London's*

Account confesses his own ambivalence about the cause, that he "admire[s] what those men can alledge, that craved, and had this Act passed, to curb the prerogative of Kings," but finds himself disgusted that the same men "are the first violators of the same Law themselves" (5–6). The Parliament had, according to this analyst, "ruined the kingdome" (2) not just with "shedding Innocent Blood" (2) in wasteful wars but with fraudulent practices of collecting funds, such as "Taxations, Impositions, Excises, [and] Contributions" (title page). Milton complains too of the Parliament's work pertaining to "nothing els but new impositions, taxes, excises" (*CPW* 5:445). These are the primary concern of the pamphlet, which actually lists the collections made in four years, which amount to "seventeene millions, five hundred thousand pounds a yeere" (11), such that the reader may see "the bignesse of the Paw, of what a huge bulk and body the Beast is" (1). Like Milton, this author suggests that the Parliament prolongs its business for the sake of personal gain: "It is worth your consideration to remember how peny-wise you were at the beginning of this long-winded Parliament, refusing the loane of but 100000.l. except His Majesty would condescend, some conceive, to an everlasting parliament, for an assurance of your repayment" (7). The "covetous sharks, and griping men, (such as never knew faire dealing)" that had infiltrated Parliament had, with their officers "fleeced away" "neere halfe the said Collections" (7). The pamphlet uses some of the same terms as Milton, as when it asperses how vastly "the Publique Faith stands indebted" (11), the phrase Milton used in the August sonnet to Fairfax and in his indictment in the "Digression" that "the public faith" has been "swallow'd up into a private gulfe." Milton's characterization of Parliament fearing "the dreaded na[me] of just account" (*CPW* 5:445) seems to look back on such demands for impeachment as that suggested in *London's Account*. Here, too, there is a call for "just account," as when the pamphlet arraigns Parliament's "sharking Committee-men" who "resolve to give no good account of" the "Loanes, plunder, and the many Sequestrations" (7). The pamphlet ends with a poem comparing this work of accounting to that of an astronomer counting stars: if they could "Make a just balance to this large Account, / The Danish Tycho Brahe they'l surmount" (12).

Another short pamphlet circulated in late July 1647, *The Grand Account*, approaches the same problem of parliamentary corruption from a populist angle, often referring, as the Leveller pamphlets do, to the injustice of the army's unpaid arrears.[70] It uses many of the same arguments as Milton's "Digression," and, like *London's Account*, it provides an actual tally of the parliamentary plunder, in this case by rougher means, such as the numbers of wagonloads of silver. The grand total comes to a similar figure as *London's*

Account: "sixteen Millions, sixteen hundred thousand pounds of Silver" (5). As the report broadcasts on its title page, it is "a remonstrance, wherein is plainly discovered the vast summes of money levyed upon the kingdome by ordinance of Parliament, since the beginning of the late warre: as also an accompt of the disposall of the greatest part thereof." *The Grand Account* provides a "glasse for all honest and true hearted English-men to present the deformities of corruption unto, and to cause them to think it is high time to enquire what is become of these vast sums of treasure: what Lord but may justly require or demand a just account of his Steward?" (5). The increasing pressure from such "just" demands for account remaining unfulfilled, a popular revolution became the only way to establish the kind of "just and well-amended common-wealth" that Milton imagines.

Appended to this account is the *Vox Populi,* a broader cry against the injustices of the Parliament, suggesting that the revolution can only be realized by purging the land not only of the monarch—now almost a secondary issue—but also by removing the corrupt Parliament. As in the "Digression," there is a sense here of missed opportunities:

> How comes it to passe, . . . we reape not the harvest of this promising seed time? How comes it to passe wee beseech you, that such faire blossomes, yeeld such slender fruit? Whence growes this muttering, nay we may say groaning under, and exclamation against oppression, tyrannie, and injustice in our street, nay Courts of (in-justice) justice we cannot call them; even at the Parliament dore, nay within the Parliament House? How comes it to passe that so many irregular, illegall, and we may say, un-parliamentary Votes, Orders, Declarations, and Ordinances, passe for currant coyne one day, and counterfit the next? Whence proceeds this spirit of Ambition, contention, oppression, and sedition, which reigns so powerfully amongst you? We cannot be seduced to believe that ever this proceeds from Parliament Principles; from Principles of Law and justice; but from Principles of Ambition, usurpation, pride, covetuousnesse, and the like, from the power of which, Good Lord deliver us." (6–7)

In the "Digression," the nation's Celtic ancestors are depicted in a state of potential, and as a set of people—not magistrates or lords of any kind—who might have chosen a system of self-governance that would have preserved liberty. The comparison with England in this distant, almost prehistoric state enables Milton to explore the relative strength of various political architectures without reference to settled traditions, either legal or theological. These early English inhabitants are not unlike the state-of-nature humans imagined in the emerging field of anthropological politics, such as Milton's own "state of Man" in *Areopagitica,* derived from Eden, or Hobbes's "state of nature" descriptions. Although Milton calls them "Christian" when he reuses this moment in *The Tenure of Kings and Magistrates,* their religion is not mentioned here, nor did the native inhabitants need Christianity to enable them to understand what God had decreed regarding social order. This is for Milton an entirely separate concern. In this anthropological field of inquiry, Milton continues the exploration of political choice conducted in the Commonplace Book in ways that would inform his defense of the coup d'état. He articulates the sovereign freedom of the people not only in terms of the right to choose a leader—as it is expressed in *The Tenure*—but also in terms of the right to choose a system of government, again exemplifying the more pronounced republicanism in his private work, suggesting that Milton strategically mutes his republicanism in his public polemics. As he writes in the "Digression":

> It may withal bee enquir'd, since god afte[r] 12 ages and more had drawne so neare a parallel betweene their state and ours in the late commotions, why they who had the chiefe management therin having attain'd, though not so easilie, to a condition which had set before them civil government in all her formes, and giv'n them to bee masters of thir own choise, were not found able after so many years doeing and undoeing to hitt so much as into any good and laudable way that might shew us hopes of a just and well amended common-wealth to come. (*CPW* 5:441)

These revolutionaries are "masters of thir own choise," yet, like their Celtic ancestors, unable, with all the forms of government before them, to choose an enduring and "just" model. The value given to choice here extends the argument for rational choice in *Areopagitica,* and in both cases Milton challenges Calvinist and Reformation political theology.

Milton repeats in *The Tenure* this argument about the natural condition of choice. He also returns to this moment of British history, but no longer with the regret that the early Britons had not chosen, like the Romans after the Tarquins, an enduring model of republican government. Instead he transforms this failure into a monumental event in history: the Britons had chosen a ruler, and in doing so, they had confirmed the legitimacy of popular choice. The "first Christian Brittish" king of the most ancient historian was not chosen by God, but (albeit poorly) by the people. "But far before these days," Milton writes in *The Tenure of Kings and Magistrates,* in a comparative formulation that might have been lifted from the "Digression," although with significant changes:

> *Gildas* the most ancient of all our Historians, speaking of those times wherein the Roman Empire decaying quitted and relinquishd what right they had by

Conquest to this Iland, and resign'd it all into the peoples hands, testifies that the people thus re-invested with their own original right, about the year 446, both elected them Kings, whom they thought best (the first Christian Brittish Kings that ever raign'd heer since the Romans) and by the same right, when they apprehended cause, usually depos'd and put them to death. This is the most fundamental and ancient tenure that any King of England can produce or pretend to. (*CPW* 3:221)

Milton's reversal of purpose with this moment of history—in the "Digression" it is an example of England's inability, but in *The Tenure* of its possibility—reflects the stark difference between public and private discourse, between a political discourse with a specific audience and a speculative digression. In *The Tenure,* the ancient Britons' poor choice in 446 demonstrates not a failure to establish a republic, but the "most fundamental and ancient tenure" of kings, a tenure given by the people. This relationship between the two texts continues, suggesting further evidence of a sequential relationship from the manuscript to the printed tract. In the "Digression," Milton underscores the failure of the Celts to "shew us hopes of a just and well amended common-wealth to come" (*CPW* 5:441) and thus leave no memorial for the emulation of future ages. Milton turns this failure on its head in *The Tenure,* where the very problem of a missing memorial provides the polemicist with a possibility: that England's present acts might provide just such a memorial. "In future ages," he comments in *The Tenure,* if the present republic "prove not too degenerat," our descendants "will look up with honour, and aspire toward these exemplary, and matchless deeds of their Ancestors" (*CPW* 3:237–38). It has been argued that "it was not the victory of the regicides [in 1649] but their failures which encouraged republican speculation,"[71] and that, following this, Milton's own interest in republicanism begins after the regicide. As I have suggested here and in regard to the strong republican language in the Commonplace Book, in fact it seems the other way around: Milton's republicanism was instead nurtured long before the transformations of government in the winter of 1648–49. But what emerges after the event, in the urgent attempts to bring legitimacy to what was essentially an illegal overthrow of both Parliament and the king, is a muted form of republicanism. The tactical muting is one of the many signs of rhetorical strategizing evidenced in the differences between Milton's manuscript record and what finds its way into print.

Milton participates here in the language of historical precedent, such as that illuminated in Pocock's *Ancient Constitution and the Feudal Law,* in which an "original right" is ferreted out of the archives of history. Milton's attention to this kind of constitutionalism emerges when he avers in the

Tenure that the ancient Britons' choice in 446 demonstrates the "most fundamental and ancient tenure" (*CPW* 3:221). Milton's work also participates in the constitutional debate concerning the Norman feudal imposition, as when, early in the tract, he castigates those who are "contesting for privileges, customs, forms, and that old entanglement of Iniquity, thir gibrish Lawes, through the badge of thir ancient slavery" (192–93). As in his earlier dismissal of the "norman gibbrish" in his Commonplace Book (*CPW* 1:424, CB 179), Milton means French law, left over from the Norman Conquest. These statements echo the dialogue between the ancient constitutionalists and their exaggeratedly feudalistic opponents. His use of "tenure" employs the rhetoric of ironic inversion that permeates *The Tenure of Kings and Magistrates,* in which the discourse of his opponents is so wrong as to be completely upside down: it is the kings and magistrates, and not the people, who are held in tenure; the royalist ideology would have these people "no better then slaves and vassals born, in the tenure and occupation of another inheriting Lord" (*CPW* 3:237).

Indeed, the feudal notions expressed here of "tenure" and "vassal" resonate with the language of debate in the late 1640s. Even in such a nonacademic setting as the Putney Debates between Parliament and the Council of the Army, for example, spurred by the Leveller *Agreement of the People,* would these seemingly academic historical issues preoccupy a debate. Here, Nicholas Cowling interrupts Henry Ireton's disapproving speech to insist that popular representation had existed "before the Conquest," igniting a debate: "Since the Conquest the greatest part of the kingdom was in vassalage," he insisted, after Ireton, taking a far more conservative position, had objected.[72] Yet Milton was more ambivalent about the value of historical precedent in *The Tenure,* and this ambivalence is one of the several ways in which this tract will assert a position—in this case an established method of political argument—and then later retreat from it, thus undermining the validity of precedent, if not simply offering contradictory arguments. In one instance Milton asserts precedent against the "Malignant backsliders" who insist that the "proceedings now in Parliament against the King, are without precedent" (222), responding with a few pages of European history as proof. But then he admits fully that there may well be no precedent: if the Rump parliamentarians "doe what they doe without precedent, if it appeare thir duty, it argues the more wisdom" (237).

THE CONCLUDING pages of the "Digression" drop the comparison with ancient Britain, giving more precision to the analysis of the present state of England. Milton had opened the "Digression" with the postulation that "the gaining or loosing of libertie is the greatest change to better or to worse that may befall a nation" (*CPW* 5:441). At this nadir in the course of the English revolution, he concludes that the English people have lost this potential for liberty. In a passage that provides one of the most revealing indications that the history Milton wrote was happening "now," in 1648, he reflects that the Parliament had broken the people's trust, and thus ruined the possibility of obtaining liberty. "Thus they who but of late," he writes in conclusion, "were extolld as great deliverers, and had a people wholy at thir devotion, by so discharging thir trust as wee see, did not onely weak'n and unfit themselves to be dispencers of what libertie they pretented, but unfitted also the people, *now* growne worse & more disordinate, to receave or to digest any libertie at all" (449, emphasis added). The concluding words turn to consideration of the loss of liberty, not only in ancient Britain, but also in ancient Rome: "For stories teach us that libertie sought out of season in a corrupt and degenerate age brought Rome it self into further slaverie" (449). One such story is told in the first page of the Political Index of the Commonplace Book, under "Republica," where Milton portrays the attempts of Brutus and Cassius, who "felt themselves of spirit to free an nation but consider'd not that the nation was not fit to be free, whilst forgetting thire old justice and fortitude which was made to rule, they became slaves to thire own ambition and luxurie."[73] England's "unfitness," like that of ancient Rome, figures centrally in these concluding reflections. Milton turns in the "Digression" to make an observation essentially repeated in the opening of *The Tenure,* in his words that "none can love liberty heartily, but good men," and that "bad men" (*CPW* 3:190) need tyranny: "libertie hath a sharp and double edge fitt onelie to be handl'd by just and virtuous men, to bad and dissolute it become[s] a mischief . . . good me[n] may enjoy the freedom which they merit and the bad the curb which they need" (*CPW* 5:449).

His conclusion leads to a revealing meditation on the kind of education required for a true revolution. As these words have been misread and are, as Milton writes, "not oft spok'n," they are worth quoting at length:

> For Britain (to speake a truth not oft spok'n) as it is a land fruitful enough of men able to govern justlie & prudently in peace; trusting onelie on thir Mother-witt, as most doo, & consider not that civilitie, prudence, love of the public more then of money or vaine honour are to this soile in a manner outlandish; grow not here but in minds well implanted with solid & elaborate breeding; too impolitic else and too crude, if not headstrong and intractable to the industrie and vertue either of executing or understanding true civil government: Valiant indeed and prosperous to winn a field, but to know the end and reason of winning, unjudicious and unwise, in good or bad success

alike unteachable. For the sunn, which we want ripens witts as well as fruits; and as wine and oyle are imported to us from abroad, so must ripe understanding and many civil virtues bee imported into our minds from forren writings & examples of best ages: wee shall else miscarry still and come short in the attempt of any great enterprise.

Perhaps hearing an echo in these last words of Cassius's line to Brutus about Casca's abilities "in the execution / of any bold or noble enterprise" (*Julius Caesar*, 1.2.300–301), Zera Fink used this passage as an example of Milton's civic humanism; the "foreign writings" intended here are for him either classical or classicist.[74] Milton is more likely referring to the "foreign" works of political thought such as those recorded in his Commonplace Book, which are not classical or particularly classicist—nor does his interest in them pertain to their use or revision of classical thought. These "foreign" writers include the French monarchomachs Hailian, de Thou, and Hotman, and Italian writers such as Guicciardini and Machiavelli—not so much as a classicist, but as a political interpreter of history. Milton's indictment of the English people here is astonishing in both its depth and breadth: this dark view of the national condition must have lingered even as Pride's Purge changed the course of events and Milton threw himself into a vigorous defense of popular sovereignty in *The Tenure of Kings and Magistrates*.

The "Digression" seems in several ways then to provide a ground for Milton to develop his most controversial ideas, those that lead him to support a popular revolt against both the king and the magistrates. It is different from the public treatises in the unrestrained nature of his criticism and analysis, which at times holds a diametrically opposite position to the rhetoric of his printed polemics. This inversion is especially apparent when Milton condemns the British people in the manuscript for not founding a republic in 446, and transforms this into an originary moment of political choice in *The Tenure of Kings and Magistrates*. The historical analysis of the manuscript is also revealingly not concerned, as is *The Tenure of Kings and Magistrates*, with the problem of the theological foundations of sovereignty, which is the subject of the chapter that follows. Milton's rethinking of these foundations in the public polemic took two main forms: a reconsideration of the meaning of Paul's words in Romans 13:4 that the ruler bears not a "sword for naught," and a reconsideration of who the ruler or magistrate is who bears such a sword.

Chapter 5

History and Natural Law in
The Tenure of Kings and Magistrates

He beareth not a sword for nought: but he is the minister of God, to take vengeance
on them that do evil. Wherefore ye must needs obey.

Romans 13

Take this drawn sword, saith [Trajan], to use for me, if I reigne well, if not,
to use against me.

Milton, *The Tenure of Kings and Magistrates*

AT THE end of Marvell's "Horatian Ode upon Cromwell's Return
from Ireland," written in the late spring of 1650, Marvell bids Cromwell to
keep his "sword erect," not only because the gesture has, according to myth,
the power to ward off evil spirits, but also because the sword has become
necessary to maintain the state: "The same arts that did gain / A pow'r must
it maintain."[1] Evocative of the stark realism of Machiavelli, the lines are
often seen to suggest that seventeenth-century England has entered into a
new way of legitimating power, marked by the execution of the king.[2] Milton's *Tenure of Kings and Magistrates,* written on just the other side of this
historical divide, refers nonetheless to the image of the magistrate's "sword"
some fourteen times, and in ways that show that this new political language
may derive as much from the "purge" of Parliament that preceded the execution, when the sword was used as a threat to prune the Long Parliament of
all members who might obstruct the deposition. That Milton's reentry into
the public arena occurred in reaction to Pride's Purge as well as to its consequence helps to explain his tract's remarkable title: not *The Tenure of Kings,*
which would involve only an inquiry into the theory of monarchy, but *The
Tenure of Kings and Magistrates,* which involves as well the bonds of obligation to Parliament—and enormously complicates the argument.

After the protracted political stalemate that had occasioned the "Digression," English political history underwent a tumultuous succession of events

in late 1648 and early 1649: the forceful exclusion by the army of the majority of Parliament (December 6), the decision by the new "Rump" Parliament to put the king on trial a month later (January 6), and the condemnation and execution of the king (January 26–30). The occasion of Pride's Purge and the subsequent decision to put the king on trial brought Milton back into the theater of polemic, with an unforeseen opportunity to make use of his work on history and his extensive notes in the Political Index of the Commonplace Book. While all three events were to some extent conflated in the public eye as having a single objective, culminating in the irrevocable but not inevitable event of the king's death, Pride's Purge was in many ways not only the decisive event transforming England's political body, but also an event that required at least as much justification as the execution itself.[3] For in order for the trial and execution to have in the eyes of contemporaries even a shred of legitimacy, it would need to be conducted by a legitimate constitutional body. In many ways the Purge had every appearance of being a military coup d'état, a political body created merely by the sword: Colonel Thomas Pride with a group of armed soldiers blocked the door to the House of Parliament and excluded or arrested members who were not in favor of deposing the king. As Blair Worden relates, "Of the 470 or so M.P.s qualified to sit at the beginning of December 1648, the purge permanently removed about 270. Temporarily it removed nearly 100 more, who stayed away from Parliament in the weeks between the purge and the king's execution and who returned to join the Rump only in or after February 1649."[4] In short, only about 100 representatives were left at the time of the composition of *The Tenure*. This process of selection and exclusion remains one of the central questions behind the nature and origins of the English Civil War: Was this exclusion, which enabled the deposition, the outcome of two factions of Puritanism, the Independents ousting the Presbyterians? And if the factions could be thus identified, was the split driven by a spirit of godly reformation, or by political motives? If the latter, were the motives entirely contingent—a defensive reaction against Charles I—or were they inflected with political theory, such as republicanism?

David Underdown and Blair Worden, among others, have shown the divisions in Parliament to have been far more complex than a "straightforward outcome of the familiar party division of Presbyterians and Independents."[5] Nor is it possible to say that those remaining in power (or their advocates, such as Milton) were all of one mind: they were not all republican revolutionaries, nor were they all Puritans, nor were the Puritans of the same variety, or from the same economic or educational background. Milton's own advocacy of the Purge derives from an idiosyncratic form of independency, both political and religious. Indeed, it is important to our understanding of Milton's position that he makes every effort at this moment not to identify himself with a particular party. He rarely uses the word "Independent," and never to identify himself. Contrastingly, he frequently uses "Presbyterian" and "Presbyterial," both to identify his opponents' ideas, and to admit a "Presbyterial" element in his own thinking. His first use of the term "Independent" does not in fact appear until *Eikonoklastes,* where it is merely coupled with "Presbyterian" against the monarchy: the royalist "took advantage of Presbyterian and Independent names"; the king "meanes no good to either Independent or Presbyterian."[6] *The Tenure of Kings and Magistrates,* although it bears some remnants of the arguments concerning religious reformation of his early pamphlets, and although it positions itself largely in opposition to political as well as religious Presbyterianism, is first and foremost an argument about justice. While the ideas that inform this argument are partially motivated by a previously cultivated republicanism, the tract is ultimately fixed on defending the legitimacy of these constitutional changes rather than on establishing a new program or structure—such a structure exists, at any rate, in the form of the Rump. Milton's theory of popular sovereignty is not, moreover, arrived at by an appeal to the glorious days of Rome, but through a description of the natural condition of humanity and a comparative analysis of European constitutional history.

The trial began on January 20, and Milton began writing *The Tenure* either during the beginning of the trial or just before it started. As John Shawcross has pointed out, there is some indication early in the tract that the trial may not even have begun, as when Milton writes, "who in particular is a Tyrant cannot be determin'd in a general discours, otherwise then by supposition; his particular charge, and the sufficient proof of it must determin that: which I leave to Magistrates, at least to the uprighter sort of them, and of the people, though in number less by many . . . to judge as they find cause" (*CPW* 3:197).[7] This description of the "Magistrates" as the "uprighter sort of them . . . though in number less by many" refers to the newly purged Rump Parliament rather than to the High Court established by that Parliament to determine the case against Charles. Later in the tract, Milton refers to the trial as already in progress: "the proceedings now in Parlament against the King" (222). The king is not only alive but not yet condemned while the first edition is in process, suggesting a period of composition that spans from about January 16 to January 29, with a publication date a week or at most two later.[8]

What began then as a tract designed to support the legitimacy of Pride's Purge itself as well as the possible execution of the king was ultimately made to serve as defense of an execution that had already taken place. Besides a few hints and indications that the king was still on trial during the tract's composition, its advocacy of the regicide works on both sides of the event, and the Purge required much justification even in the wake of the execution. Sometime around October a second edition appeared with phrases and passages inserted and, as the title page advertised, a rather lengthy series of excerpts or "Testimonies" added at the end. Strangely, the words "now in Parlament against the King" were never removed.

Since England had finally obtained the "libertie, so long desir'd" that Milton had little hope of in the "Digression" (*CPW* 5:441), the tract is instilled with a sense of assured national aspiration rarely equaled in his subsequent work, which is often defensive toward those who regarded the execution of the king as sacrilege. In the midst of the tumult of late 1648 and early 1649, Milton articulates a defiant although rhetorically guarded argument for the legitimacy of popular sovereignty: the legitimacy, in other words, of an extra-parliamentary deposition. This defense ultimately rests on secular formulations, rather than relying on counterarguments drawn from scripture to refute the charge of sacrilege. Revolutionaries may act, Milton insists, "without express warrant from Scripture, to bring indifferently both King and Peasant under the utmost rigor." According to this argument, a private person—and not just Parliament or official magistrates—is entitled "without a special Text or precedent," to "extend with like indifference the civil Sword, to the cutting off without exemption him that capitally offends" (222). This was the sword used to "purge" offending members of Parliament, and ultimately to execute the king.

The "civil Sword" in this argument is one of several images in the tract taken from the most crucial proof text in the theory of divine right, Romans 13, which seems to give the monarch—or, depending on the translation, the magistracy—the exclusive, divinely endowed right to the instrument of justice symbolized by the sword. The king or the magistrate (depending on how Paul is read) "beareth not a sword for nought: but he is the minister of God." For Calvin and some other continental reformers, magistrates, such as Parliament, were endowed with this right, whereas traditional English readings—especially those coming from the Church of England—allowed only the king the exclusive right to God's sword of justice. As Milton's title itself suggests, *The Tenure of Kings and Magistrates* subverts traditional readings of this passage, as its use of *tenure* also ironically subverts the notion that kings and lords hold subjects in a structure of feudal tenure that has its origins in the Norman Conquest. One of the great paradoxes of *The Tenure* is that, in spite of its deconstruction of Romans 13 and other scriptural foundations of sovereignty that run directly counter to Continental and English readings, Milton nonetheless appeals to the political thought of Reformation theologians, advertising his use of the authority of "the best & learnedest Protestant Divines" in the title page to the second edition.

The seeming contradiction makes his argument hard to classify. Not surprisingly, there are about as many different interpretations of the nature of argument in *The Tenure* as there are of Marvell's "Horatian Ode," with similarly polarized readings. Ernest Sirluck, representing one pole, argued that "time and again Milton denies the validity of arguing positive political consequences from scripture."[9] Although this view still has some currency,[10] it seems to have given way in recent years to a view that Milton's radical Puritanism should be equated with theological politics. In *John Milton, Radical Politics, and Biblical Republicanism*, Walter Lim contends that "Milton was significantly indebted to the legacy of radical political thinking bequeathed by the Reformation, fashioning his prophetic identity with an eye focused on certain major Protestant figures." Milton accordingly "sought answers in scripture; such biblical proof-texts as Romans 13:1–2, Deuteronomy 17:14–17, and 1 Samuel 8:7–18 contributed significantly to the formulation and articulation of his republican convictions."[11]

But Milton's use of major Protestant reformers and of these biblical texts is far more ambivalent, reactive, and rhetorical than this assessment suggests. As part of the complex rhetorical strategies of the tract, he invokes the authority of reformers like Calvin when he is fundamentally opposing them. His agile explication of biblical texts is largely in reaction to the use of scripture by others. Milton resumes his public career as a Puritan polemicist, now arguing against a faction of Presbyterians and other Puritans who had it wrong, and who were in a sense no longer really Presbyterian, but, as he wrote, "subprelatical." Like many of his polemics written prior to the four-year hiatus, Milton imagines here a largely Presbyterian, or "Presbyterian and Independent," as he later couples them, audience. Milton's insistence that his Reformation authorities are "Presbyterial" (198) is not merely a concession to his "Adversaries," but to some extent an appeal to a time when there was sufficient common ground, where "our fathers in the faith we hold" (251) spoke a language that, now in this generation, has become so fractured as to threaten the stability of the nation.[12]

One such "father" cited is Thomas Cartwright (248, 249), and it is worth digging a bit below the surface of contemporary polemical culture to illustrate what Cartwright's name would have meant in late 1648 both to Milton and to his contemporaries. Cartwright was the chief voice in the Admonition Controversy of the 1570s, which was the inspiration for the great pamphlet wars of the Martinists and the anti-Martinists, and the first major exchange between Puritans and English Churchmen.[13] His status as an original English Puritan was exploited on two important occasions in the pamphlet wars of the 1640s, both of them in direct opposition to Milton. A posthumous treatise supposedly "found in the study" of Cartwright and given the title *A Directory of Church-government* was issued a few months after *Areopagitica* to support a position of intolerance and persecution. As the longer title goes on to explain, the Presbyterian position of intolerance was "Anciently contended for, and as farre as the Times would suffer, practiced by the first Non-conformists in the daies of Queen Elizabeth." The tract invoked Mosaic Law (Deuteronomy 19) to support persecution, advocating the death penalty for the "Blasphemer" or the "stubborn Idolater."[14] In a tract dated by Thomason January 24, 1648, *Helpes for Discovery of the Truth in Point of Toleration*—that is, supporting intolerance—Cartwright is used again to assert "the force of the Judiciall Lawes of Moses" concerning "the punishment of blasphemy."[15] This pamphlet would serve as part of the propaganda machine behind the Ordinance for the Punishing of Blasphemies and Heresies later that year. The marginal citations backing the pamphlet's severest positions include references to Calvin's *Institutes* and Beza's supposed *De Comburendis Haereticis,* or Concerning the Burning of Heretics, a propagandistic embellishment of Beza's actual title, *De Haereticis a Civili Magistratu Puniendis* or Concerning the Punishment of Heretics by the Civil Magistrate (1554).[16] This embellishment specifying the *burning* of heretics may reflect the fact that Beza's book was a response to Castellio's tolerationist defenses of the anti-Trinitarian Servetus, who was burned at the stake.[17] The fiery title attributed to Beza helps lend legitimacy to the most severe form of punishment used.[18] *Helpes for Discovery of the Truth* declares that "the stubborn Idolater, Blasphemer," as well as the "Murtherer" and "Incestuous person" "should be put to death."[19] Citing Romans 13 as well as Deuteronomy 19, it asserts the necessity of the magistrate's role in putting heretics to death: "the Apostle putteth a sword in the hand of the Magistrate, and in the use of it maketh him a Minister and servant of the vengeance. . . . Now seeing there is a sword in the Magistrates hand, by the doctrine of the Apostles, and that also which the Magistrate must of duty draw; I would gladly know where that necessity of drawing this sword can be found, if it be not in these crimes of Blasphemy, &c. which I have set down?"[20] This passage underscores just how stark a difference Milton would have at that moment with Cartwright, and especially with the ideological use made of him in the Presbyterian campaigns of the 1640s, particularly if, as recent research has suggested, Milton had committed to anti-Trinitarianism.[21] Those who uphold such heresies according to this new law of 1648, with Cartwright's, Calvin's, and Beza's backing, should be put to death. In spite of a degree of sincerity in Milton's appeal in such lines as "our fathers in the faith we hold," then, it is clear that he no longer identifies with those fathers—in fact, he invokes their names not so much to show his agreement with them as to defuse the authoritative use of them by his opponents. This is particularly true with the leading Reformation figure behind Presbyterianism and English Puritanism, John Calvin.

The Title

In his use of the word *Magistrates* in the title and throughout the tract, Milton closely engages Calvin's own adjustment of Romans 13. Calvin had argued at the end of the *Institutes* that deposition was allowable in extreme cases by "magistrates"—as Calvin's *magistratui* was translated by the Elizabethan member of Parliament Thomas Norton, whose translation was still used in the seventeenth century. Following a standard Reformation treatment of Romans 13, Calvin explained that "Paul teacheth that the Magistrate ought to be obeyed, not only for feare of punishment, but for consciences sake."[22] Calvin's use of "magistrate" or "magistratus," rather than "king" or "ruler," adds a distinction not usually found in English readings of Paul, or even in traditional Vulgate and Erasmian readings, which used not *magistratui* but *principes* to translate the Greek word *archontes* (rulers) in a crucial line of Romans 13.[23] As Milton wrote in *The Tenure,* this is the passage of scripture that "they most insist upon" (252), and Milton's use of the two terms in the title derives largely from two different traditions of interpretation and translation. His tract argues that neither of these, *principes* or *magistratui,* deserve an exclusive right over private men as the Protestant tradition has argued, but his elusive method of treating these two elements in the Protestant exegetical tradition—and his confusing way of using one against the other—want closer scrutiny.

The Tenure is in many ways a sustained reading and dismantling of Romans 13. The King James Version, which was designed to replace the Calvinist Geneva Bible, translates this crucial word as "rulers" rather "magistrates":

> Let every soul be subject unto the higher powers. For there is no power but of God: the powers that be are ordained of God. Whosoever therefore resisteth the power, resisteth the ordinance of God: and they that resist shall receive to themselves damnation. For rulers ["magistrates" in the Geneva text] are not a terror to good works, but the evil. Wilt thou then not be afraid of the power? Do that which is good, and thou shalt have praise of the same: For he is the

minister of God to thee for good. But if thou do that which is evil, be afraid; for he beareth not the sword in vain: for he is the minister of God, a revenger to execute wrath upon him that doeth evil. Wherefore ye must needs be subject, not only for wrath, but also for conscience sake.

All early modern English translations used the word "ruler" except, significantly, the popular Geneva Bible—illegal in England from 1616 until the 1640s—which followed Calvin.[24] In the general conception, "ruler" implied *princeps* or monarch rather than high government official. William Tyndale chose "ruler" in the first printed translation, and used it to mean "prince" in his political theory.[25] Popular representations of the passage from such sources as the Homilies, the speeches of Archbishops, the works of King James, or the Shakespearean stage treated the singular pronoun in Paul's "he is the minister of God" as connoting a single monarch, and thus John of Gaunt protests in *Richard II* that he "may never lift / An angry arm against [God's] minister."[26]

In using *magistratus* rather than *princeps,* Calvin's reading of Paul implies that the "magistrates" under the king (such as John of Gaunt) sometimes have the responsibility to take the power bestowed into their hands, and to use the sword against the king.[27] In Norton's translations, the word "Parliament" or "Parliaments" is conspicuously added in the margin, lest the English reader miss the implications of Calvin's words:

> Let Princes hear and bee afraide. . . . For though the correcting of unbridled government bee the revengement of the Lord, let us not by and by thinke that it is committed to us, to whom there is given no other commandement but to obey and suffer. I speake always of private men. For if there bee at this time any Magistrates for the behalfe of the people, (such as in old time were the Ephori, that were set against the kings of Lacedemonia, or the Tribunes of the people, against the Roman Consuls: or the Demarchi, against the Senate of Athens: and the same power also which peradventure, as things are now, the three estates have in every Realme, when they hold their principal assemblies) I doe so not forbid them
>
> **Parliaments**   according to their office to withstand the outraging licentiousnesse of kings: that I affirme that if they winke at kings willfully ranging over and treading downe the poore communalty, their dissembling is not without wicked breach of faith, because they deceitfully betray the liberty of the people, whereof they know themselves to bee appointed protectors by the ordinance of God.[28]

This is the very passage cited in Milton's Commonplace Book in the hand of Lord Preston (CB 195; see figure 2.3), although the argument is categorically not represented in Milton's own notes. He surely he knew it well, as is strongly suggested in *Pro Populo* (see chapter 6, below). Calvin believed that it was the duty of high officers in government to determine whether a king has overstepped his bounds. Contrary to the doctrine of passive obedience imposed on ordinary subjects, it was perfidious for magistrates to allow "the outraging licentiousnesse of kinges." But deposition was never allowable by "private men." When the English Parliament proved unwilling to go forward with the deposition (before Pride's Purge in 1648), it became necessary to devise a new argument legitimating the deposition of both kings and magistrates by an unparliamentary body of citizens. Milton's task in *The Tenure* was to go beyond the tradition of resistance theory in Protestant theology to show that both kings and magistrates are given power by those over whom they hold authority, that the "tenure" given them—ironically borrowing a term from feudalism—is determined by the people. *The Tenure* argues that humans have not only the capacity of choice to establish a governing body over them, but also the inherent right to limit the conditions of such a government. Milton draws from philosophical explanations of the natural conditions of humanity, and from historical realities that corroborate these explanations, to defeat the position upheld by Calvinists and royalists. "No man who knows ought, can be so stupid to deny that all men naturally were borne free," Milton declares. Such freedom gives humanity the ability to "chose [a leader or leaders] above the rest" (*CPW* 3:198–99), and to "limit the authority of whom they chose to govern them" (200). The most detailed example of such political choice occurs in the history of fifth-century Britain, deriving from *The History of Britain* and the "Digression." But one crucial passage from the ancient historian Gildas derives not from this work directly but from an entry in the Commonplace Book, under the heading "Rex." This is the third topic titled "Rex," probably entered in the mid to late 1640s.[29] "Concerning the kings of Britain," he wrote in his notes, "Gildas says that they were anointed as kings but not by God." After the citation, Milton wrote in his own voice, "Contrary to what the people now think, namely, that all kings are the anointed of God" (CB 195, *CPW* 1:474). In *The Tenure,* Milton elaborates on this entry: "If any object that Gildas condemns the Britans for so doing [that is, for overthrowing their king], the answer is as ready; that he condemns them no more for so doing, then hee did before for choosing such, for saith he, *They anointed them Kings, not of God, but such as were more bloody then the rest.* Next hee condemns them not at all for depositing or putting them to death, but for doing it over hastily, without tryal" (221). The authority cited not only bears witness to this history of political choice, but approves the action.

Defending this radical form of popular self-determination would be extremely tricky, and Milton's maneuvers have given rise to a good deal of confusion as to what he meant and how far he meant his theory to go. At one moment Milton seems to be arguing that "it is Lawfull," as he states on the title page, "for any, who have the Power, to call to account a Tyrant, or wicked KING . . . if the ordinary MAGISTRATE have neglected, or deny'd to doe it,"[30] while at others he seems to back away from this argument. The distinction here is between the people (or "any, who have the Power") and the "magistrate," members of a legitimate Parliament. Looking back at the regicide tract in the *Defensio Secunda,* Milton actually backs away from this claim, suggesting that the judges who bore the sword against the king were, in fact, "*Magistratui.*" It "was not my affair," he reflects in this later description of his purpose in writing *The Tenure,* "to determine anything about Charles," but "that of the magistrates" (*CPW* 4:626–27). Even within *The Tenure* itself, Milton confuses the claim of popular sovereignty, and he implies that the deposition must be executed by magistrates. In the passage formerly cited that was written before the trial or in its early stages, Milton writes: "But who in particular is a Tyrant cannot be determin'd in a general discourse, otherwise then by supposition; his particular charge, and the sufficient proof of it must determin that: which I leave to Magistrates, at least to the uprighter sort of them, and," he writes with tellingly convoluted syntax, "of the people, in whom faction least hath prevaild above the Law of nature and right reason, to judge as they find cause" (197). The phrase "of the people" here leaves open several possibilities. Whether it means the "Magistrates of the people," or "the uprighter sort of the people," or "the uprighter sort of the Magistrates" is, I suspect, deliberately uncertain. In the second edition of *The Tenure,* Milton also *seems* to reaffirm the exclusive right of magistrates, in a way that has brought some readers to see a kind of *volte face,* when he writes that the Protestant theological tradition has "generally" held that "to doe justice on a lawless King, is to a privat man unlawful, to an inferior Magistrate lawfull" (257). This statement flatly contradicts his view, promoted on the title page, that "it is Lawfull . . . for any, who have the Power, to call to account a Tyrant."

Milton's ambiguity over the definition of "magistrate" implicitly contradicts his explanation of what compelled him to write *The Tenure,* that he turned to write it when the magistrates were no longer adequately attending to the pursuit of justice. To add to our sense of Milton's rhetorical shiftiness, the *Defensio Secunda* obscures the focus of *The Tenure* in even more fundamental ways. Milton stresses in 1654 that he did not "write or advise anything concerning Charles, but demonstrated what was in general permissible against tyrants" (*CPW* 4:626), a statement which untenably suggests that his treatise may not have been about the actual king, and also that it was tyrants, and not kings, that concerned him. This is patently untrue: he goes so far as to suggest that deposition need not require the proof of tyranny, a classic feature of resistance theory. And though he may not mention Charles by name, it is clear, as when he writes of the futility of preserving "the useless bulke of his person" (197), to whom he refers. While Milton does "adduce not a few testimonies from the foremost theologians [*summorum Theologorum*]" (*CPW* 4:626, *WJM* 134), as he later reflects—including even Calvin—to this purpose, this is "not so much a teaching, as an intangling,"[31] as he is unable to show much theological support for his theory of popular sovereignty. Simply speaking, his central argument on popular sovereignty is not theological.

The Commonplace Book and *The Tenure of Kings and Magistrates*

Milton's reading in political history needs to be taken into account as an essential element in his theory of popular sovereignty. In addition to the extensive historical research into political institutions that he had undertaken since the late 1630s, he had recently been engaged in the large project of *The History of Britain*. In 1649, history offered him the opportunity for which he had unknown to himself been preparing all the while. The king was delivered into the hands of the Rump, so that all the indecision he had been raging about could conceivably be brought to an end—this is the period in which the material that he had accumulated in the Political Index of the Commonplace Book would be fully deployed. In *The Tenure* Milton uses a wide range of historical arguments that utilize the research in the Commonplace Book and extend the work conducted in the "Digression." There are at least twenty-four passages in his notes on the history of political constitutions that are reused in the political tract, with many more conceptual connections. These notes and their extensive reuse reveal a serious investment in the project of sketching out the phenomenon of self-determination in history and applying this synthesized knowledge to the present.

As is also true of Bodin, there is a close relationship in Milton's work between the historical and the natural, between human history and natural history.[32] Milton's historical work devotes itself to the observation of human nature for the purpose of using these facts to gauge the viability of constitutions and constitutional changes. Sometimes his intentions seem to follow the lead of English constitutional historians like Coke or Selden, to use historical facts, although more tentatively, as a way of constructing a legal or moral precedent.

The historical notes collected in the Commonplace Book reappear abundantly here. Almost all the nonbiblical authorities and events cited in the first edition of the tract derive directly from Milton's notes. For the second edition he would go beyond his notes, with an added set of theological authorities which, except for Luther in Johann Sleidan's *Commentaries,* are not in the Commonplace Book. This difference suggests that Milton was composing the first edition very quickly, and could not take the time to search out sources that were not fully treated in his notes. Except for a small handful of sources, Milton needed little more to write the first edition of *The Tenure* than his Commonplace Book and the Bible, although the extensive exegetical arguments derive largely from the pamphlets against which he positioned himself.

Beyond the discrete references, the intellectual preparation for *The Tenure* is evidenced in philosophical entries in the Commonplace Book that do not always reappear in discrete, quantifiable packages. A significant example is the following late entry on "tenures" and feudalism, attributed by Hanford to the period 1644–47, although it could just as well have been entered at a moment closer to the composition of *The Tenure:*

> Tenures of Fief or Feud thought to be brought in by Charles the great Girard. Hist. France Book 4 p[age] 229. although the original seem to be unjust. for that which was conquer'd land ought freely to be divided to the people according to merit, & to hold only by his truth & fidelity to the commonwealth. Wherein doubtles the Roman Agrarian laws are more noble. Hence that Historian confesses p[age] 232. that they who hold in fief, are in a manner servants. (CB 183, *CPW* 1:450)

Here Milton is engaging a method of political historiography popular among English constitutional thinkers who sought to ascertain the origins of feudal tenure.[33] It was generally thought that feudalism came to England with William the Conqueror, and that the feudal aspects of the English monarchical constitution hold citizens in the less "noble" condition of servitude. The history of feudalism becomes the controlling metaphor for *The Tenure,* in which Milton retraced much of the constitutional history that he sees in historical conflict with feudalism, in order to suggest it is kings and magistrates that are held in their tenure by the people.

In addition to the broader conceptual connections between the notebook and the tract, there are in *The Tenure* a remarkable number of specific citations taken directly from the Commonplace Book. There are merely five authorities cited in the first edition of *The Tenure* who do not appear in the Commonplace Book: Euripides (who frequently appears in Milton's prose),[34] Dio Cassius (for the well-known story about Trajan cited among this chapter's epigraphs), Livy, Seneca (in a passage frequently used in revolutionary pamphlets; see *CPW* 3:213n84), and Knox; three additional references derive from other portions of works cited in the Commonplace Book: Justinian, John Chrysostom, and Buchanan. The rest, thirteen named authorities and at least twelve precise historical examples, come directly from Milton's notes that derive from the previous decade of research.[35]

Early in the tract, after the philosophical disquisition on the rights of citizens according to the law of self-preservation, Milton turned to support this by invoking examples from European history. At this point he pulled out his Commonplace Book, and drew from an entry from the French historian Claude de Seissel, whose instance from French royal history was entered, perhaps mistakenly, under the topic "The King of England &C" (CB 186, *CPW* 1:458). "Therefore saith *Claudius Sesell* a French Statesman," Milton wrote in *The Tenure* (having probably scanned through the other entries under the topic on the same page in the Commonplace Book), "*The Parliament was set as a bridle to the King;* which I instance rather, because that Monarchy is granted by all to be a farr more absolute then ours."[36] Seemingly out of an accident—that he had set this French example among the problems of English kings and Parliaments in his Commonplace Book—Milton created his first cited authority in *The Tenure*. He may have wondered himself why he "instanced" this among entries on English kings, and came up with the justification for his audience. The example from a French historian gives rise to an important series of examples based on historical precedent. He continues: "That this and the rest of what hath hitherto been spok'n"—that is, the history of constitutions after the Fall, showing that "men were naturally born free" (198)—"is most true, might be copiously made to appear throughout all Stories Heathen and Christian; ev'n those Nations where Kings and Emperours have sought meanes to abolish all ancient memory of the Peoples right by thir encroachments and usurpations. But I spare long insertions, appealing to the German, French, Italian, Arragonian, English, and not least the Scottish Histories" (*CPW* 3:201). Each of these foundational histories—even the Aragonian, in a passage from Guicciardini (*CPW* 1:442, CB 182)—is enumerated in the Commonplace Book; indeed, it has been the goal of the notebook to compile such a history. Milton does not, in fact, get to all of these in *The Tenure,* but it seems by the close correspondence that he had hoped to. The fact that he had not managed to get to the "Arragonian" constitutionalism suggests he had meant to transcribe more from his notes than he does, and it points again to a hasty process of composition. Conspicuously missing from this list are the ancient constitutions of Rome, Athens, or even Israel. At the end of this list, Milton appends a bit of information, derived from an entry from Holinshed in the Commonplace Book, although not citing his English source: "not forgetting this onely by the way, that William the Norman though a Conqueror, and not unsworn at his Coronation, was compell'd the second time to take oath at S. Albanes, ere the people would be brought to obedience" (201; *CPW* 1:427, CB 179). The legal basis for monarchies was a focus of the Commonplace Book, and it is a central point of return when Milton composes *The Tenure*.

The close relation of the regicide tract to the notebook—even to where the order of entries in the notes dictates the order and logic of the tract—is evident in the use of Peter Martyr, who is one of the two cited theologians in the first edition of *The Tenure*. The oddity of this choice is explained by the process. Probably in 1644, Milton wrote under the topic "The Tyrant": "Peter Martyr, in c[hapter] 3. Jud. says: 'To those who select an officer of higher rank according to certain laws of the commonwealth which authorize them to place him in command, as the Electors of the Empire do today, it is permitted, if the officer should not adhere to his agreements and promises, to reduce him in rank and even compel him by force to satisfy the conditions and agreements which he had promised, and they may do so by arms if it cannot be done otherwise'" (CB 185, *CPW* 1:453–54). In *The Tenure,* Milton followed a statement on Richard II, which actually derives from an entry above that on Peter Martyr in the Commonplace Book, with a citation to Peter Martyr—in other words, he simply follows the order of entries in his notes in *The Tenure,* although here adding a connection between the two entries that does not exist in the notes: "Insomuch that the Parlament drew up a charge against Richard the Second, and the Commons requested to have judgement decree'd against him, that the realm might not bee endangerd. And Peter Martyr a Divine of formost rank, on the third of Judges approves thir doings" (*CPW* 3:221).

There are two aspects of this evidence in particular that reveal Milton as having been engaged in the central ideas of his regicide tract for a long time: the notebook's commitment to the limitations of kingly power, and its commitment to the right of popular choice. In both cases, though, the information in the notes is reconstructed in the composition process of *The Tenure*. Milton goes to particular length to affirm an argument concerning popular choice, as in his transformation of an entry written in the Commonplace Book prior to 1639: "Sulpicius Severus says that the name of kings has always been hateful to free peoples, and he condemns the actions of the Hebrews in choosing to exchange their freedom for servitude" (CB 182, *CPW* 1:440). In the regicide tract Milton rewrites this: "The Jews also, especially since the time they chose a King against the advice and counsel of God, are noted by wise Authors [i.e., Severus] much inclinable to slavery" (*CPW* 3:202–3). The change in wording is significant: in the private notebook, the Jews "choose to exchange their freedom for servitude"; here, they "chose a King." The earlier wording contains a more explicitly republican sentiment, as it suggests that freedom is by definition nonmonarchical and servitude is equated with the choice of a king. Yet, as is distinctly the case with similar passages rewritten from the "Digression," Milton seems to be damping down the republican sentiment in his manuscript work in order not to risk what is still a more crucial argument in 1649, the right and capacity of political choice: they have the right to chose *not* to have this king—what they establish in his place is another issue.

In addition to Severus and others, Milton pursues the right of choice from more modern historical examples. In an entry in the Commonplace Book attributed to the mid to late 1640s, he cites de Thou's account of when "the Estates General of Holland take away Philip's power, in a treatise, moreover, published at The Hague, and the provinces are commanded to disclaim obedience to him" (CB 183, *CPW* 1:445). This passage is reused in *The Tenure,* which cites the same spot in de Thou, but Milton returns to the source to provide a more detailed account: in "the yeare 1581," he writes, "a general assembly at the *Hague,* abjur'd all obedience and subject onto *Philip* King of *Spaine;* and in a Declaration justifie thir so doing; for that by his tyrannous government against faith so many times giv'n & brok'n he had lost his right to all the Belgic Provinces; that they therefore depos'd him and declar'd it lawful *to choose another* [emphasis added] in his stead. *Thuan.* 1. 74" (226–27). Again, the concept of choice is added to the evidence; if the Dutch "disclaim obedience" to Philip of Spain, then they are enabling political choice; to say that they "depos'd" the ruler of another country who would not lose his life in the act, is, of course, very different from the deposition enacted upon Charles. Milton ends this citation with an admonition to the Dutch, who, having prospered from their own freedom more than any "State or Kingdom in the world," should not now look toward England "with an evil and prejudicial eye" for "walking by the same rule" (227)—the republicanism is present, but subtle.

The notes that did not make it into print are revealing in their absence. Milton carefully avoided the many explicitly republican notes. The regicide tract would have read very differently had he invoked the spirit of the "noble Brutus and Cassius," who existed in a Rome "ripe for a more free government then monarchy," or if he had cited Machiavelli and argued that "more excellent men come from a commonwealth than from a monarchy" (*CPW* 1:420–21, CB 177). The tract would read considerably differently had he voiced the proposition written by a close scribe in his notes that "it is permissible to kill him," a question answered by Machiavelli's contention that for the ills of the prince "the sword is necessary."

Secularizing the Sword

The image of the sword at the center of political rule had an increasingly pervasive presence in English political discourse just prior to the composition of "An Horatian Ode." It appears more frequently in Milton's two tracts of the previous year, *The Tenure of Kings and Magistrates* and *Eikonoklastes*, than in the combined total of all his other English prose tracts.[37] Although the "naked sword," as Pocock calls it, is suggestive of barefaced power, its extensive presence in English discourse of the period derives from a biblical image with a long history in theological politics. These are St. Paul's startling words in Romans 13, that the magistrate "beareth not a sword for nought: but is the minister of God," in which Paul reinforces the terms of obedience and the divine right of those in power. While this sword had a constant presence in Protestant biblical imagery—appearing in the monarchs' hands in the title pages of English Bibles and in other works—in the years 1648–1650 it became a central feature in debates over the nature of political legitimacy. Attuned to this contemporary discourse, Milton uses the sword among other terms from the biblical language of the Presbyterians to deconstruct the old theological method of legitimating power.

Historians of political thought have long understood the moment of Charles's execution and the "de facto controversy" or "engagement controversy" that ensued to be a radical turning point in the history of English politics.[38] The engagement controversy is so named for a couple of contracts that the new government sought to impose, first on February 13, 1649, when an "engagement" was submitted to be signed by every member of the Council of State "approving all that was done concerning the king and kingship, and for the taking away of the House of Lords."[39] This had the ominous refusal rate of 50 percent: twenty-two of forty-one members refused to sign.[40] More official resolutions followed in October 1649, and again in January 1650, calling for an official commitment to the new government's legitimacy: "I do declare and promise that I will be true and faithful to the Commonwealth of England, as the same is now Established, without king or House of Lords." As Pocock writes,

The "Engagement Controversy" or the "de facto controversy" . . . came about when the regicide regime set out to impose an 'engagement' to do nothing against it. There ensued debate on how far the injunction of Romans 13, 'let every soul be subject to the higher power, . . .' obligated the conscience to obedience when the powers that be exercised authority *de facto* and not *de jure*. In this setting there was no point in debating the antiquity of the government, since to discuss what was ancient was by definition to discuss what was *de jure*. The factum which set up a regime with no legal title was necessarily modern, the deed of a *principe nuovo* or a naked sword. . . . They postulated an individual in this 'state of nature' and inquired what there was in his state of nature which might oblige him to obey a government, even if (given the state of nature) he had to constitute it in order to obey it.[41]

This historical shift is suggested in the genres and contents of the printed tracts in these years. In his careful analysis of print history, Amos Tubb shows that sermons, once the "most effective tools in print, were neutered by the regicide," and that "theological arguments [became] implicit rather than explicit after the king's death."[42] *The Tenure* plays an intriguing early role in the development of this new discourse, since it essentially straddles the execution, with the first edition written with the "proceedings now in Parliament against the King" (222), and with some—the eighteen pages of added material that appeared in the second edition—written after the execution. Contrary to the timeline Pocock has set up, it is in the first edition, prior to the execution, that Milton replaces Romans 13 with a state of nature and a historical argument; the second edition attempts ostensibly to add theological justification.

Prior to the turning point in late 1648, the symbol of the sword in political thought has an almost exclusively biblical orientation, as it derives from Romans 13:1–8. Although the precise words "sword of justice" seem to have had little use before the late 1630s, when they suddenly had considerable circulation, the concept was much alive in the sixteenth century, particularly in Protestant royal iconography, where it appears prominently in English Bibles. An allegorical figure called "Justice" bears a sword on the right of Queen Elizabeth's portrait on the title page of the Bishops' Bible, for example.[43] Elizabeth's iconography followed that of Henry VIII, who asserted his role as the theocratic head of the church with a portrait by Holbein in the Coverdale Bible.[44] Later writers continue to assert the special God-given right over mortality symbolized by the sword: "We read of a threefold Sword in Scripture," writes one sermonizer in 1660: "1. The Sword of the Spirit, which is the Word of God, Ephes. 6.17. 2. The Sword of Justice, which is the Magistrates Sword, Rom. 13.4[.] 3. The Sword of Steel, usually so called, which is the

Sword of slaughter, Isa. 1.20. Ezek. 9.1,2 . . . as for the Sword of Justice, or the Magistrates Sword, we are to be subject to it, as we have fully declared, and not resist it."[45] In an address to Cromwell, George Fox wrote, "To thee Oliver Cromwell into whose hands God hath committed the sword of Justice."[46] The same iconography in Tudor biblical representations informs the engraving of Cromwell by William Faithorne, himself a printer of royal portraits,[47] in which Cromwell bears the sword in his right hand and, like the Tudor monarchs, a book in his left, with his feet crushing the whore of Babylon—a picture influenced by the Reformation iconography from Foxe's *Acts and Monuments,* in which Henry is holding the sword and book and crushing the pope under his feet.[48] Marvell likely had the sword of justice in mind when he bids Cromwell to keep his "sword erect," although Marvell's point is that this sword is divested of divine power.

Romans 13 was particularly central to arguments made by the majority of Presbyterians before and during the trial of King Charles.[49] For them, as for the majority in Commons before Pride's Purge, the outcome of the revolution should have been to negotiate with and reinstate the vanquished king. According to Reformation theology, an anointed king cannot be tried or executed, particularly by members of an illegitimate purged Parliament. To do so was to go against the commands of God established in such verses as Psalms 105 ("Touch not the lords anointed"), 1 Samuel 24:10–26:11 (when David spares Saul's life because he was the "Lord's anointed"), and Romans 13. Milton's task in *The Tenure* was to challenge his contemporaries' reading of these scripturally based arguments, and to show the hypocrisy in the use of these passages by those who label the king "the Lords anointed, not to be touch'd, though by themselves imprison'd" (197). At the same time, he strives to show that there are scriptural precedents for private men rising to resist tyrants, such as Ehud's revolt against King Eglon (Judges 3:13–26) and Jehu's slaying of Jehoram (2 Kings 9:1–2). But, as Martin Dzelzainis shows in his analysis of this tract, Milton uses biblical precedent only to offer different, less literalistic hermeneutics, as if he is more interested in showing the limitations of the strictly scripture-based argumentation than in countering scripture with scripture. Jehu's actions in slaying "a successive and hereditary tyrant," Milton argues, are "grounded so much on natural reason," that the "*addition* of a command from God" only helps to "establish the lawfulness of such an act" (*CPW* 3:216, emphasis added). Like the endorsement of reason found in *Areopagitica* and the divorce tracts, this tract presents scripture not as the source for moral law, but as the confirmation of laws that are produced by "natural reason."[50]

The level of defiance toward biblical precedent is at times surprising, given both the audience and the tract's dependence on biblical language. In

making a case for the right of a commonwealth to depose a king, in lines
that derive from entries in the Commonplace Book, Milton asserts that because a "King or Magistrate holds his authoritie of the people, both originaly
and naturally for their good in the first place, and not his own, then may the
people as oft as they shall judge it for the best, either choose him or reject
him, retaine him or depose him though no Tyrant, meerly by the liberty and
right of free born Men." This argument, he goes on to say, can stand by reason alone, without the backing of scripture: "This, though it cannot but
stand with plain reason, shall be made good also with Scripture" (206). Milton's phrasing suggests a demotion of scripture in this context: plain reason
is sufficient in letting an argument stand. Scripture in this instance merely
persuades readers who are uncomfortable with reason alone, and it confirms
rather than dictates what has already been arrived at through reason.

The scripture Milton uses to confirm regime change by the people also
suggests freedom of choice. Milton asserts that the right "to choose or reject"
a magistrate "though no tyrant" is confirmed by a biblical line: the phrase
from Deuteronomy 17:14, "I will set a King over me," which "*confirme* us that
the right of choosing, yea of changing thir own Government is by the grant
of God himself in the People" (*CPW* 3:206–7, emphasis added). This passage
was singled out by Milton's contemporary reader Sir Robert Filmer, who attacked his use of scripture. Filmer argued that "the [biblical] text not war-
ranting this right of the people," the very "foundation of [Milton's] defense
of the people is quite taken away—there being no other grant or proof of
it pretended."[51] For Filmer, Milton's fallacious attempt to find a scriptural
proof to indicate popular choice is enough to debunk the very "foundation"
of his "defense of the people." Yet for Milton this is hardly the foundation of
his argument, but merely an "addition," a supplement to an argument for
which he had given ample instances in secular history and constructed from
reason. Indeed, this addition is really meant as a rhetorical deconstruction
of his opponents' methods—such as Filmer's—and not as a foundation in any
sense. Filmer's method—and even his "proof"—consists of finding in scripture a prescriptive decree.

Milton's method differs sharply from Filmer's, as does the theory created
by this method. Milton's view of the necessity of political choice runs counter to Protestant political theology, which had drawn deep connections
between a predestined universe and the arbitrary right of sovereignty.[52] Although Calvin may grant an exception to magistrates, for subjects, and even
for magistrates—who must be enacting God's will when they depose a
tyrant—the "wicked ruler" is "a judgment of God," and even "obedience to
bad kings" is "required in scripture."[53] Calvin's theology enables deposition

through the actions of a certain social group, the "magistracy," but even they do not act by their own freedom of will. Magistrates may be "sent by God's lawful calling to carry out such acts, of taking up arms against kings," but, "though directed by God's hand whither he pleased, and executed his work unwittingly, yet planned in their minds to do nothing but an evil act" (1517). To have authority solely from God means that God, and not the people, chooses who rules. For the most part, a bad king is simply God's punishment. "When we hear that a king has been ordained by God," counsels Calvin, "let us at once call to mind those heavenly edicts with regard to honoring and fearing a king; then we shall not hesitate to hold a most wicked tyrant in the place where the Lord has deigned to set him" (1513).

Milton's theory of natural freedom, that "men were naturally born free," as they are the "image and resemblance of God" (198) as he writes later in the tract, is a radical break from Reformation theology, although it is one increasingly made by revolutionaries. In the Putney Debates of late October 1647, for example, the Leveller sympathizer Maximilian Petty declared, "I judge every man is naturally free," which gives men among other things the power to choose representatives.[54] Milton's idea of this freedom stemming from the image of a free God is a subtle insertion of anti-Calvinism—far from "Orthodoxal," as Milton claims of his authorities early in the tract. Objections to such a theology were raised by Filmer. At the beginning of *Patriarcha,* he argues against the mistaken idea that "mankind is naturally endowed and born with freedom from all subjection, and at liberty to choose what form of government it please"—those who espouse such a position, he writes, never remember that "the desire of liberty was the cause of the fall of Adam,"[55] a liberty, as mainstream Protestants believed, that Adam lost after the fall.

Milton's frustration with King David's words in Psalm 51 reveal impatience with the politically oriented hermeneutics of his contemporaries. After a short struggle with a royalist interpretation of the Psalm, he concludes, "*Whatever* his meaning were, any wise man will see that the pathetical words of a Psalme can be no certain decision to a poynt that hath *abundantly more certain rules* to goe by" (205, emphasis added). The surprising tone helps set in relief Milton's own hermeneutics: the psalm is "pathetical," able to evoke pathos, emotion, pity (like the execution itself). The pathetical words, like the "unmaskuline Rhetorick" of a "puling Priest or Chaplain" (*CPW* 3:195), persuade through pathos rather than by "more certain" and presumably more rational "rules" that should elicit assent.

What does Milton hope to accomplish in this break away from his opponents' methodology, when, as he says, his position can "be made good also with scripture"? Part of the explanation seems to lie in an attempt to scuttle the Presbyterian and prelatical arguments on their own biblical terms, and then to scuttle the methodology entirely, allowing him to refute not just their claims, but the hermeneutic assumptions—and assumptions in thinking—that created these claims. Another explanation for Milton's extra-scriptural argument is that he sought independence from the methods presented by his opponents, and independence from what was needed to gain rhetorical victory. The appeal to "natural reason" is an appeal to a philosophical explanation that supersedes what is—in the case of his opponents' use of psalms, at least—not true theology but "unmasculine Rhetorick." This is one of the few moments where Milton registers the kind of distain for rhetoric typified by the new philosophy of Hobbes; "rhetoric" here has the connotation of being merely empty words, capable of persuasion but not of conveying the truth.

Milton's approach to Romans 13 in *The Tenure of Kings and Magistrates* represents a powerful break from the Calvinist hermeneutic tradition. He begins by subtly dismantling a biblical text and then turns to provide an argument based on natural law. Before any biblical interpretation occurs, Milton renders the conventional approaches to Romans 13 untenable while structuring a new argument according to the "Law of Nature and right reason" (*CPW* 3:197). The sword of Justice functions as a controlling metaphor of the text. Milton begins by challenging the Presbyterians: "On a sudden and in a new garbe of Allegiance, which thir doings have long since cancell'd; they plead for him, pity him, extoll him, protest against those that talk of bringing him to tryal of Justice, which is the Sword of God, superior to all mortal things, in whose hand soever by apparent signs his testified will is put to it" (193). Before reinterpreting Romans 13 directly, Milton here begins to drive a wedge between the anointed king and the sword—which belongs to God, not the civil magistrate—and, as he goes on to suggest, Paul's "magistrate," or the recipient of the sword of justice, may be a private citizen. The "pity" that has resulted from the prospect of a captured and executed king seems to Milton to have taken on the trappings of a kind of false Christianity—an affective piety, swayed by icons and by "pathetical Psalms": "But certainly if we consider who and what they are, on a suddain grown so pitifull, wee may conclude, thir pitty can be no true, and Christian commiseration, but either levitie and shallowness of minde, or else a carnal admiring of that worldly pomp and greatness" (193).

Unlike many of the biblical citations in the text, Milton's complex reconsideration of Paul's supposed doctrine of passive obedience employs allusion without any indication of source. Scripture in this case clearly has a different function in his argument, and is also perhaps designed for a more subtle reader.

"Be he King, or Tyrant, or Emperour, the Sword of Justice is above him," he asserts, again dismissing the necessity of determining the question of king or tyrant. "For if all human power to execute, not accidentally but intendedly, the wrath of God upon evil doers without exception, be of God; then that power, whether ordinary, or if that faile, extraordinary so executing that intent of God, is lawfull, and *not to be resisted*" (197–98, emphasis added). Milton has managed here to turn the line crucial to divine-right absolutism—"They that resist, shall receive to themselves damnation"—into an almost comic insistence on the irresistibility of revolution. It is unlawful, Milton goes so far to suggest, in an ironic twist of conventional exegesis, to resist the just course of action: the private man is "not to be resisted" when he overthrows both kings and magistrates. Rather than explicating a biblical verse in a top-down fashion, Milton allows himself to rethink the biblical texts by weaving them loosely into his own construction: although Paul says that the magistrate bears not the sword for naught, reason tells us that the sword *precedes* the magistrate—a sword given by God to the righteous bearer of power, whoever that is. Paul's line that all power comes from God must apply to any human being that rightly embraces that power, and therefore his words about resistance in 13:2 may not apply to the magistrate, but to the rightful wielder of that sword, whose resistance to unworthy rule should not be resisted. It is a complete reversal of the standard reading.

The reworking of the language of Romans 13 has the additional effect of destabilizing scriptural certainty. Milton directly approaches the same passage later in the treatise, and offers yet another unconventional reading. When he finally approaches Romans 13 explicitly, by quoting it, he has already engaged its concepts and terms, and, at least for the more discerning reader, offered a new reading. The use of the quoted text almost seems directed toward another audience: "*There is no power but of God,* saith *Paul, Rom.* 13. As much as to say God put it into man's heart to find out that way at first for common peace and preservation, approving the exercise thereof; els it contradicts *Peter* who calls the same authority on Ordinance of man" (209–10). The chronology implied by "at first for common peace" seems to suggest "first" in the historical sense, when Paul preached to the early Christians in Neronian Rome, and thus Paul's preaching "for peace and preservation" was meant to keep the early church alive in its infancy under pagan rule. This is a historicist approach to Romans 13 used by pre-Reformation humanists but rarely by English Protestants.[56] Milton also brings another verse to contradict the verse at hand, 1 Peter 2:13, which, Milton writes, calls "it an ordinance of man." The line in Peter is "submit yourselves to every ordinance of man for the Lord's sake."

Milton follows his initial subversion of the unquoted lines from Romans with an extraordinary defense of the sword of justice in the hands of a private citizen:

> No man who knows ought, can be so stupid to deny that all men naturally were borne free, being the image and resemblance of God himself, and were, by privilege above all the creatures, born to command and not to obey: and that they liv'd so. Till from the root of *Adams* transgression, falling among themselves to doe wrong and violence, and foreseeing that such courses must needs tend to the destruction of them all, they agreed by common league to bind each other from mutual injury and joyntly to defend themselves against any that gave disturbance or opposition to such agreement. Hence came Cities, Townes and Common-wealths. (198–99)

Moving beyond the stunning reversal of the Pauline lines "not to resist" in his argument that the revolutionaries are "not to be resisted" (198), Milton flatly negates the Pauline doctrine of obedience. He answers Paul's injunction "ye must needs obey" with a dismissive correction: we were "born to command and not to obey." This is in direct contradiction to Calvin's argument quoted earlier, in which Calvin writes that the Lord has given "no other commandement but to obey and suffer." Milton's statement employs one biblical line to negate another—God's commandment that humans had dominion over the earth in Genesis 1:26 supersedes the doctrine of passive obedience in Romans 13:5.

Having invalidated the central biblical text on which early modern authority constructed itself, Milton proceeds in this passage to build an argument on purely nonbiblical terms:

> And because no faith in all was found sufficiently binding, they [i.e., these early humans] saw it needful to ordaine som authoritie, that might restrain by force and punishment what was violated against peace and common right. This authority and power of self-defense and preservation being originally and naturally in every one of them, and unitedly in them all, for ease, for order, and least [i.e., lest] each man should be his own partial Judge, they communicated and derived either to one, whom for eminence of his wisdom and integritie they chose above the rest, or to more than one whom they thought of equal deserving: the first was call'd a King; the other Magistrates . . . to execute, by vertue of thir intrusted power, that justice which else every man by the bond of nature and of Cov'nant must have executed for himself, and for one another. And to him that shall consider well why among free Persons, one man by civil right should beare autority and jurisdiction over another, *no other end or reason* can be imaginable. (199, emphasis added.)

After the loose allusions to Genesis and Romans, not a single biblical line has entered this argument, and by the exclusive words at the end, no line imaginable could challenge these reasons for civil right, certainly not Paul's words that we "must be subject, not because of wrath only, but for conscience sake." Dzelzainis observes that "Milton here committed himself to the view—without precedent in any vernacular work of political theory—that, in a state of nature, each and every individual can punish offenders against the law of nature, and that, in executing justice, the civil magistrate was exercising no new right but one which had initially been possessed by all pre-political individuals. He thus joined Grotius in flouting the orthodox view that the sword of justice belonged exclusively to the sovereign body."[57] There is one significant vernacular precedent to Milton's theory, Hobbes's *Elements of Law,* which circulated in 1640 in manuscript and was published in 1650. Although Hobbes's manuscript appears to have had considerable circulation, a direct influence seems unlikely. Yet the similarity to Milton is striking: even the essential words in the English texts—"sword of justice," "self-preservation," "covenant," "security"—are pervasive in both. But the point is not a question of influence, but of type: Milton has used the natural law of self-preservation to refute the Presbyterian and English Church arguments for sovereignty based on biblical precedent. This theory of natural justice has a distinct parallel in the historical and anthropological description of the "primitive" Britons, in that it is an effort to retell the story of an original human settlement, bound by necessity of nature rather than any custom or prescriptive tradition, in forming a political bond.

Hobbes first makes the argument for self-preservation in the same terms as Milton, even using the image of the sword to illustrate the transfer of the power of the sword from each individual in a state of nature to the sovereign. One major difference—suggesting that Milton is in an oppositional dialogue with the monarchist natural law theorists—is that Hobbes does not readily allow for this transferred power to be revoked. As in Milton's account, the sword is conferred on the sovereign by the people, and not by God through a special exclusive relationship. "It followeth therefore, that no man in any commonwealth whatsoever hath right to resist him, or them, on whom they have conferred this power coercive, or (as men call it) the sword of justice."[58] With the words "right to resist him," Hobbes subtly interweaves the words from Romans 13, which he then begins to reaffirm after having demonstrated the point through natural law: "Now seeing that everyman hath already transferred the use of his strength to him or them, that have the sword of justice; it followeth that the power of defence, that is to say the sword of war, be in the same hands wherein is the sword of justice: and consequently those two swords are but one, and that inseparably and essentially annexed to the sovereign power."[59] This is, of course, what Marvell poignantly suggests, that the sword of war is the same sword that "must maintain" the state.

Milton employs toward the end of the tract a Presbyterian who in 1643 himself made a powerful case against the royalist appeal to natural law. Herbert Palmer's *Scripture and Reason Pleaded for Defensive Armes* (1643) argued for the legitimacy of taking up arms against the king using both scripture and rational explanations. Palmer was an interesting choice for Milton from many standpoints, one being that his ties to Presbyterianism may be suspect; he seems to have sided with the Presbyterians late in his church career as much for political reasons as religious, and thus might be termed, as Underdown defines the category, "Presbyterian or covert Episcopalian."[60] Palmer's book had been "ordered [to be printed] by the Committee of the House of Commons in Parliament,"[61] and it had made an impact on Milton's thinking since 1643, when he had attacked *The Doctrine and Discipline of Divorce*. Palmer had preached to Parliament against his divorce pamphlet in a sermon that was then ordered to be published,[62] and in the introduction to *Tetrachordon* Milton upbraided him for his hypocrisy, for Palmer sought himself to "make good the same opinion which I there maintain, by inevitable consequences drawn parallel from his own principal arguments in that of *Scripture and Reason;* which I shall pardon him, if he can deny, without shaking his own composition to peeces" (*CPW* 2:582).

Though Milton knew that Palmer was the author of *Scripture and Reason,* since he referred to him as such in 1645, he chooses in *The Tenure* to refer to the book as "published by divers reverend and learned divines," its own self-advertisement. Milton's repudiation was added in the second edition, at the end of the treatise, following his engagement with the sixteenth-century theologians. Significantly, the passage contains one of the strongest arguments vindicating the right of private men to take arms against a king. "They tell us that the Law of nature justifies any man to defend himself, eev'n against the King in Person: let them shew us then why the same Law, may not justifie much more a State or whole people, to doe justice upon him, against whom each privat man may lawfully defend himself; seing all kind of justice don, is a defence to good men, as well as a punishment to bad; and justice done upon a Tyrant is no more but the necessary self-defence of a whole Common wealth" (254). These reasons follow one another, Milton writes, "as certainly and unavoydably . . . as any Probleme that ever Euclid, or Apollonius made good by demonstration" (253). It is interesting that he uses the geometric standards of Euclid as an example, as he does earlier in

Tetrachordon (*CPW* 2:618), since it is Hobbes who notably made the explicit assertion that politics could be as demonstrable as the geometry of Euclid in his *Elements of Law*. If there is an influence of Hobbes, it is most probably indirect—through parliamentary writers who might have seen *The Elements of Law* in manuscript. Regardless of the source, it is significant that Milton was keen to emulate such an objective in his own writing.

The Text's Two Editions: Negotiating the Complex Audience

If Milton needed little more to write the first edition of *The Tenure* than his Commonplace Book and a Bible keyed to contemporary pamphlets, for the second, expanded edition, he needed a handful of theological sources. The expanded edition of *The Tenure* appeared at some point between March and October 1649.[63] The essential difference between the two versions is the addition of passages from theologians at the end of the new edition. These added sections have been seen to complicate the radical claims of the early edition. Go Togashi has argued that Milton wavers almost incoherently over who is entitled to depose a government. He posits that the added theological section, which also seems to affirm a different right of sovereignty—Calvin's exclusive right given to magistrates—responds to the changing conditions in the preceding months.[64]

A change in circumstances in the months between the editions may explain some differences, yet it should be remembered that Milton makes the same ambiguous suggestion of the special authority of magistrates in the first edition, when he writes, speaking about the actual judgment against the king, "I leave [it] to the Magistrates, at least to the uprighter sort of them" (197), and yet at the same time asserts the right of "each privat man" to "lawfully defend himself," and "do justice upon him" (254) in a key passage added to the second edition—a passage that does not indicate any retreat from the tract's extreme view of popular sovereignty. There are other radical additions to the second edition, such as the wonderful chiastic rebuttal of his contemporaries: "Though perhaps till now no protestant State or kingdom can be alleg'd to have op'nly put to death their King, which lately some have writt'n, and imputed to their great glory; much mistaking the matter. It is not, neither ought to be the glory of a Protestant State, never to have put thir King to death; It is the glory of a Protestant King never to have deserv'd death" (237). These added words likely respond to Prynne's *A Brief Memento*, which admonishes that "no Protestant Kingdome or State ever yet defiled their hands" with "the deposition, or blood of any of their Kings or Princes."[65] Milton's response is one of the occasions where he subverts his own argument that there were precedents for England's move; in fact, he seems to admit, there is no precedent. Even in the first edition, he continued: "And if the Parlament and Miltitary Councel doe what they doe without precedent, if it appeare thir duty, it argues the more wisdom, vertue, and magnamity, that they know themselves able to be a precedent to others" (237).

Although the apparent support of the theologians' position seems to contradict Milton's claim of the people's right, it is, after all, the theologians' position, which he had promised in the first edition but never got around to, probably primarily because of his haste to publish. The language of his promise in the first edition—exaggerated, even disingenuous—reveals some of the qualities of Milton's staged public persona, which is bent on speaking the language of his adversaries, perhaps even with an ironic appropriation of their terms. He boasts that he will support his argument "by authorities and reasons, not learnt in corners among Scisms and Heresies, as our doubling Divines are ready to calumniat, but fetch't out of the midst of choicest and most authentic learning, and no prohibited Authors, nor many Heathen but Mosaical, Christian, Orthodoxal, and which must needs be more convincing to our Adversaries, Presbyterial" (198). This is a suspicious promise, with its expressed regard for those who brand others heretic and prohibit authors; for those, that is, whom he parodies in *Areopagitica* for their frenetic concern with the "fantastic terrors of sect and schism." In the eyes of his contemporaries he is far from "orthodoxal." He does not fulfill this promise. The first edition does not represent the high proportion of theological argument suggested here; in fact, there are few such authorities, save for a brief mention of Knox and Peter Martyr (a Commonplace Book author), whereas there are quite a few "heathen"—as well as barbarian—authorities drawn from his research in history.

The fact that Milton needs to advertise the addition of "Protestant Divines" in the title page of the second edition suggests that he is conscious of this omission. The addition of such authorities as Luther, Calvin, Zwingli, and Bucer in the second edition help him support a claim that lesser magistrates (and not private men) may depose a king, which he openly asserts as if this had little bearing on his own argument that private persons could lawfully depose a monarch: "I find it generally the cleere and positive determination of them all, (not prelatical, or of this late faction subprelatical) who have writt'n on this argument; that to doe justice on a lawless King, is to a privat man unlawful, to an inferior Magistrate lawfull." This is a strange statement, as it coheres neither with Milton's own argument, nor indeed his assertion in the title page. It is stranger still in asserting something not entirely supported in his collection of passages, a few of which make a populist argument, and a few, such as Calvin's judiciously selected passage from a commentary on Daniel rather than the *Institutes,* seem to support the deposition of bad kings without qualifying this allowance with the provision that only magistrates may initiate such an act.[66]

Milton's statement that it is a "positive determination of them all" that deposition "is to a private man unlawful" is often taken as also representing his own argument, but he is using the established Calvinist position in a much more complicated manner. He is using it rather to show the inconsistency of the theological argument. The deliberately tricky passage begins as an ironically positive reading of his opponents:

> I find it generally the Cleere and positive determination of them all . . . who have writt'n on this argument; that to doe justice on a lawless King, is to a privat man unlawful, to an inferior Magistrate lawfull: or if they were divided in opinion, yet greater then these here alleg'd, or of more authority in the Church, there can be none produc'd. If any one shall goe about by bringing other testimonies to disable these, or by bringing these against themselves in other cited passages of thir Books, he will not only faile to make good that fals and impudent assertion of those mutinous Ministers, that the deposing and punishing of a King or Tyrant, *is against the constant Judgement of all Protestant Divines,* it being quite the contrary, but will prove rather what perhaps he intended not, that the judgement of Divines, if it be so various and inconstant to it self, is not considerable, or to be esteem'd at all (257).

Here Milton is undercutting the legitimacy of his opponents' claims, rather than taking a position himself. In dissecting this argument, it is worth remembering how much he had already broken from Reformation theology. While he admits that the bulk of the Reformation tradition supports an argument that it is unlawful for a private man to "do Justice on a lawless king," this does not refute Milton's argument for popular sovereignty, which does not itself rely on Reformation theology. Rather, it only contradicts those who argue that Calvin or Luther condemn those who favor "the deposing or punishing of a King or Tyrant"; they do not, as he amply demonstrates, but rather suggest a manner in which the authority for such action might be determined. One of his quoted authorities, Christopher Goodman, in fact supports Milton's claim of popular sovereignty.[67] Milton suggests that his detractors do not in fact know their Reformation theology, and that this theology is far more open and more contradictory than they suppose.

Prynne and others may have once relied, earlier in the 1640s, on the radical elements of Calvin's doctrine, but such is not the case in the explicit rhetoric of 1649.[68] In a *Declaration* of 1649, Prynne wrote: "The Rule in the Old

Testament is, not to take any wicked Kings from their Thrones, and behead them: but (Rom: 13.1, 2, &c.) *Take away the wicked from before the King, and his Throne shall be established in Righteousnesse.* And the rule in the new Testament. To be subject to Kings, and the highter powers, and to submit unto them, even for Conscience and the Lords sake . . . not to depose or shed their bloud, for which there is no precept. . . . Ruminate upon it, and then be wise, both for your soules good, and the welfare of poor England."[69] The majority of the Presbyterians and moderate Independents were making the claim suggested in Milton's "mutinous Ministers," that the king could not be deposed or judged.

Milton seeks to wrest political thought from its theological and biblical moorings, and his rhetorical indeterminacy is part of a deliberate process aimed at eroding the relationship between theology and politics. At several moments he hits at the most basic claims of Protestant political theology. One passage in particular seems to touch on the monarchist writings of James I, which Milton does in a few notable instances in the tract, perhaps with the aim of discrediting the Stuart royal philosophy. James had argued famously that Kings are "accomptable to none but God onely," and Milton argues strenuously against the position that "kings are accountable to none but God" (204). "Kings are justly called Gods," James pronounced in an extreme form of Protestant political theology, "for that they exercise a manner or resemblance of Divine power upon earth. . . . God hath power to create, or destroy, make, or unmake at his pleasure, to give life or send death, to judge all and to bee judged nor accomptable to none . . . the like power have Kings."[70] Milton returns to this idea in the question, "How can any King in Europe maintain and write himself accountable to none but God" (206), which seems to point at Charles through James, since James has indeed "written himself" as such. "To say Kings are accountable to none but God," Milton insists, "is the overturning of all Law and government. For if they may refuse to give account, then all cov'nants made with them at Coronation; all oaths are in vaine, and mere mockeries, all Lawes which they sweare to keep, made to no purpose . . . we hold then our lives and estates, by the tenure of his meer grace and mercy, as from a God, not a mortal Magistrate" (204). The idea that all power comes from God seems here to have entirely lost its strength: a magistrate is a mere mortal, subject to the same laws as any one else. At this point Milton turns, in a passage added in the second edition, to "one of the best interpreters of nature," Aristotle, whom he cites from a passage in the Commonplace Book. Aristotle states that "Monarchy unaccountable, is the worst sort of Tyranny; and least of all to be endur'd by free born men" (204). Although Milton had promised not "many Heathen" authorities, but "Christian, Orthodoxal," and "Presbyterial," Aristotle is essentially his second cited authority (and his third) in a passage that is not only in conflict with Stuart royal ideology, but also, in a vital sense, against the grain of the Protestant theological tradition. The first authority happens to be another passage from the Commonplace Book from the French historian Claude Seissel.

Milton thus begins here to drive a wedge between theology and politics. For once a magistrate becomes merely mortal—neither anointed, nor deriving his power from God—and laws and obligations governing this magistrate are arrived at through agreement with the people, then the strict application of scripture becomes an unnecessary and even idolatrous exercise. He suggests this in his categorical instructions to "the Divines" to stay out of politics: "I have something also to the Divines, though brief to what were needful; not to be disturbers of the civil affairs, being in hands better able and more belonging to manage them; but to study harder, and to attend the office of good Pastors. . . . And all this while are to learn what the true end and reason is of the Gospel which they teach; and what a world it differs from the censorious and supercilious lording over conscience" (240–41).

Milton seems to suggest this same sense of the idolatrous misuse of theology and scripture in applying it to politics in his anger at the hypocrisy of the "dancing Divines, who have the conscience and the boldness, to come with Scripture in thir mouthes, gloss'd and fitted for thir turnes with a double contradictory sense, transforming the sacred verity of God, to an Idol with two Faces" (195). The frustration continues in the text, when Milton inveighs against "some who would perswade us, that this absurd opinion" of divine right "was King Davids" (205), with the use of Psalm 51. Milton's response to this is extremely telling: "How much more rationally spake the heathen King *Demophoon* in a Tragedy of Euripides" (205). Milton must, of course, mean this in jest, since the authority here is not just heathen, but a mythological character in a play. Yet the tone is important in understanding the rhetorical nature of the tract, not only in his comic disregard for the promise of "not many heathen" authorities, but in the sense that a line from Euripides is more authoritative simply because it is more rational.

The tract's desire for "more certain rules" to make a "certain decision" are part of its participation in the struggle for a new scientific language of politics. Milton's pseudo-anthropological explanations of the origins of political right and his use of reason and natural law are all attempts to find a language that "will as certainly and unavoydably bring out" the right end, "as any Probleme that ever Euclid, or Apollonius made good by demonstration" (253). These are akin to the "theorems almost mathematically demonstrative" he praised and emulated in *Areopagitica* (*CPW* 2:513). In *The Tenure of Kings and Magistrates* Milton engages in an ideologically destabilizing interrogation of the core issues and methodologies in English political thought: the scriptural basis for sovereignty, the question whether the accused is a king or tyrant, and the role of the "magistrate" over private citizens. Recent scholarship has attempted to explain this last instability as the revision of a position within editions of the tract, but this explanation is challenged by several important facts: the same indeterminacy occurs in the first edition; the first edition promises the theology that the second edition delivers; the second edition also has prominently added sections on popular sovereignty; and, finally, the indeterminacy over the definition of "magistrate" is just one of a few key elements of political thought about which Milton maintains seemingly opposite positions. His vacillations over precedent and scriptural warrant are in many ways far more corrosive to the fabric of the ideology of his contemporaries than the instability of the idea of "magistrate." Yet each of these represents a pattern of surface instability that is deliberately contrived to serve the circumstances of an uncertain moment, and to bring unity to a now profoundly fractured commonwealth.

Chapter 6

"His Book Alive"

Defending Popular Sovereignty after the Execution

It is not my plan now to construct a long account about nature and about the origin of political life.

Milton, *Pro Populo Anglicano Defensio*

In these westerne parts of the world, we are made to receive our opinions concerning the Institution, and Rights of Common-wealths, from Aristotle, Cicero, and other men, Greeks and Romanes, that living under Popular States, derived those Rights, not from Principles of Nature, but transcribed them into their books, out of the Practise of their own Common-wealths, which were Popular; as the Grammarians describe the Rules of Language, out of the Practise of the time; or the Rules of Poetry, out of the Poems of *Homer* and *Virgil*.

Hobbes, *Leviathan*

MILTON'S LATIN defense addressing Europe, satirically titled A Defense of the People of England, against Claude the Anonymous, Otherwise Known as Salmasius, begins with the promise that he will show "under what law, particularly that of the English, this judgement was made and executed" (*PW* 52). As is generally true of Milton's work written after the execution, this insistence of England's legal unassailability constitutes a new rhetorical strategy designed for a new audience. *The Tenure of Kings and Magistrates* had been fully cognizant of the dubious legality of the Rump Parliament and its proceedings against the king; Milton had boldly argued there that the "great actions" of the emergent Rump are "above the form of Law or Custom."[1] One irony in the title of *Pro Populo* is that Milton entirely avoids the argument of popular sovereignty that had been the centerpiece of *The Tenure of Kings and Magistrates*. Instead of being devoted to the rights of the people, his first polemical efforts following the establishment of a new government, culminating in *Pro Populo Anglicano Defensio*, are devoted to the rights of magistrates: their authority, their authenticity, and, most of all, their Protestant orthodoxy.[2] Early in *Pro Populo Anglicano Defensio,* Milton finds a way of fusing "the people" with the Parliament, as if to imply that both arguments were always one and the same: "I say it was the people; for why should I not say that the act of the better, the sound part of the Parliament, in which resides the real power of the people, was the act of the people?" (*CPW* 4:457). This disingenuously suggests that Milton had always meant "select part of Parliament" when speaking of the people, and it glosses over the real "act of the people"—the Army—in forcibly creating this Parliament. In the *Pro Populo,* the decision for deposition resides precisely where it had in Calvin, with God and his agents, the high magistracy. Milton writes to Salmasius that "what was decreed by our highest magistrates concerning the king you say was committed by a 'wicked conspiracy of sacrilegious men'" (*PW* 56), revealing some sense of the reason for this major rhetorical shift. England is under considerable pressure to establish the legitimacy of its government, and, as Thomas Corns has pointed out, Milton often reveals "a guileful concern not to alienate continental regimes from the new state."[3]

On a theoretical level, the different views found in *Pro Populo* and in the other tracts written after *The Tenure* do not represent a philosophical change in position; nor should the different tracts written within these two years be seen as one body of argument. Now an official spokesperson for the new regime, Milton, already adept at stepping outside of himself, now must step even further. For England's immediate ideological needs it mattered little whether those who passed judgment against the king were "highest magistrates" or good private citizens. What mattered is how these revised conceptions of sovereignty functioned in rhetorical and ideological warfare. To avoid the possibility that the deposition would seem, to Milton's undiscerning opponents, to have been committed by sacrilegious men, Milton disingenuously asserts the legitimacy of the "highest magistrates," sanctioned (as he insists in the *Defensio Secunda*) by "the foremost theologians."[4]

Milton even engages in retroactive self-revision. In the *Defensio Secunda,* he insists that he did not advocate the king's death, even to the point of stressing that the king was already dead when he published *The Tenure of Kings and Magistrates.* "This book," he protested of *The Tenure,* which most of his European audience would be incapable of reading, let alone between the lines, "was not published till after the death of the king, being intended rather to compose the minds of men, than to settle any thing relating to Charles" (*WJM* 8:137). The assertion seems almost comically deceptive: the tract appeared within two weeks of the king's death, and, given the indications in it that the king is "now" on trial (*CPW* 3:222), Milton had written the original tract prior to the event, as an advocate for it; it just happened that the king was dead by the time it came into print. A pressing set of political circumstances now at hand, there would be little practicality in stubbornly maintaining a radical explanation of the historical and anthropological origins of popular sovereignty. As a commissioned writer, Milton modified his views in his first tract after the first edition of *The Tenure,* known as the *Observations upon the Articles of Peace* (May 1649)—though to speak of this as *his* tract, as if it belonged to the same category of authorship as *The Tenure,* is misleading. The *Observations* asserts that it was not private military men who had purged Parliament, but other parliamentary members who took it upon themselves to rid the body of its corrupt parts, and thus a legitimate body of "magistrates" proceeded against the king.[5] This is also the argument of *Eikonoklastes,* which appeared in October 1649, after the second, expanded edition of *The Tenure.*[6]

The different positions taken in these three commissioned works represent more keenly the changing audiences and circumstances than they do the author's elusive politics. Milton's polemic has shifted from its focus on Presbyterians and other English Puritans to address a much broader spectrum of English and European readers. His role as a writer has also changed radically: he is now a public servant, even living for a significant period at Whitehall—erstwhile the palace—among parliamentary members and government workers.[7] As a spokesperson for this nascent regime, he was now beholden to its urgent need to create a legitimate constitutional identity.

This concluding chapter surveys the polemical work done for the new government while Milton still could see. This period witnesses the virtual end of Milton's use of the political notes in the Commonplace Book. Since these were commissioned pieces that respond specifically to the work of others—the Irish and the Scots in the *Observations on the Articles of Peace,* Charles's supposed *Eikon Basilike* in *Eikonoklastes,* and Salmasius's *Defensio Regia* in *Pro Populo*—Milton used his notes only as they suited these assigned purposes. The reading that became part of his writing in this period was therefore dictated largely by the texts he engaged. My purpose then is not to provide a thorough reading of these tracts, so much as to outline the ways in which Milton continues to defend, build on, but also obscure the positions he had collected in the Commonplace Book and developed in the "Digression" and *The Tenure of Kings and Magistrates.* The differences between these texts continue to suggest a high level of rhetorical prevarication and construction in Milton's polemical prose.

The Anonymous *Observations*

Milton's first work commissioned by the new government has no recognition of authorship on the title page: it is simply "Publisht by Autority."[8] Modern reception of the *Observations* has not only supplied the missing author's name, but it has also tidied up the bibliographic irregularity of the title. "Observations upon the Articles of Peace," the title usually listed as Milton's work, is not the title of the printed pamphlet, but a chapter heading of the last twenty-one pages of this sixty-five-page tract, appearing amid words of documents from various authors on page 45. The current title was bequeathed upon posterity by Edward Phillips, who was the first to acknowledge the work as Milton's in the "Catalogue of Mr. John Milton's Works" appended to the *Letters of State* (1694).[9] More evidence that Milton wrote the piece lies in a record of an order given on March 28, two weeks into Milton's new job as secretary of foreign languages for the Council of State. The Council ordered him "to make some observations upon the complication of interests which is now amongst the several designers against the peace of the Commonwealth; and that it be made ready to be printed with the Papers out of Ireland which the House hath ordered to be printed."[10] The bulk of this publication, therefore, is devoted to the reproduction of intercepted manuscripts that came to Milton from the government, which are let to speak largely for themselves.

Anonymity was of course common in the civil war period, and Milton himself had practiced it in 1643 and before, although after his claim in *Areopagitica* that the "Author's name, or at least the Printers [should] be register'd" (*CPW* 2:569) there was always at least a "J.M." on the title page.[11] English polemical works in the vernacular after *Areopagitica* (which carried his full name) bore initials, conveying both a partial anonymity and a sense of familiarity with his English readers. His three Latin defenses, *Pro Populo Anglicano Defensio*, *Defensio Secunda*, and *Pro Se Defensio*, fully displayed Milton's name and national identity: *Joannis Miltoni Angli*.[12] In addition to the open use of his name, in these years Milton and his assistant John Phillips deride the use of anonymity by others: the collaborative *Response of John Phillips Englishman* (1651) is addressed "to some anonymous sneak."[13] But the anonymity of the *Articles of Peace* is of a different sort from that normally practiced. It is not designed to protect the author, but to remove individual authorship from the creation of legal authority.

The tract's anonymity has been used to suggest that Milton wrote the *Observations* with reluctance. He may have been reluctant, but neither the tract's anonymity nor any of the other evidence given—its omission from

Milton's retrospective account or its delayed production—particularly supports such a verdict. The tract's anonymity is integral to its form, as a set of political documents issued under the auspices of the English government. While the six- or seven-week delay seems substantial, there are too many other factors that might have contributed to it, only some of them pertaining to Milton, including other governmental and personal duties, such as moving his household.[14] It is also the case that the final documents from the Presbyterians came in "while we [were] yet writing" (*CPW* 3:322); possibly introducing further logistical delays. Milton does not mention the *Observations* in his autobiographical account in the *Defensio Secunda*, but not out of a reluctance to acknowledge it as his—European readers would not have paid attention to an English tract of this nature, and certainly not for style. The tract's anonymity instead helped to facilitate the very impression Milton wanted to make in his defense, that there was chronological space between his work for the new government and *The Tenure of Kings and Magistrates*, and, therefore, that *The Tenure* was not government work, nor created to obtain government work, but "performed within private walls" (*WJM* 8:137).

Accordingly, the first-person singular pronoun that pervades *The Tenure*— "*I* wish better instruction," "*I* shall indeavour," "*I* leave to Magistrates," "*I* dare owne," "*I* instance," "*I* spare"[15]—is shorn from the *Observations*, except for one lapse in an interjected phrase "I think," which refers appropriately to the new government's yet unknown toleration policy. Instead, Milton refers entirely to "we" and "us," further indicating the degree to which it is designed as a governmental statement: "*We* may be confidently perswaded," "In these Articles of Peace *we* see as good as done by the late King," "But of such like stuffe *wee* meet not anywhere with more excrescence than in his own lavish pen," etc.[16] In one expressive passage, he is able to use the collective body represented in "we" in a manner that underscores this as the republican council against the individual will of a king:

> Exception we finde there of no person whatsoever; and if the King who hath actually done this, or any for him claime a Privilege above Justice, it is againe demanded by what expresse Law, either of God or man, and why he whose office is to execute Law and Justice upon all others, should sit himselfe like a demigod in lawlesse and unbounded *anarchy*; refusing to be accountable for that autority over men naturally his equals, which God himself without a reason givn is not wont to exercise over his creatures? And if God the nearer to be acquainted with mankind and his frailties, and to become our Priest, made himself a man, and subject to the Law, we gladly would be instructed why any mortal man for the good and wellfare of his brethren beeing made a King, should by a clean contrary motion make himself a God, exalted above

Law; the readiest way to become utterly unsensible, both of his human condition and his own duty. (307–8)

The writing stands out beyond the functional "austerity"[17] accorded this piece, both for its philosophical assertion of human equality in nature, and in its ironic use of God in the second part of this analogy. Milton's "men naturally his equals" recalls Hobbes's radical assertion of the same idea in the *Elements of Law,* that "men" are "by nature equal."[18] In the second part of this analogy, a King "by a clean contrary motion" makes himself a God, although what he becomes is not God, but a man lost in his own hubris.

The task of this government tract is not merely to reinforce the villainy of the late king, who negotiated with "those inhumane Rebels and Papists of *Ireland*"—the *Articles* being "one of his last Masterpieces" (301)—but also to reinforce the comparative legitimacy of the new governing body. It asserts that the revolution in government was an act done by magistrates and that England is ruled by magistrates (rather than private men). The keyword "magistracy" appears five times in twenty-one short pages, far more than any other Miltonic work. Even the words "magistrate" and "magistrates" appear at a rate about equal to that of *The Tenure of Kings and Magistrates* (page for page), although here it has the opposite purpose of affirming the legitimacy of the magistrates, rather than the legitimate overthrow of them. The keyword is a constant refrain, repeated in various forms on almost every page (16 times), and in a way that sustains a profoundly different position than that in *The Tenure of Kings and Magistrates,* in that he is here asserting their legitimacy. The government tract rails at those who "dare send such defiance to the sovran Magistracy of *England*" (333).

Milton performs the shift in position from *The Tenure* in part by avoiding the precise charges of his opponents. The Irish Articles of Ormond inveigh, for example, against the total destruction of the three estates, but hitting particularly on the function of the Army in purging Parliament. A letter from Ormond dated March 9, 1649, writes angrily of the new English government: "They have thus far compassed their ends to establish a perfect Turkish tyranny; now that of the three estates of King, Lords & Commons, whereof in all ages, Parlaments have consisted, there remains only a small number, and that they the dregs and scum of the House of Commons, pickt and awed by the Armie, a wicked remnant left for no other end; then yet further, if it be possible to delude the people with the name of a Parliament" (*CPW* 3:291–92). Circumventing the uncertain legitimacy of those whose actions he had previously defended, Milton responds by drawing on the history of Parliament from the Commonplace Book, with a true, although surely ineffective, scholarly correction of Ormond's knowledge of history: "As for Parlaments by three Estates, wee know that a Parliament signifies no more then the Supream and generall Councell of a Nation, consisting of whomsoever chos'n and assembld for the public good; which was ever practis'd, and in all sorts of Government, before the word *Parlament,* or the formality or the possibility of those three Estates" (314). The three estates therefore represent an invented construct, which Milton supports by drawing on eighth century French history, using entries from Girard and de Thou in his Commonplace Book (*CPW* 1:445–56, CB 183). "But whereas," Milton continues, shifting ground, Ormond "is bold to allege that of three Estates there remaines onely a small number, and they the *Dreggs and Scum of the House of Commons.* . . . Doubtless there must be thought a great scarcity in *England* of persons honourable and deserving, or else of Judgment, or so much as honesty in the People, if those whome they esteem worthy to sit in Parlament be no better then Scum and Dreggs in the *Irish* Dialect" (315). This nationalistic mudslinging avoids entirely the legal problem of the Purge, or the issue of what happened to the other part of England's respectable collection of representatives that the nation had esteemed "worthy to sit in Parliament."

In the *Observations,* Milton uses six entries from the Commonplace Book that continue the kind of historical politics undertaken in *The Tenure of Kings and Magistrates.* In one case, four entries from the notebook inform the writing on a single page. These entries assert the precedents in history for parliamentary sovereignty and depositions. Milton relies on facts drawn from Holinshed and de Thou, although without citing them. In challenging the late king for having sought to acquit the "province of *Ireland*" from "all true fealty and obedience to the Common-wealth of *England*" (305), Milton turns to a cluster of entries in the Commonplace Book under the topic "Rex." In around 1639–41 he recorded an entry from Holinshed: "no king can give away his k. dom without consent of the whole state. Holinsh. 191" (CB 182, *CPW* 1:441). Drawing on this in the *Observations,* Milton writes of how such an "act of any King against the Consent of his Parliament, though no other Crime were layd against him, might of itself strongly conduce to the disinthrowning him of all" (305). In the printed tract, Milton has substituted "Parliament" for the notebook's "whole state" (which itself broadens Holinshed, who speaks only of the barons). In composing this passage in the *Observations,* the evidence suggests his notes were still open in front of him, and Milton skipped over another short entry from Holingshed to one from de Thou, recorded much later: "So also it was answerd to Hen. 3 of France by the parlament at Blois. *Thuan.* hist. 63. p. 186: 'In no case can the patrimony of the crown be taken away from the king, inasmuch as the king is merely the usufructuary of the property of the realm in his possession,' &c. ibid.[19] He then wrote this into the *Observations,* immediately following the passage of history taken from Holinshed, as: "In France *Henry* the third demanded leave in greatest exigencies to make Sale of some Crown Lands onely, and that to his Subjects, was answerd by the Parlament then at *Blois,* that a King in no case, though of extreamest necessity, might alienate the Patrimony of his Crown, whereof he is but onely *Usu-fructuary,* as Civilians terme it, the propriety remaining ever to the Kingdom, not to the King" (305–6). Milton's modifications to the original in de Thou are slight but significant. The added emphatic phrase "though of extreamest necessity" reinforces Milton's constitutionalist position that even a state of emergency does not provide a ruler the right to personal jurisdiction over public property. He also adds the line "as Civilians term it" to explain de Thou's *usufructuarius* or (as Milton translates) *"Usu-fructuary."* "Civilians" specifically connotes practitioners or professors of civil law and thus Milton means to reinforce the applicability in England of this example of the king's loss of legitimacy. He then seems to consult the original passage in Holinshed that supplied the view that a king cannot give his kingdom away without consent, since the *Chronicles* tell the story of King John and his barons that Milton then goes on to recall.[20] He seems therefore less rushed than when he composed *The Tenure,* although he still follows in the printed tract the general order of entries as they were haphazardly laid down in his notes.

The use of historical sources here is perfunctory, even when Milton sometimes seems to be writing in a genre of historical analysis unsuited to his assignment. The tone reflects the legal objectives of the anonymous government publication, and perhaps the pressure on its author, who faced a still more urgent assignment. When Milton turned to repudiate the king's barely posthumous "last masterpiece," the vastly popular *Eikon Basilike* (1649), his scholarly use of sources is even more diminished, suggesting as well that he sought to reach a broader popular audience than he had in his earlier prose. Although he is identifiable as an individual author, Milton continues to maintain the collective national persona that he had developed in his first anonymous assignment.

Refuting Monarchs in *Eikonoklastes*

Ever since its creation, *Eikon Basilike* (Image of the King) has provided book historians and literary scholars with a prime example of the effect of the print revolution on history. Looking back more than a decade later, the ghostwriter of *Eikon Basilike,* John Gauden, remarked famously: "When [the book] came out, just upon the King's death, good God! What shame, rage, and despite filled his murderers! What comfort his friends! How many enemies did it convert! How many hearts did it mollify and melt! . . . In a word, it was an army and did vanquish more than any sword could."[21] Gauden suggested in the same passage that the book laid the way for the restoration of Charles II. This reflection on the event, written shortly after the Restoration, echoes the sentiment of the book's closing "Latin Motto," as Milton called it: *Vota dabunt quae Bella negarunt,* or "That what hee could not compass by Warr, he should atchieve by his Meditations" (*CPW* 3:342). Certainly this Latin inscription had, as Milton himself recognized, a ring of truth: for the parliamentarians, the war of words would be far more difficult to win than any military engagement. In spite of rather persistent attempts by Parliament to suppress it, *Eikon Basilike* appeared within days of the execution, and went through over thirty-five impressions in its first year alone.[22] Several manuscript versions and translations, including one in Welsh, are also extant.[23] Richard Helgerson writes that "never before had the words of an English monarch reached so many people."[24] It is probably the case that never before had any English book been churned out at such a remarkable rate, and this was in spite of an otherwise effective campaign to suppress royalist literature. As Amos Tubb has shown, "government censorship sharply curtailed the publications of anti-regicide works." While suppressing the voice of opposition, the new government and "the independent printers and booksellers worked hand in hand to provide an arena for the advocates of the regicide to air their views."[25]

   Where the government failed at censorship, they sought to counter royalist polemic in print. Milton's rebuttal has garnered considerably more attention than most of his English prose besides *Areopagitica,* but not always for its literary value. Samuel Gardiner wrote of it that it was "barely more than a Miltonic piece of hack-work," and that the "method adopted [that of relentless animadversion], perhaps adopted by order, was fatal to the production of a great work."[26] Nor did the mere three editions of *Eikonoklastes* in 1649 and 1650 hold a candle to the blaze of the King's mass-produced image. *Eikonoklastes* was by polemical standards a big book—the 229 pages of the slightly expanded 1650 edition mark it as Milton's largest published production thus far. To speak of it as "hack-work" may be a bit dismissive, although there are striking differences between it and the two major polemics that surround it, *The Tenure of Kings and Magistrates* and *Pro Populo Anglicano Defensio,* in the richness of allusion, the citations and scholarship, and in the complexity of argument. The formal aesthetic behind Gardiner's criticism stems as well from an anachronistically modern set of contentions. The blow-by-blow ani-madversion had been a staple of Protestant polemic, and Milton's format, as well as his icon-smashing title, appealed to the concept of an inevitable Prot-estant teleology.[27]

In *Eikonoklastes*, Milton openly recognizes the enormous power the King's Book had: this is a "Book alive" (*CPW* 3:341), a phrase that recalls his descrip-tions in *Areopagitica* of books as "not absolutely dead things, but doe contain a potencie of life in them . . . and as vigorously productive, as those fabulous Dragons teeth; and being sown up and down, may chance to spring up armed men" (*CPW* 2:492). Even while its author rests in peace, the book seemed capable of "retarding" the "generall peace, so needful to this af-flicted Nation, and so nigh obtain'd." Milton feels compelled, he writes, to answer it, that the nation "may be kept from entering the third time unad-visedly into Warr and bloodshed" (338–39). The fear of more civil war must be taken into account in understanding the extraordinary strains on Mil-ton's authorial autonomy: this is ideological triage, designed to prevent a re-turn to something that had already been, as Milton writes in the "Digres-sion," "much blood-shed, & vast expence, [leading] to ridiculous frustration" (*CPW* 5:443). *Eikonoklastes* seeks to counter and expose the King's Book at every turn, even in the material aspects of its presentation: "I must commend his op'nness who gave the title to this Book, *Eikon Basilike,* that is to say, The Kings Image; and by the Shrine he dresses out for him, certainly would have the people come and worship him" (343). The book is itself a kind of Catho-lic shrine or reliquary, destined to attract (and mislead) worshippers. Instead of meeting its own superstitious goals, however, it is full of "quaint Emblems and devices begg'd from the old Pageantry of some Twelf-nights entertain-ment at *Whitehall,* will doe but ill to make a Saint or Martyr" (343).[28] These images appeal to the Puritan dislike of masks and suggest that the book is but a set of theatrical devices gleaned from such entertainments. Devises like "the conceited portraiture before his Book, drawn out to the full measure of a Masking Scene," and "those Latin words after the end" are "sett there to catch fools and silly gazers" (342). Milton's rhetoric aims to disabuse naive readers of this effective royalist propaganda, and unlike *Pro Populo Anglicano Defensio,* or the demanding vernacular polemic of *The Tenure of Kings and Magistrates* or *Areopagitica,* this tract is not aimed at a particularly studious audience.[29]

Milton's literary-critical approach led him famously to uncover a bit of plagiaristic misuse on the part of the king. The King's Book contains "a Prayer stol'n word for word from the mouth of a Heathen fiction praying to a heathen God; & that in no serious Book, but the vain amatorious Poem of

Sᵣ *Philip Sidneys Arcadia;* a Book in that kind full of worth and witt, but among religious thoughts, and duties not worthy to be nam'd; nor to be read at any time without good caution" (362). The strangeness in Milton's dismissive treatment of Sidney is brought into relief by the revealing coincidence that Sidney's *Arcadia* is one of the English literary texts in Milton's Commonplace Book, where it appears four times. These entries have rare notes of high commendation that show Milton's admiration for Sidney. Under the topic of "Death Self-Inflicted," in the *Index Ethicus,* Milton records, "Whether lawful, disputed with exquisite reasoning. Sr. Philip Sid. Arcad. Book 4." In the *Index Politicus* he writes under the topics "Courtiers," "See also an excellent description of such an Oligarchy of nobles abusing the countnance to the ruin of royal sovranty Arcad. Sidney," and on the topic of "Political Adroitness" he records "excellently set out by Sidney"[30]—"excellent," "exquisite reasoning," and "excellently set out" being terms of praise almost never used in Milton's own hand in his usually impartial record. Surely Milton himself felt no need for the "good caution" he warns against the "Heathen" Sidney; indeed, the passage in *Eikonoklastes* demonstrates the extent to which Milton can be removed from himself in this government work. He might have used some of these passages from Sidney himself—they had, after all, been prepared for some sort of reuse—had he not excoriated Charles's use of the same. As is true of Milton's public disparagement of Machiavelli and his contrasting private interest, here he puts on a markedly different face to try to malign his opponent—and for a constructed pious readership that might already have such prejudices about Sidney. Milton seems to be playing on prejudices, perhaps even as he constructs them, that do not characterize his own more dispassionate regard for books and their authors. These contrived prejudices contradict the ideal view of the impartial reader in *Areopagitica,* which espouses the benefit "of books promiscuously read" (*CPW* 2:517).

Milton critiques Charles's use of Shakespeare in a similar manner, seeming at times to expel an author whose work had richly informed his own, even up to *The Tenure of Kings and Magistrates,* where he adroitly interweaves lines of *Macbeth*—for a very sharp readership—in order to cast the Presbyterians as Scottish witches.[31] These are allusions without citations, without explaining to the reader what he is drawing on and why. In *Eikonoklastes,* in marked contrast, Milton conspicuously invokes Shakespeare to supply an example of "pious words" in the mouth of a "Tyrant"—that of *Richard III:* "I shall not instance an abstruse Author, wherein the King might be less conversant, but one whom wee well know was the Closet Companion of these his solitudes, *William Shakespeare;* who introduces the Person of *Rich-*

ard the third, speaking in as high a strain of pietie, and mortification, as is utterd in any passage of this Book" (361). The four-line passage from *Richard III* ends with Richard's ironic exclamation, "I thank God for my humilitie"— illustrating how a tyrant can misuse religious sentiment. The passage is not entirely unlike Milton's use of Chaucer in the antiprelatical tracts, where he calls on a well-known literary figure to show the hypocrisy of his opponents' views. Yet while Shakespeare serves the function here of speaking for Milton, his invocation of the great dramatist seems inflected with some misgiving about Shakespeare's cultural role. Milton's cast-aside remark that he will "not instance an abstruse Author, wherein the King might be less conversant" is strange in several respects, not least because his presumed royal audience is dead. The actual audience is the reader who believes what the king writes: not bookish enough to know an abstruse author.

Milton's treatment of Shakespeare here has been the source of significant debate. On the one hand, it has been read as an example of how Milton is wrenched out of position in a strained polemical exchange; on the other hand, it is seen as an instance of his renunciation of Shakespeare in the evolution of his republican and Puritan art. Taking the former position, Steven Zwicker writes that "the association of the king's person with learning and aristocratic refinement . . . forced Milton to trivialize the artistic forms and genres most closely identified with Charles I." Drawing attention to the extraordinary passage in which Milton dismisses the king's "whole Book" as "intended" as a "peece of Poetrie" (*CPW* 3:406), Zwicker stresses that Milton must have felt this painful: "This could not have been an easy gesture for Milton."[32] Nigel Smith and Nicholas McDowell argue from various positions that this moment (in the words of Smith) "mark[s] the beginning of his expulsion of Shakespeare from his dramatic inventiveness, and his attempt to create a new theatre for the republic."[33] Although opposing, both of these arguments are premised on Milton's personal investment in the view represented. For Zwicker, Milton is forced into a painful deviation from himself, and for McDowell and Smith this experience is avoided since the author is committed to the position represented.

Milton's ambivalent treatment of Shakespeare is, I would argue, more a product of the persona that he inhabits for this occasion than it is an accurate gauge of his complex artistic relationship with the dramatist. There is some danger in conjecturing the frame of the author's mind in constructing reader-oriented positions, especially when moral and psychological presumptions might bias interpretation. Our inclination to read these contortions of position as painful runs a risk of anachronistically imposing modern conceptions of authorial integrity on a much less integral and more flexible

condition of authorship. While there is undoubtedly some level of antago-
nism toward the Stuarts' favored poets, and some early modern form of unease in misrepresentation, Milton's treatment of Shakespeare seems to conform to a pattern of polemical argument in which the readers' positions are
far more important than the author's own. Milton's dismissals of Sidney's
and perhaps even Shakespeare's poetry are of the same ilk as his casting of
Machiavelli in his pamphlets, his invocation of Cartwright in *The Tenure,* or
his casting of himself as just another Puritan who had always loathed theatre
in the 1642 *Apology*—when he had recently written in his Commonplace
Book how "absurd beyond measure" it would be to prohibit the "dramatic
arts."[34] Given especially the degree to which other positions are clearly constructed here—the legitimacy and Calvinist orthodoxy of the English magistrates, among others—it seems more likely that this too is a construction
designed for rhetorical effect. Milton writes to a readership whose opinion
matters to him—or to the state—even while their opinions fundamentally
disagree in ways that he actively conceals.

At the same time, Milton's provocative casting of the *Eikon Basilike* as a
"peece of Poetrie" may be more revealing than Zwicker allows, and it points
to the surprising curricular preferences highlighted by the research in Milton's Commonplace Book and the use to which it has been put. In this passage in *Eikonoklastes,* Milton narrates that he was about to find fault with a
particular passage in the *Eikon,* and suggest that it was dressed "in a garb
somwhat more Poetical then for a Statist," when, "hearing him reported a
more diligent reader of Poets, then of Politicians"—that is, one versed in political theory and history—Milton began "to think that the whole Book
might perhaps be intended a peece of Poetrie" (406). The presented bias, that
the king should have been reading more in politics than in poetry, accords
somewhat with the record, at least, of Milton's own reading and writing in the
1640s: far more politics and history than poetry. This is a balance, although
necessarily conjectural, that is demonstrated not only in his recorded reading
notes, but also in the reading evident in the prose written during this period.
Milton's dismissive treatment of poetry in this context is not a renunciation so
much as an expression of the inappropriateness of the king's wholesale commitment as a politician to imaginative poetic indulgences.

Except for one line from Homer's *Iliad* (345), the passage from *Richard III*
is one of the only texts actually quoted—instead of paraphrased or vaguely
gestured toward—beyond those from the Bible and from *Eikon Basilike* or
other royal documents.[35] As is generally true of this stage in his vernacular
polemic career, Milton's use of classical literature is not terribly energetic.
Suetonius seems to have been consulted for stories about Nero (439–40),

Caligula (467), and Nero again (590), although he is not cited or quoted. There is a story about Manlius that originates in Livy, although it may come from the *Vindiciae contra Tyrannos* (565), and a story that also probably originates in Livy (again uncited) about the laws of Valerius Publicola (590). Justinian is mentioned in the statement that "[it] stands yet firme in the Code of *Justinian,* that the Law is above the Emperour" (590–91). These allusions seem loosely drawn from memory rather than from his notes or the original.

While *Eikonoklastes* is surprisingly sparse in allusions to works beyond the King's Book, Milton does engage new material, much of which is reused in more interesting ways in *Pro Populo Anglicano Defensio.* These new sources, not formerly used or recorded in his Commonplace Book, suggest that Milton is continuing a program of serious research even in the midst of his assigned work, since their brief presence in *Eikonoklastes* often suggests that it was not the composition of the tract that drove Milton to these new sources. Some of these sources seem to be the by-product of recent and perhaps ongoing research for *The History of Britain* (1670), which he may have hoped to finish sooner than he was able to—and far beyond the Norman Conquest. The extent of the new historical sources also reaffirm that Milton's recording of material in the notebook diminishes considerably in the late 1640s prior to his blindness, and even prior to his substantial reuse of these recorded notes in 1649. A survey of the new sources, taken in order, shows the range of Milton's reading: a tract by David Buchanan, which he cites as *Truths manifest;* a "Book intitl'd *The Mysterie of Iniquity* [1643]"; *A Declaration of the Commons* (July 25, 1643); *The Kings Cabinet Opened* (1645); Josephus's *Antiquities of the Jews* (used before, but here a new source for political thought);[36] a manuscript on Llan Daff, which is used in *The History of Britain.*[37] Milton refers to the recent work of John Sadler, Hebraist and member of the Council of State, who wrote *Rights of the Kingdom* (1649), a book used again in greater detail in *Pro Populo.* Milton's interest in medieval English constitutionalism intensifies, as is shown in his use of Andrew Horn's thirteenth-century book *La Somme Apellee Miroir des Justices,* translated in 1646 as *The Mirror of Justices,* first seemingly referred to in *The Tenure of Kings and Magistrates,* although with no citation but the phrase "our ancient books of Law" (*CPW* 3:219), is cited in both *Eikonoklastes* and *Pro Populo.*[38] For his parliamentary history, Milton may also be consulting Thomas May's *History of the Parliament of England: Which Began November the Third, M.DC.XL* (1647), as several passages suggest; *Eikonoklastes* seems to be his only use of this text.[39] At the end of *Eikonoklastes* he refers to "ancient Books" that are new sources for him: Henry de Bracton, whose thirteenth-century *De Legibus et Consuetudinibus Angliae,* a massive though unfinished description of medieval law and constitutional history, was published in 1569 and again by Coke in 1640.[40] This would have been of keener interest to Milton had he been able to write his own *History* beyond the Norman Conquest, although the work supplies a rich history of Roman Law and the nature of the Anglo Saxon constitution prior to 1066. Milton also refers briefly to "*Fleta*" (591), a late thirteenth-century treatise on English common law that Selden edited and put into print in 1647.

When Milton turns to *Pro Populo Anglicano Defensio,* he adopts a more reader-friendly mode of animadversion, in which the quoted material is introduced as such, and worked into Milton's own text, rather than simply dropped on the page in a different typeface. In part because decorum allows him to do so, Milton adopts a lighter satiric tone that helps deflate Salmasius's often high-blown charges against the English republic. But *Pro Populo* is also more important in terms of political thought, as it responds to a text that not only defends King Charles, but defends monarchy as a form of government.

Addressing Europe

Pro Populo Anglicano Defensio (1651) has one of the more extensive and colorful publication histories of books in the mid-seventeenth century. Within about a year of its publication in February 1651, it was published in thirteen editions and a couple of reissues in London, Amsterdam, Utrecht, and Gouda; it was translated into Dutch, and was rumored to have been translated into French.[41] It was printed in cheap quarto and duodecimo editions, as well as a "splendid" folio edition, enlarged and corrected, in October 1651.[42] The large tract—now the largest printed book produced by Milton, and by far the most extensively produced—ranged from 104 to 389 pages in its various editions. In London, it was printed officially by William Dugard, who had been thrown in jail in the previous year for "printing several scandalous books against the Commonwealth."[43] These include *Eikon Basilike* and Salmasius's *Defensio Regia,* which he was apparently trying to print when, as the description in the Record Office reads, "he was cast into Newgate . . . and had been tried for his life by an High Court of Injustice, had not Sir James Harrington saved him from that danger, and procured his release."[44] Shortly thereafter, Dugard managed somehow to find his way into the position of "Printer to his Hignes the Lord Protector."[45]

Pro Populo responds to and was often bound with Salmasius's *Defensio Regia,* itself an imposing publication that appeared in as many editions as Milton's tract, with one in French and one in Dutch.[46] It is not certain when

Salmasius's tract first reached English shores,[47] although in late November the Council of State had ordered that ships be searched "for certain scandalous books which are there [in the Netherlands] printed against the government of this Commonwealth, entitled *Defensio Regia,* and which are designed to be sent over hither."[48] Milton was subsequently assigned the task of refuting Salmasius in early January 1650, a task that took about a year. William Parker writes that Milton's comic title "was intended, of course, to attract attention and to promise further humor inside."[49] This is a comic as well as a serious book, and its tone—part of its major success—must be taken into account in deciphering its complex political positions.

When Milton responds to Salmasius, he adopts a style vastly unlike that of *The Tenure,* although many of the ideas of this earlier tract, often originating in the Commonplace Book, are recycled in the Latin work. In addition to the material in the Commonplace Book, which he continues to use sporadically (given the size of the treatise), Milton infuses his Latin prose with references to the classics, and particularly those written in Latin. In a sense, he turns from being a Bodinian political writer to an Erasmian. Indeed, he uses excerpts from classical writers in a style of political writing almost opposite to his own, often building arguments in the manner of the "quotationists and common placers" (*CPW* 2:230) he had complained about in the 1640s. In part dictated by the satiric and animadversive genre, the use of traditional sententious quotation also helps represent the new English republic as consistent with cosmopolitan humanist values. The depth of reading exhibited here is most likely from memory reinforced by years of teaching, but there may well have been a temporary notebook for the process of composition of this treatise, possibly with contributions of one or more of his researchers and amanuenses. This is not a project that could have been undertaken without some help, given especially Milton's health. The number of references in common with the *Angli Responsio* or *The Response of John Phillips,* published later in the same year, suggests that he had help with research, as he would soon require at all times when his blindness became complete.[50]

Besides the deep use of classical literature in this text, Milton attempts to create a version of cosmopolitan Protestantism that is absent from his vernacular polemic. Here, the differences between Puritans that had played a major role in English politics are largely whitewashed to represent a broad Protestant orthodoxy to which the new English government subscribes. Milton's representation of theological politics in the treatise therefore represents English actions as conforming precisely to the terms laid down in Calvin's *Institutes:* Charles was a tyrant, and he was indicted as such—a fact not entirely available to Milton until the end of the composition process of *The Tenure*—and the magistrates who proceeded against him were just that, magistrates, who conform to the terms established in Calvin's version of Paul in Romans 13. As Milton questions his audience in *Pro Populo:* "What if a magistrate had done so? Does he not bear the sword of God for the very purpose of rendering evil to the evil?" (*PW* 102).

In *The Tenure of Kings and Magistrates,* Milton had built an elaborate reconstruction of this biblical text to show that it was private men who were entitled to hold a sword against the magistrate. In *Pro Populo,* he employs perfectly Calvinistic terms, using Calvin's very words in the description— words that *The Tenure of Kings and Magistrates,* beginning even with its title, had systematically deconstructed. In the preface to the work, Milton writes, "whenever it is most pleasing to [God's] infinite wisdom, he generally casts down proud and unbridled kings" (*PW* 52). The very terms here, and especially "unbridled" (*effrenatos reges, WJM* 7:4–6), derive from the crucial passage in the *Institutes* where Calvin pronounced that "the correcting of unbridled government" (*effrenatae dominationis correctio*) is "the revengement of the Lord."[51] The Lord, that is, who works through the "magistrates" when a king has become "unbridled": "If there bee at this time any Magistrates for the behalfe of the people, . . . I doe so not forbid them according to their office to withstand the outraging licentiousnesse of kings: that I affirme that if they winke at kings willfully ranging over and treading downe the poore communalty, their dissembling is not without wicked breach of faith, because they deceitfully betray the liberty of the people, whereof they know themselves to bee appointed protectors by the ordinance of God."[52]

Milton's conformity with Calvin does not indicate a change of position so much as a rhetorical compromise. We can gauge this as rhetorical rather than theoretical from the simple fact that Milton is looking back on a fact of history—members of the army "purged" Parliament—and writing around it, with the chief aim of countering the damning accusations of Salmasius. The royal apologist wrote with revulsion of the "horrible message" that had struck not just the ears but the minds of Europe "with a terrible wound, about a parricide committed in England in the character of a king by a wicked conspiracy of sacrilegious men" (*PW* 55). Milton therefore does everything to show that England's actions are "orthodox": "Luther for certain, Zwingli, Calvin, Bucer, Paraeus, (along with many others) have asserted that a tyrant 'must be removed'" (*PW* 76), he asserts. "By bringing out into the battle line Luthers, Zwinglis, Calvins, Bucers, Martyrs and Paraeuses," he writes again, "I will set against you even your Leyden friends, whose university, whose most flourishing state, once the dwelling place of freedom . . . you have not one orthodox theologian on your side—you may name one at your leisure—stripped of all Protestant support, you do not blush to flee for refuge to the Sorbonne: a college which you know quite well is totally devoted to popish doctrine and has no authority among the orthodox" (*PW* 125).[53] This is no longer a world divided between Presbyterians and Independents, but between Protestants and Catholics.

In addition to the accusation of sacrilege, there are serious military and political consequences of the world's perception of England's revolutionary act. While Milton dismisses Salmasius's power to kindle war in foreign princes, the threat is, of course, necessary to defuse:

> So far am I from fearing any war or danger for us, most cowardly man, which you can kindle among foreign kings by that raving and at the same time silly eloquence of yours—you who, in jest surely, lay accusations against us before them that "we treat kings' heads" like "balls, play with crowns like hoops, care no more for imperial sceptres than fools' staffs topped with heads." But meanwhile, most foolish head, you are yourself most worthy of topping a fool's staff—you who think kings and princes are persuaded to go to war by such childish arguments. (*PW* 64)

The amount of research, reading, and gathering of apt statements from classical authors is no less than extraordinary, especially for a man on the verge of blindness, and entirely without the use of his left eye.[54] There are just under 230 explicit citations to classical authors in *Pro Populo*, which utterly dwarfs the numbers in previous English tracts, *The Tenure of Kings and Magistrates* being a particularly telling comparison—with a mere five classical citations in the first edition. *Eikonoklastes* also contains a mere handful. (The rate of biblical references remains nearer that of *The Tenure*, although it is still only about one-half that of the regicide tract.)[55] Even when we account for the greater length of the Latin treatise by increasing that number some fourfold, there is no comparison: *Pro Populo* uses dramatically different sources to accomplish different rhetorical aims. These sources are literary as well as political writers—in addition to such appropriately political writers as Livy, Suetonius, Sallust, Tacitus, Cicero, and Aristotle (the two most cited), there are extensive excerpts from poets, such as Horace, Catullus, Terence, Martial, Ovid, Euripides, Aeschylus, Sophocles, Virgil, and Homer (with these epic writers in greater abundance, not surprisingly, in the 1658 edition, when Milton would have been read to during the early stages of *Paradise Lost*). In addition to this list, Milton mentions without citation figures from classical history well over fifty times—Tiberius, Marcus Aurelius, Claudius, Nero, Tarquin, and so forth—which derive from an unattributed source.

Unlike the far more occasional use of source material in *Eikonoklastes,* these authors as well as others are generally quoted and cited—it is a much more scholarly work that aims at a more sophisticated audience—but also, it fair to say, a work given vastly more attention in composition.

Milton reuses the entries in his Commonplace Book at least twenty-three times, twenty-two entries from the Political Index and one from the Ethical Index. One of these is written in by Jeremie Picard, the chief amanuensis for *De Doctrina Christiana.* This entry from Augustine corresponds to a small addition made to *Pro Populo* for the 1658 edition—one of the most interesting scribal entries, as it is the only one I have been able to find in the Political Index that distinctly corresponds to a printed work in the later stage of Milton's political career, allowing us to reconstruct fairly closely the chronology and manner of a scribal entry, but also revealing an aspect of Milton's relationships with his assistants.[56] This added note in the Commonplace Book is a tangible indication of the kind of editorial and even compositional help in producing later polemics that must have been extensive. But even in 1650, when, as Milton writes, "I have quite limited strength, and am forced to apply myself to this bit by bit with difficulty and break off almost every hour, when it is a matter which I ought to have pursued with uninterrupted composition and attention" (*PW* 54), we imagine that he has employed researchers—which scholars with full vision might have done in even less urgent circumstances—to collect commonplaces or historical facts to integrate into his rebuttal of Salmasius. The number of books referred to in *Pro Populo* that Milton cited here for the first and only time far surpasses that of any other printed work—there are twenty-one books that he never cites anywhere else, and seven additional books are introduced as sources, to be reused in the *Defensio Secunda* and occasionally in a few later cases in the *Response of John Phillips* (December 1651).[57] The implication here would be either that Milton helped write the *Responsio,* as is normally thought, or that Phillips helped write the Latin defenses, which makes even more sense, although surely some combination of both would be expected.[58] The number of twenty-one new and unique citations in *Pro Populo* might be compared to a mere two sources unique to the *Defensio Secunda,* six in *The History of Britain,* two in *Observations,* six in *Eikonoklastes,* seven in the second edition of *The Tenure,* and three in *Areopagitica.* The only other work that comes close in the number of unique sources is Milton's Commonplace Book, which also cites twenty sources that are not cited elsewhere (though in this case many of them clearly inform his work).[59] Some of the weight of this figure is attributable to the Latin treatise's mere length, as it is around four times the length of *The Tenure,* but it still represents a remarkable industry on Milton's part.

Many if not most of these first-used sources (or at least first-cited sources) are classical—Aeschylus, *Supplices;* Sallust, *Bellum Iugurthinum;* Plato, *Letters;* Theognis, *Elegies;* Pliny, *Panegyrics;* Philo Judaeus, *Legum allegoria;* Claudian Claudianus (fourth century), *De IV consulatu Honorii;* Herodian of Antioch, *Historiae Romanae scriptores Latini minores;* Diotogenes the Pythagorean, *Librum de regno,* a fragment preserved in Stobaeus, from *Ioannis Stobaei Sententiae, ex Thesauris Graecorum Delectae* (1609); Xenophon, *Hiero;* M. Junianus Justinus, *Epitoma historiarum Philippicarum Trogi Pompeii.* In addition to these uniquely cited sources, there are several cited sources that appear again in later works (in the *Defensio Secunda* or the *Responsio* almost exclusively), which include Terence, *Eunuchus;* Ovid, *Metamorphoses;* Sophocles, *Antigone;* Plautus, *Aulularia;* and Horace, *Odes* and *Satires.*

Some explanation for the unusual number of first citations is provided by the simple fact that Milton is quoting Salmasius and quoting the books that Salmasius uses to show his misreadings. But there are, nonetheless, some new signs of research: Fortesque's *Laws of the English People* is used here for the first time, as is the "ancient manuscript . . . titled Modus Parlamenti" (*PW* 211). And unlike *The Tenure,* which shows signs of being written in a fantastic hurry, with at times three passages taken directly from his notes, here Milton frequently returns to consult Holinshed and Socrates' *Ecclesiastical History* (*PW* 143), and conducts new research where in the heated composition process of *The Tenure* he usually would have made do with what he had already written in his notes. The difference may again reflect the possible existence of devoted research assistants, an expense easily justified given the immensity of the task, the public office, and the encroaching blindness of the author.

If the numbers of citations in this treatise were used as a gauge, one might well argue that Milton's politics were deeply classical or indeed that he matured to write something more recognizably classical (or classically republican) after the events of 1648 and early 1649. But while there are certainly signs of theoretical development of a kind, Milton's use of classical texts is largely rhetorical and accommodating. Most of this is not political theory but literary prowess. Milton argues here with a professor who had spent his career issuing editions of Greek and Roman works. Salmasius would nowadays be a classicist or a philologist; Milton pejoratively calls him a "grammarian," both to stress his expertise in words rather than deeds and to indicate his incompetence in what he does—that he is "clearly lacking in common sense and Latinity" (*PW* 209). A great part of the satiric achievement of this work lies in Milton's success in showing himself a better humanist than his exalted professorial opponent. "Let us come to the Romans," he writes in one of many such passages. "You return first of all to that statement, made not by Sallust, but by Gaius Mennius in Sallust: 'to do with impunity whatever you like.'" Once Milton shows that Salmasius misquotes Sallust, he goes on to show how Sallust is in fact an advocate for his own arguments, and not those of Salmasius: "Sallust himself is the authority in clear words for the statement that 'the Romans had a government by law, though a regal name for their government'"—citing *Bellum Iugurthinum,* which is used uniquely in *Pro Populo*—"and when it 'became a tyranny,' as you know, they thrust it out." In a procedure repeated through out the tract, Milton then draws on at least one more classical author to refute Salmasius, citing Cicero's *In Pisonem* (*PW* 166).

Again showing himself a better classicist, Milton demonstrates that Salmasius quotes Tacitus out of context: "But, you say, 'Tacitus who flourished under the empire of a single man' wrote thus: 'The gods have granted the supreme authority over affairs to a prince, to subjects there remains the honour of obeying.' And you do not say where it comes from—no doubt because you are conscious of imposing remarkably upon your readers. This indeed I at once smelt out, though I did not at once find that passage." When Milton finds the quoted passage, he discovers that these are not the words of Tacitus, but of a "Roman knight" brought before Tiberius on "a capital charge." Instead of criticizing Salmasius for willfully misreading Tacitus, although this is implied, Milton criticizes his sloppy note-taking, and his reliance on the unreliable "somewhere" that produced this excerpt: "If you preferred to read Tacitus himself rather than copy an excerpt from somewhere too carelessly, he would have taught you the origin of that right of emperors" (*PW* 167–68). Milton goes on to show just what Tacitus really has to say about the rights of emperors, and calls on a few other classical passages, in Dio Cassius, Cicero, the Codes of Theodosius and Valentinian, and Pliny (cited exclusively in *Pro Populo*).

Now that the kingdom of England had been transformed into a republic, Milton seems at greater liberty to discuss Roman Republican ideas, although often this happens in passing rather than directly. In two passages, indeed, he passes over the most important theoretical questions of the moment—the natural condition of human political life and the broad but central question of which system of government, republic or monarchical, is superior. His disappointing statement, "It is not my plan now to construct a long account about nature and about the origin of political life" (*PW* 149) is followed shortly thereafter with the similar statement: "It is not now the place to discuss what is the better form of governing the commonwealth, by one person or by many. Many famous men have indeed praised monarchy, but only if he who is sole ruler is the best man of all and most worthy of ruling. If this does not eventuate, nothing slips more readily than monarchy into a tyranny which is worst" (*PW* 153). Of course, both of these statements enact the rhetorical technique known as *praeteritio* or *occultatio,* of saying what one means by introducing it as a topic one is not going to speak of; Milton goes on, in both cases, to expound somewhat on these issues, as the first statement is used to open a chapter on the Law of Nature, and the second touches on an issue frequently returned to throughout the text. Yet these rhetorical gestures nonetheless register what is in fact too true about both of these topics, that if it were not the case that Milton needed to devote his intellectual energies toward putting out fires of internal and international rage against England's nascent government, he might have been able to theorize it.

Milton had, of course, used an "account about nature and about the origin of political life" as the foundation for his argument in *The Tenure.* This account was devoted, as is the case here, to establishing the fundamental right of national self-determination. The account went only so far as to suggest inferentially that a republic would be the best form, although without articulating how such a government would function or establish itself. Arguments for a republican form often come as asides, slipped in by way of a relentless argument for the legitimacy of the decisions of December and January 1648–49. At one moment, Milton uses Salmasius misquoting Cicero as a way of reasserting his argument through Cicero—but not in a way that he would take responsibility for in his own voice:

> You say "it was the less good kings that used to employ the right of freedom they were granted." But I have proved that this right was introduced by you for the destruction of the human race and was not granted by God. . . . You say "this freedom grants the power, if you wish" and your excuse is that you have Cicero as the authority on this right. I never regret quoting your evidence; for you yourself usually destroy your case by means of your own witnesses. So hear the words of Cicero in 4 *Philip.:* "What reason for waging war is more just than to drive off slavery? In this situation, even though the master is not troublesome, yet it is most wretched that he has the power to be so if he wants."[60]

Milton is letting the respected Cicero speak in his stead. By quoting Cicero's words, "even though the master is not troublesome," Milton subtly weaves into this otherwise more cautious text his own radical argument in *The Tenure,* where he opines that the monarchy "though not illegal, or intolerable, hangs over them as a Lordly scourge, not as a free government." In such a government, "[the people] can in due esteem be thought no better than slaves and vassals born, in the tenure and occupation of another inheriting Lord" (*PW* 32). As political philosophy, this position is more modern—in spite of its classical orientation—than Protestant resistance theory, since it mandates systemic change without regard for the legal (or spiritual) status of the ruler. Dzelzainis points out that the Ciceronian passage may be behind this formulation in *The Tenure,* and this may be so; but it is of particular interest that *The Tenure* asserts the position as a central argument (without Cicero), and *Pro Populo* instead lets Cicero make the argument for Milton, but only in passing and in a way that leaves Milton without responsibility for it. The powerful phrase "even though the master is not troublesome" is a gratuitous part of the Ciceronian passage on slavery, extraneous to Milton's rebuttal of Salmasius.

In another poignant moment, Milton draws from his unattributed meditation on the first page of the Political Index, in which he reflects that "the form of state to be fitted to the peoples disposition some live best under monarchy others otherwise. so that the conversions of commonwealths happen not always through ambition or malice. as among Romans who after thire infancy were ripe for a more free government then monarchy, being in a manner all fit to be Ks" (CB 177, *CPW* 1:420). In *Pro Populo Anglicano Defensio,* in a passage probably shaped by this formative entry, Milton states: "For it is agreed that the same form of government does not suit every people nor the same people all the time, but sometimes this form, sometimes that one, accordingly as the virtue and industry of the citizens sometimes increases and sometimes diminishes. But whoever removes from a people their power of choosing for themselves the form of government they want, removes for certain that in which civil liberty is almost wholly rooted" (*PW* 121). In the printed treatise, Milton removes all the conspicuous references to a republican "form of government," although an astute reader would have little trouble ascertaining which "form of government" corresponds to "the virtue and industry of the citizens," and which to a less virtuous and industrious citizenship: these two poles of political behavior map conventionally onto a republican-monarchy binary. Milton's suggestion that this proposition is "agreed," as if this were an axiom, however, remains a bit tricky. Still, in this broad formulation, in which we are asked only to accept that there are different forms of government that work for different people at different times (according to each society's virtue and industry), it is hard not to accept Milton's terms. The second sentence and proposition, deriving from this stated axiom, adds the right of choice to the first: without the right of choice to determine the form of government, the very prospect of civil liberty is itself precluded. There is a circularity to this formulation, as it takes as a given that "civil liberty" or "civitas libertas" (*WJM* 7:192)—itself a new concept in English politics[61]—is an inalienable right. Yet Milton is making a different and much stronger argument than that made by the bulk of this treatise, which focuses on the orthodoxy of actions committed by legitimate magistrates. Milton subtly suggests here a far more radical, if not also more modern, idea: this choice of the "people" depends not on the degree of their obligation to a malignant king, but on their strengths and needs as a nation.

To make such an argument acceptable to the nation would prove, of course, unattainable. In Milton's last polemic cry for liberty, *The Readie and Easie Way to Establish a Free Commonwealth* (1660), he seems in the midst of proposing this "easy way" to recognize that perhaps another way must come first: "To make the people fittest to chuse, and the chosen fittest to govern, will be to mend our corrupt and faulty education, to teach the people faith not without virtue" (*CPW* 7:423). At a similarly revealing moment in *Pro Populo*, Milton confesses that the constitution of the Rump Parliament and the political structure of England was perhaps far from ideal: "this constitution is what our time and dissensions allow; that it is not such as to be wished, but such as the persistent discords of wicked citizens allow it to be" (*PW* 61). These persistent discords, and the ideological efforts required to counter them, may help explain the dearth of programmatic thinking at this moment. In 1660 Milton would also look back and complain that after the dissolution of the monarchy in 1649 "the form of a commonwealth should have forthwith been framed, and the practice thereof immediately begun."[62] In the same general period, Milton wrote "A Letter to a Friend," an unpublished manuscript offering a somewhat different perspective. He surmised there that "whether the civill government be an annuall democracy or a perpetuall Aristocracy, is too nice a consideracion for the extremeties wherein wee are" (*CPW* 7:331). To pause and deliberate over the niceties of political constitutions was, in 1659, as was surely the case in 1649, nearly impossible: all that the members of the new government could do was struggle to throw together something that, in the extremities of the moment, would keep the state from collapsing.

Conclusion

Historical Politics and the Instability of Print Culture

The revolution in modern bibliographical studies has in large measure been effected
through a willingness to notice what had been unnoticeable, to find evidence in the
hitherto irrelevant.

Stephen Orgel

In the course of the period covered in this book, Milton moves
from being a polemicist whose chief purported audience is the Parliament,
to a polemicist justifying the overthrow of this Parliament, to a counterpropagandist—perhaps even a propagandist—for the newly constructed
Rump Parliament. Soon after composing his greatest effort at addressing the
Long Parliament in the early 1640s, *Areopagitica,* Milton retreated from his
first parliamentary audience and from the public altogether. From "within
private walls," he devoted himself in the late 1640s to several projects, including *The History of Britain,* a manuscript containing the trenchant "Digression" among other lost passages. When he reemerged four years later as a
polemicist, with the hurriedly written but thunderous *Tenure of Kings and
Magistrates,* many of the rhetorical strategies developed in the prior stage of
his polemical career still inhered in his work, although in this case he was no
longer trying to reform the policies of a now defunct Parliament, in a sense
forcibly "reformed" by Pride's Purge. He sought rather to justify the Purge
and the impending execution of the king. His position as author, as a private
man writing to the public, also remained unchanged from the earlier polemic of the 1640s. Unlike the earlier polemic, however, *The Tenure of Kings
and Magistrates* was inflected by the historical work he had undertaken in
the interim, as well as by his (often cynical) sense of the constitutional potential of the British people. This powerful argument for popular sovereignty
deeply utilized the historical research of the previous ten years.

The two manuscripts remaining from this period of political prose—the
Commonplace Book and the "Digression"—are essentially bits of preserved

refuse left over from the compositional and publication processes. They were, of course, both preserved and valued for a time by Milton's near contemporaries; the "Digression" in particular seems to have been shared by a limited circle of readers, and somehow managed, as its copyist had evidently hoped, to survive the ravages of time. Readers may now add the "Digression" to the *History* where it is instructed for insertion, on page 110, after "from one misery to another." For us, of course, these shreds of nearly discarded evidence are of immeasurable value, not just as museum pieces, but for the glimpse they give us, however tantalizing at times, of what happened behind the scenes of textual production. We can and should dream of finding additional shards of evidence to fill in the story—another example of the distinctive scribal hand that produced the "Digression," for instance, or a match for the other Machiavelli Scribe, or a copy of *The History of Britain* with marginal marks on page 110, or even the lost Theological Index(es?)—but for the time being, we must work with what we have.

In different ways these two manuscripts suggest a great deal about the process of composition and publication, and about the public work that was the result of this process. Fundamentally, the manuscripts allow us to see a highly developed historical component in Milton's political thought. Our reconstruction of Milton's research agenda began as he articulated it in 1637 to Diodati, when he wrote of being "occupied for a long time by the obscure history" of European constitutions, and studying such subjects as the "time when liberty was granted" the Germans "by Rudolph, King of Germany." Milton stated here that his interest thereafter would be "to read separately about what each State did by its own Effort" (*CPW* 1:327). This he did, voluminously over the course of many years, often recording notes on constitutional history in his Commonplace Book. Milton's historical note-taking was quite different from that practiced by most of his contemporaries, as it was concerned more with facts and deeds than with sententiae and aphorisms. These preferences suggest that the lack of "brief sententious precepts"[1] in his commonplacing habits has a much deeper influence—even on his prosody— than has been explored. His practices of reading can be seen in useful contrast to the methods of others, a contrast that further suggests that the models we have to describe early modern reading practices remain incomplete.

Invoking a truth universally acknowledged about seventeenth-century thought, Blair Worden once wrote that "the civilisation of seventeenth-century England rests, we may broadly say, on two intellectual pillars: the Bible, and the literature of classical antiquity."[2] This well-worn notion of the structures and sources of early modern writing has justifiably shaped perceptions of Milton, as in the claim cited in my introduction that he "immersed himself in the literature and writings of the classical republicans" and "also sought answers in scripture."[3] Yet while the classics and the Bible indisputably shaped this late humanist's vocabulary, he was deeply invested in a program of reading that does not fit within these categories. Milton's Commonplace Book brings to the fore several issues regarding his scholarship. Fundamentally, it suggests that he was in fact immersing himself in a surprisingly different corpus of reading than preconceived notions about early modern reading might have suggested.[4] Perhaps the greatest surprise in the body of now relatively obscure books and manuscripts is Milton's commitment to history. While we can only guess at what the actual balance of reading during the 1640s was for Milton—poetry, history, drama, theology, classical literature—the evidence in his notes and the books referred to in his printed work, as well as the contents of the work itself, make a compelling case that the bias of political reading over "poetrie" (*CPW* 3:406) in his charge in *Eikonoklastes* against the King's poetic reading habits represent a bias quite close to Milton's own reading in these years. Yet while there is close affinity between the use of source material in the Commonplace Book and the sources in his printed texts of the period, there are also surprising patterns of difference between manuscript and print. These differences have led me to the conclusion that there was not only a different Milton in the manuscript notes, but a different private Milton from the public persona that he created for his polemical prose. Finally, close scrutiny of these notes demonstrates that this record of reading is not a random collection of scraps haphazardly put together—my own initial impression of the Commonplace Book—but a program of research that had its own ideology, an ideology which itself responded to the reading habits and practices of Milton's contemporaries.

Milton's habits of note-taking are Bodinian rather than Erasmian, focused far more on the facts of constitutional history than on the sayings and apothegms that might find rhetorical reuse. It seems unlikely, given the structure of his Commonplace Book, his general interest in Bodin, and the popularity of Bodin's *Methodus ad Facilem Historiarum Cognitionem* (1566), that Bodin's method would not have been a shaping force. But whether this influence is direct or indirect matters far less than the ideological position about reading that this method represents, which Milton's practices and his stated opinions about "aphorisms" affirm. Early in Milton's career, he turned away from the form of reading that privileged the "sentence"—the short, aphoristic phrase stylistically transformed in poetry into the tightly end-stopped Jonsonian couplet. Instead, rejecting in practice Erasmus's emphasis on the phrase recorded from classical and vernacular literature, Milton follows Bodin in reading for historical example. In a largely chronological approach, he collates the same kind of pan-European history with some of the same goals: describing the origins and evaluating the successes of political constitutions in history, with the aim of bringing the conclusions of this research to bear on the present and future state of affairs.

In many ways, Milton's Commonplace Book is not a commonplace book in the normal sense of the term—a collection of useful sayings or commonplaces—but a structured research tool designed to organize and interpret facts about social history. In my search through archives holding early modern commonplace books and notebooks, I consulted more or less randomly—for the cataloging of anonymous manuscripts remains undeveloped—about two hundred manuscripts that might fit the category of notebook or commonplace book. While I have yet to find another notebook that follows the patterns of Milton's, there are records of people like the members of the Sidney family who were influenced by Bodin and took historical rather than rhetorical notes.[5] In addition to the large archive of unexplored reading notebooks, these case histories suggest that Milton may be less singular in his reading habits than he now appears. More commonplace books similar to Milton's will likely emerge from the archives of unexplored (and uncatalogued) manuscripts, and this will help us draw from a larger body of evidence the relationships between reading methods and writing in early modern England.

Milton's long-term interest in constitutional history seems to bear fruit in two projects in particular, started, at least, at around the same time: *The History of Britain,* which eventually appeared as a Restoration text, shorn of its digressive and not-so-digressive political language, and *The Tenure of Kings and Magistrates.* While his research into British constitutional history continued in significant ways in the initial work done for the new regime—and particularly in his Latin magnum opus, the satiric *Pro Populo Anglicano Defensio*—the nature of argument changes considerably. In *Pro Populo,* the major achievement of this period, Milton blends the more experimental form of historical inquiry that had preoccupied him in the prerevolutionary period with a traditional Erasmian style of commonplacing.

Work on Milton's prose has increasingly sought to understand how it operated within an ideological and historical battle, waged at first between Puritans and royalists, and then largely between factions of Puritans—Presbyterians and various forms of Independency. In many ways, Milton fits in this latter category, and tracts such as *Areopagitica* (1644) and *The Tenure of Kings and Magistrates* (1649) must be understood as being deeply involved in a network of communication of Puritans writing to other Puritans. Yet in other significant ways, this category does not sufficiently describe Milton or his audience, real or perceived. The *Poems of Mr. John Milton, both English and Latin* (1645), published right in the middle of the same crisis, does not easily fit into the same discursive context. The "Digression" is so inconspicuously Puritan that it was readily adapted as Tory propaganda in its pirated publication in 1681. If the large collection of reading notes recorded in the Commonplace Book were found with no distinctive marks of the owner's identity, it would not have been identified as the work of a radical Puritan: there are no references to Puritans in it, nor any references to the sort of theological reading one might expect of an English Puritan. The great range of reading found there demonstrates what Milton would appreciatively call "books promiscuously read" (*CPW* 2:517). Even the printed texts of *Areopagitica* and *The Tenure* suggest that the work of other Puritan writers constitutes only a fraction of Milton's own reading, and indeed, as I argue in this book, most of the Puritans Milton cites in these tracts, such as Thomas Cartwright or William Prynne, are writers he never actually seems to have agreed with—perhaps outside of a brief period around 1640–42.

Indeed, Milton is a master of the art of negative representation, and there is a great deal of disagreement—pronounced or concealed for rhetorical purposes—with the Puritan contemporaries he refers to. Famously, he seldom mentions sects by name, and after his explicit break with the Presbyterians in the mid-1640s, he does not assign to himself any sectarian identity.[6] The way in which we understand Milton as participating in Puritanism needs, following the major biography of Campbell and Corns, to be seriously rethought. The label should be applied to him with caution, as it unnecessarily narrows our sense of the world that shaped him and to which he responded. Nor is "Puritan" particularly useful historically, without further qualification, since in many ways the struggle that tore the state apart in the late 1640s was a struggle waged among Puritans—Puritans who wanted, among other things, to put other Puritans to death for heresy. Some of these Puritans we might call "radical," but most of them are more truly "conservative" and certainly more fundamentalist, than their Laudian opponents.[7]

Milton's avoidance of party mentality is reinforced by his wide correspondence with Puritans and non-Puritans. This is particularly true in the formative years of the 1630s, when he initiated a major plan of historical research and circulated among or visited a diverse group of influential intellectuals in both England and abroad, including such figures as Henry Lawes, Henry Wotton, and the celebrities Grotius and Galileo. The larger point to make here is that literary historians have so often painted the "Puritan" literature of the revolutionary period and the Interregnum in a binary opposition to royalist literature, when not only are the individual players more complicated when one moves the lens closer, but the culture itself cannot be seen as operating in a binary fashion. In addition to these cultural tensions, England experienced a series of administrative changes far more complex than simply the rise and fall of the monarchy, in which—in the case of Milton and many others—the less frequently told story of the rise and fall of Presbyterian extremism had a more pronounced impact on the conditions of writing in the 1640s.[8]

One of the most pressing questions with respect to the interpretation of these tracts is whether their different positions represent shifts or even incoherencies in political theory or a flexible rhetorical strategy, designed to conform to the needs of a changing and multifaceted audience. An inquiry into the motivations behind ideological representation can, of course, be rife with complications. On a simple level, this question can boil down to the issue of whether Milton's most radical arguments in *The Tenure of Kings and Magistrates* were really about justice, or were devised merely for the purpose of advancing a party whose rise to power must then be protected with the very arguments he had once dismantled. It is this kind of question that gave rise to claims that Milton's London in the 1640s could be compared to "Petrograd in 1919 and Havana in 1965"[9] or that his work possessed "the most repellent aspects of fascism."[10]

Although meaning and intent are never entirely separable, in this book I have generally sought to avoid approaching the problem from this moralizing intentionalist angle, not only because it seems biographical and psychological rather than literary or historical in its orientation, but also because the question is simply too hard to answer accurately, and is thus susceptible to the most preposterous forms of subjective judgment. It is hard enough to work out the "real motivation"—if there is such a thing—of figures yet living. To use Milton as a subject for psychological or historical information of this character is not only to pick a poor subject to answer a question hard enough without the gap of four hundred years, it is also to give literature a lamentably reductive role, when the point is to understand how the literature—and not the author—works.

Yet sometimes, in search of literary meaning, we must ask how the author works, or find, as D. F. McKenzie insisted of bibliography, "the human presence" in textual evidence.[11] Here I have sought to understand not just How Milton Works, to invoke a recent book title on the subject, but how Milton work*ed*—how he took information from books in his library or another's, copied it at one point into his notebook, and then recycled it at some other point into a writing project—or did not recycle it, or recycled only some part of it, or changed it in the process of reusing it. My conclusion, based on a reading of the evidence that places an interpretive bias on the manuscript materials, is that Milton's polemical prose is highly constructed to negotiate his readers' opinions in ways that are often entirely dissociated from Milton's own. This dissociation raises, I believe, a vital question with regard to moralizing intentionalism, since there is often an implicit ethical judgment that must accompany our gauging, often for lack of better words, Milton's disingenuousness and rhetorical prevarication. Our unease with rhetoric and even rhetorical disingenuousness is largely the product of a critique of rhetoric that has emerged since the 1660s.

In attempting to historicize Milton's forms of discourse, I have also sought to understand what impediments, either cultural or legal, may have prevented him from publishing beliefs such as republicanism or anti-Calvinism that he nonetheless possessed. In some cases, such as the ideas of Machiavelli's recorded in his Commonplace Book, he may never have thought the private record would ever be used publicly—these notes may always have functioned merely as background machinery in the private construction of ideas. But in the important cases of *De Doctrina Christiana* and the censored parts of *The History of Britain,* Milton obviously hoped at one time to publish views that became, through the course of changing events, impossible to print. Political pressures therefore changed the way in which he could represent ideas even in texts that he was in the very process of creating.

Our view of early modern censorship has now been reshaped by a couple of major revisionist studies, Debora Shuger's *Censorship and Cultural Sensibility* (2006) and Cyndia Clegg's *Press Censorship in Caroline England* (2008), the latter the last in an instructive series that began with books on Jacobean and Elizabethan England. Both of these scholars have from different perspectives challenged the "Whig" interpretation of the history of censorship, seeing the early modern condition of writing as far less circumscribed than the work of Annabel Patterson and others has suggested.[12] Shuger and Clegg look with great attention at the administrative mechanisms and stated intentions behind the control of belief to reassess the nature of this control. Remarkably, both of these books end where this study begins, in 1641, which Clegg calls in her final chapter "the end of censorship." Where Shuger's point of departure lies in the surprising rarity of Milton's contention in *Areopagitica* that the press should be free, her study, too, ends with what has been seen as the "breakdown of censorship," or—as Shuger writes correctly, when "press controls" were "dismantled."[13] Yet the period after 1641 deserves more attention. The problem with this traditional watershed moment in the history of the press, as I hope this study has made clear, is that serious pressures on authorial freedom continue through the 1640s and during the Restoration.

Indeed, Milton's writing career can be seen as a series of punctuated moments, in which he responds by changing, or muting, or being forced to mute what he puts into print. As may be the case in 1645, after being widely decried as a heretic for his views on divorce, he may have similarly responded to these restrictions on free speech by simply going into retreat. Some of the most obvious administrative acts in this period include the Licensing Act of 1643, the extraordinarily severe Ordinance for the Punishment of Blasphemies and Heresies in 1648, and the Act of Indemnity and Oblivion in 1660, and the Press Act of 1662. Added to these public acts of policy were individual cases or charges against Milton, such as the petition of the Company of Stationers against unlicensed books (including *The Doctrine and Discipline of Divorce*) of August 1644, the incident in which he was questioned for publishing the Racovian Catechism in 1650, the recalling and burning of his books by royal proclamation in 1660, and the reported acts of censorship of *Paradise Lost* (1667) and *The History of Britain* (1670).[14] These instances in Milton's particular story suggest the value of looking more closely at the material evidence for the ways in which writers used different media in different ways. Material textual analysis provides a valuable way of rethinking the nature of expressive freedom in early modern writing.

The relationship between the internal forces of authorial creation and external forces of censorious opposition would distinctly shape Milton's writing, as would the frequent need to concentrate authorial performance on the specific needs of a given audience and context. As I have suggested here, Milton's Commonplace Book, in spite of a long tradition in the use of such books as rhetorical tools, is in many crucial respects not rhetorically oriented. Milton is not interested in collecting aphorisms in a way that can be recycled into an effective act of persuasion; in fact, in spite of his publication of Raleigh's supposed maxims, he is revealingly opposed to this common practice of his contemporaries. The Commonplace Book is a scholarly research tool, a system of note-taking that reveals a great deal about the nature of Milton's historically oriented political argument. Fundamentally, it shows that his arguments are not adequately described as a series of observations taken from other authorities—classical, biblical, or even modern—and fitted together as though in some sort of pastiche, as is conspicuously the case, for example, with the *Cabinet Council*. And yet Milton's writing is deeply rhetorical. In most cases, where he is most rhetorical he is not using the evidence in his notebook, in part because this kind of historical evidence was not the common political parlance of his less sophisticated contemporaries, and when he argued rhetorically it was most often to engage or reframe the language of his opponents.

The extent to which Milton's polemic is deliberately indirect—even tactically deceptive—is, I believe, underappreciated. His republican encomiums and public treatises often endorse people or ideas about which the same text insinuates very different meanings. The rhetoric of praise, the most basic form of rhetoric in public oratory, is the most prominent among many complex strategies Milton devised to engage contemporaries and contemporary discourse, using language that performed a more complicated function than representing literal meaning. Authorities such as Bacon, Machiavelli, Cartwright, Arminius, and even Calvin are also employed not for what they meant to Milton, but what he thought they would mean to his audience—sometimes diametrically different things. At the same time, as I have sought to show in the analysis of the Commonplace Book and the "Digression," he deliberately omitted ideas, beliefs, and authorities that would not produce the right impression in his audience.

Yet at the same time that Milton's polemic is richly rhetorical, it is also invested in the philosophical developments of the seventeenth century. The hermeneutic and methodological difference between "rhetoric" and "political theory" was recognized in various ways in the history of political philosophy. While Milton rarely engages these categories in his writing at this stage, it is of interest here that some contemporaries—and particularly Hobbes—were increasingly keen to draw a categorical distinction. Writers such as Hobbes and later Thomas Sprat, historian of the Royal Society, criticized rhetoric as a dangerous and shallow tool for the pursuit of knowledge.[15] Indeed, in one instance in *Behemoth*, Hobbes dismisses the work of both Milton and his royalist opponent Salmasius: the books were, according to him, "very good Latine both, and hardly to be judged which is better; and both very ill reasoning, and hardly to be judged which is worst"; these political treatises were, he goes on to say, mere exercises in "Rhetorick."[16] Hobbes's own professedly rational political theory is not, of course, entirely devoid of rhetoric.[17] And while Milton is not a political philosopher so much as a literary polemicist, the two modes of argument—philosophical argument and rhetorical disingenuousness—coexist in his work. Milton experiments with the very form of argument that Hobbes had used to counter the rhetorical tradition, the rules of reason and the laws of nature. These become particularly important in the argument for popular sovereignty in *The Tenure of Kings and Magistrates,* and would remain a core element in his political theory.

Appendix A

The *Index Politicus* of Milton's Commonplace Book

Authors, Texts, and Citations

Any quantitative analysis of the Commonplace Book's sources is beset by a variety of qualitative distinctions. For example, should a reference to Stow's *Annales* that includes page numbers deserve equal statistical consideration with the more ambiguous reference indicated by "and Sto."? How does one quantify the difference between a single entry that includes a cluster of distinct citations—such as the many clustered citations to Holinshed—and separate, individual entries with separate and singular citations? Is Cyprian of the same weight as his companions when his name precedes the phrase "or someone else"? And to which genre of source material does the citation "as happens today" belong? Although quantitative analysis has its limitations, it should be stressed that the Commonplace Book is itself committed to a quantitative valuation: "about a dozen times by this P[age]," clarifies one entry from Speed.

In spite of these often subjective distinctions, this appendix presents two figures that emerge from an empirical and reproducible inventory of the Commonplace Book's sources. The difference between these two figures lies in their treatment of multiple citations within a single entry: the first, "conservative" figure does not take multiple citations of a single author within a single entry into account, while the second, "liberal" figure incorporates the number of citations within each entry into its data. The clustered entries seem to have been entered all at once, in a relatively long reading session. The conservative figure, therefore, which counts each of these sittings as one entry, provides a measure of numbers of different volumes Milton consulted at different times. The liberal count records each citation as a single event. This provides an important corrective to the first, conservative statistic, for any investigation into the preoccupations of Milton's research would suffer by ignoring the interest indicated by a single entry on Holinshed that occupies half of a page with multiple citations and arguments.

These two figures, then, constitute both ends of a spectrum along which we might quantify the Commonplace Book's sources. Any more accurate figure depends on interpretive acts that cannot be easily quantified—breaking down thought clusters and the rhetorical structures of commonplacing, or analyzing the structural partitioning of the sources themselves.

A note on the dating of topics and entries: In the table of citations that begins on page 210, the dating is based on several scholars, with some revisions, including Mohl, in *CPW* I, whose own dating is based on Hanford, "Chronology of Milton's Private Studies." I have assigned to topics the dates of the earliest entry, since it always matches the hand and period of the first entry after it ("Chronology," 257). Shawcross has suggested some emendations to the earlier dates (which are relatively few), and I have noted these accordingly. I have indicated by note where the dating needs to be reconsidered, although there are a few broad revisions that should be noted here: I believe that some dates need to be assigned to 1638–39, when Milton traveled through Europe. I agree with Shawcross that the dating of most of the amanuenses/ students should be moved to the period when they were students. For those written by Edward and (possibly) John Phillips, the Machiavelli entries, I have moved from the conventional place in the early 1650s to 1646–49. There is a paucity of evidence suggesting Milton's use of his Commonplace Book after 1652. One concrete citation in the *Likeliest Means to Remove Hirelings* (1659) corresponds to an entry from John Selden in the Economic Index (*CPW* 7:299; CB 109, *CPW* 1:402), but this seems to be the only occurrence in the political literature of the late 1650s, suggesting that either the Commonplace Book was brought out by an assistant in an rare moment, or that Milton's marked copy of Selden's *Uxor Hebraica* was consulted.

All original topic headings are in Latin, although around 50 percent of Milton's entries are English. The original headings are retained where possible. I have also noted a few exceptional cases where Milton comments at some length, and where these commentaries go beyond the cited material (thus giving him authorial credit below). This is necessarily an incomplete measure of Milton's authorial presence in the entries.

(Conservative estimate) Percentage of block entries from histories: 72% (170/236)
(Liberal estimate) Percentage of citations from histories: 79% (292/370)
Percentage of amanuensis entries: 9% (22/236; 14/22 are to Machiavelli, *Discorsi*)
Percentage of history in Milton's hand from the conservative: 80%
Percentage of history by other hands: 18% (4/22)
Number of different amanuenses/students/scribes: 7
Percentage of foreign imprints (by titles, rather than numbers of entries): 73% (48/66)
Percentage of British imprints (including Edinburgh and Dublin): 26% (17/66)

Abbreviations and Symbols

All citations to "later use" works are to the Yale prose edition, except where noted.

*	not cited directly, but recognizable as probable source
°	written by a hand other than Milton's (but not by Graham, who is omitted here); see the corresponding note for identification.
cit.	citations
A	*Animadversions* (1641), *CPW* I

AR	*Areopagitica* (1644), *CPW* 2
BT	Outlines for "British Tragedies" (1639?–42?), *CPW* 8
D	"The Digression" (1648), *CPW* 5
DDD	*The Doctrine and Discipline of Divorce* (1643/44), *CPW* 2
1D	*Defence of the English People* (1651); pages correspond to *PW*
2D	*Pro Populo Anglicano Defensio Secunda* (1654), *CPW* 4
E	*Eikonoklastes* (1649), *CPW* 3
ED	*Of Education* (1644), *CPW* 2
H	*History of Britain* (1648–70), *CPW* 5
O	*Observations upon the Articles of Peace* (1649), *CPW* 3
R	*Of Reformation* (1641), *CPW* 1
T	*The Tenure of Kings and Magistrates* (1649), *CPW* 3
Vane	"To Sir Henry Vane the Younger" (1652), *CSP* 330–31

Table of Citations begins on next page

Index Politicus

Topic and work cited	Probable date	Language	Later use
Respublica, "Republic" (p. 177)	**1637**		
Eusebius, *Historia Ecclesiastica* (*HE*)	1637[1]	Latin	*R*
Milton and possibly Smith	1640–42	English	*D, 449; *1D, 121; *H, 131.
Camden, *Annales* (1615–27)	1639–40	Latin	
De Thou, *Historia* (Geneva, 1620)	1642–44	Latin	*AR
Machiavelli, *Arte di Guerra* in *Tutte le Opere*	1640–42	Latin & Italian	*T, 190.

Notes
1. Shawcross; Mohl, 1635–37.

Topic and work cited	Probable date	Language	Later use
Love of Country (p. 178)	**1639–40**		
Lactantius, *Seven Books* in *Opera* (Lyons, 1548)	1639–40	Latin	
Holinshed, *Chronicles* (1587) (4 cit.)	1639–41	English	
Leges, "Laws" (p. 179)	**1639–40**		
Savonarola, *Oracolo della Renovatione della Chiesa* (1560)	1638–39 (trip)	Italian	*DDD, 265
Lambard, *Commentary upon the High Courts* (1635)	1641–42	English	
Sarpi, *Istoria* (1619) as "Concil. Trident"	Summer/fall 1643[1]	Italian & English	*DDD, 308
Stow, *Annales* (1615)	1639–41	English	H, 27, 31; T, 193
Holinshed, *Chronicles* (1587)	1639–41	English	H, 27
Holinshed, *Chronicles* (1587)	1639–41	English	H, 31
Holinshed, *Chronicles* (1587)	1639–41	English	H, 31–32, 229
Holinshed, *Chronicles* (1587)	1639–41	English	H; 1D
Justinian, *Institutes* (uncertain)	1641–43	Latin	E; *1D, 181
Holinshed, *Chronicles* (1587)	1639–41	English	
Speed, *Historie* (1623) (3 cit.)	1639–41	English	
Holinshed (2 cit.), margin	1639–41	English	
Speed, *Historie* (2 cit.), margin	1639–41	English	
Holinshed, *Chronicles* (1587) (27 cit.)	1639–41	English	

Notes
1. Smith, "Milton and the Index," 104.

Topic and work cited	Probable date	Language	Later use
Customs of Foreign Nations (p. 180)	**1639–41**		
Stow, *Annales* (1615)	1639–41	English	H, 337
Speed, *Historie* (1623)	1639–41		
Rex (p. 181)	**1637**		
Historia Miscella (Ingolstadt, Bavaria, 1603) (2 cit.)	1637[1]	Latin & Greek	
Eusebius, *De Vita Constantini* in *HE* (Paris, 1544)	1637[2]	Latin	
°Sigonius, *Imperio* (Frankfurt, 1618)[3]	uncertain date, no page		

Topic and work cited	Probable date	Language	Later use
Holinshed, *Chronicles* (1587), Bede in Holinshed	1639–41	Latin, Greek	*H*, 206
Milton, commentary, substantiated by Stow	1639–41	Latin	
Stow, *Annales* (1615)	1639–41	English	
Stow, *Annales* (1615)[4]	1639–41	English	
Historia Miscella (Ingolstadt, Bavaria, 1603)	1637[5]	Latin	**E*, 587; **1D*, 123; *R*, 607
Holinshed, *Chronicles* (1587)	1639–41	English	
Socrates [Book 1. C.6], cited within Eusebius	1637		
Eusebius, *HE* (Paris, 1544) (3 cit.)	1637[6]	Latin	
Tertullian, *Apologeticus* in *Opera* (Paris, 1634) (2 cit.)	1638–39[7]	Latin	*T*, 202; *1D*, 122
Milton, commentary, marginal note by Machiavelli scribe[8]	1637 or later[9]	Latin	
Gregoras, *Byzantinae Historiae Libri X* (Basle, 1562?)	1637 or later[10]	Latin	
Holinshed, *Chronicles* (1587)	1639–41	English	*1D*, 200
Camden, *Annales* (1615–27) (4 cit.)	1639–41	Latin	
Holinshed, *Chronicles,* margin	1639–41	English	
Stow, *Annales* (2 cit.)	1639–41	English	
Holinshed, *Chronicles* (1587) (2 cit.)	1639–41	English	*E*, 415
Jovius, *Opera* (Basle, 1578)	1642–44	Latin	**E*, 444
Cuspinian, *Historia Caesarum* (Frankfurt, 1601)	1642–44	English	
Sleidan, *Commentaries* (Strassburg, 1555)	1641–42	English	
Cuspinian, *Historia Caesarum* (Frankfurt, 1601)	1642–44	Latin	**H, T*
Sleidan, *Commentaries* (1555)	1641–42	Latin	
Codinus, in *Byzantinae Historiae Scriptores* (Paris, 1648?)	1648	Latin	

Notes

1. Shawcross; Mohl, 1635–37.
2. Shawcross; Mohl, 1635–37.
3. Amanuensis F.
4. Milton writes three sentences on how "kings scarcely recognize themselves as mortals."
5. Shawcross; Mohl, 1635–37. Shawcross has suggested a later date for the second entry for *Historia Miscella* here, I believe because of the existence of one Greek ε (Shawcross, *John Milton,* 283). Yet it seems highly likely that this entry would have occurred at the same sitting. The hand is otherwise the same.
6. Shawcross; Mohl, 1635–37.
7. This later inserted passage is in a larger hand, with both kinds of *e*'s (about 10 Italian and 15 Greek).
8. This long Miltonic passage is immediately substantiated by Gregoras. The scribal reference to p. 195 in the margin is written by the same hand that made the Machiavelli entries there, which is also appropriate since the subject of the entry here pertains most closely to the passage from the *Discorsi*.
9. Shawcross; Mohl, 1637–38.
10. Shawcross; Mohl, 1637–38.

Topic and work cited	Probable date	Language	Later use
Rex (p. 182)	**1637**		
Sigonius, *Imperio* (Frankfurt, 1618), and "quod alii"	1637[1]	Latin	
Justin Martyr, *Opera* (Paris, 1615)	1637[2]	Latin comment; Greek	*1D*, 121
Justinian, *Institutes* (Louvian, 1475) (2 cit.)	1641–43	Latin	
Boccaccio, *Vita di Dante* (several Italian eds.)	1638–39[3]	Latin	
Leunclavius, *Jus Graeco-Romanum* (Frankfurt, 1596)	1643–44	Latin; Greek text	*T,* 218
Berni, *Orlando Innamorato* (Venice, 1541)	1643–44	Latin; Italian text	
Stow, *Annales* (1615) probable, though not cited	1639–41	English	
Holinshed, *Chronicles* (1587)	1639–41	English	*1D*, 222
Severus, *History* (Leyden, 1635)	1637–38[4]	Latin	*T,* 202–3; *1D,* 85, 157
Smith, *Commonwealth of England,* no page number	1639–41	English	
Girard (Haillan), *Histoire* (Paris, 1576)	1644–47	English	**T*[5]
Holinshed, *Chronicles* (1587) (2 cit.)	1639–41	English	*O,* 306[6]
De Thou, *Historia* (Geneva, 1620)[7] (2 cit.)	1644–47	English & Latin	*O,* 306
Smith, *Commonwealth of England* (1621?) (2 cit.)	1639–41	English	**T; R,* 599
Guicciardini, *Historia d'Italia* (Florence, 1636)	uncertain	Italian	
Aristotle, *Ethics,* perhaps from *Opera*	same as Smith or after	Greek	*T,* 202; *1D,* 240
Smith, *Commonwealth of England* (1621?)	1639–41	English	
Machiavelli, *Art of War* from *Tutte le Opere* (1550)	1640–42	Italian	

Notes

1. Shawcross; Mohl, 1637–38.
2. Shawcross; Mohl, 1637–38.
3. Shawcross, 1637; Mohl, 1637–38. Since this is a second-hand record of several Italian imprints, it might be dated to Milton's Italian journey.
4. Shawcross and Mohl.
5. Girard's comment is that "the only reason why kings were first created and chosen was that human society was maintained and knit together by the prudence and leadership of a great person who discovered that, if the laws of those same people could control and restrict the daring of evil ones, they would suffice for the public preservation and defence," a point that is deeply important for Milton in *The Tenure of Kings and Magistrates.* See Mohl, *CPW* 1:441n11.
6. This is a case where he returned to the source in Holinshed after conferring the Commonplace Book.
7. Mohl uses the edition of 1626, but there is no reason why Milton would not have used the 1620 edition, which corresponds to his pagination.

Topic and work cited	Probable date	Language	Later use
Subject. see King see of Idolatry, and Sedition [1] (p. 183)	1637		
Sigonius, *De Regno Italiae* (Frankfurt, 1575 or 1591)	1637 [2]	Latin	*R, 578*
Sigonius, *De Regno Italiae* (Frankfurt, 1575 or 1591)	1637 [3]	Latin	*R, 578; 1D, 147, 212*
De Thou, *Historia* (Geneva, 1620 or 1626)	1644–47	Latin	*T, 227*
Holinshed, *Chronicles* (1587) (2 cit.)	1639–41	English	
Speed, *Historie* (1623)	1639–41	English	
Girard, *Histoire* (Paris, 1576), not cited (see 186)	1644–47	English	*T, 218; O, 314–15* [4]
De Thou, *Historia* (Geneva, 1620), Bodin in De Thou	1642–44	English	*O, 306, 313*
Holinshed, *Chronicles* (1587)	1639–41	English	
Holinshed, *Chronicles* (1587) (4 cit.)	1639–41	English	*T, 218; 1D, 212*
Holinshed, *Chronicles*	1639–41	English	
Speed, *Historie* (1623)	1639–41	English	
Holinshed, *Chronicles* (1587) (2 cit.)	1639–41	English	
Holinshed, *Chronicles* (1587) (9 cit.)	1639–41	English	
Speed, *Historie* (1623)	1639–41	English	
Holinshed, *Chronicles* (1587)	1639–41	English	
Lambard, *Archeion* (no page number)	1641–42	English	
Speed, *Historie* (1623)	1639–41	English	
Source unclear; "See de Conciliis." Possibly to other index.			
Girard, *Histoire* (Paris, 1576) (2 cit.)	1644–47	English	**T*

Notes

1. Subditus. Vide rex. Vide de Idolatria et Seditione. These two last topics are not listed in the index or in the book itself, and may again belong to the theological index.
2. Shawcross; Mohl, 1637–38.
3. Shawcross; Mohl, 1637–38.
4. This entry is embellished on 186; it is a case, in both *The Tenure* and the *Observations,* where Milton seems to have returned to the source after consulting the Commonplace Book.

Lenitas ("Leniency") (p. 184)	1639–41		
Malmesbury, *De Gestis Regum Anglicorum* (1596)	1639–41	English	*H, 211; *BT, 570*
Stow, *Annales* (1615)	1639–41	English	*H, 211; *BT, 570*
Bacon, *A Wise and Moderate Discourse* (1641)	1641	English	*A, 668; AR, 534*
Sarpi, *Istoria* (1619) "Council of Trent Book"	1641–43	English	*AR, 500–503*
De Thou, *Historia* (Geneva, 1620)	1642–44	Latin	
Tyrannus °vide 248 [1] (p. 185)	1639–41		
Malmesbury, *De Gestis Regum Anglicorum* (1596)	1639–41	English	*H, 234–35; BT, 569*
Stow, *Annales* (1615)	1639–41	English	

Topic and work cited	Probable date	Language	Later use
Stow, *Annales* (1615)	1639–41	English	
Holinshed, *Chronicles* (1587)	1639–41	English	*E,* 407
Smith, *Commonwealth of England* (2 cit.)	1639–41	English	
Basil, *Opera* (Paris, 1618)	uncertain	English & Greek	*T,* 212
Holinshed, *Chronicles* (1587) (11 cit.)[2]	1639–41	English	**T,* 201; *E,* 407
Speed, *Historie* (1623), and "our writers"	1639–41	English	
Smith, *Commonwealth of England*	1639–41	English	*T,* 221; *1D,* 198
Girard, *Histoire* (Paris, 1576)	1644–47	English	*T,* 218; *O,* 314–15
De Thou, *Historia* (Geneva, 1620)	1642–44	Latin	*T,* 223–25 (cites Buchanan)
Holinshed, *Chronicles* (1587)	1639–41	English	*T,* 220–21
Martyr, *In Librum Iudicum* (Zurich, 1571)	1642–44	Latin	*T,* 221
°Machiavelli, *Discorsi* from *Tutte le Opere?*[3]	after 1644[4]	Italian w/ Latin	**T,* etc.
Sleidan, *Commentaries* (1555)	1641–42	Latin	*E,* 443–44
Comines, *Memoires* (Paris, 1552?)	1644–47	Latin	
De Thou, *Historia* (Geneva, 1620)	1642–44	Latin	*O,* 313; *E*
De Thou, *Historia* (Geneva, 1620)	1644–47	Latin	*T,* 228–30

Notes

1. Amanuensis F wrote this when adding a new heading, "Tyrannus," on page 248, thus suggesting a later date for the entries there. These are the only five occurrences of F's hand, which was once confused by Horwood as the same hand as C, the scribe who also wrote the *Christian Doctrine.* Hanford, "Chronology of Milton's Private Studies," 285.

2. See Patterson, *Reading Holinshed's Chronicles,* 116.

3. J. Phillips?

4. Mohl, 1651–52.

Rex Anglicae &c. "King of England" (p. 186)	1639–41		
Holinshed, *Chronicles* (1587) (2 cit.)	1639–41	English	
Speed, *Historie* (1623)	1639–41	English	
Speed, *Historie* (1623)	1639–41	English	
De Seissel, *De Monarchia Franciae* (Lyon, 1626) (2 cit.)	1642–44	Latin	*T,* 200; **1D,* 203
Camden, *Annales* (1615–27)	1639–41	English	
De Thou, *Historia* (Geneva, 1620)	1642–44	Latin	
[Hotman, *Franco-Gallia,* through de Thou]	1642–44	Latin	*1D,* 147
Cuspinian, *Historia Caesarum* (Frankfurt, 1601)	1642–44	Latin	
Schickard, *Jus Regium Hebraeorum* (Strassburg, 1625)	1639–50	Latin	*1D,* 85[1]
Buchanan, *Rerum Scoticarum* (Edinburgh, 1582)?[2]	1639–41	English	**T; 1D,* 202
De Thou, *Historia* (Geneva, 1620), margin	1642–44	Latin	**T*
[Hotman, *Franco-Gallia,* through de Thou]	1642–44	Latin	*1D,* 202
Girard, *Histoire* (Paris, 1576) (3 cit.)	1642–47	French & English	*1D,* 147, 202
Girard, *Histoire* (Paris, 1576) (5 cit.)	1644–47	English	**T*

Topic and work cited	Probable date	Language	Later use
De Thou, *Historia* (Geneva, 1620)	1644–47	Latin	*$1D$

Notes

1. Schickard's book is cited again at $1D$, 91, from a passage not in the Commonplace Book, which suggests that Milton had the book and—since he never uses it elsewhere—that he may have made this entry in 1650.
2. This same book is cited on 198 by an amanuensis. Milton does not give the source. It may be from Holinshed. See *CPW* 1:460–61n9.

Aulici, [et Consiliarii] "Courtiers" (p. 187)	**1639–41**		
Speed, *Historie* (1623)[1]	1639–41	English	*E
Sidney, *Arcadia* (1633), p. 119	1641–42	English	*T
°Berni/Boiardo, *Orlando* (Venice, 1541, 1608)[2]	1641–42[3]	Italian	

Notes

1. Cross reference "Leges in this book."
2. Amanuensis A.
3. See Shawcross, *John Milton*, 81.

Astutia politica "Political Adroitness" (p. 188)	**1639–41**		
Camden, *Annales* (1615) (3 cit.)	1639–41	Latin	
Sidney, *Arcadia* (1633)	1641–42	English	
Camden, *Annales* (1615–27) (with Milton comment)	1639–41	Latin	*Moscovia*
Spenser, *History of Ireland* (the *View*) (Dublin, 1633)	1642–44	English	
De Thou, *Historia* (Geneva, 1620) (4 cit.)	1642–44	Latin	*T*
°Rivet, *Commentarius*[1]	1658	Latin	

Notes

1. Jeremie Picard. There are two entries by this hand (see also 195), once labeled Amanuensis C. This is the amanuensis, Jeremie (or Jeremy) Picard, whom Milton used for *De Doctrina Christiana* and for several other projects, including the second edition of the *1D*.

De Legibus "Of Laws"[1] (p. 189)	**1641–43**		
Sarpi, *Istoria* (1619) "concil. Trident"	1641–43	Latin	*DDD*, 300
Boccalini, *Ragguagli* (Venice, 1612) (3 cit.)	1643–44	Latin	
Tomasini, *Petrarcha Redivivus* (Padua, 1635)	1643–44	Latin	*ED, 375
Tassoni, *Pensieri Diversi* (Venice, 1636)	1643–44	Italian	
Tassoni, *Pensieri Diversi* (Venice, 1636)	1643–44	Italian	

Notes

1. The full title is "Of Laws, Dispensations from them, and Indulgences," or in the original. "De Legibus earum dispensationibus et indulgentiis."

Libertas (p. 190)	**1642–44**		
Cuspinian, *Historia Caesarum* (Frankfurt, 1601)	1642–44	Latin	$2D$, 683–84
Justinian, *Institutes* (Geneva, 1589; uncertain)[1]	1642–44	Latin	*T, 198; E

Topic and work cited	Probable date	Language	Later use
Justinian, *Institutes* (Geneva, 1589; uncertain)[2]	1642–44	Latin	*1D*
Justinian, *Institutes* (Geneva, 1589; cluster)	1642–44	Latin	*1D*
Justinian, *Institutes* (Geneva, 1589; cluster)	1642–44	Latin	*1D*
Guicciardini, *Historia* (Florence, 1636)	uncertain	Italian & Latin	

Notes

1. Milton does not use page numbers for Justinian. Mohl suggests the 1475 edition, which seems unlikely, since there were much more modern editions (Geneva, 1589 and Frankfurt, 1587); see Boswell, *Milton's Library,* 148.

2. This is a cluster of three citations, separated in the following two entries for reference purposes. Milton does not use page numbers for Justinian, as it is divided into sections; he appears to own the book, as there is not sufficient information given from the passages. This is a clustered citation with three entries, which are individually listed here so as to provide more precise references to ultimate use.

Nobilitas "Nobilitas" (p. 191)	**1637–38**		
Prudentius, *Opera* (Antwerp, 1564), ed. uncertain	1637–38	Latin	
Dante, *Convivio* in *Divina Comedia* (Venice, 1568)	1637–38	Latin	
Chaucer, *Workes* (ed. Speght, 1602)	1637–38	English	
Romance of the Rose	1637–38	English	
Guillim, *Display of Heraldrie* (London, 1632 or 1638)	uncertain	English	
Girard, *Histoire* (Paris, 1576) (6 cit.)	1644–47	English	*T,* 219–20
Severitas (p. 193)	**1642–44**		
Cuspinian, *Historia Caesarum* (Frankfurt, 1601)	1642–44	Latin	
Rex (p. 195)	**1640–42**		
Gildas in Commenlin, *Rerum Britannicarum* (Lyon, 1587)	1640–42	Latin	*H,* 140; *T,* 221
°Augustine, *De Civitate Dei* (Venice, 1475?)[1]	1658	Latin	*1D* (1658), 146
°Machiavelli, *Discorsi*[2]	1646?	Italian	
°Machiavelli, *Discorsi*[3]	1646?	Italian	

Notes

1. Jeremie Picard. Hanford and Mohl suggest 1658–60, though as Mohl notes, "Milton quotes this passage from Augustine in *A Defence,* Chapter IV, as well as another chapter from Book IV, chap 4 of *De Civitate Dei.*" This fact is of particular interest as it is the only explicitly cited passage in Milton's work that corresponds with an entry by an amanuensis. What has not been pointed out, in part because modern editions of the Defense have silently conflated the 1651 and 1658 editions or simply used the 1658, is that the cited passage is *added* to the 1658 edition to *Pro Populo Anglicano Defensio,* which appeared in October, or earlier. This would indicate several things, primarily that we have tangible evidence of the help of an amanuensis, and that the entry must be dated early in 1658 or before.

2. John Phillips? See Shawcross, *John Milton,* 80; also Shawcross, "Notes on Milton's Amanuenses," and Miller, *John Milton & the Oldenburg Safeguard,* 293–95.

3. John Phillips?

Topic and work cited	Probable date	Language	Later use
Of Religion. to what extent it concerns the state (p. 197)	1651–52?		
°Machiavelli, *Discorsi*[1]	1646?	Italian	
°Dante, *Divina Comedia* (?)[2]	uncertain[3]	Italian	*AR
°Machiavelli, *Discorsi*[4]	1646?	Italian	*AR

Notes

1. Amanuensis B, Edward Phillips. Shawcross, *John Milton,* 80.
2. Amanuensis D (*PL*).
3. Mohl, 1650–67.
4. Amanuensis B, Edward Phillips. Shawcross, *John Milton,* 80.

Various Forms of Government (p. 198)	1651–52?		
°Machiavelli, *Discorsi* (2 cit.)[1]	1651–52?	Italian	
°Machiavelli, *Discorsi*[2]	1651–52?	Italian	
°Buchanan, *Historia* (Edinburgh, 1582)[3]	after 1652?	Latin[4]	

Notes

1. John Phillips?
2. John Phillips?
3. Amanuensis E.
4. This is another suspicious entry in a hand other than Milton's, as it is full of errors and corrections, and very badly written. Just how Milton might have been overseeing this entry is rather unclear.

Property and Taxes (p. 220)	1637–38		
Sigonius *De Regno Italiae* (Frankfurt, 1591)	1637–38	Latin	
Camden, *Annales* (1615)	1639–41	English	*1D
Stow, *Annales* (1615) (2 cit.)	1639–41	English	H, 370, 377
Speed, *Historie* (1623)	1639–41	English	
Speed, *Historie* (1623)	1639–41	English	H, 371
Holinshed, *Chronicles* (1587), margin	1639–41	English	
Stow, *Annales* (1615)	1639–41	English	
Holinshed, *Chronicles* (1587)	1639–41	English	
Holinshed, *Chronicles* (1587) (3 cit.)	1639–41	English	
Stow, *Annales* (1615)	1639–41	English	
Holinshed, *Chronicles* (1587)	1639–41	English	
Camden, *Annales* (1615) (2 cit.), margin	1639–41	Latin	
Holinshed, *Chronicles* (1587)	1639–41	English	
Evagrius, in *Ecclesiasticae Historiae Autores* (Paris, 1544)	1637[1]	Latin	
Comines, *Memoires* (Paris, 1552)	1644–47	English	
Holinshed, *Chronicles* (1587), "and in other pages"	1639–41	English	
Chesne, *Histoire* (Paris, 1634)	1639–41	English	
Gregoras, *Byzantine History* (Basle, 1562)	1637–38 Italy?	Latin	
Camden, *Annales* (1615–27) (2 cit.)	1639–41	English	

Topic and work cited	Probable date	Language	Later use
Stow, *Annales* (1615)	1639–41	English	
Camden, *Annales* (1615–27) (2 cit.)	1639–41	English	

Notes
1. Shawcross; Mohl, 1635–37.

Robbery or Extortion[1] **(p. 221)**	**1639–41**		
Holinshed, *Chronicles* (1587), margin	1639–41	English	
Holinshed, *Chronicles* (1587) (8 cit.)	1639–41	English	
Speed, *Historie* (1623), margin	1639–41	English	
Holinshed, *Chronicles* (1587) (4 cit.)	1639–41	English	
Speed, *Historie* (1623) (2 cit.)	1639–41	English	
Speed, *Historie* (1623) (2 cit.)	1639–41	English	
Speed, *Historie* (1623)	1639–41	English	
Holinshed, *Chronicles* (1587)	1639–41	English	

Notes
1. Rapina seu extorsio; is followed by "see Pope, 42, in other index," which is very likely the *Index Theologicus.*

Plague (p. 230)	**1637**		
Procopius, *De Bello,* in *Historiarum* (Ausburg, 1607)	1637[1]	Latin	

Notes
1. Shawcross; Mohl, 1637–38.

Gymnastica (p. 240)	**1637**		
Gregoras, *Historia* (Basle, 1562)	1637–38	Latin	
Cantacuzene, *Historiarum Libri IV* (Ingolstadt, 1603)	1637–38	Latin	
Sigonius, *De Regno Italiae* (Frankfurt, 1591) (2 cit.)	1637–38	Latin	

Spectacula. "Public Shows" (p. 241)	**1637**		
Tertullian, *De Spectaculis* in *Opera* (Paris, 1634)	1637–38	Latin	
Cyprian, *Epistles* in *Opera* (Paris, 1593), "or someone else"	1637–38	Latin	
Lactantius, *Opera* (Lyons, 1548) (2 cit.)	1639–41	Latin	*ED, 400–401
Milton, commentary throughout with long rebuttal of Lactantius		Latin	

De disciplina militari (p. 242)	**1639–41**		
Stow, *Annales* (1615)	1639–41	English	*H,* 321
Camden, *Annales* (1615–27)	1639–41	English	
Milton, commentary supported by Jovius	1642–44	Latin	
Jovius, *Historia* in *Opera* (Basle, 1578)	1642–44	Latin	

Topic and work cited	Probable date	Language	Later use
Holinshed, *Chronicles* (1587) (2 cit.)	1639–41	English	
Jovius, *Historia* in *Opera* (Basle, 1578)	1642–44	Latin	
Jovius, *Historia* in *Opera* (Basle, 1578)	1642–44	Latin	
Speed, *Historie* (1623)	1639–41	English	
Seissel, *De Monarchia* (Lyons, 1626)	1642–44	Latin	
Speed, *Historie* (1623) (2 cit.)	1639–41	English	
Holinshed, *Chronicles* (1587)	1639–41	English	
°Machiavelli, *Discorsi*[1]	1646?	Italian	
De Seissel, *De Monarchia* (Lyons, 1626)	1642–44	Latin	*T*
Hardyng, *Chronicle* (1543)	1642–44	English	
Spenser, *History of Ireland* (the *View*) (Dublin, 1633)[2]	1642–44	English	
°Machiavelli, *Discorsi*[3]	1646?	Italian	
°Machiavelli, *Discorsi*[4]	1646?	Italian	

Notes

1. John Phillips?
2. Cited as "dialogue of Ireland."
3. John Phillips?
4. John Phillips?

De Bello (p. 243)	**1639–41**		
Holinshed, *Chronicles* (1587)	1639–41	English	
Gower, *Confessio Amantis* (1532)	1642–44	English	
Sleidan, *Commentaries* (Strassburg, 1555) Zwingli (3 cit.)	1641–42	Latin	*T*
Theodonit., *Historia Ecclesiastica* (*HE*) (Paris, 1544) (2 cit.)	after 1639	Latin	
Holinshed, *Chronicles* (1587), unidentified source	1639–41	English	
°Machiavelli, *Discorsi*[1]	1646?	Latin	Vane
°Machiavelli, *Discorsi*[2]	1646?	Latin	

Notes

1. John Phillips?
2. John Phillips?

De bello Civili (p. 244)	**1639–41**		
Holinshed, *Chronicles* (1587) (2 cit.)	1639–41	English	
Sleidan, *Commentaries* (Strassburg, 1555)	1641–42	Latin	*T*, 223, **E*
Sarpi, *Istoria* (1619) (2 cit.)	1641–43	Latin	
De Thou, *Historia* (Geneva, 1620) (2 cit.)	1641–43	Latin	**T* (to the event)
De Thou, *Historia* (Geneva, 1620)	1641–43	Latin	
[Hotman, *Franco-Gallia* in De Thou.]	1641–43	Latin	**1D* (Hotman)[1]
Sarpi, *Istoria* (1619)	1641–44	Latin	**E* (to the event)
Sarpi, *Istoria* (1619)	1641–43	Latin	

Notes

1. See discussion in chapter 2.

Topic and work cited	Probable date	Language	Later use
De Foederatis "Of Allies" (p. 245)	1639–41		
Ascham, *Toxophilus* (1545)	1639–41	English	*R
Speed, *Historie* (1623)	1639–41	English	
Camden, *Annales* (1615–27) (9 cit.)	1639–41	Latin	
Camden, *Annales* (1615–27) (3 cit.)	1639–41	Latin	
Camden, *Annales* (1615–27)	1639–41	Latin	*R, 586
Hayward, *King Edward the Sixt* (1630)	1639–41	English	R, A
°Machiavelli, *Discorsi* [1]	1646?	Latin, Italian	

Notes
1. John Phillips?

Topic and work cited	Probable date	Language	Later use
Of Sedition. [1] And on Civil War (p. 246)	1641–42		
Sleidan, *Commentaries* (Strassburg, 1555)	1641–42	Latin	
Sleidan, *Commentaries* (Strassburg, 1555)	1641–42	Latin	T
Sleidan, *Commentaries* [2]	1641–42	Latin	T, 223
°Machiavelli, *Discorsi* [3]	1646?	Latin, Italian	

Notes
1. De Seditione vide Idololatria. Et Ecclesia. "See Idolatry and the Church." Another reference to an outside index, presumably the *Index Theologicus.*
2. On Magistrates—"as happens today."
3. John Phillips?

Topic and work cited	Probable date	Language	Later use
Of Besieging a City and a City Besieged (p. 247)	1642–44		
Jovius, *Opera* (Basle, 1578)	1642–44	Latin	
Jovius, *Opera* (Basle, 1578)	1642–44	Latin	
°Tyrant (p. 248)	**Uncertain**		
°Costanzo, *Historia* (Aquila, 1581) [1]	uncertain	Latin and Italian	

Notes
1. Amanuensis F.

Topic and work cited	Probable date	Language	Later use
°Of Navigation and Shipwrecks (p. 249)	1647?		
°Choniate, *Imperii Graeci Historia* (Paris, 1647) [1]	1647?	English [2]	

Notes
1. Amanuensis D.
2. This is another case in which Milton's scribe enters a bit of information similar to that entered here. *Eikonoklastes* (10), has "Andronicus Comnenus the Byzantine Emperor, though a most cruel Tyrant, is reported by Nicetas to have bin a constant reader of St. Paul" (*CPW* 3:361). Though a similar phrase "though otherwise a most cruell tyrant" appears in this entry, the source for the history of Comnenus is not the same, nor indeed is there any mention of either anecdote in either reference.

Appendix B

The Scribal Entries in Milton's Commonplace Book
Amanuenses, Students, Researchers, or Visitors?

An analysis of the evidence follows this list of entries for each of the amanuenses originally labeled by Hanford in "Chronology of Milton's Private Studies," with the later attributions given in parentheses. The dates provided are from Ruth Mohl's annotations in the Yale edition. The page numbers supplied follow those of the Commonplace Book itself, and after these I've listed whether or not the scribe has listed a page number for the citation. Except for the page number supplied on page 195 and a strangely garbled page number on page 198, no page numbers are given in the scribal citations, which is very unusual in entries in Milton's hand. There is only one entry in English, thirteen in Italian with occasional Latin and one English comment, and thirteen in Latin.

Symbols
* = on a page with other scribes
\# = on a page without any writing of Milton

Amanuensis A; same hand found in Milton's copy of Giovanni della Casa, *Rime*
Berni, *Orlando Inamorato,* p. 71; after Milton's entries. Latin, Italian.
\# Boiardo, *Orlando Inamorato,* p. 77. Latin, Italian.
Berni and Boiardo compared, p. 187; after Milton's entries. Latin, Italian.

Amanuensis B or Edward Phillips
*# Machiavelli, *Discorsi;* p. 197, on an exclusive page of amanuenses (see Amanuensis D). Latin.
*# Machiavelli, *Discorsi;* p. 197. Latin, Italian.

Machiavelli Scribe (John Phillips?)
\# Machiavelli, *Discorsi;* p. 148, by itself on the page. Latin.
Machiavelli, *Discorsi;* p. 185, squeezed between Milton's entries. Italian.
* Machiavelli, *Discorsi;* p. 195, after Milton's entries, with other amanuenses (see C). Italian.

* Machiavelli, *Discorsi;* p. 195, after Milton's entries, with other amanuenses (see C). Italian.

*# Machiavelli, *Discorsi;* p. 198, on an exclusive page of amanuenses (see E). Latin.

*# Machiavelli, *Discorsi;* p. 198, on an exclusive page of amanuenses (see E). Latin.

Machiavelli, *Discorsi;* p. 242, squeezed between Milton's entries. English, Italian.

Machiavelli, *Discorsi;* p. 242, after Milton's entries. Latin.

Machiavelli, *Discorsi;* p. 242, after Milton's entries. Latin.

Machiavelli, *Discorsi;* p. 243, after Milton's entries. Latin.

Machiavelli, *Discorsi;* p. 243, after Milton's entries. Latin.

Machiavelli, *Discorsi;* p. 245, after Milton's entries. Italian.

Machiavelli, *Discorsi;* p. 246, after Milton's entries. Italian.

Amanuensis C or Jeremie Picard, whose hand appears in: *De Doctrina Christiana;* Milton's *Bible,* in which Picard recorded the death of Milton's wife, Katherine, in February 1658 and the birth of his daughter in March 1658 (BL MS Additional 32310); and the Trinity Manuscript's copy of "Me thought I saw my late espoused saint," (Cambridge Trinity College MS R.5.5, p. 47; 1658–60). At least one of these entries, to Augustine, can be dated more precisely to sometime before October 1658, when the second edition of *Pro Populo Anglicano Defensio* was printed.

Rivet, *Commentarius;* p. 188, no page; after Milton's entries. Latin. Only known use of this book in Milton's corpus.

*#Augustine, *De Civitate Dei;* p. 195, after Milton's entry, with others (see Machiavelli Scribe). Latin. This passage is used in *Pro Populo,* in a passage added to the 1658 edition (*CPW* 4:419, *PW* 146). Picard cites the same chapter of Augustine cited in *Pro Populo.* Milton also cites passages not cited here, and cites Augustine more generally (for the first and only time in his corpus in other passages in 1651, at *CPW* 4:375).

Amanuensis D (the same hand is found in the *Paradise Lost* ms; hence Mohl's date of "1650–1667")

*# Dante, *Divina Comedia* (?); p. 197, an exclusive page of amanuenses (see E). Italian.

Choniate, *Historia* (Paris, 1647); p. 249 after Preston; heading in scribe's hand. Page number. English.

Amanuensis E "after 1652"

*# Buchanan, *Historia* (Edinburgh, 1582); p. 198, page supplied, although totally off. Latin.

Amanuensis F "after ca. 1650"

Costanzo, *History di Napoli;* p. 5, after Milton's entries; page number. Italian.

Sigonius, *Imperio* (Frankfurt, 1618?); p. 19, page number (203). Latin.
Sigonius, *Imperio* (Frankfurt, 1618?); p. 181, no page; squeezed between M's entries "date uncertain."
#Costanzo, *History di Napoli;* p. 248. after Milton's entries; page number. Italian.

The Scribal Hands: An Analysis of the Evidence

Once the posthumous entries by Lord Preston are excluded, the hands other than Milton's do not amount to a substantial number. There are 27 entries total in 7 hands; of these, 4 appear in the Ethical Index, 1 in the Domestic Index, and 22 in the Political Index. All of these entries seem to have been made after those by Milton on the same page, although in many cases the entries belong to topics made by the scribe on a page with no writing by Milton, making the chronology unclear. Still, the scribal entries that are on the same page as Milton's consistently come after Milton's own entries, thus suggesting that while a few late entries by Milton may have been made at the same time as these by the scribes, the scribal entries generally seem to postdate most if not all of Milton's entries. However, this chronology cannot be determined with accuracy, since there are relatively few entries by other hands, and even among these only 17 of the 27 appear on pages that Milton has also written on, reducing the numbers still further. But the layout of these 17 entries, with the additional fact that several of these hands match those of Milton's future amanuenses and scribes, has left the general impression that these scribal entries began at or after the onset of Milton's blindness. The conventional dating, established by Hanford and Mohl, shows Milton making a few entries around 1646–47, such as the entry from Selden's *Uxor Ebraica,* published in 1646 (CB 109), and then the amanuenses picking up after 1650, with a few references to Berni and Boiardo by an amanuensis who also inscribed Milton's Italian Sonnet in Milton's copy of Giovanni della Casa's *Rime et Prose* (Venice, 1563),[1] then many references to Machiavelli by two different hands, then—skipping ahead almost a decade, according to this established dating—two entries are added by Jeremie Picard (1658–60), and then, skipping forward another five to eight years, two more entries are made by the scribe whose hand is also preserved in a manuscript of *Paradise Lost.* Mohl and Hanford feel less confident about the date of the five remaining entries, and Mohl simply writes "date uncertain" for most of these.

There are many reasons to question both the proposed dating and the proposed function of these other hands. The fundamental problem with the dating lies in explaining why Milton would have used his notebook in such an extremely sporadic manner after some point in the early 1650s when he had supposedly dictated entries from Machiavelli. With nine or fewer entries written between approximately 1652 and 1667, the chronology proposed by Mohl and Hanford suggests that Milton had the book taken down by different people at a rate of much less than one short entry per year. If Milton used the book this sporadically, it should also be noted that the blind poet would have directed these scribes in almost every case suggested by Mohl and Hanford to set the note only on pages where previous amanuenses had written over a decade before. This picture seems even less compelling when the substance of these entries is considered: A passage from Rivet's biblical commentary, a passage from Augustine's *City of God,* an excerpt from Dante, a passage from Nicetas's Greek History, and a poorly recorded passage from Buchanan, among others—books that Milton knew and had used (though only Dante appears in the Commonplace Book in his hand), but little can be traced with certainty to Milton's own projects. The best correspondence we have is between an entry made by Jeremie Picard and an added passage in the 1658 edition of *Pro Populo Anglicano Defensio,* which expands on a passage of Augustine already used in this section of the book. It suggests that Picard added the passage from Augustine after he helped Milton fill in a section of the book, rather than before, as is the common practice.

Further patterns in the scribal entries show that they do not follow Milton's own practice. Only 18 percent of the entries by scribal hands are to histories, where about 80 percent of Milton's entries are historical—representing a very different use. Only one of the scribal notes is in English, with the rest divided evenly between Latin and Italian, a language with peculiarly extensive representation here. In comparison, Milton wrote 112 out of 224 of his entries in the Political Index in English, or 50 percent. And only 5 out of 27 of the scribal entries supply page numbers, while the vast majority of Milton's do. In every respect, Milton is not using his amanuenses here to continue his project. Being more literary and random, the scribal entries seem to follow traditional English commonplace-book practice, rather than the specific, historical purpose in Milton's personal research agenda, possibly suggesting that the entries are the work of students or of people following the more conventional habits that they may have used in their own commonplace books. The entries generally conform to more standard commonplace-book usage, in which sententious passages are fully excerpted onto the page, ready for quotation. On page 195 of the Commonplace Book, for example, the so-called Machiavelli Scribe takes down two important passages from Machiavelli's *Discorsi,* and on p. 197, the next page used in the book, another scribe paraphrases another passage from Machiavelli, and then another copies down two relatively lengthy passages from Dante—all of which are quite unlike Milton's own entries. Further, if Milton were dictating, he would likely use the topics and pages already established by himself. Instead, there is a strange camaraderie in the entries by these hands: 10 out of 27 entries are on pages without any writing of Milton's, and 6 out of these 10 have entries by other scribes, thus showing a high propensity for scribes to write on the same page as each other, as if they were working together. There are 66 pages and 66 topics, with the scribal hands thus densely clustered on pages that are often created by scribes. In only two cases does more than one scribal hand occur on the same page on which Milton has written. The very fact that over a third of the entries appear on pages where Milton appears not to have written at all—thus indicating that he is not returning to his own headings—further challenges the explanation that entries constitute the work of amanuenses under direct supervision.

Rather than the being the results of strict supervision, many of these entries seem to be the work of free agents, perhaps acting in the capacity of a student rather than an amanuensis. One such example is the third entry to Berni's revision of Boiardo's *Orlando Innamorato,* possibly from the Venetian version of 1541 or the Milanese version of 1542.[2] Under the topic "Of Evil Speaking," itself written by this other hand, and the only entry under this topic, the much-corrected Latin reads: "Especially fine are those little verses in which the Italian poet Bioardo, in the *Orlando Innamorato,* begins book 2, canto 21, and wisely admonishes that no one should heedlessly slander anyone."[3] The original wording with corrections helps illustrate the point: "Belli sunt imprimis versiculi isti quibus Poeta Italus Boiardus in Orlando Inamorato. Lib: 2di cantum 21mum incipit, ~~contra maledicem~~ monetque prudenter ~~ut maledicdicendiam vide~~ ne quis temere ~~mal~~ cuiquam maledicat." Milton seldom strikes words out in his Commonplace Book. This entry appears to be the work of a struggling young Latinist, and highly unlikely the result of dictation. It is clear even in the style of citation that it is not Miltonic. Milton cites authors in a much more perfunctory manner—in the case of his own Berni quotation, for example, he writes "see also the Orlando Innamorato of Berni cant. 7. stanz. 3:. . . & c."[4] The multiple uses in the scribal entry of appreciative modifiers, "especially fine," "little verses," "wisely," "heedlessly," resemble another manner and purpose from those of Milton's entries, especially at such a late date as 1650, the date attributed, when the book had long since become a scholarly tool rather than a collection of sentences and verses. Milton seldom writes more than "excellent," his most common form of praise. In addition, if he were dictating this entry, he would probably have said "Berni," as he does in the other two entries in his own hand, rather than "Boiardo."[5] There is, in short, no reason to believe that this entry derives from direct oversight; it is rather the work of a student or free agent. Another entry to Buchanan, the single entry by Amanuensis E and written after the scribal Machiavelli entries on the same page, is, as Hanford writes, "badly written and badly spelled"[6]—unlikely the product of direct supervision, let alone dictation.

Although it has been thought that the amanuenses—as I believe they should hesitantly be called, if that—were continuing the work just as Milton had started it, in fact there are many differences between those entries in Milton's hand and the others: another stark one being the slim correspondence between these scribal entries and Milton's printed work. It is especially unlikely that Milton would have made use of amanuenses at a stage when he had become increasingly utilitarian with his Commonplace Book, and then not actually used their passages. Since the passages account for a very small fraction of the Political Index, this is not of major consequence, although over half of these entries are from Machiavelli's *Discorsi,* and the nature of Milton's relationship to that work is particularly worth investigating in this context.

Almost all of these hands are recognizable as those of the amanuenses Milton employed before and after he had lost his sight, but—to make matters more confusing—these are often the hands of his students. Some of these students were also family members, provoking the question of whether the entries made by these young men in their capacity as amanuenses, as students, or as nephews? And if as students, were they merely fulfilling an exercise, or were they behaving more like research assistants? Certainly students were used this way. Bacon wrote in a letter advising Fulke Greville about employing students for research: "He that shall out of his own Reading gather [notes] for the use of another, must (as I think) do it by Epitome, or Abridgment, or under Heads or Common Places."[7] William Drake employed an amanuensis to assist him, although not by taking dictation, but by actually doing the reading and taking notes for Drake. As Kevin Sharpe points out, Drake even recorded his intention in one of his notebooks: "Have a scholar to read my ordinary printed books and still to be discoursing at meals with him or walking in the garden, to reserve the strength of my own mind for things material and most important."[8] Drake's eyesight was also apparently waning.[9] The large collection of commonplace books of John Evelyn are mostly in his hand, but they were begun by a professional scribe whom Evelyn had brought to Paris in 1649 to help "reduce my studies into a method."[10] All seventeen notes taken by the so-called Machiavelli Scribes are from the *Discorsi.* The entries are usually thought to have been added shortly after Milton's blindness, and thus used loosely to inform the republican thought of the later treatises. Maurice Kelley has convincingly shown that one of these is his nephew Edward Phillips,[11] and it has been argued that the other Machiavelli scribe is his brother John, although this is uncertain.[12] These could easily have been added, however, in the late 1640s, when Milton's own use of the manuscript as an active reading notebook (rather than a retrieval system) had significantly waned. In one case, when Machiavelli is used to weigh the question of killing the king (CB 185), it seems particularly likely that the entry was made in the late 1640s, rather than after the death of the king.

One of the most determinable dates of entry is one by Jeremie Picard, the scribe employed to copy much of last half of *De Doctrina Christiana,* probably around 1658–1560, although that date is itself determined by other evidence, and two years may still not be enough time for "Picard's protracted involvement with Milton's working manuscript."[13] Picard's hand is seen in a several other places in Milton's literary and documentary remains, all clustered around this span of time (see above). We can now confidently add a 1657 or 1658 date to Picard's entry on Augustine, as this corresponds closely with an addition made to the 1658 edition of that text.

The precise entries and numbered references cannot literally "derive from Milton's reading,"[14] of course, but—even in the most direct circumstances—from Milton's being read to, and then, presumably from his instructing his reader to then make entries in the Commonplace Book. (Possibly, they derive from Milton's *re*-reading, in which he is getting help from his students in recalling a precise moment in a book that he remembers from a previous reading.)[15] But this process could have been much less direct, and indeed, although Kelley and Hanford claim that the style of the entries follow Milton's,[16] in fact there are many differences, including the omission of page numbers, which are seldom left out of Milton's own entries, leaving it also impossible to tell, for example, whether the Machiavelli entries come from the same edition, *Tutte Le Opere Di Nicolo Machiavelli* (1550?), as the Miltonic excerpts from *Dell'Arte della Guerra*.[17] Milton might simply have instructed his researcher (as Bacon suggested to Greville) to copy what Phillips thought to be important from Machiavelli, or to continue using (if he wished) the Commonplace Book. Phillips might well have written these entries in the book entirely of his own accord. It is highly likely that Milton would have instructed his nephew and the rest of his students in the art of keeping a commonplace book, and that he shared his own notes with his nephew. Peter Beal observes that "there is evidence of multiple compilations: that some miscellanies [and commonplace books] were passed around and made common use of within restricted circles—such as in a single family or among a group of students or courtiers."[18]

Milton himself makes a few citations to Machiavelli's *Art of War,* whose page numbers indicate that he used an edition that may also have supplied passages from the *Discorsi,* and indeed (though there are none), it could have supplied passages from the *Prince: Tutte Le Opere Di Nicolo Machiavelli* (1550). Shawcross's idea that some of the other hands in the Commonplace Book may have been students during Milton's schoolmaster period is well taken. The observation might, I think, be taken one step further: that these students are writing in his book *as* students, and not strictly speaking amanuenses, and that—like those mentioned by Beal—Milton is sharing his book either for pedagogical purposes or to benefit his own research. In the case of Machiavelli, the most extensively recorded and most pertinent to Milton's politics, this is indeed "far above the Pedantry of common publick Schooles,"[19] as Edward Phillips later boasts of his education. Phillips does not record having read Machiavelli with Milton—nor would he have been likely to, given public opinion and his defensiveness about Milton—but he does mention reading Italian authors, such as the historian Villani, who does appear the Commonplace Book.[20] Surely we need not depend on the question of whether the hands are those of students or amanuenses to imagine that Milton had explored the rest of an important tome of political philosophy, that he had flipped through more than merely the *Art of War.*

That these entries are part of a pedagogical exercise or allowance would also help to explain why they are made by so many hands, why there are so few entries in these hands, and why Milton rarely if ever uses the entries written in these hands, even though there are some passages in his later work that could well be influenced by Machiavelli. There are at least seven non-Miltonic hands in the manuscript, the same number in the Political Index, and, with the exception of the Machiavelli Scribes, they each rarely make more than two entries apiece. For Milton to employ a scribe to make two rather simple entries (as most of them are) would seem a strange use of his resources; it seems especially unlikely that he would have employed such an amanuensis to make one or two miscellaneous notes after years of not using the Commonplace Book. The Machiavelli Scribes do seem to have had a function more obviously germane to Milton's own purposes; in one instance, Edward Phillips actually supplies a detailed marginal cross reference to a apparently missing notebook of Milton's, "See the Theological Index, Of Not Forcing Religion" (CB 197, *CPW* 477), the only reference that names this missing book, the others—there are twelve in all—merely point to topics and to "another index."[21]

It is thus likely that the entries from the *Discorsi,* since they are far more extensive, professional, and pertinent, were made under different circumstances from the others, the students here perhaps behaving more like researchers than students. To what extent Milton directed or dictated these passages remains unclear—although he surely would have known them.

Notes

Introduction

1. See, for example, Steven Zwicker's work on the annotations of *Paradise Lost* in "What Every Literate Man Once Knew"; and, on *Paradise Regained* and *Samson Agonistes*, see Knoppers, "General Introduction," lvii–lxxiv. On readers of Sidney's *Arcadia*, see Hackel, *Reading Material*, chap. 4.

2. These studies include Sharpe, *Reading Revolutions;* Robert C. Evans, *Habits of Mind;* Jardine and Grafton, "Studied for Actions"; and Sherman, *John Dee.* For a more complete bibliography, see Sherman, *Used Books*, xi, 185–86.

3. See Zwicker, "Reading the Margins" and "What Every Literate Man Once Knew"; and Sherman, *Used Books.* Hackel also traces the reading habits of a wide demographic in *Reading Material.*

4. For recent examples, see Dobranski, *Milton, Authorship, and the Book Trade;* Sauer, *"Paper-contestations" and Textual Communities;* Joseph Loewenstein's work on *Areopagitica* in *Author's Due*, 152–91; and McKenzie's work on the same text in *Making Meaning*, 126–43.

5. See Beal, *Index,* 2.2:78–80; Hackel, "Countess of Bridgewater's London Library"; Harrison and Laslett, *Library of John Locke;* and Carley, *Books of King Henry VIII.* Boswell's useful but misleadingly titled *Milton's Library: A Catalogue of the Remains of John Milton's Library and an Annotated Reconstruction of Milton's Library and Ancillary Readings* is a rough list of texts that Milton read or may have read, not what was actually on his shelves.

6. One important reading record on the royalist side is the notebooks of Edward Hyde, Earl of Clarendon, Bodleian Clarendon MSS 126, 127; see Sharpe, *Reading Revolutions*, 300.

7. Beal, *In Praise of Scribes*, v. Recent studies of manuscript culture in this period include Love, *Scribal Publication;* Love, *English Clandestine Satire;* Marotti, *Manuscript, Print, and the English Renaissance Lyric;* Woudhuysen, *Sir Philip Sidney;* and McKitterick, *Print, Manuscript, and the Search for Order.*

8. Sirluck in *CPW* 2:18.

9. Milton, *Poems of Mr. John Milton* (London, 1645), 57.

10. This chapter derives partially from an article that appeared several years ago, which explores the tract's relationship with its immediate discursive context. In weighing the relationship between the records of Milton's thinking in his

Commonplace Book and *Areopagitica*, I have reconsidered how it should be understood to operate in this context. Fulton, *"Areopagitica* and the Roots of Liberal Epistemology."

11. Zagorin, *History of Political Thought*, 106.

12. Achinstein, *Milton and the Revolutionary Reader*, 6.

13. Achinstein, *Milton and the Revolutionary Reader*, 6.

14. Skinner, "'Social Meaning' and the Explanation of Social Action," 95.

15. For some discussions of Milton's rhetorical strategies, see Corns, "Milton's Quest for Respectability"; Corns, "John Milton, Roger Williams, and the Limits of Toleration," 84; Dzelzainis, "Milton and the Protectorate"; Wittreich, "Milton's *Areopagitica*"; and Achinstein, *Milton and the Revolutionary Reader*, esp. 161–62.

16. See Skinner, *Reason and Rhetoric*.

17. Lim, *Milton, Radical Politics, and Biblical Republicanism*, 23.

18. Shelley and Hazlitt provide examples of this dual vision. Shelley invoked Milton as an example of what England might produce, were it divided into "institutions not more perfect than those of Athens." Milton represented a Promethean liberator, who "shook to dust the oldest and most oppressive form of the Christian religion," since he was "a republican, and a bold inquirer into morals and religion." Hazlitt described Milton as one who "had his thoughts constantly fixed on the contemplation of the Hebrew theocracy, and of a perfect commonwealth." *Prometheus Unbound*, 123–24; Hazlitt, *Lectures on the English Poets* (London, 1818), 111.

19. Darbishire, *Early Lives*, 14.

20. Dzelzainis, "Milton's Classical Republicanism," 7. Aubrey's relationship to Hobbes is recounted in *Aubrey's Brief Lives*, 147–59.

21. Livy is merely mentioned in *The Tenure* (*CPW* 3:208) and in *Areopagitica* (*CPW* 2:499, although Milton seems here to mean Tacitus; see 2:499n51). Livy may be the source for the historical moments recounted in a few other places: *Eikonoklastes* at *CPW* 3:565, 590. I will discuss *Pro Populo* in chapter 6.

22. Hobbes, *Behemoth*, 168. Hobbes repeats this view in *Leviathan*, 150. For an important discussion, see Skinner, "Classical Liberty," 14–15.

23. An important echo of the eighth Philippic is discussed by Dzelzainis in "Milton's Classical Republicanism," 17. A distinct line from *De legibus* is inserted in the text of the second edition; see *PW* 9. Milton later cites this explicitly in *Pro Populo* (*PW* 113). For other echoes or uses of Cicero in *The Tenure*, see *PW* 3n1, 17n71 (also used explicitly in *Pro Populo*, 163), 18n74, 33n138.

24. This is from *Bellum Catilinae*; see *PW* 3n2.

25. *CPW* 1:182; see chapter 3 for discussion.

26. See *Of Education*, *CPW* 2:396–99.

27. *CPW* 2:550. On this passage see McKeon, "Politics of Discourses," 47.

28. A list of entries in the Commonplace Book is supplied in Appendix A.

1. A Material History of Texts in Milton's England

1. Howe, "Uses of Uncertainty," 181.

2. BL MS Cotton Nero A.x. See Andrew and Waldron, *Poems of the Pearl Manuscript,* 1.

3. Folger Shakespeare Library, MS V.a.354. *Everyman,* which might also be included, is preserved in a printed copy of around 1519. Translated from the Dutch, it is itself a strange anomaly. See Harbage, *Annals of English Drama,* 8–13, 20.

4. The lines are from a translation of Donne's poem by Blunden in "Some Seventeenth-Century Latin Poems," 11; Donne's original is "Parturiunt madido quae nixu praela, recepta, / Sed quae scripta manu, sunt veneranda magis" (*Satires, Epigrams, and Verse Letters,* 112). See Beal, *Index,* 1:244–49, and "John Donne and the Circulation of Manuscripts," 122; Kelliher, "Donne, Jonson, Richard Andrews and The New Castle Manuscript," 134; Garrod, "The Latin Poem Addressed by Donne to Dr. Andrews"; and Ioppolo, *Dramatists and Their Manuscripts,* 191n32.

5. Nicholas Barker, "Donne's 'Letter to the Lady Carey and Mrs. Essex Riche.'"

6. On scribal culture see Saunders, "Stigma of Print"; Ezell, *Patriarch's Wife,* 62–100; Woudhuysen, *Sir Philip Sidney;* Beal, *In Praise of Scribes;* Love, *Scribal Publication;* and Coiro, "Milton and Class Identity"; see also the useful discussion in Hackel, *Reading Material,* 17–43.

7. *Pro Populo Anglicano Defensio, PW* 211; *Eikonoklastes, CPW* 3:588, see n17; on Nennius, see Glicksman, "Sources of Milton's *History of Britain,*" 106. On parliamentary antiquarianism see Sharpe, *Sir Robert Cotton;* and Woolf, "Selden: From Antiquarianism to History."

8. [Charles Dallison,] *The Royalist's Defence: Vindicating the King's Proceedings in the Late Warre Made against Him* (London, 1648), A2, verso. On similarly derogatory treatments of "moth-eaten" manuscripts, see Hackel, *Reading Material,* 33.

9. Bodleian MS Rawl. Essex 11 (Holman collections), fol. 89r, cited in Woolf, *Reading History,* 49.

10. Letter to Sir Robert Ker, 1619, in Donne, *Selected Prose,* 152.

11. Donne, *Selected Prose,* 140.

12. Donne, *Biathanatos* (licensed in 1644; published in 1647), dedicatory epistle. For the complex bibliographic history of this text, see Keynes, *Bibliography of Dr. John Donne,* 111–20.

13. Creaser, "Editorial Problems in Milton," 280.

14. Love, *Scribal Publication,* vi. See also Achinstein, "Texts in Conflict," 55–56.

15. Hill, *Intellectual Origins,* 32. English editions in Italian of both *I Discorsi* and *Il Principe* were printed in the 1580s, unlicensed and with the imprint "Palermo" to elude authorities. See also Raab, *English Face of Machiavelli,* 52–53. On the manuscript editions of *The Prince,* see Orsini, "Elizabethan Manuscript Translations of Machiavelli's *Prince,*" and Craig, *Machiavelli's "The Prince."*

16. See Beer, *Sir Walter Ralegh and His Readers,* esp. 179–85.

17. Malcolm, *Aspects of Hobbes,* 28.

18. Quoted by Gaskin in Hobbes, *Elements of Law,* xii.

19. Quoted in Gaskin, *Elements of Law,* 235.

20. See Beal, *Index,* 2.1:578–80.

21. This is BL Egerton 1910. The complexities of Hobbes's alliance and in particular his use of this gift are discussed in Collins, *Allegiance of Thomas Hobbes,* 143–47. See also Trevor-Roper, *Catholics, Anglicans, and Puritans,* 182–84.

22. Edward Hyde, *A Brief View and Survey of the Dangerous and Pernicious Errors to Church and State, in Mr. Hobbes's Book entitled Leviathan* (Oxford, 1676), 8–9; Kirton to Verney, February 3, 1652, *Historical Manuscripts Commission,* 7th Report, 458, cited in Collins, 145n180.

23. On extant copies of Milton's works, see Parker's useful appendix in *Milton,* 1209–13. As Joad Raymond writes, the *Epitaphium Damonis* was probably printed "for circulation among select friends." Raymond, "Milton," 377. This copy is BL C.57.d.48.

24. On the declining percentages of registered books that were recorded, see Clegg, *Press Censorship in Elizabethan England,* 17–18. See also Willard, "Jaggard's Catalogue of English Books"; and Willard, "Survival of English Books Printed before 1640." Adam Hooks kindly pointed me toward these articles.

25. McKenzie, "London Book Trade in 1644," 131.

26. See Parker, *Milton,* 1213.

27. McKenzie, *Making Meaning,* 129. Joad Raymond has calculated a similar rate of loss for the early modern period, in which "modern bibliographies may record no more than two-thirds of all the books actually published." Raymond, *Pamphlets and Pamphleteering,* 165. A wonderful example of the problems of enumerative bibliography for this period is illustrated in the five thousand or so "ghosts" listed by Wing in *Gallery of Ghosts.*

28. McKenzie, *Making Meaning,* 23–25, 39–41. McKenzie points out that modern conceptions of early print runs are largely based on the "1587 ordinance of the Stationers' Company which, with one or two exceptions, forbade the printing of more than 1250–1500 copies of any books from the same setting of type" (23–24), although it remains uncertain how rigorously or for how long this rule was observed. See also Sharpe, *Reading Revolutions,* 46; on *Paradise Lost* see Raymond, "Milton," 382.

29. Examples include BL Additional 45154, which has an unpublished tract among other miscellaneous notes and excerpts, and BL MS Sloane 63, which contains at least two short manuscript prose tracts, one called "A Discourse Touching the Present Consultacion concerning the peace with Spaine and the retaining of the Netherlands in society written by Sir Walter Raleigh, 1602" (fols. 58–68); and the other titled "Christs Monarchicall, and Personall Reigne upon Earth over all the Kingedoms of this World," with a signed epistle to the reader.

30. See Fulton, "Edward Phillips and the Manuscript of the 'Digression.'"

31. Love, *Scribal Publication,* 46–47.

32. Fulton, "Edward Phillips and the Manuscript of the 'Digression.'"

33. Ezell, *Social Authorship*, 154n1.

34. Quoted in McKeon, *Secret History of Domesticity*, 55.

35. For an excellent summary of Milton's relationship to print, see Raymond, "Milton."

36. David Harrison Stevens, "Bridgewater Manuscript of *Comus*," 316; see also Coiro, "Anonymous Milton," 609–11.

37. Bodleian MS Ashmole 36/37, fol. 22. For the notes in the Trinity MS, see Fletcher, *John Milton's Complete Poetical Works*, 1:395.

38. BL MS Sloane 1446, fols. 37v–38v.

39. Fletcher, *Milton's Complete Poetical Works*, 1:389.

40. Parker, "Milton's Hobson Poems," 396; see also G. Blakemore Evans, "Two New Manuscript Versions."

41. James Grantham Turner, "Libertinism and Toleration," 113.

42. MS. Lat. Misc. d. 77. See Achinstein, *Citizen Milton*, 6.

43. Fletcher, *Milton's Complete Poetical Works*, 1:396–97.

44. Fletcher, *Milton's Complete Poetical Works*, 1:368; see *CSP* 294.

45. Fletcher, *Milton's Complete Poetical Works*, 1:43.

46. Fletcher, *Milton's Complete Poetical Works*, 1:446–47.

47. [George Sikes,] *The Life and Death of Sir Henry Vane* (London, 1662), 93.

48. Ellwood, *History of Thomas Ellwood*, 199–200. Ellwood's wording suggests the manuscript was untitled.

49. Nor do any copies carry Milton's title. Oxford Wadham College MS 29 has "Sr Walter Rawglies Arts of Empire" added in a later hand, following the title of the 1692 printed edition. See Strathmann, "A Note on the Ralegh Canon." The manuscripts are instead mostly signed by "T. B.," suggested by Strathmann to be Thomas Bedingfield, although the name Tho. Bushell appears on the top of the first page of Bodleian MS Don. D. 93. As Strathmann shows, the manuscript was first circulated around 1596–1600. One poor copy has the attribution "written by Sr. Frances Bacon, Knight and Barronett," although this is written in a later ink and therefore shows signs of not being in the copied ms; BL MS Harley 1853, fol. 41v. This version is not individually bound, but copied into a larger collection of prose works. See also Beal, *Index*, 1.2:367.

50. Huntington MS EL 1174. Milton's printed copy measures approximately 3 by 5 inches.

51. See Paul Stevens, "Milton's 'Renunciation' of Cromwell." Milton "would have easily recognized," as Stevens points out, "the numerous echoes and sometimes whole passages" lifted from Machiavelli (382).

52. Minnis, *Medieval Theory of Authorship*, 94–103.

53. *Politica* (1589), page 3 of the *Breves notae* paginated separately at the end of the book; I quote from the translation of Ann Moss in "The *Politica* of Justus Lipsius," 422.

54. Huntington MS EL 1174, "The Argument"; same wording as BL MS Additional 27320, fol. 2v.

55. *The Cabinet-Council: Containing the Cheif ARTS OF EMPIRE, And MYSTERIES of STATE; DISCABINETED In Political and Polemical Aphorisms, grounded on Authority, and Experience; And illustrated with the choicest Examples and Historical Observations. By the Ever-renowned Knight, Sir WALTER RALEIGH, Published By JOHN MILTON, Esq* (London, 1658), A2r, v. For discussion of this, see Dzelzainis, "Milton and the Protectorate."

56. Bredvold, "Milton and Bodin's *Heptaplomeres*"; see also Nigel Smith, "Milton and the European Contexts of Toleration," 25.

57. There are two seventeenth-century copies at the British Library: Sloane 2859 and Sloane 2998 fols. 1–136. Sloane 2859 was created by many scribal hands and has many corrections. Sloane 2998 is copied on much larger paper. On the circulation of manuscripts of this work, and some extant copies, see Kuntz's edition of Bodin, *Colloquium of the Seven about Secrets of the Sublime,* lxvii–lxxii; on the date, see xxxviii n69; Popkin, "Dispersion of Bodin's Dialogues."

58. Kuntz in Bodin, *Colloquium,* lxx.

59. Kuntz in Bodin, *Colloquium,* lxviii n135.

60. See James Grantham Turner, "Libertinism and Toleration," 113. Turner does not give a source here for his statement that Milton brought Bodin's manuscript back from the continent.

61. Lewalski, *Life of Milton,* 351; Popkin, "Dispersion of Bodin's Dialogues."

62. Henry Oldenburg to Samuel Hartlib, August 13, 1659, in Oldenburg, *Correspondence,* 1:302, quoted in Popkin, "Dispersion of Bodin's Dialogues," 157. On Milton's connections with Oldenburg, see von Maltzahn, "Royal Society and the Provenance of Milton's *History of Britain,*" 91.

63. Oldenburg, *Correspondence,* 1:307.

64. James Grantham Turner, "Libertinism and Toleration," 120, 109.

65. As the editor of Wotton's letters points out, Hales's full name is spelled out "in old handwriting in a copy of the *Reliquiae* (1672)." Logan Pearsall Smith, *Life and Letters of Sir Henry Wotton,* 2:381n1. On the significance of Hales in this context, see Nigel Smith, "Milton and the European Contexts of Toleration," 29, 42; and von Maltzahn, "Milton, Marvell and Toleration," 94; *Oxford Dictionary of National Biography;* Yates, "Paolo Sarpi's 'History of the Council of Trent,'" 134–35. See also Sells, *Paradise of Travellers,* 52–76.

66. Poole, "Shelf-List of John Hales." I thank William Poole for sharing this paper with me.

67. Trevor-Roper, *Catholics, Anglicans, and Puritans,* 175, 186.

68. On the Tew Circle, see Barbour, *Literature and Religious Culture,* 56–90; Trevor-Roper, *Edward Hyde,* 5–6; Trevor-Roper, *Catholics, Anglicans, and Puritans,* 166–230; and Elson, *John Hales,* 24, 123–25.

69. The manuscript made it to Laud himself, although surely against Hales's anti-Laudian intentions, as Laud peremptorily summoned the author for an interview at Lambeth Palace. The interview, however, seems to have resulted in a friendly subsequent relationship. Elson, *John Hales,* 24, 123–25.

70. Mede, *Works of Joseph Mede* (London, 1677), 883.

71. See Zagorin, *Religious Toleration*, 94–97, 115. Castellio's first printed toleration tract, also responding to Servetus's execution, *Concerning Heretics and Whether They Should Be Persecuted*, appeared anonymously in 1553 with a false imprint and printer's name. Zagorin, *Religious Toleration*, 102.

72. The full Latin title is *Contra libellum Calvini in quo ostenditur conatur haereticos jure gladii coercendos esse;* the book it refutes is Calvin's *Defense of the Orthodox Faith*, or *Defensio orthodoxae fidei de sacra Trinitate* ([Geneva], 1554).

73. Zagorin, *Religious Toleration*, 124. For a discussion of the discovery of Latin and French texts in manuscript in the Remonstrants Library in Rotterdam, see Becker and Valkhoff's introduction in Castellion, *De l'impunité des hérétiques;* Zagorin, *Religious Toleration*, 334n65.

74. See Bouwsma, *Concordia Mundi*, 19–23; Bodin, *Colloquium*, xx–xxi, 177, 462.

75. See Kuntz in Bodin, *Colloquium*, lxi.

76. Bodin, *Colloquium*, 365. On Saloman and Bodin, see Kuntz in Bodin, *Colloquium*, xliv, and Rose, *Bodin and the Great God of Nature*, 138, 144–45, and on Socinianism, 188.

77. Trevor-Roper, *Catholics, Anglicans and Puritans*, 194.

78. Hunter, *Visitation Unimplor'd*, 39–40, quoted in Shawcross, *Rethinking Milton Studies*, 118.

79. Shawcross, *Rethinking Milton Studies*, 118–19.

80. Campbell et al., *Milton and the Manuscript of "De Doctrina Christiana,"* 39–58; on Milton's intentions for publication, see 33, 64–65.

81. Campbell et al., *Milton and the Manuscript of "De Doctrina Christiana,"* 53.

82. Campbell et al., *Milton and the Manuscript of "De Doctrina Christiana,"* 51. The corrections are listed and shown in facsimile in Kelly, *This Great Argument*, 218–51.

83. The Latin phrase is "Haec si omnibus palam facio, si fraterno quod Deum testor atque amico erga omnes mortales animo, haec, quibus melius aut pretiosius nihil habeo, quam possum latissime libentissimeque imperio" (*WJM* 14:8).

84. The Latin for "Concealment is not my object" is "Latibula non quaero" (*WJM* 14:10).

85. Firth and Rait, *Acts and Ordinances of the Interregnum*, 1:1133–34, 1135.

86. Nigel Smith, "And if God was one of us," 164; Coffey, "Ticklish Business," 118.

87. See Coffey, "Ticklish Business," esp. 111; and David Loewenstein, "Toleration and the Specter of Heresy."

88. For instances of these attacks, see Campbell, *Chronology*, 87, 90, 94.

89. Dzelzainis, "Milton and Antitrinitarianism," 182–84.

90. French, *Life Records*, 3:206; see also Dobranski, "Licensing Milton's Heresy"; and Nigel Smith, "And if God was one of us," 168.

91. Campbell et al., *Milton and the Manuscript of "De Doctrina Christiana,"* 157–58. Many "incriminating papers," as David Norbrook has written, would have been frantically destroyed in this year. Norbrook, *Writing the English Republic*, 4.

92. This history is recounted in Campbell et al., *Milton and the Manuscript of "De Doctrina Christiana,"* an extensive defense of the manuscript's authenticity. For an excellent overview, see Dobranski and Rumrich, "Introduction: Heretical Milton."

93. For an excellent discussion of this, see Rogers, "*Paradise Regained* and the Memory of *Paradise Lost.*" I thank the author for sharing this prior to publication.

94. Campbell et al., *Milton and the Manuscript of "De Doctrina Christiana,"* 92.

95. See Rajan, "Poetics of Heresy," 39.

96. Sewell, *Study in Milton's Christian Doctrine,* 77–85. As Sewell writes, *De Doctrina Christiana* is "to some extent . . . merely epiphenomenal. Milton's deeper needs and more lasting satisfactions are to be found elsewhere. . . . The poems report the more integral truth of Milton's spiritual development" (83).

97. *Paradise Lost,* 7.25–26. See Rajan, "Poetics of Heresy."

98. Discussed in Nigel Smith, *Literature and Revolution in England,* 1; and Norbrook, *Writing the English Republic,* 1–22.

99. Treadwell, "The Stationers and the Printing Acts," 755–57.

100. *By the King. A Proclamation for Calling in, and Suppressing of Two Books By John Milton* (August 13, 1660), single page.

101. Those printed in 1694 are reproduced in Fletcher, *Milton's Complete Poetical Works,* 1:372–73; Toland may be using this earlier publication (since his versions are much closer to Phillips than to the manuscript). Toland, *Life of Milton* (Amsterdam, 1699), 72–73, 111–12.

102. Patterson, "Why Is There No Rights Talk in Milton's Poetry?" 197. See also Dobranski, *Milton, Authorship and the Book Trade,* 175.

103. *CSP* 323–25, 328–31, 346–47. Subsequent line numbers to Milton's short poems come from this edition unless otherwise noted.

104. [Sikes], *Life and Death of Sir Henry Vane,* 94; Fletcher, *Milton's Complete Poetical Works,* 1:373, 454–55.

105. Fletcher, *Milton's Complete Poetical Works,* 1:451.

106. Fletcher, *Milton's Complete Poetical Works,* 1:452–55.

107. Wilding, "Marvell's Horatian Ode," 1.

108. On the republican language in the sonnet to Skinner, see Campbell and Corns, *John Milton,* 191.

109. Woolrych, "Date of the Digression," 217.

110. See Fulton, "Edward Phillips and the Manuscript of the 'Digression.'"

111. Darbishire, *Early Lives,* 75.

112. Dobranski, *Milton, Authorship, and the Book Trade,* 59. The date of the licensing is presented before the title-page.

113. Oddly, unlike *Paradise Regained* and *Samson Agonistes,* the *History* has no imprimatur, so it is unclear exactly when the licensing happened. The *History* appears around November 1, 1670; see von Maltzahn, "Royal Society and the Provenance of Milton's *History*," 91. Entries in the Stationers' Register seem to postdate its publication; see Arber, *Transcript of the Registers,* 2:451–52.

114. Raymond, "Milton," 382.

115. French, *Life Records,* 4:429–31; BL Additional MS 18861, quoted in Raymond, "Milton," 382.

2. Combing the Annals of Barbarians: The Commonplace Book and Milton's Political Scholarship

1. *CPW* 1:491, CB 241. For contrasting Miltonic views, see *CPW* 1:887–88.

2. Hanford, "Chronology of Milton's Private Studies"; Mohl, *John Milton and His Commonplace Book;* although see now Poole, "Genres of Milton's Commonplace Book."

3. Jardine and Grafton, "Studied for Actions"; Moss, *Printed Commonplace-books;* Blair, *Theater of Nature;* see also Crane, *Framing Authority;* Havens, *Commonplace Books;* Beal, "Notes in Garrison"; Thomas, "Reading and Writing the Renaissance Commonplace Book"; Clark, "Wisdom Literature of the Seventeenth Century"; Shephard, "Political Commonplace Books of Sir Robert Sidney"; Warkentin, "Humanism in Hard Times"; and Poole, "Genres of Milton's Commonplace Book."

4. This is described in greater detail by Shawcross, "Survey of Milton's Prose Works."

5. See Appendix A for details and for a description of the challenges of quantification. The figures provided for the *Index Ethicus* and the *Index Economicus* derive from Mohl, who gets slightly different numbers for the *Index Politicus;* Mohl, *Milton and His Commonplace Book,* 31. Parker gives slightly different numbers for the total numbers, as well; *Milton,* 802.

6. Hanford, "Chronology of Milton's Private Studies." Hanford indicates 92; Poole ("Genres of Milton's Commonplace Book") gives the figure as 95. A complete list of the entries in the Political Index with their probable dates of composition is supplied in Appendix A.

7. The foundations for the chronology of studies in Milton's notes have been established by James Holly Hanford and Ruth Mohl, and these have been revised by William Riley Parker and John Shawcross. While I have relied on some of these dates, there remain many uncertainties and assumptions that deserve more attention. Parker, *Milton,* 145–50, 801–4; Shawcross, *John Milton,* esp, 76–82, 122–26, 281–88; see also Shawcross, "Survey of Milton's Prose Works."

8. The letter to Charles Diodati, November 23, 1637, in which Milton writes of his reading in Italian, French, and German history (such as Sigonius); see Parker, *Milton,* 150, and Shawcross, *John Milton,* 76–77. Shawcross argues that Milton began the Commonplace Book around September 1637 (77); see also Campbell and Corns, *John Milton,* 89.

9. After 1637 or 1638, a shift begins to occur in Milton's from a Greek ε to an Italian *e,* which gives some sense of chronology, although Shawcross has shown that this shift is far less precise than was once thought. See Shawcross, *John Milton,* 241–44. A few handwriting specimens can be dated with certainty from Milton's European trip,

so it is inaccurate to suggest, as Hanford and Mohl do, that every Italian *e* must be subsequent to 1639; at any rate, there are Italian *e*'s that occur in the manuscripts before this date, such as in *Lycidas.* Italian *e*'s are seen in the signature and a few lines written in the *liber amicorum* of Camillus Cardoinus of Naples, dated June 10, 1639, and a letter to Holstenius, dated by Milton March 29, 1639, and written from Florence (Milton returns to England in July or August 1639). Bottkol, "Holograph of Milton's Letter to Holstenius." For the Carduini family inscription, see the facsimile reprint in Sotheby, *Ramblings in the Elucidation of the Autograph of Milton,* plate XIV (after 98); for discussion see Beal, *Index,* 2.2:102; Hanford, "Chronology of Milton's Private Studies," 256.

10. A full analysis of this and the other evidence pertaining to the scribal entries is provided in Appendix B.

11. Shawcross, *John Milton,* 81–82. Milton took John and Edward Phillips as boarders in 1639 and 1640. Milton downsized in 1647, closing his academy, but possibly continued tutoring his nephews; Lewalski, *Life of Milton,* 210. Cyriack Skinner, whose comment that Milton used students as amanuenses is evidenced in the Trinity Manuscript, does not himself appear in the Commonplace Book. Darbishire, *Early Lives,* 33.

12. *CPW* 1:475n4, and Mohl, *Milton and His Commonplace Book,* 43.

13. This is discussed in Mohl, *Milton and His Commonplace Book,* 11–24. See also Havens, *Commonplace Books,* 13–31.

14. Quoted in Henry S. Turner, *English Renaissance Stage,* 53; Turner quotes from Jardine, "Gabriel Harvey," 38.

15. Aristotle, *Basic Works,* 1419.

16. As Mohl points out in *Milton and His Commonplace Book,* 62; see also 155.

17. Poole, "'The Armes of Studious Retirement'?" I thank William Poole for sharing this manuscript with me.

18. Chaucer, *The Workes of our Ancient and Lerned English Poet, Geffrey Chaucer* (1602), fols. 25–31. For evidence this was Milton's text, see *CPW* 1:402n31.

19. CB 109, *CPW* 1:402; CB 191, *CPW* 1:472; CB 150, *CPW* 1:416.

20. Moss, "The *Politica* of Justus Lipsius," 424–25.

21. *Politica* (1589), *Breves notae,* 4 and 3, respectively; translated by Moss, "The *Politica* of Justus Lipsius," 424, 428.

22. Passages were trimmed such that "many falsities, inconsistencies and variations in a historical account will escape the reader as a result of this process of 'cutting up' the text into small pieces." Waszink, "Inventio in Lipsius' Politica," 154; see also 159–62.

23. Lipsius, *Six Bookes of Politickes,* trans. William Jones (1594), Epistle to the Reader.

24. Lesser and Stallybrass, "First Literary Hamlet."

25. See also Stallybrass and Chartier, "Reading and Authorship," 46–47. On the emergence of the vernacular commonplace in the late sixteenth century, see also Moss, *Printed Commonplace Books,* 209.

26. BL Additional MS 42518, fol. 422v, incorrectly foliated as 394; see Fulton, "Speculative Shakespeares," 395–96.

27. See Kiséry, "Politicians in Show," 179–80. Holinshed, *The Third Volume of Chronicles* (London, 1586), 546; Shakespeare, *Comedies, Histories, and Tragedies* (London, 1623), 71.

28. Kiséry, "Politicians in Show," 185; see also Sharpe, *Reading Revolutions,* 259–60.

29. BL Additional MS 42518, fol. 422v, incorrectly foliated as 394.

30. Jonson, *Sejanus* (1605), "to the Readers."

31. I owe these observations to David Quint. See Geraldi Cinthio, *Cleopatra* (Venice, 1583), or Robert Garnier, *Cornelie* (Paris, 1574). Neither the Italian nor the French set off the sentences with rhyme.

32. Jonson, *Sejanus: His Fall,* Act 1, ll. 70–72, 396–97.

33. Altman, *Tudor Play of Mind,* 3.

34. Chaucer, *Workes,* title page.

35. Chaucer, *Workes,* fol. 31v; Sherman, *Used Books,* 25–67.

36. CB 111, under a topic on "Education." This entry may, in fact, be the only one of the Chaucerian passages in the Commonplace Book that Milton reuses. See *Of Education, CPW* 2:372.

37. *CPW* 1:570, 579, 580; Chaucer, *Workes,* fol. 89r.

38. *CPW* 3:411; *Paradise Regained,* 4.264, in *CSP* 494.

39. John Brinsley, *Ludus Literarius; or, The Grammar Schoole Shewing How to Proceed from the First Entrance into Learning* (London, 1612), 187–88. See also Charles Hoole, *A New Discovery of the Old Art of Teaching Schoole* (London, 1661), 131, 133, 174. See also "Of Common places or memoriall books," Bodleian MS Rawlinson D 208, fols. 45ff.

40. Brinsley, *Ludus Literarius,* 188, 189.

41. See Erasmus, *On Copia,* 2.

42. Erasmus, *On Copia,* 68.

43. Erasmus, *On Copia,* 68.

44. Baldwin, *William Shakespere's Small Latine & Lesse Greeke,* 1:351, quoted in Mohl, *Milton and His Commonplace Book,* 17.

45. Mohl, *Milton and His Commonplace Book,* 17–18.

46. Aristotle, *On Rhetoric,* 190–204; see also 45, 329.

47. Drexel, *Aurifodina Artium et Scientiarum Omnium* (Antwerp, 1638), 3, quoted in Blair, "Note Taking," 98.

48. BL Additional MS 63781, title page.

49. Sharpe, *Reading Revolutions,* 101. On Drake's own notes, see 99–103.

50. On Harvey, see Jardine and Grafton, "Studied for Actions."

51. R. Dallington, *Aphorismes Civill and Militarie,* 2nd ed. (London 1629). Raleigh's tract was published in 1642 as *The Prince; or, Maxims of State* (London, 1642), and then in 1650 as *Maxims of State.*

52. These passages are quoted in Dzelzainis's revealing analysis in "Milton and the Protectorate," 194. *CPW* 1:571–72, 573, 582, 598.

53. Bodin, *Method for the Easy Comprehension of History*, x. Heywood includes a translation of chap. 4 of the *Methodus* in his Sallust in *Two Most Worthy and Notable Histories* (London, 1608 [i.e., 1609]). See Fehrenbach and Leedham-Green, *Private Libraries in Renaissance England* 4:320, 5:342, 6:286. Leedham-Green, *Books in Cambridge Inventories*, 2:132.

54. Woolf, *Idea of History*, 67–69, 88, 124, 208–9. Woolf traces the influence of Bodin on Daniel, although "he never explicitly cites" Bodin (88).

55. Shephard, "Political Commonplace Books of Sir Robert Sidney," 2, 12–13, 16. Since the Sidney library catalog is extant, we know that the *Methodus* was there. Some 82–83 percent of Sidney's entries refer to medieval history (10).

56. Warkentin, "Humanism in Hard Times," 241–45.

57. See Beal, "Notes in Garrison," 145. Bacon's essays, which are themselves deeply shaped by the commonplace-book tradition, were published in Lyon in 1641 and clustered under the same general rubrics: *Sermones Fideles Ethici, Politici, Oeconimici*. Mohl, *Milton and His Commonplace Book*, 23. On Bacon, see Beal, "Notes in Garrison," 145. On the philosophical origins of these categories, see Poole, "Genres of Milton's Commonplace Book."

58. The Latin is "de locis historia rum recte instituendis." *Methodus ad Facilem Historiarum Cognitionem* (Paris, 1566), 24; *Method*, 28.

59. *Method*, 28; I have corrected the loose translation in a couple of instances. Bodin, *Methodus* (Paris, 1566), 24.

60. Blair, *Theater of Nature*, 3.

61. See, for example, BL Additional MS 78333, which Evelyn categorizes as "Historical, Physical, Mathematical, Mechanicall etc. promiscuously set downe as they occur in Reading, or Causual discourse," to which he adds in the margin, "also some particular notes in my Travells" (fol. 1r). I'm indebted to Elizabeth Yale for pointing this out.

62. Bodin, *Method for the Easy Comprehension of History*, 31; the Latin is from Bodin, *Methodus ad Facilem Historiarum Cognitionem* (1566), 29.

63. Bodin, *Method for the Easy Comprehension of History*, 34–35.

64. Poole suggests the influence of the *Method* of the Oxford historian Degory Wheare, who seems a strong indigenous possibility. See "'The Armes of Studious Retirement'?"

65. See Poole, "'The Armes of Studious Retirement'?"

66. *CPW* 6:119, *WJM* 14:4. See also the editorial introduction, *CPW* 6:16–17. Gordon Campbell has argued that the *Index Theologicus* cross-referenced in the extant Commonplace Book was created for polemical purposes; see Campbell, "Milton's *Index Theologicus*," and the discussion of this in Poole, "Genres of Milton's Commonplace Book."

67. See Parker, *Milton*, 804n6.

68. *CPW* 1:467–68. See Yates, "Paolo Sarpi's 'History of the Council of Trent,'" 123.

69. CB 187; Milton refers again to the *Arcadia* on 188, 16 and 17.

70. BL MS Additional 36354, 195. Preston is taking this from Bodin's *De Republica*. CB 195; citations to Luther are also on 195.

71. Edward Phillips writes of being assigned "Frontinus his Stratagems" by Milton. See Phillips in Darbishire, *Early Lives,* 60.

72. These are on CB 19, 109, and 182.

73. This is unfortunately done by Jackson Boswell in his otherwise useful bibliography, *Milton's Library,* x. On the topic of libraries Milton may have consulted, see Jones, "Filling in a Blank in the Canvas"; and Poole, "'The Armes of Studious Retirement'?" On Milton's borrowing books from friends, see, for example, *CPW* 1:328.

74. Horwood, *Common-place Book of John Milton,* xv–xvi.

75. As Horwood also notes; *Common-place Book of John Milton,* xvi. The letter is now prefixed to the Commonplace Book, glued with an aperture to reveal the interesting neoplatonic tetrameter on its back: "Fixe here yee overdaled spheras / That wing the restless foote of time."

76. Milton, *Epistolarum familiarium* (1674), 27. I am grateful to Peter Stallybrass for elucidating this passage. On writing tables, see Stallybrass et al., "Hamlet's Tables."

77. Here editors of Milton's Commonplace Book have mistakenly misread the manuscript's "969" as "909," thus not identifying this note with the two that followed. See *CPW* 1:501, which follows Horwood (1877), 53. As a consequence, Mohl incorrectly dates these entries, 1642–1644 for the first and 1641–1643 for the second, illustrating the haphazard quality of the dating in general. The quarto volume cited is Francis Hotman, Juris Consulti, *Francogallia. Libellus statum veteris Reipublicae Gallicae* (Coloniae, 1574).

78. Maryr or Pietro Martire Vermigli appears in the inventories frequently, although less often with this title. The title does not appear in Fehrenbach and Leedham-Green, *Private Libraries in Renaissance England,* but it shows up eight times in Leedham-Green, *Books in Cambridge Inventories,* 2:531.

79. See Boswell, *Milton's Library,* 161.

80. See the example of Montesquieu in Blair, "Note Taking," 100.

81. Harrison and Laslett, *Library of John Locke,* 20.

82. For some valuable studies of shelf lists, see Hackel, "Countess of Bridgewater's London Library," 144–45; and Poole and Henderson, "Library Lists of Francis Lodwick." See also Fehrenbach and Leedham-Green, *Private Libraries* (and on the proportions of continental imprints, see Index V, "Places of Publication," where London plays a surprisingly small role); Jayne, *Library Catalogues of the English Renaissance;* and Leedham-Green, *Books in Cambridge Inventories.*

83. Leedham-Green, *Books in Cambridge Inventories,* 2:428. Ingolstadt also seldom appears as a place of publication; there is only a tiny handful in *Private Libraries in Renaissance England,* 1:213, 3:279 5:345. WorldCat lists this book as existing in only two libraries worldwide.

84. See Roberts, "Latin Trade."

85. See de Smet, *Thuanus,* 205–61.

86. On the functional differences between quartos and folios, see Masten, Stallybrass, and Vickers, *Language Machines,* 4; see also Altick, *English Common Reader,* 16; and on Milton's expensive taste in books, see Poole, "'The Armes of Studious Retirement'?"

87. Mohl, *Milton and His Commonplace Book,* 35.

88. *Of Reformation,* for example, is heavily dependent on Holinshed. Annabel Patterson discusses an example in *The Tenure of Kings and Magistrates* in *Reading Holinshed's Chronicles,* 116.

89. Parker, *Milton,* 802.

90. *CPW* 1:327. See Hanford, "Chronology of Milton's Private Studies," 260–65.

91. Mohl suggests Smith's *Commonwealth of England* (*CPW* 1:420n2).

92. See Skinner, "Classical Liberty," 10.

93. Milton invokes both of these men in the *Defensio Secunda.* Yet his mention of "Nicolaus Rentius," as Milton spells his name in print, and "Crescentius Nomentanus," is so loose as to have been easily reconstructed by memory, as the reference to Rienzio is originally.

94. See Pocock, *Machiavellian Moment,* 51.

95. On the importance of Justinian, see Dzelzainis, "John Milton, *Areopagitica,*" 155, and Skinner, *Liberty before Liberalism,* 40–41.

96. The passage referred to in the *Defensio Secunda,* for example, is "book 4, concerning injuries, tit. 4," a wholly different section than those covered in his notes (*CPW* 4:713). See also *PW* 181.

97. This is Mohl's translation, *CPW* 1:471n3.

98. These writers are discussed in Pocock, *Ancient Constitution.*

99. For example, Milton's interest in common-law history is indicated in a note on how King John "promiseth to abolish the unjust laws of the Normans and to restore the laws of K. Edward" (CB 179, *CPW* 1:428), or a note about how "Alfred 'turn'd the old laws into english,'" (*CPW* 1:424), or "Edward the Confessor reduc't the laws to fewer, pick't them, and set them out under the name of common law" (426).

100. *CPW* 1:409, 834. In the Commonplace Book, he refers to "Bodin. Repub. Book 1 c 3" (409); he is referred to again on 446 as speaking something "displeasing to the courtiers" in the "great Parlament at Blois 1576." In *Reason of Church Government,* Milton uses a comment Bodin made in the first part of the sixth book of the *Six Livres de la République* (1577) that the commonwealth of Geneva will flourish as an endorsement of the "presbyterial government," although Bodin is "a papist" (834).

101. Published in London in 1721. The Latin text is Hotman, *Francogallia* (1574).

102. *CPW* 4:420–21. Milton cites Hotman again in *CPW* 4:659.

103. Hotman, *Franco-Gallia; or, An Account of the Ancient Free State of France, and Most Other Parts of Europe before the Loss of their Liberties* (London, 1721), iv–v.

104. Hotman, *Franco-Gallia* (1721), 1; The Latin is in *Francogallia* (1574), 1: "Principio exponendum videtur qui Gallia status fuerit, antequam a Romanis in Provinciae formam redigeretur."

105. Hotman, *Franco-Gallia* (1721), 6. See, for example, *CPW* 1:461–62, 473; but see also 441, 446.

106. *CPW* 1:908. The bogeyman "Matchiavel" also appears in *The Doctrine and Discipline of Divorce* as a way of disparaging the unsound position of Beza's of "regulating sinne by a politick law": "but what politick law I know not, unlesse one of Matchiavel's, may regulate sin" (*CPW* 2:321).

107. On this early modern habit of reading, see Sharpe, *Reading Revolutions*, 39–45.

108. Mohl translates this as "Gentleness" (*CPW* 1:450).

109. *CPW* 1:450, and [Francis Bacon], *A Wise and Moderate Discourse, Concerning Church-Affairs* (1641), 11. How Milton knew this was by Bacon is an interesting question, as his identity is nowhere in the pamphlet. The 1641 pamphlet derives from *An Advertisement Touching the Controversies of the Church of England*, written in 1589 but only circulated in manuscript.

110. [Bacon], *A Wise and Moderate Discourse*, 11–12.

111. See Nigel Smith, "Milton and the Index," and "Milton and the European Contexts of Toleration," 32.

112. Nigel Smith, "Milton and the Index," 103.

113. *Animadversions* (July 1641), in *CPW* 1:669; Nigel Smith draws attention to this in relation to an edition of Sarpi issued by the printer of Milton's 1645 poems, Humphrey Mosley ("Milton and the Index," 104).

114. See the entries under "Tyrant," 185 in the Commonplace Book, and *The Tenure*, 220–21. The topic "Rex," on 181–82 in the Commonplace Book is used three times in *The Tenure*, 202.

3. *Areopagitica:* Books, Reading, and Context

1. Belsey, *John Milton: Language, Gender, Power*, 78, quoted in Kolbrener, *Milton's Warring Angels*, 15. Kolbrener provides a detailed survey of the critical traditions.

2. Laski, "*Areopagitica* after Three Hundred Years," 175.

3. See Foucault, *Power/Knowledge*, 109–33; and Lyotard, *Postmodern Condition*, xxiv, 8–9, 27–37, 46.

4. Illo, "Misreading of Milton," 183.

5. Rapaport, *Milton and the Postmodern*, 172.

6. Fish, "Driving from the Letter," 235.

7. Worden, "Toleration and the Cromwellian Protectorate," 199.

8. See Davis, "Religion and the Struggle for Freedom"; Lamont, "Pamphleteering"; and Condren, "Liberty of Office."

9. Davis, "Religion and the Struggle for Freedom," 515.

10. Coffey, *Persecution and Toleration,* 5; see also Coffey, "Puritanism and Liberty Revisited."

11. Tournu and Forsyth, introduction to *Milton, Rights and Liberties,* 5. Milton first used the term in *An Apology against a Pamphlet* (*CPW* 1:923–24).

12. For an important discussion of the role of London in Puritan polemic culture, see Manley, *Literature and Culture,* 531–82.

13. Mueller, "Contextualizing Milton's Nascent Republicanism," 281.

14. Norbrook, "*Areopagitica,* Censorship, and the Early Modern Public Sphere," 15; see also Norbrook, *Writing the English Republic,* 118–39; Dzelzainis, "John Milton, *Areopagitica.*"

15. See Kahn, *Machiavellian Rhetoric,* 172. See also Worden, "Milton's Republicanism."

16. Kahn, *Machiavellian Rhetoric,* 172.

17. See Zurbuchen, "Republicanism and Toleration." On this issue, see Achinstein and Sauer, introduction to *Milton and Toleration,* 15.

18. *Mercurius Aulicus,* August 19, 1643, quoted in the *Oxford Dictionary of National Biography.* Norbrook, "*Areopagitica,* Censorship, and the Early Modern Public Sphere," 17; see also Hirst, *England in Conflict,* 212.

19. Plato is mentioned six times, on 495, 522, 523, and 526. The nearest second is Cicero, who appears four times, although not in theoretically pertinent passages: 494, 498, and 510. Aristotle, far more important to the argument, is mentioned once, on 521. Plato is the subject of two source studies: Agar, *Milton and Plato,* and Samuel, *Plato and Milton.* In particular, see Agar, 1–2, 56–68; and Samuel, 12–25.

20. Tuck, *Natural Rights Theories,* 101–18; Rosenblatt, "Milton, Natural Law, and Toleration."

21. I have formerly suggested that these are "liberal" because a similar theory of knowledge motivates Locke and other major representatives of liberalism (such as Spinoza), and because the relationship here between methodology, epistemology, and politics is more like Locke than it is akin to Renaissance or classical political theory. Yet the neologism may misleadingly invoke a progressivist set of values. See Fulton, "*Areopagitica* and the Roots of Liberal Epistemology."

22. CB 4, *CPW* 1:363; see later discussion.

23. *CPW* 2:158–83; see also Arthur Barker's pioneering contextualism in *Milton and the Puritan Dilemma,* 80–97. More recent studies include Nigel Smith, "*Areopagitica:* Voicing Contexts" (on Plato, see 103); and the essays in Achinstein and Sauer, *Milton and Toleration.*

24. *CPW* 7:252. On Milton and Erastianism, see Campbell and Corns, *John Milton,* 161.

25. Sirluck, *CPW* 2:170–78. Annabel Patterson explores the tract's rhetorical function in relation to Parliament in *Censorship and Interpretation,* 111–19. Reid Barbour points out complications that follow from calling Selden an "Erastian" in *John Selden,* 3.

26. CB 177, *CPW* 1:421. Milton quotes from Thuanus [de Thou], *Historiarum sui Temporis* (Geneva, 1626), 2:74 (and not 71, as Mohl suggests).

27. Coffey, "Puritanism and Liberty Revisited," 969, although Coffey's inclusion of Vane is not quite right; see Dzelzainis, "Milton and Antitrinitarianism," 180n25; see also Nigel Smith, "Milton and the European Contexts of Toleration," 29; and Corns, "Milton, Roger Williams, and the Limits of Toleration." The problem of Milton's more limited toleration is frequently recognized by Miltonists; see Arthur Barker, *Milton and the Puritan Dilemma*, 93–97.

28. On de Thou's religious beliefs, see de Smet, *Thuanus,* 85, 131, 241, 283.

29. Dobranski, "Letter and Spirit"; Hoxby, *Mammon's Music,* 25–52; Joseph Loewenstein, *Author's Due,* 152–91.

30. See Nigel Smith, *"Areopagitica:* Voicing Contexts," 105. On the significance of the title page, see Blum, "Author's Authority," 85; see also Dobranski, "Letter and Spirit," 135–36.

31. See Fulton, *"Areopagitica* and the Roots of Liberal Epistemology."

32. Patterson, "Milton and the D-Word"; see her *Milton's Words.*

33. Fish, "Driving from the Letter," 246. See Dobranski, "Letter and Spirit," 132.

34. The ordinance expresses concern with the "great defamation of Religion and Government," but it is ultimately concerned to protect property, the "Books belonging to the Company of Stationers." Firth and Rait, *Acts and Ordinances of the Interregnum,* 1:184.

35. Joseph Loewenstein, *Author's Due,* 152–91; Hoxby, *Mammon's Music,* 25–52.

36. Arber, *Transcript of the Registers,* 1:584. The printed speech is dated "Aprill 1643" by Thomason, E. 669 (584).

37. Paolo Sarpi, one source for Milton's ideas on the Inquisition, is cited several times in the Commonplace Book. On Milton's possible use of Parker, and on situating *Areopagitica* among other parliamentary speakers, see Nigel Smith's analysis in *"Areopagitica:* Voicing Contexts," 103–13.

38. Arber, *Transcript of the Registers,* 1:586–88.

39. Wanklyn and Jones, *Military History,* 199; see also Woolrych, *Britain in Revolution,* 291.

40. Wanklyn and Jones, *Military History,* 190–214; Woolrych, *Britain in Revolution,* 290.

41. For a full account, see Jordan, *Development of Religious Toleration,* and more recently, Zagorin, *How the Idea of Religious Toleration Came to the West,* esp. 145–239. The English movement was preceded by the Dutch, whose toleration policy had an exemplary influence. See, for example, [Roger Williams], *Queries of Highest Consideration* (London, 1644), 12; [William Walwyn], *The Compassionate Samaritane* (London, 1644), 44–45. Some of the Dutch influence comes from exiled Baptists, such as Thomas Helwys; see Coffey, "Puritanism and Liberty Revisited," 964.

42. Nigel Smith, "Milton and the Index," 101–2. For an account of the European context and prehistory, see Smith's "Milton and the European Contexts of Toleration."

43. Sirluck claims this to be the earliest wartime toleration tract, although [William Walwyn], *Some Considerations Tending to the Undeceiving Those Whose Judgements Are Misinformed* (November 10, 1642), may have the rightful claim; *CPW* 2:79–80.

44. [Henry Robinson], *Liberty of Conscience*, 133, 165–66.

45. Coffey, "Puritanism and Liberty Revisited," 965.

46. Sirluck, in *CPW* 2:86.

47. On the influence of this tract on *Areopagitica*, see *CPW* 2:87; see especially *The Compassionate Samaritane*, 47 and 55–56.

48. Walwyn, *The Compassionate Samaritane*, 55.

49. This has been insightfully discussed by Jason Rosenblatt in "Milton, Natural Law, and Toleration."

50. Campbell and Corns, *John Milton*, 149. On Milton's early Arminianism, see also Corns, "Milton's Antiprelatical Tracts"; and Corns, "Milton before 'Lycidas.'"

51. Höpfl in *Luther and Calvin on Secular Authority*, xxiii; see also xliii.

52. For an excellent discussion of Bucer and his fusion of Mosaic and Platonic law, see Shuger, *Political Theologies*, 11–47.

53. Lewalski, *Life of Milton*, 175–76. The extensive contemporary reaction to Milton's divorce tracts, especially *The Doctrine and Discipline of Divorce*, is documented in Campbell, *Chronology*, 78–99. It is of particular interest that the Company of Stationers mentions this tract in a petition to Parliament against unlicensed books on August 24, 1644; see Campbell, *Chronology*, 81.

54. Bucer, *De Regno Christi*, 162.

55. See Burnett, "Church Discipline and Moral Reformation."

56. Bucer, *De Regno Christi*, 181.

57. On his deathbed, Bucer expressed a hope that England would not follow Germany in falling asunder, which was the reason for his writing of church discipline ("de disciplina Ecclesia") and prescribing it to England. Martin Bucer, *Scripta Anglicana* (Basel, 1577), 875. The earliest Puritan pamphlets, such as the Presbyterian *Admonition to the Parliament* (1572), echoed this imperative of "ecclesiastical discipline," which, the pamphlet demands, means "correction of faults severlie." *Admonition to the Parliament* (London, 1572), sig. A1v.

58. Calvin, *Institutes of the Christian Religion* (trans. Battles), 2:1229.

59. CB 4, *CPW* 1:363; here I use Poole's adjustment of Mohl's translation, found in "Genres of Milton's Commonplace Book." For discussion of the connections between Lactantius, the Commonplace Book, and *Areopagitica*, see Hartwell, *Lactantius and Milton*, 18–34.

60. These are *CPW* 1:573, 746, 846, 879, 880, 881, 891.

61. *CPW* 1:752, emphasis added; see also 755.

62. The words of Corns, *Uncloistered Virtue*, 11.

63. White, "Rise of Arminianism Reconsidered," 34. The Baptists also broke with Calvinism and adopted Arminianism. See Tyacke, "'Rise of Puritanism,'" 31; and Hill, *Milton and the English Revolution*, 272–73. For a full account of Armin-

ianism among Puritan sectarians and others, see Wallace, *Puritans and Predestination*, 104–57.

64. Marshall, *A Sermon Preached before the Honourable House of Commons* (London, 1641), 22–23. For discussion of this, see Kahn, *Wayward Contracts*, 116.

65. Prynne, *The Church of England's Old Antithesis to New Arminianisme* (London, 1629), sigs. A4v, c3v, quoted in Tyacke, "Arminianism and English Culture," 94. As Tyacke shows, "Englishmen labeled Arminian by their compatriots did usually espouse the cause of man's free will" (95); see White, "Rise of Arminianism Reconsidered," 34; and John Owen, *Theomachia autexousiastike; or, A display of Arminianisme. Being a discovery of the old Pelagian idol free-will* (London, 1643).

66. See, for example, *CPW* 1:533–34, 917. See Lewalski, *Life of Milton*, 139; Corns, "Milton, Roger Williams, and the Limits of Toleration," 83. On Milton's early Arminianism, see Corns, "Milton's Antiprelatical Tracts"; and Corns, "Milton before 'Lycidas.'"

67. Hooker, *Laws of Ecclesiastical Polity*, 1:35. Hooker's *Laws* were recycled in different forms during the church government debates of the early 1640s, as in a pamphlet called *The Dangers of New Discipline* (1642).

68. Hooker, *Laws of Ecclesiastical Polity*, 1:188; see also 1:33, 190.

69. For discussion of reason and scripture in Hooker, see Lake, *Anglicans and Puritans*, 145–54. As Lake argues, Hooker disagreed with the common merger of "the minister and the magistrate," and suggested instead that the "right to rule came directly from men and only indirectly from God" (203).

70. Lake, *Anglicans and Puritans*, 153.

71. Tuck, *Natural Rights Theories*, 101.

72. Tuck, *Natural Rights Theories*, 101–18.

73. *His Majesties Answer to a Book* (London, 1642). This pamphlet is generated, Charles writes, because Parliament "thought fit to assault us with a newer Declaration, *indeed of a very new Nature and Learning,* which must have another answer" (2, emphasis added).

74. John Bramhall, *Serpent Salve; or, A remedie for the Biting of an Aspe* (1643). For discussion of this see Nigel Smith, *Literature and Revolution*, 41. The controversy around the "Observator" seems to have spawned more than just one Hobbesian defender of Charles's right. For another royalist writer possibly influenced by Hobbes's 1640 manuscript, see Dudley Diggs, *An Answer to a printed book, intituled, Observations* (Oxford, 1642). See also J. M., *A Reply to the Answer* (London, 1642), 19.

75. John Bramhall, *Castigations of Mr. Hobbes* (London, 1657), 507.

76. Herbert Palmer, *The Glasse of Gods Providence Towards His Faithfull Ones* (London, 1644), 57. It is possible that Milton would have heard about Palmer's sermon in August; Milton may respond to the printed tract, as Palmer's tract was dated in Arber, *Transcript of the Registers*, 1:136, as November 7, and could have appeared very soon thereafter; *Areopagitica* appeared on November 23. See *Chronology*, 81–82; Lewalski, *Life of Milton*, 179; discussed in Joseph Loewenstein, *Author's Due*, 171–72.

77. Lewalski, *Life of Milton,* 182.

78. The changes in methodology in *The Doctrine and Discipline of Divorce* have been observed in several studies, including Arthur Barker, *Milton and the Puritan Dilemma,* 63–74; Haskin, *Milton's Burden of Interpretation,* 45–49, 59–76; Sirluck, *CPW* 2:145–58; and Fish, *How Milton Works,* 215–55.

79. On Selden, Hobbes, and the Tew Circle, see Sommerville, "John Selden," and Tuck, "Ancient Law of Freedom"; see also Rosenblatt, "Milton's Chief Rabbi," esp. 46–66; and Eivion Owen, "Milton and Selden on Divorce." On natural law, see Tuck, "'Modern' Theory of Natural Law"; and Tuck, *Philosophy and Government.* For a discussion of toleration, Grotius, and the Tew Circle, see Trevor-Roper, *Edward Hyde,* 5–6. For Grotius's influence on Milton, see Hill, *Milton and the English Revolution,* 54, 117, 276, and 288; Lewalski, *Life of Milton,* 87, 89, 167; and most recently Rosenblatt, "Milton, Natural Law, and Toleration." On Milton's "Seldenic language," see Nigel Smith, *"Areopagitica:* Voicing Contexts," 106–8.

80. For another important parliamentarian natural law theorist see Nathanael Culverwel, *An Elegant and Learned Discourse on the Light of Nature* (London, 1652), published after his death in 1652 but probably written in the mid-1640s.

81. These positions are represented, for example, in Joshua Hoyle, *Jehojadahs Justice against Mattan, Baals Priest; or, The Covenanters Justice against Idolaters* (London, 1645), 7; George Gillespie, *A Late Dialogue betwixt a Civilian and a Divine Concerning the Present Condition of the Church of England* (London, 1644), 33; Herbert Palmer, *The Glasse of Gods Providence* (London, 1644), 58.

82. William Prynne, *Histrio-mastix, The Players Scourge* (London, 1633), 917. See also Thomas Beard, *Theatre of Gods Judgements* (London, 1642), 72.

83. Roger Williams, *The Bloudy Tenent of Persecution,* 4.

84. [Robinson], *Liberty of Conscience,* 109.

85. *A Short Discourse Touching the Cause of the Present Unhappy Distractions . . . and Ready Means to Compose, and Quiet Them* (1643), 1, 3.

86. [Robinson], *Liberty of Conscience,* 116.

87. Underhill, *Tracts on Liberty of Conscience and Persecution,* 10.

88. Underhill, *Tracts on Liberty of Conscience and Persecution,* 27.

89. Underhill, *Tracts on Liberty of Conscience and Persecution,* 34.

90. [Williams], *Queries of Highest Consideration,* 3. He repeats this in *Bloudy Tenent of Persecution,* 182.

91. Wolseley, *Liberty of Conscience . . . Asserted and Vindicated,* 27, quoted in Worden, "Toleration and the Cromwellian Protectorate," 231.

92. D. P. P., *An Antidote against the Contagious Air of Independency* (London, February 18, 1644), 12, 9, 16.

93. D. P. P., *An Antidote,* 17.

94. The Presbyterian heresiographer Thomas Edwards registered horror at the "many plausible reasons" given to support "total liberty of all Religions." *Gangreana* (London, 1646) 1:124, quoted in Coffey, "Puritanism and Liberty Revisited," 971.

95. Robinson, *An Answer to Mr. William Prynn's Twelve Questions* (London, 1644), 2.

96. Robinson, *An Answer to Mr. William Prynn's Twelve Questions*, 9.

97. [Robinson], *Liberty of Conscience*, 141–42.

98. [Walwyn], *The Compassionate Samaratine*, 12, emphasis added.

99. See Sirluck, *CPW* 2:177; and Nigel Smith, "*Areopagitica:* Voicing Contexts," 106–18. As Sirluck points out, Milton strategically cites Selden and Lord Brooke, an Independent who believed in toleration, but he cites no Presbyterians (177). See also Parker, *Milton,* 269; *CPW* 2:521.

100. For a discussion of the influence of this book on Hobbes, see Malcolm, *Aspects of Hobbes,* 96–97. Selden wrote that his new methodology was analogous to the revolution in astronomy brought about by "Copernicus, Tycho, Galileus, Kepler," showing a conscious attempt to draw a relation between the scientific revolution and new kinds of political argument. *Titles of Honor* (1631) sig. ¶ 2r, quoted in the *Oxford Dictionary of National Biography.*

101. See, for example, the 1644 edition of *The Doctrine and Discipline of Divorce* (*CPW* 2:350).

102. For a discussion of the Cartesian elements of this passage, see Francis Barker, "In Wars of Truth," 117.

103. On this tradition, see Ferguson, *Trials of Desire.*

104. See Nigel Smith, "Milton and the European Contexts of Toleration," 36.

105. Aristotle, *Nicomachean Ethics* (1112a), in *Basic Works of Aristotle,* 968.

106. A surprising parallel exists in Hobbes: "There are few things in this world, but either have a mixture of good and evil, or there is a chain of them so necessarily linked together, that one cannot be taken without the other." *Elements of Law,* 45.

107. Prynne, *The Antipathie of The English Lordly Prelacie* (London, 1641), 469; see also 126, 503, 521. See also *The Path Way to Peace; or, A Sure Means to Make Wars to Cease. According to the Prescription of the Lord* (London, 1643). Thomas Beard wrote in *The Theatre of God's Judgements,* "And unto him [God] belongeth the direction and principall conduct of humane matters, in such sort that nothing in the world commeth to passe by chance or adventure, but onely and always by the prescription of his will." To the Reader, second page (not paginated).

108. Norbrook, *Writing the English Republic,* 135.

109. Filmer, *Patriarcha and Other Writings,* 2. For further examples, see his contradictions of Hobbes in *Observations concerning the Originall of Government Upon Mr Hobs Leviathan, Mr Milton against Salmasius, H. Grotius De Jure Belli* (1652), 187ff., and *The Anarchy of a Limited or Mixed Monarchy* (1648), 138.

110. Davenant, *Sir William Davenant's Gondibert,* 30.

111. *Leviathan,* 159.

112. *The Compassionate Samaritane,* 42, emphasis added.

113. David Loewenstein, "Toleration and the Specter of Heresy."

114. David Loewenstein, "Toleration and the Specter of Heresy," 67. See Zagorin, *How the Idea of Religious Toleration Came to the West,* 18–19; Zagorin writes of

Paul's association of heresy or *hairesis* with schism or *schismata,* as in 1 Corinthians 1:10.

115. Sirluck points out a similar passage in Walwyn's *Compassionate Samaritane,* 41–42. See *CPW* 2:84–87.

116. Coffey, "Puritanism and Liberty Revisited," 963. See also Corns, "Milton, Roger Williams, and the Limits of Toleration," 80–81.

117. See Coffey, *Persecution and Toleration,* 146; see Firh and Rait, *Acts and Ordinances of the Interregnum,* 1:1133–35.

118. Thomas Sprat, *The History of the Royal-Society of London for the Improving of Natural Knowledge* (London, 1667), 111, 113. See Vickers, "Royal Society and English Prose Style."

119. Lewalski, *Life of Milton,* 190. See also Achinstein, *Milton and the Revolutionary Reader,* 59.

120. Achinstein, *Milton and the Revolutionary Reader,* 59.

121. Corns, "Milton's Quest for Respectability," 773.

122. *Complete Works of St. Thomas More,* 2:59 and 4:98–99.

123. *Correspondence of Erasmus,* 81.

124. Skinner, "'Social Meaning' and the Explanation of Social Action," 86.

125. See Wittreich, "Milton's *Areopagitica,*" 103.

126. Habermas, *Communication and the Evolution of Society,* 34; Austin, *How To Do Things with Words,* 118. See Tully, *Meaning and Context,* 8.

127. See Wittreich, "Milton's *Areopagitica.*"

4. "The Digression" and Milton's Return to Polemics

1. The date on the title page is 1645; it appears on January 2, 1646. See Campbell, *Chronology,* 86.

2. John Milton, *Poems of Mr. John Milton, both English and Latin, compos'd at several times* (London, 1645), a3r–a3v. Milton's courtly connections are stressed on the title page, which advertises that "the Songs were set in Musick by Mr. Henry Lawes Gentleman of the Kings Chappel, and one of this Maiesties Private Musick." For a discussion of the ideological uncertainty of Milton's career between 1645 and 1647, see Patterson, "Forc'd Fingers," esp. 19–22; Patterson, "Why Is There No Rights Talk in Milton's Poetry?"; Corns, "Milton's Quest for Respectability"; and Coiro, "Milton and Class Identity." On Moseley's publications and advertisements of Milton, see French, "Moseley's Advertisements."

3. *CSP* 297, l. 10; Leonard, "Revolting as Backsliding in Sonnet XII."

4. *CSP* 303. I use the translation of Merritt Hughes in *John Milton: Complete Poems and Major Prose,* 146, ll. 8–10.

5. Patterson, "Forc'd Fingers," 20.

6. See Hampshire, "An Unusual Bodleian Purchase." The Bodleian was not (nor is it still) a lending library. See also Craster, "John Rous"; Campbell, *Chronology,* 85.

7. Hughes, *John Milton: Complete Poems and Major Prose,* 147.

8. Respectively: *Accidence Commenc't Grammar* (London, 1669), *Artis Logicae Plenior Institutio* (London, 1672), *A Brief History of Moscovia* (London, 1682).

9. On the politics of the *History of Britain,* see Dzelzainis, "Conquest and Slavery in Milton's *History of Britain,*" which the author kindly shared prior to publication; and von Maltzahn, *Milton's History of Britain.* For political elements in the other works, see Herendeen, "Milton's *Accidence Commenc't Grammar*"; on *Moscovia,* see Lewalski, *Life of Milton,* 212.

10. Masson, *Life of John Milton,* 6:808–11. Masson did not, however, know about the existence of the manuscript acquired by Harvard in 1926, and had to base his judgment on the *Character* discussed below. Even after the discovery of the manuscript, Don Wolfe wondered whether "Milton's condemnation of the Long Parliament is authentic." Wolfe, *Milton in the Puritan Revolution,* ix.

11. See Dzelzainis's excellent discussion in "Dating and Meaning."

12. Von Maltzahn, *Milton's History,* chap. 2.

13. Although the manuscript was discovered in 1874, it did not appear in the accounts of Firth or Masson. See von Maltzahn, *Milton's History,* 2.

14. French Fogle, editor of the Yale Prose, posits a date of 1647–48 (*CPW* 5:407); Christopher Hill dates it roughly to 1647–48 (*Milton and the English Revolution,* 102). This date is also argued by Fink, *Classical Republicans,* 191–94; and Firth, "Milton as an Historian," esp. 100.

15. Woolrych, "Date of the Digression."

16. Von Maltzahn, "Dating the Digression," 950, and *Milton's History,* chap. 2. The disagreement between von Maltzahn and Woolrych is revisited in Woolrych, "Dating Milton's *History of Britain,*" and von Maltzahn, "Dating the Digression"; see Fulton, introduction to "John Milton's 'Digression.'"

17. Worden, *Literature and Politics,* 419.

18. Lewalski, *Life of Milton,* 212–16. See also Norbrook's discussion of the dating in *Writing the English Republic;* he favors a date prior to 1649 (188–91).

19. Fulton, introduction to "John Milton's 'Digression.'"

20. *A Brief Inference upon Guicciardines Digression, in the fourth part of the first Quarterne of his Historie* (London, 1629; first printed 1613), title page. This short text was bound with Dallington, *Aphorismes Civill and Militarie,* 2nd ed. (London 1629; first printed 1613).

21. See Fulton, "Edward Phillips and the Manuscript of the 'Digression,'" and the introduction to "John Milton's 'Digression.'"

22. For these differences, see Fulton, "Edward Phillips and the Manuscript of the 'Digression.'"

23. See Dobranski, *Milton, Authorship, and the Book Trade,* 44–49; Fletcher, *Milton's Complete Poetical Works,* 1:452–55; see chapter 1, above.

24. As Fogle argues, *CPW* 5:411; see also Masson, *Life of John Milton,* 6:808. And see the reconstruction of Worden, in *Literature and Politics,* 414–25.

25. Darbishire, *Early Lives,* 75.

26. On this library, see Patterson and Dzelzainis, "Marvell and the Earl of Anglesey." John Toland, a less reliable source since he was born in 1670, writes about this in greater detail; Darbishire, *Early Lives*, 185, 75. See *CPW* 5:411–14; and Fulton, "Edward Phillips and the Manuscript of the 'Digression.'"

27. Greene, "Arthur Annesley," 98, quoted in Patterson and Dzelzainis, "Marvell and the Earl of Anglesey," 707.

28. John Toland, *The Life of Milton* (Amsterdam, 1699), 83–93; *Eikon Basilike* (ed. Knachel), xxv–viii.

29. *Bibliotheca Angleseiana, sive catalogus variorum librorum* [London], 1686, sig. A2, quoted in Patterson and Dzelzainis, "Marvell and the Earl of Anglesey," 712.

30. Patterson and Dzelzainis, "Marvell and the Earl of Anglesey," 708–9, 713–26.

31. Patterson and Dzelzainis, "Marvell and the Earl of Anglesey," 712.

32. BL Additional MS 18730, fol. 2, quoted in Patterson and Dzelzainis, "Marvell and the Earl of Anglesey," 711.

33. Love, *Scribal Publication*, 71.

34. *Journals of the House of Commons*, 8:636. An attempt had been made ten years earlier in Cromwellian England on the same grounds; see Burton, *Diary of Thomas Burton*, 1:349.

35. Love, *Scribal Publication*, 71.

36. Toomer, "Selden's History of Tithes," quoted in Serjeantson and Woolford, "Scribal Publication," 149n108. I am grateful to the authors for sharing this essay with me prior to publication.

37. Serjeantson and Woolford, "Scribal Publication," 130–49. For further discussion of printed books that were finished by hand, see Hackel, *Reading Material*, 29–30; and Woudhuysen, *Sir Philip Sidney*, 20–25.

38. "Hybrid" is Serjeantson and Woolford's useful term; see "Scribal Publication," 145.

39. They are often smaller, presumably due to trimming. Copies of this dimension include one at the Beinecke Library at Yale University (Ij M642 670hb), which is the 1671 printing, sold by Spencer Hickman.

40. Woolrych, "Date of the Digression," 219. Worden argues that the preamble to book 3 was added at the same time as the "Digression" in a late revision, and then just the "Digression" was cut; see *Literature and Politics*, 420–26.

41. See Fulton, introduction to "John Milton's 'Digression.'"

42. Indeed, Edward Phillips's dictionary defines the rare word *interreign* as interregnum, the space between monarchs. "In Latin Interregnum, the space between the death of one Prince or Ruler, and the succession or election of another." Phillips, *The New World of English words* (London, 1658).

43. For further discussion see French, *CPW* 5:431–33.

44. Worden, *Literature and Politics*, 425.

45. Here I respectfully disagree with Worden, 417–19.

46. Woolrych, "Date of the Digression," 227. Woolrych is a bit unclear on the date of the composition of the *History*, however; see 217, 231.

47. *Oxford Latin Dictionary, Converto,* 6c: "to turn (or return) to some given activity, topic, etc."

48. This is pointed out by Woolrych, "Date of the Digression," 228.

49. Darbishire, *Early Lives,* 68–69.

50. Milton shows that Salmasius had formerly taken a Presbyterian position against the bishops, even while he hypocritically contradicts this in the hired defense (*PW* 59–60); he also shows Salmasius to have formerly taken a republican position (*PW* 120–21).

51. Parker, *Milton,* 352.

52. Turnbull, *Hartlib, Dury and Comenius,* 40.

53. Woolrych, "Date of the Digression," 226–27.

54. See Sharp, *English Levellers,* 131n1.

55. Sharp, *English Levellers,* 131.

56. Sharp, *English Levellers,* 133–34.

57. Skinner, "Classical Liberty," 18. Henry Parker notably uses it, citing Cicero, in the *Observations upon Some of his Majesties Late Answers* (July 1642); see Skinner, 21–22. For further discussion, see Achinstein, *Milton and the Revolutionary Reader,* 29.

58. *A Remonstrance of His Excellency Thomas Lord Fairfax . . . held at St Albans the 16th of November 1648,* reprinted in Kenyon, *Stuart Constitution,* 281.

59. *A Remonstrance of His Excellency,* 282–83.

60. *A Remonstrance of His Excellency,* 285.

61. Woolrych, "Date of the Digression," 233.

62. Dzelzainis, "Milton and Antitrinitarianism," 182–84.

63. Firth and Rait, *Acts and Ordinances of the Interregnum,* 1:1133.

64. See, for example, the 1648 publication of Thomas Cartwright's supposed *Helpes for Discovery of the Truth in Point of Toleration,* discussed in the following chapter. Calvin's position of intolerance was supported by other reformers, such as Beza, whose *De Haereticis a Civili Magistratu Puniendis,* or Concerning the Punishment of Heretics by the Civil Magistrate (Geneva, 1554), appeared just after Servetus was burned at the stake, and in defense of that act.

65. See Nigel Smith, "And if God was one of us."

66. On the republicanism of this sonnet, see Campbell and Corns, *John Milton,* 191; and Norbrook, *Writing the English Republic,* 182–85.

67. *Milton's Sonnets* (ed. Honigmann), 142. Honigmann cites the use of "Public Faith" in Scobell, *A Collection of Acts and Ordinances* (1658), 40, and *Journals of the House of Commons,* 7:79; he also cites a 1647 pamphlet that, like Milton, criticizes the abuse of this faith, *The Mysterie of the Two Iunto's, Presbyterian and Independent,* 3 (*Milton's Sonnets,* 142). On the context (and text) of the sonnet, see Shawcross, "Milton's 'Fairfax' Sonnet."

68. Fogle cites the instance of Francis White, *A Copie of a Letter,* June 21, 1647; see *CPW* 5:454n17. One might also consider the demands in the *Remonstrance of Many Thousand Citizens* (1646), written by Milton's friend Richard Overton with

the help of William Walwayn, or *The Case of the Armie Truly Stated* (1647), *To the Right Honourable and Supreme Authority of this Nation, the Commons in Parliament Assembled* (1647), and the *Agreement of the People* (1647). See also *A Solemn Engagement of the Army* ([London], 1647), 9–10.

69. The full title is illuminating: *London's account; or, A calculation of the arbitrary and tyrannicall exactions, taxations, impositions, excises, contributions, subsidies, twentieth parts, and other assessements, within the lines of communication, during the foure yeers of this unnaturall warre. What the totall summe amounts unto, what hath beene disbursed out of it, and what remaines in the accomptants hands* ([London], 1647). Page references are cited parenthetically in the text.

70. *The Grand Account; or, A Remonstrance, wherein is plainly discovered the vast summes of money levyed upon the kingdome by ordinance of Parliament, since the beginning of the late warre: as also an accompt of the disposall of the greatest part thereof, for the service of the Parliament, &c. Also vox populi, or the cry of the commons against committee-men. In all humility tendered unto the consideration of the body representative, now sitting in Parliament at Westminster* (Oxford [i.e., London?], 1647). Thomason dates this July 29, 1647. Page references are cited parenthetically in the text.

71. Worden, "Milton's Republicanism," 226.

72. Sharp, *Leveller Tracts*, 102.

73. CB 177, *CPW* 1:420. Fogle suggests a resonance with another passage in the Commonplace Book, Milton's uncited reference to the story of Niccolo Rienzio, whose attempt to restore Rome to its ancient republican form failed in 1354 (CB 190, *CPW* 1:470). While this may have been in Milton's mind, the first passage is more to the point. Fogle, *CPW* 5:456n29.

74. Fink, *Classical Republicans*, 93–94.

5. History and Natural Law in *The Tenure of Kings and Magistrates*

1. Nigel Smith, *Poems of Andrew Marvell*, 273, ll. 119–20.

2. Thomas M. Greene, "Balance of Power in Marvell's 'Horatian Ode,'" 385–95; on the Machiavellianism of this passage especially, see also Norbrook, "Marvell's 'Horatian Ode' and the Politics of Genre"; Worden, "Andrew Marvell, Oliver Cromwell, and the Horatian Ode"; Worden, "Classical Republicanism," 195–99; and on the connection to the "sword" in Pride's Purge, see Wilding, "Marvell's Horatian Ode," 9–12.

3. As Nicholas McDowell points out, recent scholarship has suggested that the outcome of the trial was in no way a foregone conclusion; see McDowell, headnote to *The Tenure*; see also Kelsey, "Politics and Procedure"; Kelsey, "Death of Charles I"; and Tubb, "Printing the Regicide."

4. Worden, *Rump Parliament*, 23.

5. Underdown, *Pride's Purge*, 2. See Worden, *Rump Parliament*, 8.

6. *CPW* 3:560, 562; Milton uses "Independent" or "Independents" a few more times in the tracts written ten years later, but still not to identify himself; see *CPW*

7:247, 318, 458. On Milton's omission of names and sects in his writing, see David Loewenstein, "Milton among the Religious Radicals and Sects."

7. Shawcross, "Milton's *Tenure*," 2.

8. Thomason's copy is dated February 13, but this could be a bit late. Shawcross suggests the short compositional span of January 20–29; see "Milton's *Tenure*," 3. On the issue of Thomason's date, see McDowell, headnote to *The Tenure*.

9. Sirluck, "Milton's Political Thought," 215.

10. See Dzelzainis's work in his introduction to the *Political Writings*.

11. Lim, *Milton, Radical Politics, and Biblical Republicanism*, 22–23.

12. Milton addresses "the party calld Presbyterian, of whom I believe very many to be good and faithfull Christians, though misledd by some of turbulent spirit, I wish them earnestly and calmly not to fall off from thir first principles" (238). Christopher Goodman and William Whittingham are "true Protestant Divines of England, our fathers in the faith we hold" (251).

13. See McGinn, *Admonition Controversy*. On the significance of the Marprelate tracts to the pamphlet wars of the 1640s, see Achinstein, *Milton and the Revolutionary Reader*, 12; see also Lander, *Inventing Polemic*, 80–109.

14. [Cartwright], *A Directory of Church-government* (London, 1644 [1645]), 5.

15. Thomas Cartwright, *Helpes for Discovery of the Truth in Point of Toleration* (1648), "to the reader." These are excerpts from Cartwright, *The Second Replie of Thomas Cartwright: against Maister Doctor Whitgifts second answer touching the Church Discipline* ([Zurich?], 1575).

16. Cartwright's original also cites the book loosely: "Bez. In his booke of putting Here. to death." Cartwright, *The Second Replie*, xcvi.

17. Zagorin, *How the Idea of Toleration Came to the West*, 122.

18. See David Loewenstein, "Toleration and the Specter of Heresy."

19. Cartwright, *Helpes for Discovery of the Truth*, A2v.

20. Cartwright, *Helpes for Discovery of the Truth*, 6.

21. See Dzelzainis, "Milton and Antitrinitarianism."

22. *The Institution of Christian Religion* (London, 1561), fol. 58 (4.10); see also fol. 214 (3.19).

23. Desiderius Erasmus, *Novum Testamentum Omne* (Basel: Froben, 1527), 338.

24. After 1616, the Geneva Bible had to be smuggled into England from abroad (at least one man was arrested for smuggling it), and Laud later confessed to suppressing it in his trial. See Hill, *English Bible*, 58; and Betteridge, "Bitter Notes," 44.

25. *Tyndale's New Testament* (1534), 238. Tyndale is here employing Exod. 20:12. Tyndale, *The Obedience of a Christian Man* (1528), 201–2.

26. *An Homilie against Disobedience and Wylfull Rebellion* (London, [1570]), B3v; Chester, *Selected Sermons of Hugh Latimer*, 101; James, *True Lawe of Free Monarchies* (London, 1603), B3r–v, C4v–C5r; *Richard II* (1.2.40–41).

27. In a key moment in the *Institution of Christian Religion*, for example, Calvin translates Romans 13:4 with *magistratui*: "Minime id vero: siquidem magistratus vindictam, non hominis, sed Dei esse cogitamdum est, quam per hominis ministerium

in bonum nostrum (ut ait Paulus) exerit atque exercet." ("Rom. 13.4" is in the margin.) Calvin, *Institutio Christianae Religionis* (Geneva, 1609), fol. 308v (book 4, chap. 20, 19). For Calvin's use of the "republican word" *magistratus,* see Harro Höpfl's useful glossary in *Luther and Calvin on Secular Authority,* xli.

28. The gloss "The revenge of unbridled government belongeth not to private men" appears also in the margin of this passage. Calvin, *The Institution of Christian Religion* (London, 1634), 748. The original is essentially the same, using *magistratus* in the sense distinct from the prince and the people. Calvin, *Institutio Christianae Religionis* (Geneva, 1609), fol. 311r (book 4, chap. 20, 19).

29. Following Hanford, Mohl attributes this topic to 1640–42, but because the entry is quite far from others in the book, other entries in the earlier "Rex" topics are later than 1642, and it seems more appropriate to what Milton is reading (Gildas and British history) and the historical situation after 1643, a date after 1643 seems more likely.

30. Dzelzainis writes of this passage as "amounting to almost a *volte face,*" although he rightly adds that Milton does "not unequivocally make the distinction his own" (*PW* xviii–xix). See also Togashi, "Milton and the Presbyterian Opposition." See the astute analysis of this problem in Fallon, "'The strangest piece of reason': Milton's *Tenure of Kings and Magistrates.*" I am grateful to the author for sharing this essay with me prior to publication.

31. As Milton writes of scripture in *Tetrachordon* (*CPW* 2:642); see Fish, *Surprised by Sin,* 1–56.

32. See the study of Bodin's political science in Blair, *Theater of Nature.*

33. Pocock, *Ancient Constitution.*

34. See Achinstein, "Medea's Dilemma."

35. More specifically, the five authors and works cited in the first edition that are not in the Commonplace Book are Euripides' *Heraclidae* (205); Dio Cassius, *Roman History* (Trajan; 205–6); Livy, possibly from Machiavelli's *Discourses on Livy* (208); Seneca's *Hercules furens* (213), possibly taken from the end of John Canne's *The Golden Rule* (1649) or another regicide tract (see *CPW* 3:213n84); and Knox, *History of the Reformation of the Church of Scotland* (1644) (224–25). The three remaining authorities cited who do appear in the Commonplace Book but not the precise passages cited in *The Tenure* are Justinian, *Codex Justinianus* (*PW* 13n52, *CPW* 3:206); John Chrysostom, in a passage that may come from Grotius's *De Jure Belli ac Pacis* (Amsterdam, 1631), 74 (see *CPW* 3:211n79); and parts of Buchanan's *History of Scotland* that are not in the Commonplace Book, although others are (223, 225, 226—these events are covered by de Thou in the Commonplace Book—and 239). All of the thirteen mutual citations are by name, save one to Sulpicius Severus, merely cited as "noted by wise Authors" (*CPW* 3:203), cited from *CPW* 1:440, CB 182. There is one additional author quoted in the second edition of *The Tenure,* Luther from Sleidan, which has already been discussed above in chapter 2.

36. *CPW* 3:200. I cite from the first edition.

37. Sterne and Kollmeier, *Concordance to the English Prose,* 1313–14.

38. See Skinner, "History and Ideology," "Ideological Context," and "Conquest and Consent." For discussion of the engagement controversy and Milton, see Togashi, "Milton and the Presbyterian Opposition"; and Achinstein, "Milton Catches the Conscience of the King."

39. *Calendar of State Papers, Domestic Series, 1649–1660,* 1:6; Whitelocke, *Memorials of the English Affairs,* 2:537; see the discussion in Togashi, "Milton and the Presbyterian Opposition," 63.

40. *Commons Journal,* 6:15.

41. Pocock, *Ancient Constitution,* 325.

42. Tubb, "Printing the Regicide," 505.

43. The Bible is also held by "Mercy" to her left. Most editions of the Bishops' Bible feature the Mercy and Justice allegorized on the title page. These include edition of 1569 (STC 2105), the 1573 version (STC 2108), and two later editions, 1575 (STC 2114) and 1577 (STC 2121), which include Justice and Mercy among other allegorical figures.

44. See John King, *Tudor Royal Iconography,* 54.

45. Henry Adis, *A Fannaticks Mite Cast into the Kings Treasury* (London, 1660), 55. See also Nicholas Byfield, *A Commentary upon the Three First Chapters of the First Epistle Generall of St. Peter* (London, 1637), 426.

46. George Fox, *To Thee Oliver Cromwell* (London, 1655).

47. His *Effigies Regum Anglorum a Wilhelmo Conquestore* ([London], 1640) is a collection of pictures of English Kings, some bearing the sword in their right hands. See also *The Portrait of his Majesty Charles the Second* (London, 1660). For discussion of Cromwell portraiture, see Knoppers, *Constructing Cromwell.* As Knoppers points out, Milton never mentions Cromwell in *The Tenure* or *Eikonoklastes* (64).

48. John Foxe, *Actes and Monumentes of Martyrs* (London, 1570), 2:1201.

49. See, for example, William Prynne, *A Briefe Memento* (London, 1649), 11; *A Serious and Faithful Representation of the Judgements of Ministers of the Gospell* (London, 1649), 4.

50. See Dzelzainis, *PW* xv; and see Victoria Kahn's important reading of Milton's hermeneutics in *The Tenure* in *Wayward Contracts,* 120–24.

51. Filmer, *Observations Concerning the Original of Government Upon Mr Hobs Leviathan, Mr Milton against Salmasius, H. Grotius De Jure Belli,* in *Patriarcha and Other Writings,* 199.

52. On the "theology of arbitrary rule," see Rogers, *Matter of Revolution,* 4–8.

53. Calvin, *Institutes,* 2:1512–13; see also 1517–18. Page references are cited parenthetically in the text.

54. From the Putney Debates, excerpted in Sharp, *English Levellers,* 112.

55. See Filmer, *Patriarcha,* 2.

56. For pre-Reformation historicist readings of Paul, see Colet, *Lectures on Romans,* 91–98. Erasmus writes, for example, that Romans 13 "is to be taken as referring to pagan princes" in *The Education of a Christian Prince,* 235–36.

57. Dzelzainis, *PW* xvi.

58. Hobbes, *Elements of Law,* 112.

59. Hobbes, *Elements of Law,* 112.

60. Underdown, *Pride's Purge,* 362.

61. *Scripture and Reason Pleaded for Defensive Arms* (1643), title page.

62. Palmer, *Glasse of Gods Providence* (London, 1644); see Lewalski, *Life of Milton,* 178–79, 598n90.

63. On dating, see Shawcross, "Milton's *Tenure,*" and see now McDowell, headnote to *The Tenure,* where he convincingly dates the second edition of *The Tenure* prior to the appearance of *Eikonoklastes.*

64. See Togashi, "Milton and the Presbyterian Opposition," 59, 61. See also Dzelzainis, "Milton's Politics."

65. Prynne, *A Brief Memento,* 12.

66. Thomas Corns points out a similar phenomenon in *Areopagitica,* in which Milton "lines up the opinions of men regarded by the mainstream of English Puritanism as authorities of impeccable standing in order to demonstrate that his own heterodoxy falls inside the range of those opinions." Corns, "Milton, Roger Williams, and the Limits of Toleration," 84.

67. Milton quotes Goodman's claim that bad kings "ought no more to be accounted Kings or lawfull Magistrates, but as privat men to be examind, accus'd, condemn'd and punisht by the Law of God, and being convicted and punisht by that law, it is not mans but Gods doing" (250).

68. For Prynne's early rebellious arguments against the king, see Prynne, *Soveraigne Power of Parliaments & Kingdomes* (1643), 137. Prynne's arguments in *A Brief Memento* (1649) were largely legal rather than biblical (2–4).

69. Prynne, *Mr. Pryn's Last and Final Declaration* (London, 1649), 3.

70. James VI and I, *Political Writings,* 181.

6. "His Book Alive": Defending Popular Sovereignty after the Execution

1. *CPW* 3:194. For a discussion of "Law" see Sirluck, "Milton's Political Thought," 211–12.

2. See, for example, *PW* 125, and in Latin (simply *Orthodoxus*), *WJM* 7:202, 204.

3. Corns, "Milton and the Characteristics of a Free Commonwealth," 26.

4. *CPW* 4:626; the Latin original is in *WJM* 8:134.

5. Togashi, "Milton and the Presbyterian Opposition," 70. On the relationship between *Observations upon the Articles of Peace* and *The Tenure,* see also Sirluck, "Milton's Political Thought," 213.

6. On the sequence of these tracts, see McDowell, headnote to *The Tenure.*

7. He had a residence in Whitehall from November 1649 to December 17, 1651; Parker, *Milton,* 367, 393. Campbell, *Chronology,* 103.

8. *Articles of Peace . . . upon all which are added observations* (London, 1649), title page. On the subject of the tract's anonymity, see Corns, *Uncloistered Virtue,* 202; and Daems, "Dividing Conjunctions," 53.

9. *Letters of State* (1694), unpaginated here, but it should be xlix.

10. Masson, *Life of John Milton,* 4:87.

11. On anonymous publication in early modern England, see North, *Anonymous Renaissance;* for Milton, see 28, 98. On the rates of anonymity in the Thomason Tracts—which were around 45–60 percent—see Raymond, *Pamphlets and Pamphleteering,* 168–69; the rates of anonymity were higher for controversial literature.

12. Milton wrote most of his antiprelatical tracts anonymously, as well as the first edition of *The Doctrine and Discipline of Divorce,* but after this, he never appeared anonymously except in the *Observations.* The translated documents, *A Declaration; or, Letters Patents of the Election of the present King of Poland* (1674) and *Judgment of Martin Bucer* (1644), lack any indication of their translator, but the translation of Bucer explicitly draws connection to "a late Book restoring the *Doctrine and Discipline of Divorce*" on the title page.

13. *Joannis Philippi Angli Responsio ad Apologiam Anonymi cuiusdam tenebrionis pro Rege & Populo Anglicano infantissimam, CPW* 4:887. On the collaborative work between Milton and John Phillips, see Coiro, "Milton & Sons," 13, 24–30.

14. Raymond, "Complications of Interest," 316; Campbell, *Chronology,* 97. Milton moves across London from High Holborn to Charing Cross in March and to Whitehall in November; Campbell, *Chronology,* 103.

15. *CPW* 3:194, 197, 200, 201, emphasis added.

16. *CPW* 3:311, 301, 307, 315, emphasis added. See also 316, 310, 320, 322.

17. Corns, "Milton's *Observations upon the Articles of Peace,*" 123.

18. Hobbes, *Elements of Law,* 80.

19. *CPW* 1:441. The passage quoted from de Thou is in Latin; CB 182.

20. Holinshed, *Third Volume of Chronicles,* 191–92.

21. Wordsworth, *Documentary Supplement,* 16, quoted in Helgerson, "Milton Reads the King's Book," 1.

22. Madan, *New Bibliography,* 2–3. The Thomason copy of *Eikon Basilike* is dated February 9, which is four days before Thomason dates *The Tenure.* See Campbell, *Chronology,* 97. For more on parliamentary attempts to suppress the work, see Sauer, *"Paper-contestations" and Textual Communities,* 65–67; Tubb, "Printing the Regicide," 506–7.

23. See Madan, *New Bibliography,* 114. Madan lists BL Sloane 1907, a Latin translation; BL Additional MS 32280, a transcript; Harvard MS English 125, a commonplace book with partial transcription; and a Welsh manuscript in the National Library of Wales, Aberystwyth.

24. Helgerson, "Milton Reads the King's Book," 8. For further discussion see Merritt Hughes's introduction, *CPW* 3:150; and Madan, *New Bibliography.*

25. Tubb, "Printing the Regicide," 502–3.

26. Gardiner, *History of the Commonwealth and Protectorate,* 1:195.

27. See Gilman, *Iconoclasm and Poetry;* David Loewenstein, *Milton and the Drama of History;* Guibbory, "Charles's Prayers"; Cable, "Milton's Iconoclastic

Truth"; Sandler, "Icon and Iconoclast"; and Helgerson, "Milton Reads the King's Book," 9.

28. On pageantry and the "Stage-work" of Charles, see Sauer, *"Paper-contestations" and Textual Communities,* 57–124.

29. On Milton's engagement with his readership, see Achinstein, *Milton and the Revolutionary Reader,* 136–76; see also Norbrook, *Writing the English Republic,* 205.

30. CB 16, *CPW* 1:371; CB 187, *CPW* 1:463; CB 188, *CPW* 1:464; see also CB 17, *CPW* 1:372.

31. On Milton's expulsion of Shakespeare in the regicide tracts, see Nigel Smith, *Literature and Revolution,* 16–17. See also Walker, "Eclipsing Shakespeare's Eikon." On Milton's use of Macbeth, see Dzelzainis, "Milton, Macbeth, and Buchanan"; and McDowell, "Milton's Regicide Tracts."

32. Zwicker, *Lines of Authority,* 39; see also 45.

33. Nigel Smith, *Literature and Revolution,* 16–17; McDowell, "Milton's Regicide Tracts," 256.

34. *Apology, CPW* 1:886–88; CB 241; *CPW* 1:491.

35. Milton quotes Charles's words in *His Majesties Declaration* of August 12, 1642; 380n15.

36. He had used this text in *The Reason of Church Government* and *The Doctrine and Discipline of Divorce,* but returns to it here and in *Pro Populo* for political purposes.

37. *CPW* 3:439, 476, 477, 511, 589, 513, 526, 537–44, 534, 535, 582, 588 (see n17).

38. The first cited reference to the *Mirror of Justices* occurs within the quoted passage from Sadler's *Rights of the Kingdom (CPW* 3:398–99).

39. See Merritt Hughes's notes at *CPW* 3:350n2, 391n30, 393n35, 400n7, 436n9; and Whiting, "Sources of *Eikonoklastes.*"

40. *CPW* 3:591. See Plucknett, *Concise History of the Common Law,* 258–65.

41. On this publication history, see *PW* xxvii; Madan, "Milton, Salmasius, and Dugard," 133–34; Madan, "Revised Bibliography."

42. As it is described in a letter of Gronovius in October 17, which describes it as "enlarged and splendid form"; Masson, *Life of John Milton,* 4:344.

43. Madan, "Milton, Salmasius, and Dugard," 119.

44. Almack, *Bibliography of the King's Book,* 7, quoted in Madan, "Milton, Salmasius, and Dugard," 135–36.

45. Madan, "Milton, Salmasius, and Dugard," 119.

46. Madan, "Milton, Salmasius, and Dugard," 123, 143–45; "Revised Bibliography," 103–10.

47. The Thomason copy (E. 1386–87) is dated May 11, 1649, but this is disputed, since there is evidence suggesting the tract appeared in November. Raymond, *Pamphlets and Pamphleteering,* ascribes to the May 11 date, 317n4; Parker, *Milton,* 360, 962, where the November date is upheld, yet Campbell accepts the May 11 date in *Chronology,* 100. The chronological puzzle lies not only in Thomason's strangely

early date, but also in the fact that some sections of the second edition of *The Tenure* seem to respond to Salmasius; see *PW* 33n140.

48. Madan, "Milton, Salmasius, and Dugard," 120; Parker, *Milton*, 962.

49. Parker, *Milton*, 378–79.

50. On the collaborative work between Milton and his nephews, see Coiro, "Milton & Sons."

51. Calvin, *Institutio Christianae Religionis* (Geneva, 1609), fol. 311r.

52. The gloss "The revenge of unbridled government belongeth not to private men" appears also in the margin of this passage. Calvin, *Institution* (London, 1634), 748.

53. See again *PW* 177.

54. Parker, *Milton*, 376.

55. There are sixty-eight references to the Bible, a figure that includes repetitions, which is around twice the number in *The Tenure*, although *Pro Populo* is four times the length.

56. These are all in Appendix A, except for the reference from de Thou in *CPW* 1:380 (CB 53), which appears in *PW* (79). Milton had quoted Augustine in a rebuttal of Salmasius's own use, but he did not cite the specific passage in the 1651 edition; see *Pro Populo Anglicano Defensio* (London, 1651), Wing, *Short-Title Catalogue*, 2168B, 126–27.

57. This is true of Ovid's *Metamorphoses*, which appears four times in *Pro Populo* for the first time, then four times again in *Defensio Secunda*, and twice in the *Response* (the work had influenced Milton, but was not precisely referred to); it is true also for Horace, *Satires* and *Odes*, which follow a similar pattern of citation in each of the Defenses and in the *Response* (see Boswell, *Milton's Library*, 184), and Seneca, *Ad Lucilium*. In addition, there are many other references that are shared between the defenses and the *Response* and just one or two other, much unrelated works, which adds to this evidence; these include Martial, *Epigrams*, and Plutarch, *Lives*.

58. See Parker, *Milton*, 391, 990–91; Phillips in Darbishire, *Early Lives*, 70–71.

59. The sources tallied here are those Boswell categorizes as "verifiable" in *Milton's Library* (the books actually cited by Milton); I exclude the list of unique works enumerated in *Of Education*, since the manner of citation there is different. For books used in composing *Pro Populo*, I have moved one book from Boswell's "possible" category into "verifiable," and that is John Cook, *King Charles His Case*, which, as Dzelzainis shows, is a source (*PW* xix, 97); I have also added Selden, *Fleta* (1647), which Milton refers to on 210 and elsewhere, although this source is not listed in Boswell.

60. Milton's citation seems off; this is not from *Philippics* 4. The source is *Philippics* 8.12.4; *PW* 87–88 with n36.

61. The first attested use of "civil liberty" in the *OED* is in *Areopagitica*, although it occurs in earlier Miltonic tracts. Tournu and Forsyth, introduction to *Milton, Rights and Liberties*, 5.

62. *CPW* 7:443. For discussion, see Worden, "Milton's Republicanism," 235.

7. Conclusion: Historical Politics and the Instability of Print Culture

1. *Paradise Regained*, 4.264, *CSP* 494.

2. Worden, "Classical Republicanism," 182.

3. Lim, *Milton, Radical Politics, and Biblical Republicanism*, 23.

4. See the eloquent discussion of this general issue in Zwicker, "What Every Literate Man Once Knew."

5. Shephard, "Political Commonplace Books of Sir Robert Sidney"; Warkentin, "Humanism in Hard Times."

6. See David Loewenstein, "Milton among the Religious Radicals and Sects."

7. For a rethinking of protestant history along these lines, see Simpson, *Burning to Read.*

8. For an invigorating discussion of this historiography, see Martin, "Unediting Milton."

9. Illo, "Misreading of Milton," 183.

10. Rapaport, *Milton and the Postmodern,* 172.

11. McKenzie, *Bibliography and the Sociology of Texts,* 29.

12. Patterson, *Censorship and Interpretation.*

13. Shuger, *Censorship and Cultural Sensibility,* 38.

14. Campbell, *Chronology,* 81.

15. Sprat, *The History of the Royal-Society of London for the Improving of Natural Knowledge* (London, 1667), 111, 113. See Vickers, "Royal Society and English Prose Style."

16. *The History of the Civil Wars of England [Behemoth]* (London, 1679), 229–30.

17. Kahn, *Rhetoric, Prudence, and Skepticism,* 152–81; and Skinner, *Reason and Rhetoric.* An extensive bibliography on this subject can be found in the notes of both of these books.

Appendix B: The Scribal Entries in Milton's Commonplace Book

1. On fol. 28; the copy is in the possession of the New York Public Library Rare Book Room, KB 1529. See Beal, *Index,* 79; Hanford, "Chronology of Milton's Private Studies," 280–81; Kelley, "Milton's Dante–Della Casa–Varchi Volume."

2. As is often true with poetic entries, all of these use canto numbers, making it hard to know if the two hands cite the same edition, though Milton cites canto and stanza, whereas the amanuensis cites book and canto.

3. CB 77, *CPW* 1:391–92.

4. CB 182, *CPW* 1:439. Hanford ("Chronology," 277–78) simply thinks the passage is after 1643. Mohl and Hanford suggest that one of the entries in Milton's own hand dates from around 1643–44, in which Milton cites the work as by Berni. This same work is quoted as by Boiardo on another page by Amanuensis A, who is dated by Mohl as 1650, and again on 187 as "date uncertain," though surely at about the same time as the first, since these are the only two entries by this hand. Mohl; see

CPW 1:463n4. It is apparently the same hand that copied an Italian sonnet "on p. 28 of Milton's copy of the Rime of Giovanni della Casa, now in the possession of the New York Public Library." Hanford, "Chronology," 280–81. Shawcross dates these entries after 1641–42, and believes this scribe to be John Phillips. See Shawcross, *John Milton,* 81.

5. While the subsequent entry by the same scribe distinguishes between Berni and Bioardo, it is in a way that does not fit naturally with the explanation that Milton had dictated these after having written the former. It seems unlikely that Milton would have called Boiardo "the Italian poet," or written at this stage of his "witty verses," revised by "Berni of Tuscany." These words seem the efforts of a young man, explaining something to himself that the older Milton would not have needed to record or bothered to write. If not written after Milton's blindness, the passage is still most likely written after 1641–42 (if the passages above do indeed come from this period, as they probably do), when Milton's entries have little more than the economic deposit of ideas. The entries also compare two authors and two editions—Boiardo's *Orlando,* book 2, canto 21, stanza 40 (Venice 1608) with Berni's book 2, canto 21, 40 and 41, of 1541—in the way that a young man or a student assigned to do so would.

6. Hanford, "Chronology," 285. This is on CB 198, *CPW* 1:477.

7. Quoted from Blair, "Note Taking," 86, who quotes it from Snow, "Francis Bacon's Advice to Fulke Greville," 370; these same words—likely copied by Essex—are used in an address by the Earl of Essex to Greville; see Sherman, *John Dee,* 64, 19n60–61.

8. University College London Ogden MSS (Bacon-Tottell MSS 7/7f. 164v. Quoted in Sharpe, *Reading Revolutions,* 73.

9. Sharpe, *Reading Revolutions,* 73, 173.

10. Evelyn to Sir Richard Browne, June 14, 1649; BL MS Additional 78221. See, for example, the small Latin commonplace book, BL MS Additional 78327, an exceptional example of scribal work.

11. Kelley, "Milton and Machiavelli's *Discorsi,*" 125–27. Kelley shows that the entries are in the same hand as that used to write a letter dated February 13, 1651 (i.e., 1652), by Phillips, but it does not follow that Phillips would have written the entry and the letter at the same time. This is the letter to Mylius, which is numbered in the *Columbia Works* LXIII, and is kept in the Niedersächsische Staatsarchiv at Oldenburg under the pressmark Bestd. 20 (Grafschaft Oldenburg), Tit. 38, No. 73, Fasc. 5, no. 8.

12. Shawcross makes a case for John Phillips in "Notes on Milton's Amanuenses" and *A Milton Encyclopedia,* 1:41–43; but see Peter Beal's more skeptical analysis of the evidence in *Index,* 2.2:84–85.

13. Campell et al., *Milton and the Manuscript of "De Doctrina Christiana,"* 58.

14. Kelley, "Milton and Machiavelli's *Discorsi,*" 124.

15. This is suggested by Shawcross in *John Milton,* 81.

16. Hanford's assertion that the notes "follow the exact form established by Milton himself" ("Chronology," 253) has obviously been influential, but this is untrue,

and it should also be said that—once small differences are omitted—the style of entry is relatively standard to other commonplace books. Lord Preston, for example, uses a similar method, though he indicates page numbers with "pag" instead of "p," as he does in his entries in Milton's book; see BL MS Additional 63781.

17. For a less sceptical discussion of this evidence, see Mohl, *CPW* 1:414–15n1.

18. Beal, "Notions in Garrison," 133.

19. Darbishire, *Early Lives*, 60. It worth noting, however, that Phillips does invoke Machiavelli in a safer context in the beginning of his biography, as an author of a biography to be emulated: "among the Moderns, *Machiavel* a Noble *Florentine*, who Elegantly wrote the Life of *Castrucio Castracano*, Lord of *Luca*" (49).

20. In the Ethical Index in CB 12, *CPW* 1:366; dated by Mohl as 1643–45, which would correspond to the approximate time of Villani's being taught, though Shawcross is skeptical—rightly, I believe—of this date, suggesting instead that it belongs to the period right after Milton returned from Italy. Shawcross, *John Milton*, 78.

21. See *CPW* 1:365n1 for a list (Mohl errs in saying that there are "six cross references," though she goes on to list most of them). See Parker, *Milton*, 804n6. It is possible that some of these are not to the lost index, but to another, although most of them, except "De Conciliis" (CB 183), seem to be on theological issues, though this could be the name of an unknown source, as well.

Bibliography

Achinstein, Sharon. *Citizen Milton: An Exhibition Celebrating the 400th Anniversary of the Birth of John Milton (1608–1674).* Oxford: Bodleian Library, 2008.

———. *Milton and the Revolutionary Reader.* Princeton: Princeton University Press, 1994.

———. "Milton Catches the Conscience of the King: *Eikonoklastes* and the Engagement Controversy." *Milton Studies* 29 (1993): 143–63.

———. "Medea's Dilemma: Politics and Passion in Milton's Divorce Tracts." In *Rethinking Historicism: Essays in Early Modern English Literature and Culture,* edited by Ann Baines Coiro and Thomas Fulton, forthcoming.

———. "Texts in Conflict: The Press and the Civil War." In Keeble, *Cambridge Companion to Writing of the English Revolution,* 50–68.

Achinstein, Sharon, and Elizabeth Sauer, eds. *Milton and Toleration.* Oxford: Oxford University Press, 2007.

Adis, Henry. *A Fannaticks Mite Cast into the Kings Treasury.* London, 1660.

An Admonition to the Parliament. London, 1572.

Agar, Herbert. *Milton and Plato.* Princeton: Princeton University Press, 1928.

Agreement of the People. [London], 1647.

Altick, Richard D. *The English Common Reader.* Chicago: University of Chicago Press, 1957.

Altman, Joel. *The Tudor Play of Mind.* Berkeley: University of California Press, 1978.

Andersen, Jennifer, and Elizabeth Sauer, eds. *Books and Readers in Early Modern England.* Philadelphia: University of Pennsylvania Press, 2002.

Andrew, Malcolm, and Ronald Waldron. *The Poems of the Pearl Manuscript.* Exeter: University of Exeter Press, 2002.

Arber, Edward, ed. *A Transcript of the Registers of the Company of Stationers of London, 1554–1640 A.D.* 5 vols. London, 1875–77.

Aristotle. *The Basic Works of Aristotle.* Translated and edited by Richard McKeon. New York: Random House, 1941.

Aristotle. *On Rhetoric.* Translated and edited by George A. Kennedy. Oxford: Oxford University Press, 1991.

Armitage, David, Armand Himy, and Quentin Skinner, eds. *Milton and Republicanism.* Cambridge: Cambridge University Press, 1995.

Aubrey, John. *Aubrey's Brief Lives.* Edited by Oliver Lawson Dick. 1949. Reprint, Ann Arbor: University of Michigan Press, 1957.

Austin, J. L. *How to Do Things with Words.* Edited by J. O. Urmson. Oxford: Oxford University Press, 1962.

[Bacon, Francis]. *A Wise and Moderate Discourse, Concerning Church-Affairs.* 1641.

Baldwin, T. W. *William Shakespere's Small Latine & Lesse Greeke.* 2 vols. Urbana: University of Illinois Press, 1944.

Barbour, Reid. *John Selden: Measures of the Holy Commonwealth in Seventeenth-Century England.* Toronto: University of Toronto Press, 2003.

———. *Literature and Religious Culture in Seventeenth-Century England.* Cambridge: Cambridge University Press, 2002.

Barker, Arthur. *Milton and the Puritan Dilemma.* Toronto: University of Toronto Press, 1942.

Barker, Francis. "In Wars of Truth." *Southern Review* 20.2 (1987): 111–25.

Barker, Nicolas. "Donne's 'Letter to the Lady Carey and Mrs. Essex Riche.'" In *Form and Meaning in the History of the Book: Selected Essays,* 7–14. London: British Library, 2003.

Barnard, John, and D. F. McKenzie, eds. *The Cambridge History of the Book in Britain,* vol. 4, *1557–1695.* Cambridge: Cambridge University Press, 2002.

Beal, Peter. *In Praise of Scribes: Manuscripts and Their Makers in Seventeenth-Century England.* Oxford: Clarendon Press, 1998.

———. *Index of English Literary Manuscripts.* 4 vols. London: Mansell, 1980–.

———. "John Donne and the Circulation of Manuscripts." In Barnard and McKenzie, *Cambridge History of the Book in Britain,* 4:122–26.

———. "'Notes in Garrison': The Seventeenth-Century Commonplace Book." In *New Ways of Looking at Old Texts: Papers of the Renaissance English Text Society, 1985–1991,* edited by W. Speed Hill, 131–47. Binghamton, N.Y.: Medieval and Renaissance Texts and Studies, 1993.

Beard, Thomas. *The Theatre of God's Judgements.* London, 1642. First printed 1597.

Beer, Anna R. *Sir Walter Ralegh and His Readers in the Seventeenth Century.* London: Macmillan, 1997.

Belsey, Catherine. *John Milton: Language, Gender, Power.* New York: Basil Blackwell, 1988.

Betteridge, Maurice S. "The Bitter Notes: The Geneva Bible and its Annotations." *Sixteenth Century Journal* 14.1 (1983): 41–62.

Bèze, Théodore de. *De Haereticis a Civili Magistratu Puniendis.* Geneva, 1554.

Blair, Ann. "Note Taking as an Art of Transmission." *Critical Inquiry* 31 (2004): 85–107.

———. *The Theater of Nature: Jean Bodin and Renaissance Science.* Princeton: Princeton University Press, 1997.

Blum, Abbe. "The Author's Authority: *Areopagitica* and the Labor of Licensing." In Ferguson and Nyquist, *Re-membering Milton,* 74–96.

Blunden, Edmund. "Some Seventeenth-Century Latin Poems by English Writers." *University of Toronto Quarterly* 25 (1955–56): 10–22.

Boccalini, Traiano. *I Ragguagli di Parnasso; or, Advertisements from Parnassus.* Translated by Henry Carey. London, 1669.

Bodin, Jean. *Colloquium of the Seven about Secrets of the Sublime.* Edited and translated by Marion Leathers Daniels Kuntz. Princeton: Princeton University Press: 1975.

————. *Method for the Easy Comprehension of History.* Translated and edited by Beatrice Reynolds. New York: Octagon Books: 1966.

————. *Methodus ad Facilem Historiarum Cognitionem.* Paris, 1566.

————. *Six Livres de la République.* Paris, 1577.

Boswell, Jackson. *Milton's Library: A Catalogue of the Remains of John Milton's Library and an Annotated Reconstruction of Milton's Library and Ancillary Readings.* New York: Garland, 1975.

Bottkol, Joseph McG. "The Holograph of Milton's Letter to Holstenius." *PMLA* 68.3 (1953): 617–27.

Bouwsma, William J. *Concordia Mundi: The Career and Thought of Guillaume Postel (1510–1581).* Cambridge: Harvard University Press, 1957.

Bramhall, John. *Castigations of Mr. Hobbes.* London, 1657.

————. *Serpent Salve; or, A Remedie for the Biting of an Aspe.* N.p., 1643.

Bredvold, Louis I. "Milton and Bodin's *Heptaplomeres.*" *Studies in Philology* 21.2 (1924): 399–402.

A Brief Inference upon Guicciardines Digression, in the fourth part of the first Quarterne of his Historie. London, 1629. First printed 1613.

Brinsley, John. *Ludus Literarius; or, The Grammar Schoole Shewing How to Proceede from the First Entrance into Learning.* London, 1612.

Brooke, Robert Greville. *A Discovrse opening the Natvre of that Episcopacie.* London, 1641.

Bucer, Martin. *Common Places of Martin Bucer.* Translated and edited by D. F. Wright. Abingdon: Sutton Courtenay Press, 1972.

————. *De Regno Christi.* In *Melanchthon and Bucer,* edited by Wilhelm Pauck. Philadelphia: Westminster Press, 1969.

————. *Scripta Anglicana.* Basel, 1577.

Burnett, Amy Nelson. "Church Discipline and Moral Reformation in the Thought of Martin Bucer." *Sixteenth Century Journal* 22.3 (1991): 438–56.

Burton, Thomas. *Diary of Thomas Burton.* Edited by John Towill Rutt. 4 vols. London: Henry Colburn, 1828.

Byfield, Nicholas. *A Commentary upon the Three First Chapters of the First Epistle Generall of St. Peter.* London, 1637.

By the King. A Proclamation for Calling in, and Suppressing of Two Books By John Milton. 1660.

Cable, Lana. *Carnal Rhetoric: Milton's Iconoclasm and the Poetics of Desire.* Durham: Duke University Press, 1995.

———. "Milton's Iconoclastic Truth." In Loewenstein and Turner, *Politics, Poetics, and Hermeneutics in Milton's Prose,* 135–51.

Calendar of State Papers, Domestic Series, 1649–60. 13 vols. 1875–86. Reprint, Vaduz: Kraus, 1965.

Calvin, John. *Calvin: Institutes of the Christian Religion.* Edited by John T. McNeill and translated by Ford Lewis Battles. 2 vols. Philadelphia: Westminster Press, 1960.

———. *Defensio orthodoxae fidei de sacra Trinitate.* [Geneva], 1554.

———. *Institutio Christianae Religionis.* Geneva, 1609.

———. *The Institution of Christian Religion.* London, 1561.

———. *The Institution of Christian Religion.* London, 1634.

———. *The Institution of Christian Religion, written in Latine by M. John Calvine.* Translated by Thomas Norton. London, 1587.

Campbell, Gordon. *A Milton Chronology.* London: Macmillan, 1997.

———. "Milton's *Index theologicus* and Bellarmine's *Disputationes de controversiis Christianae fidei adversus huius temporis haereticos.*" *Milton Quarterly* 11.4 (1977): 12–16.

Campbell, Gordon, and Thomas N. Corns. *John Milton: Life, Work, and Thought.* Oxford: Oxford University Press, 2008.

Campbell, Gordon, Thomas Corns, John Hale, and Fiona Tweedie. *Milton and the Manuscript of "De Doctrina Christiana."* Oxford: Oxford University Press, 2007.

Carley, James. *The Books of King Henry VIII and His Wives.* London: British Library, 2008.

[Cartwright, Thomas]. *A Directory of Church-government.* London, 1644 [1645].

Cartwright, Thomas. *Helpes for Discovery of the Truth in Point of Toleration.* London, 1648.

———. *The Second Replie of Thomas Cartwright: against Maister Doctor Whitgifts second answer touching the Church Discipline.* [Zurich?], 1575.

The Case of the Armie Truly Stated. [London], 1647.

Castellion, Sébastien. *De l'impunité des hérétiques. De haereticis non puniendis.* Edited by Bruno Becker and M. Valkhoff. Geneva: Droz, 1971.

Chartier, Roger. *Cultural History: Between Practices and Representations.* Cambridge: Cambridge University Press, 1988.

Chaucer, Geoffrey. *The Workes of our Ancient and Lerned English Poet, Geffrey Chaucer.* 1602.

Chester, Allan G., ed. *Selected Sermons of Hugh Latimer.* Charlottesville: University Press of Virginia, 1968.

Clark, Stuart. "Wisdom Literature of the Seventeenth Century: A Guide to the Contents of the 'Bacon-Tottel' Commonplace Books." *Transactions of the Cambridge Bibliographical Society* 6.5 (1976): 291–305; and 7.1 (1977): 46–73.

Clegg, Cyndia Susan. *Press Censorship in Caroline England.* Cambridge: Cambridge University Press, 2008.

————. *Press Censorship in Elizabethan England.* Cambridge: Cambridge University Press, 1997.

Coffey, John. *Persecution and Toleration in Protestant England, 1558–1689.* New York: Longman, 2000.

————. "Puritanism and Liberty Revisited: The Case for Toleration in the English Revolution." *Historical Journal* 41.4 (1998): 961–85.

————. "A Ticklish Business: Defining Heresy and Orthodoxy in the Puritan Revolution." In Loewenstein and Marshall, *Heresy, Literature, and Politics,* 108–36.

Coiro, Ann Baynes. "Anonymous Milton, or, A Maske Masked." *ELH* 71 (2004): 609–29.

————. "Milton and Class Identity." *Journal of Medieval and Renaissance Studies* 22 (1992): 261–89.

————. "Milton & Sons: The Family Business." *Milton Studies* 48 (2008): 13–37.

Collins, Jeffrey R. *The Allegiance of Thomas Hobbes.* Oxford: Oxford University Press, 2005.

Collinson, Patrick. "The Reformer and the Archbishop: Martin Bucer and the English Bucerian." In *Godly People: Essays on English Protestantism and Puritanism,* 19–47. London: Hambledon Press, 1983.

Condren, Conal. "Liberty of Office and Its Defense in Seventeenth-Century Political Argument." *History of Political Thought* 18.3 (1997): 460–82.

Corns, Thomas N. "John Milton, Roger Williams, and the Limits of Toleration." In Achinstein and Sauer, *Milton and Toleration,* 72–85.

————. "Milton and the Characteristics of a Free Commonwealth." In Armitage, Himy, and Skinner, *Milton and Republicanism,* 25–42.

————. "Milton before 'Lycidas.'" In *Milton and the Terms of Liberty,* edited by Graham Parry and Joad Raymond, 23–36. Cambridge: D. S. Brewer, 2002.

————. "Milton's Antiprelatical Tracts and the Marginality of Doctrine." In Dobranski and Rumrich, *Milton and Heresy,* 39–48.

————. "Milton's *Observations upon the Articles of Peace:* Ireland under English Eyes." In Loewenstein and Turner, *Politics, Poetics, and Hermeneutics in Milton's Prose,* 123–34.

————. "Milton's Quest for Respectability." *Modern Language Review* 77.4 (1982): 769–79.

————. *Uncloistered Virtue: English Political Literature, 1640–1660.* Oxford: Clarendon Press, 1992.

Craig, Hardin. *Machiavelli's "The Prince": An Elizabethan Manuscript Translation.* Chapel Hill: University of North Carolina Press, 1944.

Crane, Mary Thomas. *Framing Authority: Sayings, Self, and Society in Sixteenth-Century England.* Princeton: Princeton University Press, 1993.

Craster, Edmund. "John Rous, Bodley's Librarian 1620–52." *Bodleian Library Record* 5 (1956): 130–46.

Creaser, John. "Editorial Problems in Milton." *Review of English Studies,* n.s., 34.135 (1983): 279–303.

Culverwel, Nathanael. *An Elegant and Learned Discourse on the Light of Nature.* London, 1652.

Cummings, Brian. *The Literary Culture of the Reformation.* Oxford: Oxford University Press, 2002.

Daems, Jim. "Dividing Conjunctions: Milton's *Observations upon the Articles of Peace.*" *Milton Quarterly* 33.2 (1999): 51–55.

Dallington, R. *Aphorismes Civill and Militarie.* 2nd ed. London, 1629. First printed 1613.

[Dallison, Charles]. *The Royalist's Defence: Vindicating the King's Proceedings in the Late Warre Made against Him.* [London], 1648.

Darbishire, Helen, ed. *The Early Lives of Milton.* 1932. Reprint, New York: Barnes and Noble, 1965.

Davenant, William. *Sir William Davenant's Gondibert.* Edited by David F. Gladish. Oxford: Clarendon Press, 1971.

Davis, J. C. "Religion and the Struggle for Freedom in the English Revolution." *Historical Journal* 35.3 (1992): 507–30.

Dobranski, Stephen B. "Letter and Spirit in Milton's *Areopagitica.*" *Milton Studies* 32 (1995): 131–52.

———. "Licensing Milton's Heresy." In Dobranski and Rumrich, *Milton and Heresy,* 141–46.

———. *Milton, Authorship, and the Book Trade.* Cambridge: Cambridge University Press, 1999.

Dobranski, Stephen B., and John P. Rumrich. "Introduction: Heretical Milton." In Dobranski and Rumrich, *Milton and Heresy,* 1–17.

———, eds. *Milton and Heresy.* Cambridge: Cambridge University Press, 1998.

Donne, John. *Biathanatos.* London, 1647.

———. *The Satires, Epigrams, and Verse Letters.* Edited by W. Milgate. Oxford: Oxford University Press, 1967.

———. *Selected Prose.* Edited by Evelyn Simpson, Helen Gardner, and Timothy Healy. Oxford: Clarendon Press, 1967.

Dzelzainis, Martin. "Conquest and Slavery in Milton's *History of Britain.*" In McDowell and Smith, *The Oxford Handbook of Milton,* 407–23.

———. "Dating and Meaning: *Samson Agonistes* and the Digression in Milton's *History of Britain.*" *Milton Studies* 48 (2008): 160–77.

———. "John Milton, *Areopagitica.*" In *A Companion to Literature from Milton to Blake,* edited by David Womersley, 151–58. Oxford: Blackwell, 2000.

———. "Milton and Antitrinitarianism." In Achinstein and Sauer, *Milton and Toleration,* 171–85.

———. "Milton, Macbeth, and Buchanan." *The Seventeenth Century* 4 (1989): 55–66.

———. "Milton and the Protectorate in 1658." In Armitage, Himy, and Skinner, *Milton and Republicanism*, 181–205.

———. "Milton's Classical Republicanism." In Armitage, Himy, and Skinner, *Milton and Republicanism*, 3–24.

———. "Milton's Politics." In *The Cambridge Companion to Milton*, 2nd ed., edited by Dennis Danielson, 70–83. Cambridge: Cambridge University Press, 1999.

Edwards, Thomas. *Gangreana*. London, 1646.

Ellwood, Thomas. *The History of Thomas Ellwood*. London: George Routledge and Sons, 1885.

Elson, James Hinsdale. *John Hales of Eton*. New York: King's Crown Press, 1948.

Erasmus, Desiderius. *The Correspondence of Erasmus*, vol. 2 of *The Collected Works of Erasmus*. Toronto: University of Toronto Press, 1975.

———. *The Education of a Christian Prince*, vol. 27 of *The Collected Works of Erasmus*. Toronto: University of Toronto Press, 1986.

———. *Novum Testamentum Omne*. Basel, 1527.

———. *On Copia of Words and Ideas*. Translated by Donald B. King and H. David Rix. Milwaukee: Marquette University Press, 1999.

———. *Opus Epistolarum Des. Erasmi Roterodami*. Edited by P. S. Allen. 11 vols. Oxford: Oxford University Press, 1906–47.

———. *The Praise of Folly*. Translated and edited by Clarence H. Miller. New Haven: Yale University Press, 1979.

Evans, G. Blakemore. "Two New Manuscript Versions of Milton's Hobson Poems." *Modern Language Notes* 57.2 (1942): 192–94.

Evans, Robert C. *Habits of Mind: Evidence and Effects of Ben Jonson's Reading*. Lewisburg: Bucknell University Press, 1995.

Eyre, G. E. B., and H. R. Plomer. *A Transcript of the Registers of the Company of Stationers from 1640–1708 A.D.* 3 vols. London, 1913–14.

Ezell, Margaret. *The Patriarch's Wife*. Chapel Hill: University of North Carolina Press, 1987.

———. *Social Authorship and the Advent of Print*. Baltimore: Johns Hopkins University Press, 1999.

Fallon, Stephen M. *Milton among the Philosophers: Poetry and Materialism in Seventeenth-Century England*. Ithaca: Cornell University Press, 1991.

———. "'The strangest piece of reason': Milton's *Tenure of Kings and Magistrates*." In McDowell and Smith, *The Oxford Handbook of Milton*, 241–51.

Fehrenbach, R. J., and E. S. Leedham-Green. *Private Libraries in Renaissance England*. 7 vols. Binghamton, N.Y.: Medieval & Renaissance Texts and Studies, 1992– .

Ferguson, Margaret W. *Trials of Desire: Renaissance Defenses of Poetry*. New Haven: Yale University Press, 1983.

Ferguson, Margaret W., and Mary Nyquist, eds. *Re-membering Milton: Essays on the Texts and Traditions*. London: Methuen, 1988.

Filmer, Robert. *The Anarchy of a Limited or Mixed Monarchy*. [London?], 1648.

————. *Observations concerning the Originall of Government Upon Mr. Hobs Leviathan, Mr. Milton against Salmasius, H. Grotius De Jure Belli.* London, 1652.

————. *Patriarcha and Other Writings.* Edited by Johann P. Sommerville. Cambridge: Cambridge University Press, 1991.

Fink, Z. S. *The Classical Republicans.* 2nd ed. Chicago: Northwestern University Press, 1962.

Firth, Charles H. "Milton as an Historian." In *Essays, Historical and Literary,* 61–102. Oxford: Clarendon Press, 1938.

Firth, Charles H., and R. S. Rait, eds. *Acts and Ordinances of the Interregnum, 1642–1660.* 3 vols. London: H. M. Stationery Office, 1911.

Fish, Stanley. "Driving from the Letter: Truth and Indeterminacy in Milton's *Areopagitica.*" In Ferguson and Nyquist, *Re-membering Milton,* 234–54.

————. *How Milton Works.* Cambridge: Harvard University Press, 2001.

————. *Surprised by Sin: The Reader in Paradise Lost.* 2nd ed. Cambridge: Harvard University Press, 1997.

Forsyth, Neil, and Christophe Tournu, eds. *Milton, Rights and Liberties.* Bern: Peter Lang, 2007.

Fletcher, Harris, ed. *John Milton's Complete Poetical Works Reproduced in Photographic Facsimile.* 4 vols. Urbana: University of Illinois Press, 1945.

Foucault, Michel. *Power/Knowledge, Selected Interviews and Other Writings 1972–1977.* Edited by Colin Gordon. Brighton: Harvester Press, 1980.

Foxe, John. *The First (Second) Volume of the Ecclesiasticall History, Contaynyng the Actes and Monumentes of Martyrs.* London, 1570.

French, J. Milton. *The Life Records of John Milton.* 5 vols. New Brunswick, N.J.: Rutgers University Press, 1949–66.

————. "Moseley's Advertisements of Milton's Poems, 1650–1660." *Huntington Library Quarterly* 25.4 (1962): 337–45.

Fulton, Thomas. "*Areopagitica* and the Roots of Liberal Epistemology." *English Literary Renaissance* 37.1 (2004): 42–82.

————. "Edward Phillips and the Manuscript of the 'Digression.'" *Milton Studies* 48 (2008): 95–112.

————. "Historicism, Rhetoric, and Ideology: Erasmus, Colet, and the Present." In *Rethinking Historicism: New Essays on Early Modern History and Literature,* edited by Ann Baines Coiro and Thomas Fulton, forthcoming.

————. "John Milton's 'Digression' in *The History of Britain*: An Online Facsimile Edition of Harvard MS Eng 901." http://scholarworks.umass.edu/umpress/HM

————. "Speculative Shakespeares: The Trials of Biographical Historicism." *Modern Philology* 103.3 (2006): 385–408.

Gardiner, Samuel Rawson. *History of the Commonwealth and Protectorate, 1649–1660.* 4 vols. London: Longmans, 1894.

Garrod, H. W. "The Latin Poem Addressed by Donne to Dr. Andrews." *Review of English Studies* 21.81 (1945): 38–42.

Gilman, Ernest B. *Iconoclasm and Poetry in the English Reformation: Down Went Dagon.* Chicago: University of Chicago Press, 1986.

Glicksman, Harry. "The Sources of Milton's *History of Britain*." *University of Wisconsin Studies in Language and Literature* II, ser. 2 (1920): 105–44.

Goodwin, John. *Right and Might Well Met.* London, 1648.

The Grand Account; or, A Remonstrance, wherein Is Plainly Discovered the Vast Summes of Money Levyed upon the Kingdome by Ordinance of Parliament. Oxford [i.e., London?], 1647.

Greene, Douglas G. "Arthur Annesley, First Earl of Anglesey, 1614–1686." Ph.D. diss., University of Chicago, 1972.

Greene, Thomas M. "The Balance of Power in Marvell's 'Horatian Ode.'" *ELH* 60 (1993): 379–96.

Guibbory, Achsah. "Charles's Prayers, Idolatrous Images, and True Creation in Milton's *Eikonoklastes.*" In Stanwood, *Of Poetry and Politics,* 283–94.

Habermas, Jürgen. *Communication and the Evolution of Society.* Translated by Thomas McCarthy. Cambridge: Polity Press, 1976.

Hackel, Heidi Brayman. "The Countess of Bridgewater's London Library." In Andersen and Sauer, *Books and Readers,* 138–59.

———. *Reading Material in Early Modern England.* Cambridge: Cambridge University Press, 2005.

[Hales, John]. *A Tract Concerning Schisme and Schismaticks wherein is briefly discovered the Original Causes of all Schisme.* London, 1642.

H[all], J[ohn]. *Peri Hypsous; or, Dionysius Longinus of the Height of Eloquence.* London, 1652.

Hampshire, Gwen. "An Unusual Bodleian Purchase in 1645." *Bodleian Library Record* 10.6 (1982): 339–48.

Hanford, James Holly. "The Chronology of Milton's Private Studies." *PMLA* 36.2 (1921): 251–314.

Harbage, Alfred. *Annals of English Drama, 975–1700.* Revised by S. Schoenbaum and Sylvia Wagonheim. 3rd ed. London: Routledge, 1989.

Harrison, John, and Peter Laslett. *The Library of John Locke.* 2nd ed. Oxford: Oxford University Press, 1971.

Hartwell, Kathleen. *Lactantius and Milton.* Cambridge: Harvard University Press, 1929.

Haskin, Dayton. *Milton's Burden of Interpretation.* Philadelphia: University of Pennsylvania Press, 1994.

Havens, Earle. *Commonplace Books: A History of Manuscripts and Printed Books from Antiquity to the Twentieth Century.* New Haven: Beinecke Rare Book and Manuscript Library, 2001.

Hazlitt, William. *Lectures on the English Poets.* London, 1818.

Healy, Thomas, and Jonathan Sawday, eds. *Literature and the English Civil War.* Cambridge: Cambridge University Press, 1990.

Helgerson, Richard. "Milton Reads the King's Book: Print, Performance, and the Making of a Bourgeois Idol." *Criticism* 29.1 (1987): 1–25.

Herendeen, Wyman. "Milton's *Accidence Commenc't Grammar* and the Deconstruction of 'Grammatical Tyranny.'" In Stanwood, *Of Poetry and Politics,* 295–312.

Hill, Christopher. *The English Bible and the Seventeenth-Century Revolution.* 1993. Reprint, New York: Penguin, 1994.

———. *Intellectual Origins of the English Revolution.* Oxford: Oxford University Press, 1965.

———. *Milton and the English Revolution.* London: Faber and Faber, 1977.

———. *Puritanism and Revolution.* London: Secker and Warburg, 1958.

Hirst, Derek. *England in Conflict, 1603–1660.* New York: Oxford University Press, 1999.

His Majesties Answer to a Book, Entituled, The Declaration, or Remonstrance of the Lords and Commons, of the 19th of May, 1642. London, 1642.

Hobbes, Thomas. *Behemoth: A History of the Causes of the Civil Wars of England.* In *The English Works of Thomas Hobbes of Malmesbury,* edited by William Molesworth, 11 vols., 6:161–418. London: John Bohn, 1839–45.

———. *The Elements of Law.* Edited by J. C. A. Gaskin. Oxford: Oxford University Press, 1994.

———. *The History of the Civil Wars of England* [*Behemoth*]. London, 1679.

———. *Leviathan.* Edited by Richard Tuck. Cambridge: Cambridge University Press, 1996.

Holinshed, Raphael. *The Third Volume of Chronicles, Beginning at Duke William the Norman.* London, 1586.

Höpfl, Harro, ed. *Luther and Calvin on Secular Authority.* Cambridge: Cambridge University Press, 1991.

Hooker, Richard. *Of the Laws of Ecclesiastical Polity.* Edited by Georges Edelen. 3 vols. Cambridge: Harvard University Press, 1977.

Hoole, Charles. *A New Discovery of the Old Art of Teaching Schoole.* London, 1661.

Horwood, Alfred J. *A Common-place Book of John Milton.* Rev. ed. London: Camden Society, 1877.

Hotman, François. *Francogallia. Libellus statum veteris Reipublicae Gallicae.* Coloniae, 1574.

Hotman, Francis [i.e., François]. *Franco-Gallia; or, An Account of the Ancient Free State of France, and Most Other Parts of Europe before the Loss of their Liberties.* London, 1721.

Howe, Nicholas. "The Uses of Uncertainty: On the Dating of *Beowulf.*" In *Beowulf: A Prose Translation,* 2nd ed., edited by Nicholas Howe and E. Talbot Donaldson, 179–90. New York: Norton, 2001.

Hoxby, Blair. *Mammon's Music: Literature and Economics in the Age of Milton.* New Haven: Yale University Press, 2002.

Hunter, William. *Visitation Unimplor'd: Milton and the Authorship of "De Doctrina Christiana."* Pittsburgh: Duquesne University Press, 1998.

Hyde, Edward. *A Brief View and Survey of the Dangerous and Pernicious Errors to Church and State, in Mr. Hobbes's Book Entitled Leviathan.* Oxford, 1676.

Illo, John. "The Misreading of Milton." In *Radical Perspectives in the Arts,* edited by Lee Baxandall, 178–92. Harmondsworth, England: Penguin, 1972.

Ioppolo, Grace. *Dramatists and Their Manuscripts in the Age of Shakespeare, Milton, and Heywood.* London: Routledge, 2006.

James VI and I. *Political Writings.* Edited by Johann P. Sommerville. Cambridge: Cambridge University Press, 1994.

Jardine, Lisa. "Gabriel Harvey: Exemplary Ramist and Pragmatic Humanist." *Revue des Sciences Philosophiques et Théologiques* 70 (1986): 36–48.

Jardine, Lisa, and Anthony Grafton. "'Studied for Actions': How Gabriel Harvey Read His Livy." *Past and Present* 129 (November 1990): 30–78.

Jayne, Sears. *Library Catalogues of the English Renaissance.* 2nd ed. Godalming, Surrey: St. Paul's Bibliographies, 1983.

Jones, Edward. "'Filling in a Blank in the Canvas': Milton, Horton, and the Kedermister Library." *Review of English Studies* 53.209 (2002): 31–60.

Jones, Frank, and Malcolm Wanklyn. *A Military History of the English Civil War, 1642–1646.* London: Pearson, 2004.

Jonson, Ben. *Sejanus: His Fall.* Edited by Philip J. Ayers. Manchester: University of Manchester Press, 1990.

Jordan, Wilbur K. *The Development of Religious Toleration in England.* 4 vols. Cambridge: Harvard University Press, 1932–40.

Journals of the House of Commons. London, 1802. www.british-history.ac.uk/catalogue .aspx?type=2&gid=43.

Kahn, Victoria. *Machiavellian Rhetoric.* Princeton: Princeton University Press, 1994.

———. "Political Theology and Reason of State in *Samson Agonistes.*" *South Atlantic Quarterly* 95.4 (1996): 1065–97.

———. *Rhetoric, Prudence, and Skepticism in the Renaissance.* Ithaca: Cornell University Press, 1985.

———. *Wayward Contracts: The Crisis of Political Obligation in England, 1640–1674.* Princeton: Princeton University Press, 2004.

Keeble, N. H., ed. *The Cambridge Companion to Writing of the English Revolution.* Cambridge: Cambridge University Press, 2001.

Kelliher, Hilton. "Donne, Jonson, Richard Andrews and The New Castle Manuscript." *English Manuscript Studies 1100–1700* 4 (1993): 135–73.

Kelley, Maurice. *This Great Argument: A Study of Milton's De Doctrina Christiana as a Gloss upon Paradise Lost.* Princeton: Princeton University Press, 1962.

———. "Milton and Machiavelli's *Discorsi.*" *Studies in Bibliography* 4 (1951–52): 123–27.

———. "Milton's Dante–Della Casa–Varchi Volume." *Bulletin of the New York Public Library* 66 (1962): 499–504.

Kelsey, Sean. "The Death of Charles I." *Historical Journal* 45 (2003): 727–54.

———. "Politics and Procedure in the Trial of Charles I." *Law and History Review* 22.1 (2004): 1–25.

Kenyon, J. P., ed. *The Stuart Constitution.* 2nd ed. Cambridge: Cambridge University Press, 1986.

Keynes, Geoffrey. *A Bibliography of Dr. John Donne.* 4th ed. Oxford: Clarendon Press, 1973.

King, John. *Tudor Royal Iconography: Literature and Art in an Age of Religious Crisis.* Princeton: Princeton University Press, 1989.

Kirby, W. J. Torrance. *Richard Hooker's Doctrine of the Royal Supremacy.* Leiden: E. J. Brill, 1990.

Kiséry, András. " 'Politicians in Show': The Circulation of Political Knowledge in Early Seventeenth-Century English Drama." Ph.D. diss., Columbia University, 2008.

Klinge, Markus. "The Grotesque in *Areopagitica.*" *Milton Studies* 45 (2006): 82–128.

Knachel, Philip A., ed. *Eikon Basilike: The Portraiture of His Sacred Majesty in His Solitudes and Sufferings.* Ithaca: Cornell University Press, 1966.

Knoppers, Laura Lunger. *Constructing Cromwell: Ceremony, Portrait, and Print, 1645–1661.* Cambridge: Cambridge University Press, 2000.

———. "General Introduction." *The Complete Works of John Milton,* vol 2: *The 1671 Poems: Paradise Regain'd and Samson Agonistes,* xix–lxxv. Oxford: Oxford University Press, 2008.

Kolbrener, William. *Milton's Warring Angels: A Study of Critical Engagements.* Cambridge: Cambridge University Press, 1997.

Lake, Peter. *Anglicans and Puritans? Presbyterianism and English Conformist Thought from Whitgift to Hooker.* London: Unwin Hyman, 1988.

Lamont, William. "Pamphleteering, the Protestant Consensus, and the English Revolution." In *Freedom and the English Revolution: Essays in History and Literature,* edited by R. C. Richardson and G. M. Ridden, 72–92. Manchester: Manchester University Press, 1986.

Lander, Jesse M. *Inventing Polemic: Religion, Print, and Literary Culture in Early Modern England.* Cambridge: Cambridge University Press, 2006.

Laski, Harold J. "The *Areopagitica* after Three Hundred Years." In *Freedom of Expression: A Symposium,* edited by Hermon Ould, 168–76. London: Hutchinson International Authors, 1945.

Leedham-Green, S. *Books in Cambridge Inventories.* 2 vols. Cambridge: Cambridge University Press, 1986.

Leonard, John. "Revolting as Backsliding in Sonnet XII." *Notes and Queries* 43.3 (1996): 269–73.

Lesser, Zachary, and Peter Stallybrass. "The First Literary Hamlet and the Commonplacing of Professional Plays." *Shakespeare Quarterly* 59.4 (2008): 371–420.

Lewalski, Barbara. *The Life of Milton: A Critical Biography.* Oxford: Blackwell, 2000.

Lieb, Michael, and John T. Shawcross, eds. *Achievements of the Left Hand.* Amherst: University of Massachusetts Press, 1974.

Lim, Walter S. H. *John Milton, Radical Politics, and Biblical Republicanism.* Newark: University of Delaware Press, 2006.

Loewenstein, David. "Milton among the Religious Radicals and Sects: Polemical Engagements and Silences." *Milton Studies* 40 (2001): 222–47.

————. *Milton and the Drama of History: Historical Vision, Iconoclasm, and the Literary Imagination.* Cambridge: Cambridge University Press, 1990.

————. *Representing Revolution in Milton and His Contemporaries: Religion, Politics, and Polemics in Radical Puritanism.* Cambridge: Cambridge University Press, 2001.

————. "Toleration and the Specter of Heresy in Milton's England." In Achinstein and Sauer, *Milton and Toleration,* 45–71.

Loewenstein, David, and John Marshall, eds. *Heresy, Literature, and Politics in Early Modern English Culture.* Cambridge: Cambridge University Press, 2006.

Loewenstein, David, and James Grantham Turner, eds. *Politics, Poetics, and Hermeneutics in Milton's Prose.* Cambridge: Cambridge University Press, 1990.

Loewenstein, Joseph. *The Author's Due: Printing and the Prehistory of Copyright.* Chicago: University of Chicago Press, 2002.

London's Account; or, A Calculation of the Arbitrary and Tyrannicall Exactions [London], 1647.

Love, Harold. *English Clandestine Satire, 1660–1702.* Oxford: Oxford University Press, 2004.

————. *Scribal Publication in Seventeenth-Century England.* Oxford: Oxford University Press, 1993.

Lyotard, Jean-François. *The Postmodern Condition: A Report on Knowledge.* Translated by Geoff Bennington and Brian Massumi. Minneapolis: University of Minnesota Press, 1984.

Madan, F. F. "Milton, Salmasius, and Dugard." *The Library* 4.2 (1923): 119–45.

————. *A New Bibliography of the "Eikon Basilike" of King Charles the First.* Oxford: Oxford University Press, 1950.

————. "A Revised Bibliography of Salmasius's *Defensio Regia* and Milton's *Pro Populo Anglicano Defensio.*" *The Library* 5.9 (1954): 101–21.

Malcolm, Noel. *Aspects of Hobbes.* Oxford: Oxford University Press, 2002.

Manley, Lawrence. *Literature and Culture in Early Modern London.* Cambridge: Cambridge University Press, 1995.

Marotti, Arthur F. *Manuscript, Print, and the English Renaissance Lyric.* Ithaca: Cornell University Press, 1995.

Martin, Catherine Gimelli. "Unediting Milton: Historical Myth and Editorial Misconstruction in the Yale Prose Edition." In Tournu and Forsyth, *Milton, Rights and Liberties,* 113–30.

Masson, David. *The Life of John Milton.* 7 vols. Cambridge: Macmillan, 1859–94.

Masten, Jeffrey, Peter Stallybrass, and Nancy Vickers, eds. *Language Machines: Technologies of Literary and Cultural Production.* New York: Routledge, 1997.

McDowell, Nicholas. *The English Radical Imagination: Culture, Religion, and Revolution, 1630–1660.* Oxford: Oxford University Press, 2003.

————. Headnote to *The Tenure of Kings and Magistrates.* In *The Complete Works of John Milton,* vol. 6: *Vernacular Regicide and Republican Tracts,* edited by N. H. Keeble and Nicholas McDowell. Oxford: Clarendon Press, forthcoming.

————. "Milton's Regicide Tracts and the Uses of Shakespeare." In McDowell and Smith, *Oxford Handbook of Milton,* 252–71.

McDowell, Nicholas, and Nigel Smith, eds. *The Oxford Handbook of Milton.* Oxford: Oxford University Press, 2009.

McGinn, Donald Joseph. *The Admonition Controversy.* New Brunswick, N.J.: Rutgers University Press, 1949.

McKenzie, D. F. *Bibliography and the Sociology of Texts.* Cambridge: Cambridge University Press, 1999.

————. *Making Meaning: "Printers of the Mind" and Other Essays.* Edited by Peter D. McDonald and Michael F. Suarez. Amherst: University of Massachusetts Press, 2002.

McKeon, Michael. "Politics of Discourses and the Rise of the Aesthetic in Seventeenth-Century England." In *Politics of Discourse: The Literature and History of Seventeenth-Century England,* edited by Kevin Sharpe and Steven N. Zwicker, 35–51. Berkeley: University of California Press, 1987.

————. *The Secret History of Domesticity.* Baltimore: Johns Hopkins University Press, 2006.

McKitterick, David. *Print, Manuscript, and the Search for Order, 1450–1830.* Cambridge: Cambridge University Press, 2003.

McLachlan, H. J. *Socinianism in Seventeenth Century England.* Oxford: Oxford University Press, 1951.

Mede, Joseph. *Works.* 4th ed. London, 1677.

Miller, Leo. *John Milton & the Oldenburg Safeguard.* New York: Loewenthal Press, 1985.

A Milton Encyclopedia. Edited by William B. Hunter Jr. 9 vols. Lewisburg: Bucknell University Press, 1978–83.

Milton, John. *Accidence Commenc't Grammar.* London, 1669.

[Milton, John.] *Articles of Peace . . . upon all which are added observations.* London, 1649.

Milton, John. *Artis Logicae Plenior Institutio.* London, 1672.

————. *A Brief History of Moscovia.* London, 1682.

————. *Complete Shorter Poems.* Edited by John Carey. Rev. 2nd ed. London: Longman, 2007.

————. *Epistolarum familiarium.* London, 1674.

————. *John Milton: Complete Poems and Major Prose.* Edited by Merritt Hughes. New York: Macmillan, 1957.

————. *Letters of State, Written by Mr. John Milton, to Most of the Sovereign Princes and Republicks of Europe.* London, 1694.

————. *Milton's Sonnets.* Edited by E. A. J. Honigmann. New York: St. Martin's Press, 1966.

————. *Paradise Lost.* Edited by Alastair Fowler. London: Longman, 1971.

————. *Poems of Mr. John Milton, both English and Latin, compos'd at several times.* London, 1645.

————. *Pro Populo Anglicano Defensio.* London, 1651. (Wing 2168B.)

————. *Pro Populo Anglicano Defensio.* London, 1658.

Minnis, Alastair. *Medieval Theory of Authorship: Scholastic Literary Attitudes in the Later Middle Ages.* 2nd ed. Aldershot: Scolar Press, 1984.

Mohl, Ruth. *John Milton and His Commonplace Book.* New York: Frederic Unger, 1969.

More, Thomas. *Richard III.* Edited by Richard S. Sylvester. Vol. 2 of *The Complete Works of St. Thomas More.* New Haven: Yale University Press, 1963.

————. *Utopia.* Edited by Edward Surtz and J. H. Hexter. Vol. 4 of *The Complete Works of St. Thomas More.* New Haven: Yale University Press, 1965.

Moss, Ann. "The *Politica* of Justus Lipsius and the Commonplace-Book." *Journal of the History of Ideas* 59.3 (1998): 421–36.

————. *Printed Commonplace-Books and the Structuring of Renaissance Thought.* Oxford: Oxford University Press, 1996.

Muddiman, J. G. *Trial of King Charles the First.* London: William Hodge, 1928.

Mueller, Janel. "Contextualizing Milton's Nascent Republicanism." In Stanwood, *Of Poetry and Politics,* 263–82.

Norbrook, David. "*Areopagitica,* Censorship, and the Early Modern Public Sphere." In *The Administration of Aesthetics: Censorship, Political Criticism, and the Public Sphere,* edited by Richard Burt, 3–33. Minneapolis: University of Minnesota Press, 1994.

————. "Marvell's 'Horatian Ode' and the Politics of Genre." In Healy and Sawday, *Literature and the English Civil War,* 147–69.

————. *Writing the English Republic.* Cambridge: Cambridge University Press, 1999.

North, Marcy. *The Anonymous Renaissance: Cultures of Discretion in Tudor-Stuart England.* Chicago: University of Chicago Press, 2003.

Oldenburg, Henry. *The Correspondence of Henry Oldenburg,* vol. 1. Edited by A. Rupert Hall and Marie Boas Hall. Madison: University of Wisconsin Press, 1965.

Orgel, Stephen. "Records of Culture." In Andersen and Sauer, *Books and Readers,* 282–89.

Orsini, Napoleone. "Elizabethan Manuscript Translations of Machiavelli's *Prince.*" *Journal of the Warburg Institute* 1.2 (1937): 166–69.

Overton, Richard, and William Walwyn. *Remonstrance of Many Thousand Citizens.* [London], 1646.

Owen, Eivion. "Milton and Selden on Divorce." *Studies in Philology* 43 (1946): 233–57.

Owen, John. *Theomachia autexousiastike; or, A Display of Arminianisme.* London, 1643.

Oxford Dictionary of National Biography. www.oxforddnb.com.

Oxford Latin Dictionary. Edited by P. G. W. Glare. Oxford: Clarendon Press, 1982.

Palmer, Herbert. *The Glasse of Gods Providence towards his Faithfvll Ones Held Forth in a Sermon Preached to the Two Houses of Parliament at Margarets Westminster, Aug. 13, 1644.* London, 1644.

———. *Scripture and Reason Pleaded for Defensive Arms.* London, 1643.

Parker, William Riley. *Milton: A Biography.* Rev. ed. by Gordon Campbell. 2 vols. Oxford: Oxford University Press, 1996.

———. "Milton's Hobson Poems: Some Neglected Early Texts." *Modern Language Review* 31.3 (1936): 395–402.

Patterson, Annabel. *Censorship and Interpretation: The Conditions of Writing and Reading in Early Modern England.* Madison: University of Wisconsin Press, 1984.

———. "'Forc'd Fingers': Milton's Early Poems and Ideological Constraint." In *The Muses Common-Weale: Poetry and Politics in the Seventeenth Century,* edited by Claude J. Summers and Ted-Larry Pebworth, 9–22. Columbia: University of Missouri Press, 1988.

———. "Milton and the D-Word." Hilda Hulme Memorial Lecture, University of London, July 9, 2008.

———. *Milton's Words.* Oxford: Oxford University Press, 2009.

———. *Reading Holinshed's Chronicles.* Chicago: Chicago University Press, 1994.

———. "Why Is There No Rights Talk in Milton's Poetry?" In Tournu and Forsyth, *Milton, Rights and Liberties,* 197–200.

Patterson, Annabel, and Martin Dzelzainis. "Marvell and the Earl of Anglesey: A Chapter in the History of Reading." *Historical Journal* 44.3 (2001): 703–26.

Phillips, Edward. *The New World of English Words.* London, 1658.

Pocock, J. G. A. *The Ancient Constitution and the Feudal Law: A Study of English Historical Thought in the Seventeenth Century.* 1957. Reissue with retrospect, Cambridge: Cambridge University Press, 1987.

———. *Machiavellian Moment: Florentine Political Thought and the Atlantic Republican Tradition.* Princeton: Princeton University Press, 1975.

Poole, William. "'The Armes of Studious Retirement'?": Milton Scholarship, 1632–1641." Unpublished manuscript.

———. "The Genres of Milton's Commonplace Book." In McDowell and Smith, *Oxford Handbook of Milton,* 367–81.

———. *Milton and the Idea of the Fall.* Cambridge: Cambridge University Press, 2005.

———. "The Shelf-List of John Hales, c. 1623: Unedited Transcript for 'Young Milton,' presented at Oxford University, 24 March 2009." Unpublished manuscript.

Poole, William, and Felicity Henderson. "The Library Lists of Francis Lodwick, FRS (1619–1694): An Introduction to Sloane MSS. 855 and 859, with a Searchable

Transcript." *Electronic British Library Journal* 1 (2009): 1–162. www.bl.uk/eblj/2009articles/article1.html.

Popkin, Richard H. "The Dispersion of Bodin's Dialogues in England, Holland, and Germany." *Journal of the History of Ideas* 49.1 (1988): 157–60.

The Portrait of his Majesty Charles the Second. Faithfully taken to the life. London, 1660.

Prynne, William. *The Antipathie of The English Lordly Prelacie, Both to Regall Monarchy, and Civill Unity.* London, 1641.

———. *A Briefe Memento to the Present Unparliamentary Junto Touching their Present Intentions and Proceedings to Depose and Execute, CHARLES STEWART, their Lawfull KING.* London, 1649.

———. *The Church of England's Old Antithesis to New Arminianisme.* London, 1629.

———. *Histrio-mastix, The Players Scourge.* London, 1633.

———. *Mr. Pryn's Last and Final Declaration to the Commons of Engand.* London, 1649.

———. *Soveraigne Power of Parliaments & Kingdomes.* London, 1643.

Raab, Felix. *The English Face of Machiavelli.* London: Routledge & K. Paul, 1964.

Rajan, Balachandra. "The Poetics of Heresy." In *Milton and the Climates of Reading: Essays by Balachandra Rajan,* edited by Elizabeth Sauer, 33–45. Toronto: University of Toronto Press, 2006.

Raleigh, Walter. *The Cabinet-Council . . . In Political and Polemical Aphorisms.* London, 1658.

Rapaport, Herman. *Milton and the Postmodern.* Lincoln: University of Nebraska Press, 1983.

Raymond, Joad. "Complications of Interest: Milton, Scotland, Ireland, and National Identity in 1649." *Review of English Studies* 55.220 (2004): 315–45.

———. "Milton." In Barnard and McKenzie, *Cambridge History of the Book in Britain,* 4:376–87.

———. *Pamphlets and Pamphleteering in Early Modern Britain.* Cambridge: Cambridge University Press, 2003.

Riddell, James A., and Stanley Stewart. *Jonson's Spenser: Evidence and Historical Criticism.* Pittsburgh: Duquesne University Press, 1995.

Roberts, Julian. "The Latin Trade." In Barnard and McKenzie, *Cambridge History of the Book in Britain,* 4:141–73.

Robinson, Henry. *An Answer to Mr. Prynne's Twelve Questions.* London, 1644.

[Robinson, Henry]. *Liberty of Conscience.* In *Tracts on Liberty in the Puritan Revolution, 1638–1647,* edited by William Haller, vol 3. New York: Columbia University Press, 1934.

Rogers, John. *Matter of Revolution: Science, Poetry, and Politics in the Age of Milton.* Ithaca: Cornell University Press, 1996.

———. "*Paradise Regained* and the Memory of *Paradise Lost.*" In McDowell and Smith, *Oxford Handbook of Milton,* 589–612.

Rose, Paul Lawrence. *Bodin and the Great God of Nature.* Geneva: Librairie Droz, 1980.

Rosenblatt, Jason P. "Milton, Natural Law, and Toleration." In Achinstein and Sauer, *Milton and Toleration,* 126–48.

———. "Milton's Chief Rabbi." *Milton Studies* 24 (1984): 43–71.

Rumrich, John. *Milton Unbound: Controversy and Reinterpretation.* Cambridge: Cambridge University Press, 1996.

———. "Radical Heterodoxy and Heresy." In *A Companion to Milton,* edited by Thomas Corns, 141–56. Oxford: Blackwell, 2001.

Samuel, Irene. *Plato and Milton.* 1947. Reprint, Ithaca: Cornell University Press, 1965.

Sandler, Florence. "Icon and Iconoclast." In Lieb and Shawcross, *Achievements of the Left Hand,* 160–84.

Sauer, Elizabeth. *"Paper-Contestations" and Textual Communities in England, 1640–1675.* Toronto: University of Toronto Press, 2005.

Saunders, J. W. "The Stigma of Print: A Note on the Social Bases of Tudor Poetry." *Essays in Criticism* 1 (1951): 139–64.

Sells, A. Lytton. *The Paradise of Travellers: The Italian Influence on Englishmen in the Seventeenth Century.* London: George Allen & Unwin, 1964.

A Serious and faithful Representation of the Judgements of Ministers of the Gospell within the Province of London. London, 1649.

Serjeantson, Richard, and Thomas Woolford. "The Scribal Publication of a Printed Book: Francis Bacon's *Certain considerations touching . . . the Church of England* (1604)." *The Library,* 7th ser., 10.2 (2009): 119–56.

Sewell, Arthur. *A Study in Milton's Christian Doctrine.* Oxford: Oxford University Press, 1939.

Sharp, Andrew, ed. *The English Levellers.* Cambridge: Cambridge University Press, 1998.

Sharpe, Kevin. "'An Image Doting Rabble': The Failure of Republican Culture in Seventeenth-Century England." In Sharpe and Zwicker, *Refiguring Revolutions,* 25–56.

———. *Reading Revolutions: The Politics of Reading in Early Modern England.* London: Yale University Press, 2000.

———. *Sir Robert Cotton, 1586–1631: History and Politics in Early Modern England.* Oxford: Oxford University Press, 1979.

Sharpe, Kevin, and Steven N. Zwicker, eds. *Refiguring Revolutions: Aesthetics and Politics from the English Revolution.* Berkeley: University of California Press, 1998.

Shawcross, John T. *John Milton: The Self and the World.* Lexington: University of Kentucky Press, 1993.

———. "Milton's 'Fairfax' Sonnet." *Notes and Queries* 200 (1955): 195–96.

———. "Milton's Spelling: Its Biographical and Critical Implications." Ph.D. diss., New York University, 1958.

———. "Milton's *Tenure of Kings and Magistrates:* Date of Composition, Editions, and Issues." *Papers of the Bibliographical Society of America* 60 (1966): 1–8.

———. "Notes on Milton's Amanuenses." *Journal of English and Germanic Philology* 58 (1959): 29–38.

———. *Rethinking Milton Studies.* Newark: University of Delaware Press, 2005.

———. "A Survey of Milton's Prose Works." In Lieb and Shawcross, *Achievements of the Left Hand,* 369–74.

Shelley, Percy Bysshe. *Prometheus Unbound: A Variorum Edition.* Edited by Lawrence John Zillman. Seattle: University of Washington Press, 1959.

Shephard, Robert. "The Political Commonplace Books of Sir Robert Sidney." *Sidney Journal* 21.1 (2003): 1–30.

Sherman, William. *John Dee: The Politics of Reading and Writing in the English Renaissance.* Amherst: University of Massachusetts Press, 1995.

———. *Used Books: Marking Readers in Renaissance England.* Philadelphia: University of Pennsylvania Press, 2008.

Shuger, Debora. *Censorship and Cultural Sensibility.* Philadelphia: University of Pennsylvania Press, 2006.

———. *Political Theologies in Shakespeare's England: The Sacred and the State in "Measure for Measure."* New York: Palgrave, 2001.

[Sikes, George]. *The Life and Death of Sir Henry Vane.* London, 1662.

Simpson, James. *Burning to Read: English Fundamentalism and Its Reformation Opponents.* Cambridge: Harvard University Press, 2007.

Sirluck, Ernest. "Milton's Political Thought: The First Cycle." *Modern Philology* 61.3 (1964): 209–24.

Skinner, Quentin. "Classical Liberty and the Coming of the English Civil War." In Gelderen and Skinner, *Republicanism,* 2:9–28.

———. "Conquest and Consent: Thomas Hobbes and the Engagement Controversy." In *The Interregnum: The Quest for Settlement, 1646–1660,* edited by G. E. Aylmer, 79–98. London: Macmillan, 1972.

———. "History and Ideology in the English Revolution." *Historical Journal* 8 (1965): 151–78.

———. "The Ideological Context of Hobbes's Political Thought." *Historical Journal* 9 (1966): 286–317.

———. *Liberty before Liberalism.* Cambridge: Cambridge University Press, 1998.

———. *Reason and Rhetoric in the Philosophy of Thomas Hobbes.* Cambridge: Cambridge University Press, 1996.

———. "'Social Meaning' and the Explanation of Social Action." In Tully, *Meaning and Context,* 79–96.

Smet, Ingrid A. R. de. *Thuanus: The Making of Jacques-Auguste De Thou.* Geneva: Librairie Droz, 2006.

Smith, Logan Pearsall. *The Life and Letters of Sir Henry Wotton.* 2 vols. Oxford: Clarendon Press, 1907.

Smith, Nigel. "'And if God was one of us': Paul Best, John Biddle, and Anti-Trinitarian Heresy in Seventeenth-Century England." In Loewenstein and Marshall, *Heresy, Literature, and Politics*, 160–84.

———. "*Areopagitica*: Voicing Contexts, 1643–5." In Loewenstein and Turner, *Politics, Poetics, and Hermeneutics in Milton's Prose*, 103–22.

———. *Literature and Revolution in England, 1640–1660*. New Haven: Yale University Press, 1994.

———. "Milton and the Index." In *Of Paradise and Light: Essays for Alan Rudrum*, edited by Holly Nelson and Donald R. Dickson, 101–22. London: Associated University Presses, 2004.

———. "Milton and the European Contexts of Toleration." In Achinstein and Sauer, *Milton and Toleration*, 23–44.

———. *Perfection Proclaimed: Language and Literature in English Radical Religion, 1640–1660*. Oxford: Clarendon Press, 1989.

———, ed. *The Poems of Andrew Marvell*. Rev. ed. London: Longman, 2007.

Snow, Vernon F. "Francis Bacon's Advice to Fulke Greville on Research Techniques." *Huntington Library Quarterly* 23, no. 4 (1960): 369–79.

A Solemn Engagement of the Army. London, 1647.

Sommerville, J. P. "John Selden, the Law of Nature, and the Origins of Government." *Historical Journal* 27.2 (1984): 437–47.

———. *Politics and Ideology in England, 1603–1640*. London: Longman, 1986.

Sotheby, Samuel Leigh. *Ramblings in the Elucidation of the Autograph of Milton*. London: Thomas Richards, 1861.

Sprat, Thomas. *The History of the Royal-Society of London for the Improving of Natural Knowledge*. London, 1667.

Stallybrass, Peter, and Roger Chartier. "Reading and Authorship: The Circulation of Shakespeare 1590–1619." In *A Concise Companion to Shakespeare and the Text*, edited by Andrew Murphy, 35–56. Oxford: Blackwell, 2007.

Stallybrass, Peter, Roger Chartier, J. Franklin Mowery, and Heather Wolfe. "Hamlet's Tables and the Technologies of Writing in Renaissance England." *Shakespeare Quarterly* 55.4 (2004), 379–419.

Stanwood, P. G., ed. *Of Poetry and Politics: New Essays on Milton and His World*. Binghamton, N.Y.: Medieval and Renaissance Texts and Studies, 1995.

Sterne, Laurence, and Harold H. Kollmeier, eds. *A Concordance to the English Prose of John Milton*. Binghamton, N.Y.: Medieval and Renaissance Texts and Studies, 1985.

Stevens, David Harrison. "The Bridgewater Manuscript of *Comus*." *Modern Philology* 24.3 (1927): 315–20.

Stevens, Paul. "Milton's 'Renunciation' of Cromwell: The Problem of Raleigh's *Cabinet-Council*." *Modern Philology* 98.3 (2001): 363–92.

Strathmann, E. A. "A Note on the Ralegh Canon." *Times Literary Supplement*, April 13, 1956, 228.

Taylor, Jeremy. *The Liberty of Prophesying*. London, 1647.

Thomas, Max. "Reading and Writing the Renaissance Commonplace Book: A Question of Authorship?" In *The Construction of Authorship: Textual Appropriation in Law and Literature,* edited by Martha Woodmansee and Peter Jaszi, 401–15. Durham: Duke University Press, 1994.

Togashi, Go. "Milton and the Presbyterian Opposition, 1649–1650: The Engagement Controversy and *The Tenure of Kings and Magistrates,* Second Edition (1649)." *Milton Quarterly* 39.2 (2005): 59–81.

Toland, John. *The Life of Milton.* Amsterdam, 1699.

Toomer, G. J. "Selden's History of Tithes: Genesis, Publication, Aftermath." *Huntington Library Quarterly* 65 (2002): 345–78.

Tournu, Christophe, and Neil Forsyth, eds. *Milton, Rights and Liberties.* Bern: Peter Lang, 2007.

Treadwell, Michael. "The Stationers and the Printing Acts at the End of the Seventeenth Century." In Barnard and McKenzie, *Cambridge History of the Book,* 4:755–76.

Trevor-Roper, Hugh. *Catholics, Anglicans, and Puritans.* 1987. Reprint, London: Fontana, 1989.

———. *Edward Hyde, Earl of Clarendon.* Oxford: Clarendon Press, 1975.

Tubb, Amos. "Printing the Regicide of Charles I." *History* 89 (2004): 500–524.

Tuck, Richard. "'The Ancient Law of Freedom': John Selden and the Civil War." In *Reactions to the English Civil War 1642–1649,* edited by John Morrill, 137–62. New York: St. Martin's Press, 1982.

———. "The 'Modern' Theory of Natural Law." In *The Languages of Political Theory in Early-Modern Europe,* edited by Anthony Pagden, 99–119. Cambridge: Cambridge University Press, 1987.

———. *Natural Rights Theories: Their Origin and Development.* Cambridge: Cambridge University Press, 1979.

———. *Philosophy and Government, 1572–1651.* Cambridge: Cambridge University Press, 1993.

Tully, James, ed. *Meaning and Context: Quentin Skinner and His Critics.* Princeton: Princeton University Press, 1988.

Turnbull, G. H. *Hartlib, Dury and Comenius: Gleanings from Hartlib's Papers.* London: University Press of Liverpool, 1947.

Turner, Henry S. *The English Renaissance Stage: Geometry, Poetics, and the Practical Spatial Arts, 1580–1630.* Oxford: Oxford University Press, 2006.

Turner, James Grantham. "Libertinism and Toleration: Milton, Bruno, Aretino." In Achinstein and Sauer, *Milton and Toleration,* 107–25.

Tyacke, Nicholas. "Arminianism and English Culture." *Britain and the Netherlands* 7 (1981): 94–117.

———. "The 'Rise of Puritanism' and the Legalizing of Dissent, 1571–1719." In *From Persecution to Toleration,* edited by Ole Peter Grell, Jonathan Israel, and Nicholas Tyacke, 17–50. Oxford: Oxford University Press, 1991.

Tyndale, William. *The Obedience of a Christian Man* (1528). In *The Work of William Tindale,* edited by S. L. Greenslade. London: Blackie & Son, 1938.

———, trans. *Tyndale's New Testament* (1534). Edited by David Daniell. New Haven: Yale University Press, 1989.

Underdown, David. *Pride's Purge: Politics in the Puritan Revolution.* Oxford: Clarendon Press, 1971.

Underhill, Edward, ed. *Tracts on Liberty of Conscience and Persecution, 1614–1661.* 1846. Reprint, New York: B. Franklin, 1966.

van Gelderen, Martin, and Quentin Skinner, eds. *Republicanism: A Shared European Heritage.* 2 vols. Cambridge: Cambridge University Press, 2002.

Vickers, Brian. "The Royal Society and English Prose Style." In *Rhetoric and the Pursuit of Truth: Language Change in the Seventeenth and Eighteenth Centuries,* edited by Brian Vickers and Nancy S. Struever, 3–76. Los Angeles: William Andrews Clark Library, 1985.

von Maltzahn, Nicholas. "Dating the Digression in Milton's *History of Britain.*" *Historical Journal* 36.4 (1993): 945–56.

———. "Milton, Marvell and Toleration." In Achinstein and Sauer, *Milton and Toleration,* 86–104.

———. *Milton's History of Britain: Republican Historiography in the English Revolution.* Oxford: Oxford University Press, 1991.

———. "The Royal Society and the Provenance of Milton's *History of Britain* (1670)." *Milton Quarterly* 32.3 (1998): 90–95.

Walker, Julia M. "Eclipsing Shakespeare's Eikon: Milton's Subversion of *Richard II.*" *Journal of English and German Philology* 90 (1991): 51–60.

Wallace, Dewey D., Jr. *Puritans and Predestination: Grace in English Protestant Theology, 1525–1695.* Chapel Hill, 1982.

[Walwyn, William]. *The Compassionate Samaritane.* London, 1644.

[———]. *Some Considerations Tending to the Undeceiving Those Whose Judgements Are Misinformed.* London, 1642.

Warkentin, Germaine. "Humanism in Hard Times: The Second Earl of Leicester (1595–1677) and His Commonplace Books, 1630–1660." In *Challenging Humanism: Essays in Honor of Dominic Baker-Smith,* edited by Ton Hoenselaars and Arthur F. Kinney, 229–53. Newark: University of Delaware Press, 2005.

Waszink, Jan. "Inventio in Lipsius' Politica: Commonplace Books and the Shape of Political Theory." In *Lipsius in Leiden,* edited by Karl Enenkel and Chris Heesakkers, 141–62. Voorthuizen, Netherlands: Florivallis, 1997.

White, Peter. "The Rise of Arminianism Reconsidered." *Past and Present* 101 (1983): 34–54.

Whitelocke, Bulstrode. *Memorials of the English Affairs from the Beginning of the Reign of Charles the First to the Happy Restoration of King Charles the Second.* 4 vols. Oxford: Oxford University Press, 1853.

Whiting, G. W. "The Sources of *Eikonoklastes:* A Resurvey." *Studies in Philology* 32 (1935): 74–102.

Wilding, Michael. "Marvell's 'Horatian Ode upon Cromwell's Return from Ireland,' the Levellers, and the Junta." *Modern Language Review* 82 (1987): 1–14.

Willard, O. M. "Jaggard's Catalogue of English Books." *Stanford Studies in Language and Literature* (1941): 152–72.

———. "The Survival of English Books Printed before 1640: A Theory and Some Illustrations." *The Library,* 4th ser., 23.4 (1942): 171–90.

Williams, Roger. *The Bloudy Tenent of Persecution.* Edited by Samuel L. Caldwell. 1867. Reprint in *The Complete Writings of Roger Williams.* 7 vols. New York: Russell and Russell, 1963, vol. 3.

[———]. *Queries of Highest Consideration.* London, 1644.

Wing, Donald. *A Gallery of Ghosts.* New York: Modern Language Association, 1966.

Wing, Donald. *Short-Title Catalogue of Books Printed in England, 1641–1700.* 2nd ed. New York: Modern Language Association, 1994.

Wittreich, Joseph. "Milton's *Areopagitica:* Its Isocratic and Ironic Contents." *Milton Studies* 4 (1972): 101–15.

Wolfe, Don M. *Milton in the Puritan Revolution.* New York: T. Nelson and Sons, 1941.

Woolf, Daniel. *The Idea of History in Early Stuart England: Erudition, Ideology, and "The Light of Truth" from the Accesssion of James I to the Civil War.* Toronto: University of Toronto Press, 1990.

———. *Reading History in Early Modern England.* Cambridge: Cambridge University Press, 2000.

———. "Selden: From Antiquarianism to History." In *The Idea of History in Early Stuart England,* 200–242.

Woolrych, Austin. *Britain in Revolution, 1625–1660.* Oxford: Oxford University Press, 2002.

———. "The Date of the Digression in Milton's *History of Britain.*" In *For Veronica Wedgwood These: Studies in Seventeenth-Century History,* edited by Richard Ollard and Pamela Tudor-Craig, 217–46. London: Collins, 1986.

———. "Dating Milton's *History of Britain.*" *Historical Journal* 36.4 (1993): 929–43.

Worden, Blair. "Classical Republicanism and the Puritan Revolution." In *History and Imagination: Essays in Honor of H. R. Trevor-Roper,* edited by Hugh Lloyd-Jones, Valerie Pearl, and Blair Worden, 182–200. London: Duckworth, 1981.

———. *Literature and Politics in Cromwellian England: John Milton, Andrew Marvell, Marchamont Nedham.* Oxford: Oxford University Press, 2007.

———. "Milton's Republicanism and the Tyranny of Heaven." In *Machiavelli and Republicanism,* edited by Gisela Bock, Quentin Skinner, and Maurizio Viroli, 225–47. Cambridge: Cambridge University Press, 1990.

———. *The Rump Parliament, 1648–1653.* Cambridge: Cambridge University Press, 1974.

———. "Toleration and the Cromwellian Protectorate." In *Persecution and Toleration: Papers Read at the Twenty-Second Summer Meeting and the Twenty-Third Winter Meeting of the Ecclesiastical History Society,* edited by W. J. Sheils, 199–234. Oxford: B. Blackwell for the Ecclesiastical History Society, 1984.

Wordsworth, Christopher. *Documentary Supplement to "Who Wrote Eikon Basilike?"* London: J. Murray, 1825.

Woudhuysen, H. R. *Sir Philip Sidney and the Circulation of Manuscripts, 1558–1640.* Oxford: Oxford University Press, 1996.

Yates, Frances A. "Paolo Sarpi's 'History of the Council of Trent.'" *Journal of the Warburg and Courtauld Institutes* 7, nos. 3–4 (1944): 123–43.

Zagorin, Perez. *A History of Political Thought in the English Revolution.* 1954. Reprint, Bristol: Thoemmes Press, 1997.

———. *How the Idea of Religious Toleration Came to the West.* Princeton: Princeton University Press, 2003.

Zurbuchen, Simone. "Republicanism and Toleration." In Gelderen and Skinner, *Republicanism,* 47–72.

Zwicker, Steven N. *Lines of Authority: Politics and English Literary Culture, 1649–1689.* Ithaca: Cornell University Press, 1993.

———. "Reading the Margins: Politics and the Habits of Appropriation." In Sharpe and Zwicker, *Refiguring Revolutions.*

———. "What Every Literate Man Once Knew." In *Owners, Annotators, and the Signs of Reading,* edited by Robin Myers, Michael Harris, and Giles Mandelbrote, 75–90. London: British Library, 2005.

Index

THOMAS FULTON received a PhD from Yale University and has taught at Connecticut College, Wesleyan University, and Rutgers, the State University of New Jersey, in New Brunswick. He teaches graduate and undergraduate courses in sixteenth- and seventeenth-century literature, Shakespeare and English dramatic history, Milton, and the history of the book. He has also published several articles on these topics in the *Journal of Medieval and Early Modern Studies, Milton Studies, Modern Philology, English Literary Renaissance, Studies in Philology,* and *The John Donne Journal.*